LUTHER'S WORKS

LUTHER'S WORKS

VOLUME 16

LECTURES ON ISAIAH

Chapters 1–39

JAROSLAV PELIKAN
Editor

HILTON C. OSWALD
Associate Editor

CONCORDIA PUBLISHING HOUSE · SAINT LOUIS

9 780570 064169

Library of Congress Catalog Card No. 55-9893

7 8 9 10 11 28 27 26 25 24 23

MANUFACTURED IN THE UNITED STATES OF AMERICA

Contents

General Introduction

THE first editions of Luther's collected works appeared in the sixteenth century, and so did the first efforts to make him "speak English." In America serious attempts in these directions were made for the first time in the nineteenth century. The Saint Louis edition of Luther was the first endeavor on American soil to publish a collected edition of his works, and the Henkel Press in Newmarket, Virginia, was the first to publish some of Luther's writings in an English translation. During the first decade of the twentieth century, J. N. Lenker produced translations of Luther's sermons and commentaries in thirteen volumes. A few years later the first of the six volumes in the Philadelphia (or Holman) edition of the *Works of Martin Luther* appeared. Miscellaneous other works were published at one time or another. But a growing recognition of the need for more of Luther's works in English has resulted in this American edition of Luther's works.

The edition is intended primarily for the reader whose knowledge of late medieval Latin and sixteenth-century German is too small to permit him to work with Luther in the original languages. Those who can, will continue to read Luther in his original words as these have been assembled in the monumental Weimar edition (*D. Martin Luthers Werke.* Kritische Gesamtausgabe; Weimar, 1883 ff.). Its texts and helps have formed a basis for this edition, though in certain places we have felt constrained to depart from its readings and findings. We have tried throughout to translate Luther as he thought translating should be done. That is, we have striven for faithfulness on the basis of the best lexicographical materials available. But where literal accuracy and clarity have conflicted, it is clarity that we have preferred, so that sometimes paraphrase seemed more faithful than literal fidelity. We have proceeded in a similar way in the matter of Bible versions, translating Luther's translations. Where this could be done by the use of an existing English version – King James, Douay, or Revised Standard – we have done so. Where it could not, we have supplied our own. To indicate this in each specific instance would have been pedantic; to adopt a uniform procedure would have been artificial – especially in view of Luther's own inconsistency in this regard. In each volume the translator will be responsible primarily for matters of text and language, while the responsibility of the editor will extend principally to the historical and theological matters reflected in the introductions and notes.

Although the edition as planned will include fifty-five volumes, Luther's writings are not being translated in their entirety. Nor should they be. As he was the first to insist, much of what he wrote and said was not that important. Thus the edition is a selection of works that have proved their importance for the faith, life, and history of the Christian Church. The first thirty volumes contain Luther's expositions of various Biblical books, while the remaining volumes include what are usually called his "Reformation writings" and other occasional pieces. The final volume of the set will be an index volume; in addition to an index of quotations, proper names, and topics, and a list of corrections and changes, it will contain a glossary of many of the technical terms that recur in Luther's works and that cannot be defined each time they appear. Obviously Luther cannot be forced into any neat set of rubrics. He can provide his reader with bits of autobiography or with political observations as he expounds a psalm, and he can speak tenderly about the meaning of the faith in the midst of polemics against his opponents. It is the hope of publishers, editors, and translators that through this edition the message of Luther's faith will speak more clearly to the modern church.

J. P.
H. L.

Introduction to Volume 16

This volume contains the first part of Luther's *Lectures on Isaiah,* covering chapters 1–39, or, as he called it, the First Book of Isaiah. It is translated from the lecture notes published for the first time in Weimar, XXXI-2, 1–260.

Early in May 1527, Luther wrote to Wenzeslaus Link in Nürnberg, announcing his intention to translate the Old Testament prophets into German. "At the same time," he continued, "I plan to lecture on Isaiah, to keep from being idle *[lecturus simul Iesaiam, ne otiosus sim].*" It would appear that he began the lectures in July of the same year, for Bugenhagen in a letter of that month refers to "public lectures" of Luther, presumably those on Isaiah. An outbreak of the plague forced the university to transfer operations from Wittenberg to Jena for a while in 1527, and this meant an interruption of the exposition. The reference (p. 40) to the approach of Advent surely means the Advent of 1527. Thus Luther had moved to the commentary on the third chapter shortly before the end of the year.

We are not informed in much detail about his progress after that time. On May 22, 1528, Luther wrote to Spalatin that he was busy with "translating and explaining *[vertendi et illustrandi]*" Isaiah, perhaps speaking of his lectures. The next information we have about the chronology is a marginal comment (p. 184, n. 2) in the manuscript of the lectures on chapter 23, to the effect that at this point the recording of the lectures was taken over by another scribe. Who this scribe was is indicated by a later marginal gloss (p. 312, n. 6), where "Anthony" means Anthony Lauterbach (1502–1569), best known for his role in the compilation of Luther's *Table Talk.* Lauterbach matriculated at Wittenberg in 1528, and in October of that year began to take down Luther's sermons. From this G. Buchwald, the Weimar editor, has concluded that at that time Luther must have been lecturing on Isaiah 23. The only other data, such as they are, are pertinent to the lectures on "The Second Book of Isaiah" and will appear in the Introduction to Volume 17.

As we have already mentioned, the transcribing of these lectures was not the work of a single hand. The scribe who broke off at chapter 23 was George Schmalzing, but that does not necessarily imply that he had taken down all the lectures from the beginning until that point. It would appear that Lauterbach copied the notes of Schmalzing – and of any other amanuensis who may have preserved the earlier lectures – and added his own from chapter 23 on. Lauterbach's version of Luther's lectures is characterized by the appearance of frequent personal reminiscences from Luther's youth, such as the recollection of days at Erfurt (p. 196) or of a particular celebration of the Mass (p. 216) or of the blasphemy of a girl during Luther's youth (p. 312). The parallels between these anecdotes and similar comments in Luther's *Table Talk* suggest that Lauterbach exercised the same fidelity in both. Adding to the verisimilitude of the transcription are such comments as "Martin Luther's opinion" (p. 207), as well as references to preceding lectures (e. g., p. 326, p. 335, p. 338). It is also highly plausible that the many proverbs appearing in the lectures were cited by Luther himself. As is evident from other commentaries (cf. *Luther's Works,* 13, pp. 145–224, for an outstanding example in the *Commentary on Psalm 101* of 1534), Luther did make it a practice to "explain by means of German proverbs, so that the text may be made clear" (p. 277 below). Except where such proverbs appear in the Greek and Latin classics, we have not cited their literary occurrence nor noted their use in other writings of Luther.

It was not until 1914 that these notes on Luther's lectures were published. What was available of Luther's *Lectures on Isaiah* until that time was an edition of scholia, first published at Wittenberg in 1532 and issued again in 1534 in a revised and expanded version (Weimar, XXV, 87–401; Saint Louis, VI, 1–851). Although it was recognized that this edition was anything but a verbatim transcript of Luther's exposition of Isaiah, it did come as close to his *ipsissima verba* as some of the other commentaries that we have included in the American Edition. With the discovery of the Lauterbach manuscript, however, there is neither need nor even justification for relying on the scholia, and we have decided to translate the version closest to Luther himself. On the other hand, there are occasional expansions and corrections in the scholia that clarify obscure statements or allusions in the lecture notes, and we have been able to exploit this resource in some of our footnotes (e. g., p. 245, n. 11). Additional elucidation of Luther's words has come from the exegetical tradition on which he drew in these lectures, notably from Jerome, whose commentaries he seems to have had before him throughout much of his preparation, but also the medieval exegetes cited in our notes. In the case of the latter, we have tried to determine which may have been the source of Luther's information; but since he cites them anonymously, using such terms as "many" or "the writers," it has not always been possible to decide this with any precision. Perhaps he himself would not have been able to identify the specific scholar from whom he had taken his ideas.

A special instance of Luther's relation to the exegetical tradition in these lectures is his use of the allegorical method of interpretation. Like most of his commentaries on the Old Testament from his maturer years, this exposition of Isaiah warns his hearers against the allegorical extravagances of men such as Origen (e. g., p. 327). But such warnings are usually accompanied by a brief sally of allegorization, almost reluctantly expressed and quite self-consciously held within the limits of evangelical hermeneutics. As we have indicated in our footnotes, some of these allegories are also drawn from the exegetical tradition, but Luther has often added his own characteristic application. In our footnotes we have also taken note of our deviations from the Weimar text. Some of these represent emendations of what are almost certainly misreadings of the manuscript. Others are corrections of what are probably simple typographical errors that occurred in the course either of transcription or of publication. A few are suggestions of what Luther seems to have meant, even though both Lauterbach's version and the Weimar printing may have another reading. Luther's lectures on chapters 40–66, together with special commentaries on Isaiah 9 and Isaiah 53, will appear in Volume 17.

J. P.

LECTURES ON ISAIAH

Chapters 1–39

Translated by
HERBERT J. A. BOUMAN

PREFACE TO THE PROPHET ISAIAH

Two things are necessary to explain the prophet. The first is a knowledge of grammar, and this may be regarded as having the greatest weight. The second is more necessary, namely, a knowledge of the historical background, not only as an understanding of the events themselves as expressed in letters and syllables but as at the same time embracing rhetoric and dialectic, so that the figures of speech and the circumstances may be carefully heeded. Therefore, having command of the grammar in the first place, you must quickly move on to the histories, namely, what those kings under whom Isaiah prophesied did; and these matters must be carefully examined and thoroughly studied.

The chief and leading theme of all the prophets is their aim to keep the people in eager anticipation of the coming Christ. Thus Moses, too, although he teaches many things that should be done, nevertheless always points to the well-known words in Deut. 18:15, where he also keeps the people in eager anticipation of Christ the Teacher, who will come with that authority with which He is endowed in His own right, yes, who will come as the chief Teacher and Disposer. Likewise in our time, too, whatever we teach and establish in the church, we do with a view to getting the people to await the coming of the Savior. Here we must not act in an ungodly manner, but we must live sober, upright, and godly lives (Titus 1:8; 2:12), not, however, as if we always had to stay here ("for here we have no lasting city" [Heb. 13:14] but through Christ we should await another life to come after this life). Whoever knows this will not feel ashamed of the reading and preaching in the course of which the histories must constantly be observed and treated. The prophets must be read in such a way that we prepare ourselves for the coming of Christ. But although the majority of the prophets do speak about a physical kingdom, yet they do (however tersely) lead to Christ. For this reason we must pay more attention to the designs and intentions of the prophets than to their words. Thus, therefore, Isaiah has much to say about his people and the physical kingdom; he condemns sins in one place and praises righteousness in another, and it seems that almost the entire prophecy is directed toward the people. Meanwhile, however, he also prepares the hearts of the people and causes them to look forward to the coming reign of Christ. Thus Peter says (1 Peter 1:10): "The prophets . . . searched and inquired about this salvation." The rule and government of that particular people teaches how they were helped and protected by God at one time and forsaken and punished at another, and the prophet intersperses these accounts with references to Christ and to us. We read these things as an example for us who must expect the same treatment if we live in the same way. Hence we are taught here to lead a good life in faith and love, and our faith rests on clear prophecies when we see those things that were foretold by God so many centuries ago.

Oecolampadius has translated Isaiah with adequate care.[1]

[1] Luther is referring to the commentary on Isaiah by Johannes Oecolampadius, which had appeared at Basel in 1525, under the title: *In Iesaiam prophetam Hypomnematon, hoc est, Commentariorum, Ioannis Oecolampadii Libri VI.*

CHAPTER ONE

1. *The vision of Isaiah the son of Amoz, which he saw concerning Judah and Jerusalem.*

This is the title of the book according to the custom of the Hebrews, who use the opening words of a book as its title.[1] Here we see when Isaiah prophesied, and we are informed about the historical situation. And so this title takes the place of a large commentary. The most valid interpretation of this prophet must be derived from the histories, and both Micah and Hosea were contemporaries of Isaiah.[2]

Isaiah, however, wrote this book concerning a part of the Jewish people, namely, about Judah, and he does not mention even one king of the other part, which is Israel, because when he had begun to prophesy, the kingdom of Israel had just about been done away with. But the prophet speaks of happenings in the life of the Jewish people, not only of past events but also of future events, something no histories of the Gentiles can do. The prophets condemn sins; they praise righteous deeds and point out future rewards for both. And in this respect they excel other historians.

But this whole prophecy is summed up above all in three parts, namely, the prediction of the coming captivity in Babylonia, secondly, the return from this captivity, and thirdly, what it says about Christ.

Vision. We correctly explain a vision as a prophecy, for the prophets used to be called "seers" (1 Sam. 9:9), certainly a word denoting weakness and humility, as if the prophet were saying: "I come to proclaim the things I have seen." Thus Christ says (John 3:11): "We bear witness to what we have seen." The prophet sees; the people hear.

2. *Hear, O heavens [and give ear, O earth; for the Lord has*

[1] Thus, for example, each of the books of the Pentateuch was named in Jewish usage by its opening words; on the other hand, both Joshua and Judges were given these names already in the Hebrew Bible.

[2] According to Luther's chronology, *Computation of the Years of the World* (W, LIII, 97—99), Hosea, Isaiah, Joel, Micah, and Nahum all flourished between the years 3210 and 3230 after creation, viz., 750—730 B. C.

spoken]. This is an imitation of Moses (cf. Deut. 32:1) and an intense and fiery exclamation and appeal. For Isaiah is an exceedingly eloquent prophet, endowed with a rich supply of words; he is a man who speaks with great earnestness. But this is Scripture's way: first to terrify, to reveal sins, to bring on the recognition of oneself, to humble hearts. Then, when they have been driven to despair, its second office follows, namely, the buoying up and consolation of consciences, the promises. This is how the Holy Spirit teaches. Satan, on the other hand, worms his way in by means of sweet speeches and flattering words until he infects innocent hearts. Then he leaves behind horrible terror and despair without consolation. For this reason the prophet, speaking in the Holy Spirit, moves in on the people with a loud and powerful exclamation. If anybody could ponder the individual emotions, he would see in each word a furnace and intense heat. Not just anyone can interpret the feelings of the prophets, but one must teach with the aid of the Spirit. The prophet calls on heaven and earth to hear, not to understand but to be witnesses. Do not interpret heaven to mean angels and earth to mean men,[3] but know that this is a way of speaking to make the hearers pay attention; as if to say: "Nobody is listening; everybody is ungodly." Therefore let heaven and earth hear. Why this? Because the Lord is speaking, and He is worthy to be heard. Furthermore, while the Lord is speaking, there follows the speech to which nobody listens except him who is of God; as He says (John 8:47): "He who is of God hears the words of God." Therefore wherever it is written: "The Lord speaks," it is immediately indicated who the hearers are, namely, only those who are of God. The others do not hear, even though you shout more than 600 times. And this is said chiefly against the show-off saints, not against those gross sinners. Look at the history. Uzziah, Jotham, and Hezekiah were praiseworthy kings. Under them Isaiah prophesied, and he censured them as sinners in order to comfort them afterwards. Ahaz alone was ungodly. He undoubtedly came from a line of godly kings. The family was godly, and there were many godly subjects. Yet even in their praiseworthy realm the prophet found room for such rebuking. This could justly be done

[3] Jerome, *Commentaria in Isaiam prophetam,* Book I, *Patrologia, Series Latina,* XXIV, 25. Because Luther refers to this commentary so frequently, we shall hereafter cite it simply as "Jerome, *Commentaria,*" with the number of the book in Roman numerals and the column number from Vol. XXIV of the *Patrologia* in Arabic numerals.

even today, so full of evil is everything. When, therefore, there is no one who listens, or only very few, the prophet is forced to speak either into the wind or to those who listen. Of these, however, there are two kinds: some are carnal and gross sinners; others listen spiritually and by means of a new faith want to rule over souls with their own righteous deeds, opinions, and inventions. It is the latter who are censured here. What, then, does the Lord say?

Sons have I reared. This is a reproach for ingratitude and blindness beyond measure. The words are certainly powerful; for He does not say: "I have received a people for Myself; I have assembled Israel." No, He says: "Sons have I reared, etc." It is as if He were saying: "I have omitted nothing. There is nothing I have not shown. I wanted to be their Father. I chose them to be My children. And not only this, but also I brought them up; that is, I bestowed on this people all fatherly blessings, care, protection, a very great increase in number, etc." Look at the histories. He is alluding to this, that if any king or prince of the earth were to do such things, it would be a great kindness, and it would be great ingratitude if men did not acknowledge the kindness, even though it was conferred by men. Now, when God does it, it is regarded as nothing.

Allegory.[4] "They were adopted as children, and indeed they ought to be children, because I showed Myself toward them as a Father. I not only brought them up, protected them, and increased their number; but I also exalted them, glorified them, and made much of them. I made their name holy. I gave them kings and princes, so that there was no other kingdom of this kind on earth." God is good by nature, and He does not cast His kindness in the teeth of those who acknowledge that they have received this from God their Father. On the other hand, He berates the ungodly for their incalculable ingratitude. Here, however, you have a sign of God's fatherly feeling toward us. But how do we behave toward such a great Father? Alas, He has reared us as His children and has received evil instead of good. We are ungrateful, we despise and blaspheme Him; that is to say, we are nourished by the blessings of God in order to be His enemies through these. Woe, woe to him who loves such a world! This is surely a serious matter, and therefore He says: *Hear, O heavens, etc.*

[4] On Luther's resort to allegorical interpretation in these lectures, see Introduction, p. xi.

But they have rebelled against Me. That is, "They have deserted Me; they have withdrawn from Me; and though exalted by Me, they have dropped their excrement into My hand." The world treats us in the same way, no matter how much we have done for it. Whoever wishes to live in the world and desires to imitate God, his Father, should expect from the world the same treatment that God receives. Accordingly, He says: "I have bestowed many favors on them. But they turn away from Me and go elsewhere. They blaspheme Me, and the very things with which I attract them to worship Me they prefer to misuse for the purpose of wickedness." This is a description of the world.

3. *The ox knows its owner, etc.* Among the Hebrews verbs in the past tense are explained as being in the present tense, provided that nothing interferes.[5] And this is the praise of our wisdom and our free will. In the preceding verse our righteousness and sanctity were praised, which is the height of ingratitude and blasphemy, and with this ungodliness those who want to be most saintly exert themselves above all. Now it is shown what the light of our intellect is, when we are so confounded that no one dares to lift up his eyes when he sees an ox or an ass approaching him. Is it not a great thing that an ass should be compared, yes, preferred to us – an ass that knows where it is looking and betakes itself to the house of its master? Would we not rightly bare our heads before the ass and greet it as our teacher? Therefore it is still proper to say to us: "You are an uncouth ass and more uncouth than an ass." When the Hebrews speak of the manner of having possession, they often use the word בַּעַל, which means master, husband, or lord. Baal of the sword, for instance, means one who owns a sword.[6] Thus the "master's crib" means the crib that belongs to its lord and to him who owns the ass.

But Israel does not know. Here the Lord certainly speaks plainly, for He should rather have said: "My people are foolish. They have no knowledge or understanding. They are more stupid than an ox and an ass. But what will happen?" "My people," He says at another time, "are destroyed for lack of knowledge; because you have rejected knowledge. . . . And since you have forgotten the Law of your God, etc." (Hos. 4:6). Here, therefore, you understand what

[5] Cf. *Luther's Works,* 30, p. 233.

[6] Luther is thinking of the usage in a passage such as Gen. 49:23, where "archers" is literally "lords of the arrows."

is the wisdom and godliness of men who depart from God. Certainly there is nothing they think they do not know. He who would call them ignorant would be very hard of hearing. But here the prophet proceeds especially against those very people and says that they are more uncouth than an ass. Nevertheless, they think they know everything, and the prophet calls their wisdom and knowledge sheer stupidity and ignorance. But is it not foolhardy so to open the mouth and rail at the saintly people and condemn their wisdom and light? But who listened to this? No one except him who was of God. He confesses and deprecates his guilt in terror. Other hearts are not touched. The fact that because of the word "crib" this passage is applied to the birth of Christ is an error we can put up with, since it does not conflict with the faith; it is a childish mistake and one that flows from piety.[7] "As for the man who is weak in faith, welcome him" (Rom. 14:1). The stubborn must be resisted. Christ bore with the apostles even when they erred in the faith, but not with those who erred persistently. Augustine says: "It will be possible for me to err, but I will not be a heretic." [8]

4. *Woe to the sinful nation!* Some interpret this as meaning: "Oh, how sinful this nation is!" [9] But give heed to the ability of the prophet; he strips those people of every mask. Above he said that they were ungodly and foolish; now he robs them of the glory because of which they boasted of being the people of God, a holy nation, a royal priesthood (1 Peter 2:9), the seed of Abraham, the children of God whom He led out of Egypt and to whom He gave the Law. All this the prophet overturns and says that they are indeed a nation, but a sinful one which ought to have been holy, a people chosen indeed by God and one that ought to be borne up above the stars but now lies [10] on the ground crushed with sins. Therefore their god and prince is the devil. A seed they are indeed, but an evil one and of evil parentage,

[7] The ceremonies surrounding the use of the crèche in medieval devotion included quotations and allusions from the Biblical references to "crib," whether these referred to the manger or not.

[8] In his *Rejection of Purgatory* (W, 30-II, 382), Luther also quoted these words, "Errare potero, sed hereticus non ero," which do not seem to appear in this form in Augustine's writings.

[9] This interpretation is reflected in the English translation of the verse: "Ah, sinful nation." In the Vulgate, which Luther is following here, the verse is rendered: *Vae genti peccatrici.*

[10] The Weimar text has *iacere,* but we have read *iaceret.*

not of godly Abraham. Children they are indeed, but of corrupt parents, not of God; sons of the damned, not of salvation, whose every effort is directed toward evil. This, you see, is the distinction of the Jews and of the ungodly among us too. Certainly they were not all like this; yet the great majority were, and they were involved in both gross and internal sins to such an extent that they did not accept the rebuke, namely, that they are lost and hopeless people who must be chastised by the executioner, since they refuse to be chastised by their Father. But this is their sin.

They have forsaken the Lord. That is to say, this strength of theirs has departed from the true worship of God, namely, from faith and love. Indeed, they have even forsaken the external form of worship prescribed to them and have brought sacrifices on the mountaintops. They have not feared God; but, what is more serious, they have blasphemed Him and fought against Him, and they have not only departed from obedience to Him. And such things are said against a holy people under excellent kings. If the prophet were here, what would he say to us thoroughly wicked people? After they had forsaken the faith, they invented one religion and one opinion of faith after the other. This always happens, and for that counterfeit faith they rage against the true prophets and blaspheme in them the true Word of God. For together with the Word of God sects that blaspheme the Word always arise, and thus there is always a battle with the Word of God and against the truth. Peter says (2 Peter 2:2): "Because of them they have reviled the way of truth." *The Holy One of Israel,* namely, for whose worship Israel was chosen and sanctified by Him. Therefore the prophet calls Him holy on the basis of what He effects.[11] Our Holy One is Christ, who sanctifies us through the Word of truth. Yet many attack this true and only sanctification with another sanctity that is counterfeit and false. A pig is led unwillingly to a bath because it thinks this is mud. On the other hand, it is willing to go into mud because it considers this a bath. Thus the wicked sectarians abhor the truth because they are delighted by lies.

They are utterly estranged. נָזֹרוּ; that is, they have drawn away, have separated and consecrated themselves, have sanctified themselves for something. He means, therefore, that the Jews have sanc-

[11] On the origin of this insight into Biblical usage, see *Luther's Works,* 34, p. 337.

tified themselves in reverse; that is, they are sanctified by someone else than God, who is the "Holy One of Israel," that they praise some new holiness, namely, the devil's, that is, mud, pigs. And thus he deprives them of all glory.

5. *Why will you still be smitten?* This is another rebuke, namely, that they are utterly hardened and incorrigible, even though they have been punished. And this annoys God most. When the ungodly are punished, they turn this to their own advantage as praise of martyrdom or of holiness. Thus the papists in their insurrection boasted that they had suffered for the sake of glory.[12] This is what God complains about through the prophet. It is as if He were saying: "Whether I chastise you by means of words or with blows, you always add deceit and are hardened against Me by those very blows." The scourges are turned into a strengthening of ungodliness. Therefore the final scourge must come, namely, death itself, which will put an end not only to their prevarications but also to their ungodliness and to the false righteousness which they appropriate to themselves because of suffering the blows which are inflicted more because of their sins. What, then, will be the way to proceed? With what cure will I help you? If I add blows to words,[13] you become more impenitent, stubborn, and hardened. Promises do not soften you. Threats do not frighten you. Blows do not reform you. These are hard hearts. Gross sinners can certainly be reformed, at least with punishments, because they acknowledge that they are stricken for sins which they cannot deny. But saintlets and spiritual sinners cannot be reformed; for they do not acknowledge their sins and therefore do not think that they are being punished on account of sins. Ahaz was stricken much and often, but for this reason he worshiped strange gods much more, especially the gods of the Syrians, because he saw their prosperity. Thus when a blow threatens, our people run more quickly from one place and another rather than to God, and they increase their sins, although they imagine they are seeking pardon. This is what we read in Jeremiah (44:17 ff.). There is a proverb which states: "While fools shun faults, they run into the opposite fault." [14]

[12] Luther is probably, though not certainly, referring to the Peasants' War of 1525, which occupied his mind frequently in the course of these lectures (cf. p. 42, p. 74, and p. 231 below).

[13] The Latin contains a play on words: *Si verbis addam verbera.*

[14] Horace, *Satires,* I, 2, 24.

6. *The whole head is sick, etc.* Not a part or member remains that has not been smitten. To be sure, we deserve more smiting; but there is no room, because already the whole head has been smitten enough and is sick. Even now the whole heart is faint. Even though I could undoubtedly find a place to smite you, yet I still desist, because there is no physician to provide a cure. Nor do you want to be reformed. You promise yourselves the highest seats in heaven, etc. So it is with our hypocrites. But no matter how much we have sinned, there is no reason for us to despair, provided that we acknowledge our sins and have knowledge of our Lord Jesus Christ and of God's mercy in Him. If there is no light, there will be no room for a cure. Isaiah is a rhetorician in a wonderful manner, and he uses flowery language; for he almost always employs allegories and figures of speech. The people are the body; the head, the superiors; the heart, the sages and practitioners of justice. The remaining classes of the people are the other members. Therefore He wants to say that these people are smitten and abased as much in the upper classes as in the lower classes of men. Look at the histories. When the 10 tribes were led up, how the two tribes in the land of Judah and elsewhere feared for themselves! For the words of the prophet should not be pulled apart to apply only to this or that historical situation, but the prophet speaks in a general way except when he speaks of Christ. This is the hardness of the human heart, which is deep and inscrutable, since it has been impenitent. For even though all evils are inflicted on it, yet it remains hard like the trunk of a tree and like an anvil. This is the heart that deserves to be terrified by even a flying leaf (Lev. 26:36), since it does not have the promises by which it may be buoyed up and lacks the comfort of faith and help. It is smitten within by dread, blindness, and madness. Without there are disturbances of all classes: of princes, prophets, and priests of the people, since God smites all things. There is no physician with the obligation to cure this, that is, no prophet with the obligation to proclaim and teach this. Yet there are false prophets who presume to offer comfort of a sort, but as it is in Jeremiah, the people are worse off because of the cure offered by those men.

7. *Your country lies desolate.* When Isaiah prophesied, this had not yet happened except in the land of Israel. Therefore there are some who refer this passage to the devastation of Israel when it was led into

Assyria under Jotham.[15] Accordingly, He is saying: In your presence this happened, and it will happen more completely when even your whole kingdom will be overwhelmed. Now the body politic is afflicted, and a part of the land lies desolate, to be devastated even more by the Chaldeans. In Hebrew the country is called fields, soil, אֲדָמָה, which means red and fertile earth. The prophet has put the container for the content,[16] the field for the produce.

Aliens, that is, outsiders. It is as if He were saying: "You are sons and lords of the land because the Lord hands it over to you, but because of your sins you will be forced to see outsiders rule over it and enjoy its fruits.

It is desolate, as overthrown by aliens. (This allegory may be referred to the judge of this sign +, which you see above on this same page.)[17] Oil denotes the Word of grace and the promise of good things. The wound is first cleansed and purged of bloody matter with a sponge or a cloth; then it is soothed with oil and bandaged with a plaster. This means that sins must first be shown, and penitence must be preached; then the promises must be added, and the Word of grace with which to assuage the grief of contrition.

8. *And the daughter of Zion is left.* That is, what remained of Jerusalem will not be a kingdom or a palace but huts for shepherds and cabins for the night watch. For when the whole body has been smitten to such an extent that no place is left for a blow, yet the sins remain, and there is no one to heal, to mourn, to restore. And the wounds fester. Nothing is left except that the whole kingdom is corrupted and destroyed, just as unbandaged wounds putrefy and corrupt more and more from day to day. And compared with its flourishing state, the kingdom of Judah will be devastated like a single little hut in a vineyard. After the princes and the nobles had been led away, the peasants and the rabble were left behind. Therefore you should not think that nothing at all was left in the land.

Like a besieged city. It is called a fortified city by antiphrasis, like war, a grove, etc.

9. *If the Lord of hosts had not left us a few survivors, etc.* The Hebrew word שָׂרִיד means survivors. The Septuagint has trans-

[15] Cf. Jerome, *Commentaria,* I, 30—31.

[16] The particular form of metonymy is *continens pro contento,* as in "this cup" in 1 Cor. 11:25.

[17] In the manuscript there appears a + at this point.

lated it with "seed." Paul followed this version in Rom. 9:29. He applied this passage as a general statement to his own times. God had promised that He would be the God of Abraham and of his seed forever. Because of this promise there always remain among the Jews those who belong to Christ, and a kingdom of the Jews had to remain for the sake of Christ, who wanted to be born, to preach, and to die there, namely, as the One promised to that nation. Thus that tree was cut down, yet the root and the stump remained, and this out of the pure mercy of God and the superabundance of His grace. In Sodom no survivors remained. This is a a rebuke directed against the saints and the self-righteous – a rebuke especially of those whose conversion through an offering will be impossible. But true conversion is a matter of faith, not of works.

10. *Hear the Word of the Lord, you rulers of Gomorrah!* The prophet was a man with a great and burning spirit. Paul says in Rom. 10:19 f. that after Moses Isaiah has courage, when one considers the circumstances and the importance of his words. Certainly this is an exceedingly sharp reproof. Yet it was spoken under godly King Uzziah, who is praised in Scripture. Undoubtedly there were also many good people in this nation. Under King Ahaz they would not have put up with this reproach. They do not want to be accused of being ungodly. Now, therefore, the prophet begins as a good teacher to tell them what they must do to put an end to the affliction of the head and the members, namely, that first their hypocritical and pharisaical righteousness must be done away with.

11. *What to Me is the multitude of your sacrifices?* According to the judgment of the flesh, which does not understand the Holy Spirit, these words are indeed pure blasphemies. The prophet agrees with David in Ps. 40:6 and in Ps. 50:13, and with others who reject the sacrifices offered for the purpose of appeasing God, such as Jer. 7:22; Ezek. 20:25, although the offering of sacrifices was the supreme work and was commanded by God through Moses. And this is our doctrine of faith, that God is not appeased by our works and merits; for He neither needs nor wants them in order that we may have glory. But He Himself, who has regard for nothing else than His own goodness, has the glory. Therefore whoever wants to appease God by his own merits is worse than the Sodomites, namely, an idolater. Consequently, these people are reproached here in this way because they do not understand the Law. But when the godly

bring sacrifices, they testify that they believe God; and by this faith they are justified. The ungodly disregard faith and consider sacrifice to be the supreme worship of God; that is, they despise the kernel and admire the husk. To them faith is worthless because they do not see it, but they do see the showiness of works and therefore admire them and make much of them. To be sure, sacrifices are not evil; but if on their account I wanted to boast that I am a righteous child of God, etc., then I would be misusing them. It is like this: If I wanted to boast that I am an heir of heaven because of the bright eye God gave me, I would be misusing an otherwise good eye and would be making it only an idol and making a liar of God, who says that He will be gracious for His own sake, not for the sake of anything else whatever. Therefore we must do works only for the purpose of bearing witness to faith in God – the faith by which I acknowledge that He is merciful and freely pours out His mercy on my misery. And in the end he is a true Christian who neither is presumptuous in his works nor despairs in his sins, even though he avoids sins and does good works. Nevertheless, the affections of hope must be fixed on God alone, not on a creature or a work.

I have had enough of burnt offerings. This means that He is disgusted with them; that is, that they are useless to Him and that He has need neither of eating the flesh nor of drinking the blood for the purpose of being appeased but is nauseated by them, even though they were the most praiseworthy offerings in the Law, especially the fat, which, as He has particularly mentioned, was offered to Him. Does the prophet not forbid good works here? Not the works, but the attitude.

I did not delight. "I do not delight" is better, since he is speaking of the present status of the people before God. There was not the least praise even for the offering of blood, from which they abstained completely. They smeared and sprinkled the altars. Yet He condemns even this form of worship. What, then, is holy, when the best part of the religion is removed?

12. *When you come to appear before Me.* It is as if He were complaining of the insult that by their entrance into the court they have desecrated the place. He does not consider them worthy of entrance into the court, as if they were an unbearable burden for His court. It is as if He were saying: "You enter My court as filthy peasants going into a lovely creek with their muddy boots." And

this applies properly to the priests, who entered behind the veil and appeared before the Lord. The face of the Lord was the name given to those images in the tabernacle, where God had said He would dwell. Therefore those who entered were said to see the face of the Lord. And surely such a religion handed down by God should not be despised. What God hands down is something great, even if it is physical, that men may know that they worship God through these things; for otherwise one seeks God here, another there, yet will find God nowhere except where He has bound Himself through His Word. On the other hand, however, it is insolent to condemn what Moses commanded and to say: *Who has required these things?* God requires our works, and He does not require them. How is this? I answer: He simply requires them, not as if they themselves were necessary or as if He wanted to be appeased by them. Thus, on the other hand, He does not require them. But consider the folly of men. We reverse the order and want to serve God with works and men with faith. Thus they say that that what has been presented to the sacrificing priests has been given to God and must not be turned to profane uses. Of course, it has been given to them that they might serve God. But to serve and come to the aid of neighbors, to those who are needy, this they do not consider to be a service of God. For this reason they are taken to task here.

Who has required these things? For thus man trusts man, but works do not follow. On the other hand, where God is to be believed, there the works are multiplied. What, then, does the prophet, or God, say? "Distribute the flesh of your animals to the poor, and do not disturb Me." For this is what the sacrifices are for, namely, to feed the poor priests, not to appease God. Yet they sought to do the latter with the sacrifices. מִנְחָה, that is, the sacrifices consisted properly of solid and dried foods such as bread, flour, etc. Furthermore He says that they are not only useless but are even an abomination, since they had the idea that the more often a burnt offering was brought, the more praiseworthy it was. In sum, these are statements directed specifically against the efforts and works of men. And the works are not condemned, but only their misuse, that is, false trust in them. You should rather sing (cf. Ps. 51:1): "Be merciful to me, O God, not on account of the multitude of my burnt sacrifices, not on account of the holiness and purity of Mary and others, but on account of Thy great mercy." Scripture always proclaims the mercy of God and our sin. The majesty of God is supreme; we are completely worthless. Yet we must convince ourselves that God is merciful to us, because this is what He has promised. If only our faith were strong, this gracious disposition of God would make us fearless in all things. Fear indicates weakness on God's part. A faith undaunted defies all things, and because faith is such a great thing, it condemns our efforts and works, even the best of them, as sins, because they puff us up, etc.

13. *New moon and Sabbath.* These are the things you boast of very much and proclaim, and you establish many new things. Moses called those declared festivals the chief ones. I cannot, says God, endure אָוֶן, that is, iniquity, and עֲצֶרֶת or עֲצָרָה, that is, solemn assembly. Thus the speech grows. For first He said that He was disgusted with their offerings and that they were an abomination; now He says that they are utterly useless and evil, and that He does not want them. אָוֶן, that is, trouble. This is properly transferred by a metaphor to their pursuits of piety and their idols. For those things are nothing but trouble and toil, and those hypocrites burden themselves with many ceremonies and unbearable things. Yet they gain nothing fruitful or useful. It is sheer toil, weariness, and trouble, which fruitlessly devour the worshiper himself in a restless spirit, even though otherwise they eat and drink, etc. The Jews rejoiced before the Lord on seven festive days, but on the seventh day they were called together and blessed after the Law had been read and they had prayed. Behold, this diligence is also fruitless. There is no difference between the new moon and the calends, but both mean the same thing, namely, the new moon and the first day of the month.

14. *Your.* By adding this word the prophet means that the Jews also established other festivals besides those of Moses, and those additions constantly obscure the first good institution of God. Satan always wants to be God's mimic and ape, but God hates him.

15. *When you spread forth.* It was a gesture of prayer, praise, and blessing to lift up the hands, as in the writings of Paul and in the Psalms. This, then, is the meaning: "Even though you pray with the greatest boldness, I will turn away, I will not hear." Is this not altogether bad? Not at all. But the misuse of prayer and βαττολογία (cf. Matt. 6:7) are censured. Likewise ungodliness, for He says:

Your hands are full of blood, though Paul, on the other hand, says (1 Tim. 2:8): "Lifting holy hands." And here the prophet says that they are all murderers. By the hands are meant the works which should be done for the needy neighbor. But he who does not help his neighbor destroys him. 1 John 3:15 states: "Anyone who hates his brother is a murderer." Ambrose says: "Feed your starving brother. If you have not fed him, you have killed him."[18] We read (Matt. 25:42): "I was hungry, and you gave Me no food." Again (1 John 3:17): "If anyone has the world's goods, etc." In short, he who does not practice love toward his neighbor is regarded by God as a murderer; for even though he is able to help, yet he does not do so. So far as he is concerned, he lets his brother perish. In brief, the meaning is this: "You have hands full of blood. Therefore your prayers and all your efforts are ungodly." Thus with one word he involves them in all sins and proves them guilty of damnation. This statement does not disturb us very much, but God certainly does not speak in vain. What good thing would bloodhounds pray for? Consider how many monsters there are in the world, and how much ungodliness. We do everything except what love demands; we give much for monstrous and godless religions but nothing for the need of the poor. Clean before men, but unclean, cruel, and murderers before God. Who could rest when thinking of these things? God grant that these things do not come to mind in the last hour! James says: "Come now, you rich, weep, etc." (James 5:1). One aspect of ungodliness is unfaithfulness. Another is bloodiness; that is, a lack of love, which is the fruit of faith. We neglect these, and meanwhile we busy ourselves in vain with various religions. Nobody considers how great the demand of faith and love is. What, then, is to be done? Now he sets forth a command in an affirmative manner.

16. *Wash yourselves; make yourselves clean.* Here is the whole thing. He mentions two parts. One is to put aside filth, unfaithfulness, hatred, and all ungodliness. The other is to do good. Thus David says (Ps. 37:27): "Depart from evil and do good." The filth is removed by a bath. Cleanness is a new kind of life. Therefore wash yourselves from ungodliness; cleanse yourselves through godliness. Put an end to the unclean blindness and the bloody hand.

Remove the evil of your thoughts. This pertains to the washing. "The evil of your thoughts," that is, of your plans, blindness, ungodli-

[18] Cf. Ambrose, *De officiis,* II, 28, 140—142, where some of these thoughts are expressed though not in these very words.

ness, hypocrisy. Keep quiet, stop acting spitefully and doing evil to your neighbors contrary to love. Do no harm; do not offend them.

17. *Seek justice.* שָׁפַט, he judged; מִשְׁפָּט judgment, right. Justice, however, called צֶדֶק, is the administration and the carrying out of the right, namely, when what is right is done. צְדָקָה, that is, justifying justice or alms (cf. Dan. 4:24). Such a one, says Jer. 23 and Ps. 24:5, will receive blessing from God and צְדָקָה; that is, he will be blessed and justified by the Lord. צֶדֶק seems to pertain to external righteousness, which, however, is right if it flows from internal righteousness. Now, however, justice proceeds only as far as the purse does.

Correct oppression; that is, buoy up him who suffers violence and is harrassed by perverted right, to whom might is applied, not right, by mixing up the words.[19] The world is full of wrongs, so that a just judge hardly has time left to go to the temples.

Defend the fatherless. The defense of an orphan consists in bringing it about that he is not oppressed. When there is no defender in the world, then a poor man lies exposed everywhere to every act of robbery. Consider the dealings of guardians and those who draw up wills, whether they are guilty of blood. Widows have been bereft of a defender. Here there is sinning in an extraordinary manner. Many live for themselves. Meanwhile they neglect the poor, devote themselves to prayer, and consider themselves saints. Yet it is not enough not to have harmed one's neighbor; God also demands positive uplifting of the needy through love, and one's whole substance and life must be expended for the brethren, as John 3:17 says. Would that we only realized that this is our duty! For it is evil for us to think smugly that we are living a good life. For it is a serious matter, because you hear: "The Lord says."

18. *Come now, let us reason together.* Come, and let us have a discussion. It is as if He were saying: "I will enter into judgment with you. If I do not do good and am not gracious to those who do these things, believe, are washed and clean, then accuse Me and charge falsely that I am not God. Indeed, it is God's inward feeling and His preponderant desire. How much He would want us to be good! Oh, would that we acknowledged our evils with all our hearts! Then the Spirit would finally come. But to pass away in folly in

[19] The Latin is a play on the words *uis* and *ius*.

this manner, this is regrettable. Christianity is surely a constant sobbing. Who of the two, then, is more righteous, the people, who do wrong and love their own strivings while despising God's commandments, namely, of faith and love, or God, who censures and condemns these strivings?

Though your sins are like scarlet, etc. Scarlet, Tyrian purple, shellfish purple, dye from a purple fish, purple. This is a new and strange way of speaking. Why did He not rather say black sins? Black denotes sadness, but red denotes bloodguiltiness. Sins are red when we are guilty of blood. "Deliver me," he says, "from bloodguiltiness" (Ps. 51:14), that is, from the guilt of death and of punishments. White is the sign of innocence and justice. Therefore the angels, as innocent spirits, appeared mostly in white garments. For Oriental kings, namely, for those who were rather mild, the special attire was white. But bloodthirsty Rome conducted itself as worthy of purple.[20] Therefore the meaning here is this: "Though your sins are in the highest degree deserving of punishments and death, they will be worthy of righteousness and faith; and though they are worms, they will not bite you." Certainly the fullest, finest, and sweetest consolation. Although we have very many sins, yet they will be as if they did not exist. Nor will they frighten us, even if they are present; for they are white. The Jews used white wool very often. Consequently, even in the Song of Solomon (4:2; 6:5) white teeth are compared to wool. Therefore he simply says here: "Like wool."

19. *If you are willing and obedient.* To the spiritual promise He adds a physical one. Therefore for faith He promises the forgiveness of sins, namely, a spiritual promise; and for love and clean hands He promises an abundance of temporal goods. "Give," He says in Luke 6:38, "and it will be given to you; good measure." Because you have left, etc., "a hundredfold," Matt. 19:29 says. "Seek first the kingdom of God," Matt. 6:33 says. These things are promised here, but they are regarded as something written on a wall which all pass by. No one believes that it is true. On the contrary, they say: "Give, and I will give." *You shall eat the good of the land.* In one word he expresses abundance or at least sufficiency, and the land brings forth more than we all can consume; and all of us would easily have enough, provided that we distributed things equally. But now one person grasps as much for himself as would be enough for a thousand, yet

[20] The Weimar text has *purpuram,* but we have read *purpura.*

not to distribute it, much less to enjoy it himself. The godly, however give bountifully. Therefore they also have what they need.

20. *If you refuse and embitter Me;* that is, if you are disobedient to Me. For God is embittered by disobedience. If teachings, admonitions, and promises accomplish nothing, threats will surely be effective.

You shall be devoured by the sword. "I will not let the obedient be unrewarded or the disobedient unpunished." God first gives Himself to the godly, and then He gives all good things. What more could or should He do? But this profusion bestowed even on the ungodly will make their judgments worse.

For the mouth of the Lord. He will surely proceed in this way and in no other. He adds this to frighten them. For it is not Marcolphus,[21] not Demosthenes, not Vergil who is speaking; but since He teaches, promises, and threatens in vain, for this reason He returns to Himself and again begins to expostulate. Similarly, when we see no progress of the Word, we, too, cry out: "Is it not a blow that so great a light is despised in this way?"

21. *How the faithful city has become a harlot!* He uses meaningful and emphatic words. It is as if He were saying: "Why is it that such clear blessings, promises, and threats accomplish nothing?" To commit fornication away from God is a strong expression. This is what Jerusalem, which was once loyal and upright and in which the truth shall be, is doing. He who is faithful is contrasted to hypocrisy and false religion, which is called fornication before God, where faith has been abandoned and hearts are prostituted to false teachings. Here formerly there was the true faith, which makes righteous. There were excellent rulers, such as David, Solomon, etc., who practiced justice. Superstitions and the traditions of men did not hold sway. Righteousness, that is, the carrying out of justice, dwelt here, that is, was in operation. Now, however, there are murderers. Thus it is stated above (v. 15): "Your hands are full of blood, etc." This is hard preaching for delicate ears. The truth is biting, and therefore it brings forth hatred.[22]

[21] We have been unable to identify the "Marcolphus" to whom Luther refers here.

[22] Cf. Terence, *Andria,* 68.

22. *Your silver has become dross.* This is the prophet's fullness of expression as he explains what a harlot is. The meaning is the same, but the words are different. With the word "silver" he simply refers to all ruling princes. Dross is very much like silver. Yet it is not silver, and it has no value. Thus Jerusalem has the appearance of sanctity; but in it there is sheer hypocrisy, the sediment of silver. They are criminal children of saintly fathers. And this is the great sentence against all perversions of righteousness. For among us, too, mere masks have arisen from the best bishops. It is dross, not silver. Water, not wine, except only in appearance. The people are neither refreshed nor gladdened either by doctrine or by civil government. For this allegory applies to both. Godly officials in the church as well as in the state are silver and wine, and they give strength and joy. The godless, on the other hand, oppress and destroy.

23. *Your princes are rebels and companions of thieves.* The prophet explains himself. In Hebrew "rebels" are instigators and disobedient. For סוֹרֵר [23] means rebellious, impudent, stubborn, unreliable; but חָבֵר means one who turns a stranger away and incites him to rebellion. In this way, therefore, He accuses the princes in accordance with their evil state of mind, not according to the Law. "Companions of thieves." It is a crime of high treason to apply this term to the princes. But he calls them people of this kind for the same reason that he calls them murderers above (v. 21), and here he adds the reasons why they are such people.

Everyone loves a bribe. It is not wicked to have money, and one could be glad to forgive them if the money is given to them willingly; but to chase after and look for it, this indeed is detestable, especially in princes, who on this account are called companions of thieves. They give nothing; they do nothing except in the hope of getting twice as much back. For the rabble tests friendship from the standpoint of usefulness. They seek only their own advantage to the neglect of others, whether those persons are orphans or widows; and yet it is chiefly for the sake of protecting such people that they administer their office. The law of nature is the law of God, and the prophets teach that one person owes love to the other. Therefore no one will be excused.

24. *Therefore the Lord says.* Since promises and threats accomp-

[23] We have corrected the Hebrew as it appears in the Weimar text.

lish nothing, He begins to proclaim the coming disaster, and He does this with lofty words. *The Lord of hosts.* In Hebrew: the ruling Lord, who does not rest or sleep in the heavens but rules and effectively carries out what He says. Nor does He let the matter remain in words, as people do for the purpose of terrifying. אָבִיר, strong, splendid, powerful, the God of Jacob. Above (v. 4): "the Holy One of Israel." He performs all things in His saints. In 2 Cor. 13:3 Paul says that He is powerful in us. In 1 John 4:4 John says: "He who is in you is greater than he who is in the world." *On My enemies.* Some interpret this to mean "on the Jews," [24] but it should rather be made to refer to foreign enemies to be brought in against the Jews. It is as if God were saying: "My enemies will bring it about that I give consolation." This is surely a grave and hard consolation. But when He pours Himself out completely to love us, when He has omitted nothing to attract us except love for Himself, when the sweetest promises accomplish nothing, when grave threats achieve nothing, what else should He do but let the complaint stand? It is as if He were saying: "Since they want nothing except to smash through headlong, I, too, will reveal My purpose." Surely His words have been brought to an end here with all arguments and figures of persuasion and teaching. He began by teaching, admonishing, and promising to guide the people, so that these words lack nothing that could move them. But they are hardened Pharisees and self-righteous people, and they do not think He is speaking about them. Therefore the last part of this address now follows. Here He neither promises nor threatens but simply prophesies what will happen to those who are ungodly, etc. Thus all preachers have always cried out in vain, as in Matt. 3:7: "Who warned you to flee from the wrath to come?" Because the ungodly cannot stop sinning and God does not approve of injustice, therefore He Himself does not cease to punish.

On My enemies. That is to say: "From the enemies vengeance will come upon this people, one who will comfort Me; and I will avenge Myself through My enemies." [25] For because the Jews were God's people, the enemies of the Jews were also God's enemies. "I will be an enemy to your enemies," He says (Ex. 23:22). The prophets often reminded God of this and said: "They are defiling Thy heritage," as if God were affronted by an attack on His people. For this reason

[24] Jerome, *Commentaria,* I, 40.

[25] At this point, as at several others later in these lectures, Luther breaks into German.

He says: "The persecutors of My people would also have to be My persecutors, and I would have to protect My people; but these people are living in such an abandoned manner that I am forced to summon My enemies and to reform them through My enemies." This word "I will vent My wrath has reference to what He said above (v.14), namely, "I am weary."

25. *I will turn My hand against you.* This is characteristic of divine power and the wrath of God, to chastise in such a way that nevertheless it leaves some seed that is sound. On the other hand, Satan utterly uproots everything, as the godless do in the Psalms. They say: "Let the name of Israel be remembered no more!" (Ps. 83:4) It is as if they were saying: "Let us destroy the tree together with the fruit." Moreover there is the raging of the world, together with the raging of the devil, about which we read below in chapter 14:10 ff. Thus it is the desire of the persecutors of the Gospel to destroy everybody completely without leaving anything, not even one little page that proclaims the Gospel. But God chastises in order that in spite of this one may see that the people are restored and are not destroyed but only corrected and smitten. Therefore He does not say: "I will utterly destroy all that is sick." No, He says: "I will turn My hand against you and remove the dross from you; that is, I will punish the wicked government, will remove ungodly teaching and the laws of strangers, and will take away the alloy and leave the pure silver. The silver is greatly changed in color and luster, and perhaps this is why what He called dross above (v. 22) He now calls alloy. He means the hypocrisy and the semblance of godliness with which they wanted to worship God. They say that the alloy is a stubborn metal that cannot be easily separated from others. Similarly, ungodliness is stubbornly tenacious. Lead and quicksilver are different. Therefore He preferred to say alloy here rather than lead.

26. *And I will restore your judges.* He interprets Himself by saying what He means by dross and alloy, namely, judges and counselors. This was done through King Sennacherib.

The city of righteousness, that is, of the righteousness that will flourish there where there will also be good rulers and good laws.

Faithful, that is, the city of faithfulness and uprightness, or truth. First the persons must be reformed, then both the laws and the city will be more easily reformed. First Moses appointed good judges.

Even the best laws are worthless if there are no good judges. Behold, however, it is God who gives good magistrates. They are not produced through many threats or promises, but when God looks for lice on a foolish person with a club. We indeed teach, and we do it strenuously; but we accomplish nothing. Therefore if the people are to be cleansed, they will be cleansed in the way He says: "I will turn my hand against you, etc." The stubborn refuse to believe but prefer to feel the chastisement. But by chastising He makes the wicked good.

27. *Zion shall be redeemed by justice.* This means that the Lord is always concerned about preserving the rest, lest they perish. By justice, not by laws. If the kingdom must be restored, this will certainly not be done by the laws of men; but it will be done by justice, that is, by killing the old life and turning it away from injustice, in order that we may become acceptable to God. For a reward follows righteousness, even when it is external; but punishment follows unrighteousness. This is the way to reform men so that they become upright and preserve judgment and justice. Then God will be favorably disposed toward them. Who will then be against them? Righteousness, that is, the righteousness whereby we are accounted righteous before God, although some interpret it as mercy,[26] which is justifying grace. Therefore Zion is brought back by the Spirit and by faith, and then the political administration is also restored. The Hebrews have no impersonal words, and in their place they use the third person plural.[27] Thus in the Gospel we have "they shall give good measure" (cf. Luke 6:38) instead of "it shall be given." Thus here we have "they shall restore" instead of "it shall be restored."

28. *But rebels and sinners shall be destroyed together.* This explains what was said above about dross, that is, hypocritical, greedy, and evil magistrates shall rule no more.

And those who forsake the Lord, that is, the idolaters, who follow their own desires and counsels.

29. *They shall be shamed by idols.* Some translate with "by the trees" or "by the groves," others with "by the oaks,"[28] which the

[26] Luther is apparently thinking of such passages as Hos. 2:19, where righteousness seems to be equated with mercy.

[27] That is, Hebrew, like spoken English, employs such locutions as "they say" rather than "it is said."

[28] Thus in the revision of Luther's translation of the Bible under discussion in 1538 ff., the rendition *Eichen* was suggested here (W, *Deutsche Bibel,* IV, 40).

Jews desired and which gave them pleasure. They planted and prepared them on every mountain (אֵיל means oak, or tree) and on pleasant hills, and next to them they erected altars and idols. They did everything with great zeal and at great expense. They established new kinds of worship in opposition to God after forsaking the temple in imitation of their fathers and of the Gentiles. They sought piety according to their own feelings.

You have chosen, namely, for the worship of God. But you will be a "garden" that is not desirable but parched and withered.

31. *And the strong shall become tow.* These are very beautiful comparisons. They mean that one cannot resist the wrath and the scourge of God. It is easy to set tow on fire, but it is hard to put the fire out. Thus it will be impossible to hinder the scourge of God. "Strong," or חָסֹן in Hebrew, refers to the idol in the grove, just as above (v. 24) God was called "strong" and "of Israel." Thus for the idol they devised names belonging to a deity. But the idol itself will become ashes together with its maker; or it means in general the princes and all the magistrates and heads of households to whom He threatens destruction and a burning until they are pure, both the household economy and the state.

Your work, that is, government and power together with attendants. The shepherd together with the flock. A remnant will be preserved, as stated above (v. 9). It is more pleasant and agreeable to endure discipline from God than from men, as David experienced. He said: "When Thou art angry, Thou wilt remember mercy" (cf. Heb. 3:2; Ps. 65:3), but especially toward those who know Him.

CHAPTER TWO

1. *The Word which Isaiah the son of Amoz saw concerning Judah and Jerusalem.*

AFTER the Babylonian captivity a part of the kingdom of Judah was preserved in order that it might be the seed of the coming reign of Christ, to whom it was bound. Therefore this people could not be completely rejected until the lawful reign of Christ had come. And this is why the prophets move over from the physical kingdom to the spiritual, even though they are regarded as fanatics for not preserving the order. But he who sees the continuance of those two kingdoms will also see that the prophets have written in the best way. Accordingly, in the previous chapter Isaiah dealt with the punishments of the physical kingdom because of the sin and ungodliness of those people. Later he dealt with limited restoration after the captivity. Now follows the prophecy concerning the kingdom of Christ that is to come after the return from the captivity. But these words must be carefully noted, because the prophet speaks spiritually when he describes the church of Christ and skillfully depicts it, namely, that this kingdom is ruled by one scepter, which is the Gospel. Wherever this Gospel is proclaimed with sincerity, there this kingdom of Christ is. The Word does not deceive. Works can deceive. The Holy Spirit accompanies the Word, though He may not be present in the preacher and in the hearers. The Jews are still looking for a physical kingdom of Christ in Jerusalem. Yet in that kingdom of Christ no person or mask is shown, but only a voice and a word. The Hebrews explain עַל by saying that it means "to us." We explain it more clearly with "concerning," as in the Epistle to the Hebrews. "To whom, that is, concerning whom," says Isaiah, "we are speaking." Likewise (Heb. 1:7): "To, that is, of, the angels He says, etc." דָּבָר means "word," "speech," "thing," "cause," "order," "something." The pronoun "this" is used rather frequently for the word mentioned last.

2. *It shall come to pass in the latter days that the mountain of the*

house of the Lord shall be established. You see that here the prophet speaks in a completely spiritual sense, for what he says here cannot be understood in a physical sense. Moriah is the mountain on which Solomon built the temple, on which at an earlier time Abraham was going to sacrifice his son; and he interprets it to mean "vision." Here, he says, it shall be established because it is the highest. But when did this take place? The Jews imagine that all mountains flow together and that Mt. Moriah will be the loftiest.[1] But this is not said here. It was necessary, however, for the church to begin at a definite place, where the Gospel would have its beginning and where Christ would come together with His disciples. Although the Gospel is not bound to a place, yet it had to begin at some place, and there has to be a place for hearing the Gospel, not however, for obtaining salvation. Hag. 2:9 says: "The latter splendor of this house shall be greater than the former," because there the church had to begin, namely, in a physical place, though the church itself is not physical. That mountain, He says, will be most highly praised, because from it the church receives its name and will be called Mt. Zion. Out of a physical mountain the prophet makes one that is spiritual and a kingdom that is spiritual. Therefore the church, or the kingdom of Christ, is an exalted mountain, the house of the Lord in a spiritual sense, because there it had its beginning in a physical way. *Established* is a Hebraism and means confirmed, attested, made stable. Scripture is also wont to speak this way elsewhere. In 1 Kings 2:46 we read: "So the kingdom was established in the hand of Solomon." Thus this kingdom will also be lifted up beyond all hills, all other kingdoms, principalities, and whatever is lofty on earth. No matter how much the church is sure to be harassed and trampled underfoot by death, sins, Satan, tyranny, and heretics, yet in this trampling underfoot it shall be exalted above all mountains. For no other kingdom is so firmly established, and compared with it all other kingdoms are filthy: the Assyrians, the Greeks, the Chaldeans, the Romans, etc. For that kingdom endures, overcomes, and triumphs over death, devil, and heresies. No other kingdom can do this. But this takes place by the Word alone. Very many kingdoms have been laid waste. The church remains victorious over all kingdoms and the gates of hell (Matt. 16:18).

And all the nations shall flow to it. A wonderful kingdom this!

[1] On Moriah, cf. *Luther's Works,* 4, pp. 98—101.

The others are set up by force of arms in such a way that the nations are subjugated against their will. This kingdom, however, is not established by force, and here men are not compelled against their will. But because it will be raised up, they will flow to it; that is, the virtues of the church will attract the nations so that they come of their own free will. The kingdom of Christ has been put in progress because it is placed in public view with its powers and gifts. Here one sees truth, pure doctrine, safety, peace; the Gospel is heard, and nothing can give greater joy. For it promises an abundance of things and salvation both here and hereafter, and a man stands safe in this Word against everything that opposes him, even against the gates of hell (Matt. 16:18). Behold, these virtues should influence the nations to make them come. They are proclaimed through the Word, namely, that Christ is the King of mercy and of peace. Moses preaches the Law and is the minister of sin and death. Nobody runs to him. On the contrary, they are terrified. Christ, on the other hand, is the Minister of righteousness, of life, and of peace. Therefore the people flow to Him just as water flows by its own effort and needs no one to push it. This is what Christ says in Matt. 11:12: "The kingdom of heaven suffers violence." This cannot be understood of a physical kingdom to such a degree as the Jews dream, for the nations hate the Jews. But when He says *all the nations*, this must not be understood of every nation. No, this is a figure of speech, as in Gen. 22:18: "By your descendants shall all the nations of the earth be blessed." The Gospel will be published among all nations, and some will be converted everywhere. For the Gospel sanctifies in every place and bears fruit, as Paul says in Col. 1:6 and as Isaiah says below in ch. 55:11: "My Word . . . shall not return to me empty." Therefore all nations shall come to this mountain, that is, to the church, which is called a mountain. To this place the souls gather through faith; for when the Gospel is heard, hearts grow soft, rejoice, and come running.

3. *And many peoples shall come.* Before He said "shall flow," now He says "shall come" or "shall walk." This again is a word of spontaneous sanctification. It surely will be a kingdom that is willing, free, and safe. Paul says in 2 Cor. 9:7[2]: "God loves a cheerful giver." In the other kingdoms there is force and demanding. Although here,

[2] The original has "2 Cor. 8."

in the kingdom of Christ, the body is put in subjection, yet the spirit flows freely, believes willingly, loves, does good, etc.

And say: Come, let us go up to the mountain of the Lord. The whole occupation that is praised in this kingdom is the Gospel. Here nothing but the sweetness of the Word is discussed. "Let us go up," they say. They have one work, namely, to hear and be taught. It is on the kingdom and on nothing else, that this Word rests. The Gospel is the force, power, and work of Christians, and those people are true Christians who from day to day learn the same Word more and more and do not quickly become disdainful and get sick of it. The sectarians, on the other hand, are those who think at once that they fully understand what they have heard only once. A Christian must always learn to say: "Thy will be done." To be sure, it is easy to utter words, but in this life one will never add feeling in a perfect manner. This will happen after death. Therefore one can never learn enough. Paul says in Col. 3:16: "Let the Word of Christ dwell in you richly"; that is one must ponder it constantly, and always some new fire to arouse the heart will be found. The sectarians constantly think up one novelty after another. Christians never read the same teaching enough. For the Gospel does not concern itself with knowledge; it concerns itself with feeling. We slip every day. The flesh, sin, death, and the world assail us. Not for even one moment are we safe from spiritual adultery. This is how it is because sins surround us on all sides and weaken godly feelings. Besides, the world persecutes us. Hence it is necessary to hear the Word of God constantly, to proclaim the death of Christ constantly, and to ponder constantly, in order that our feelings may be enlightened. At another place He says (Matt. 7:13): "And lead us not into temptation, but deliver, etc." For no one is safe for even one hour, but all are daily in a most precarious state. Now they stand, now they fall, etc., and now an evil conscience, etc., is immediately associated with sin. *Come, let us go up.* They have a taste of the Word of God. Therefore they have a greater desire to hear the mountain of the Lord. He will teach, etc. All the words are emphatic. For Christians live every day by the Word as the body lives by food. He who does not have the Word or ponder it soon becomes a sorry wretch. If I do not reflect on a verse of a psalm or a statement of the Gospel, my heart is completely full of sins. A return to the Word guards against sins. The heart should always grind, if not something else, then at least itself. If the grain, namely, the Word of God, is good, the flour will be good, and the bread will be good. This life of ours is certainly most wretched. There is no rest, and therefore Christianity is most truly a hearing or pondering of the Word, in order that Christ may speak to us at all times. Therefore when anyone has trials that torture him in body or in soul, it is a sign that Christ is not at home, that is, is not in that person's heart. But he who wants to be set free should place Christ before him – Christ who says in Matt. 11:28: "Come to Me, all who labor," and in John 11:25: "I am the resurrection and the life." When Christ speaks he is set free and is not afraid. But when Christ is absent, the trial returns. Then the slaughter and the misfortunes of men begin, and those thoughts terrify the heart. Then return to Christ, who says (John 6:37): "Him who comes to Me I will not cast out." Behold, you hear the joyful and saving Word.

His ways. The ways of the Lord are His works, especially the works He does in us, namely, that He destroys the works of the devil, sin, death, sadness, fear, trembling, and all evils, then also our daily lapses; and He works the opposite in us: hope, righteousness, patience, joy, peace, etc. These are the ways of the Lord which His Word brings when it is heard and believed. When the Word is missing, we begin to be offended, to judge and accuse others. But when the Word is present, I say: "God has forgiven you your sins. You, too, must likewise forgive that person his sin and pray for him." In this way the heart is filled with new thoughts through the Word and is put at rest. Then we walk in the paths of the Lord; for Christ works and rules more and more in us – Christ, who is the Word of God and King over all. Good-bye to all other paths, for they are false.

Out of Zion shall go forth the Law, and the Word of the Lord from Jerusalem. This is what will influence and draw the nations, so that they flow to Christ and learn, namely, the Word. Here there is no armed departure from Jerusalem on the part of the king, no violent clash. Ps. 110:2 says: "The Lord sends forth from Zion your mighty scepter." From this place the scepter of Christ's kingdom was sent forth through the apostles without force in supreme peace, and the sweetness of this peace takes hold of the nations. But behold here the promise of a new word, a new law, namely, one that is different from that which was given from the cloud and on Sinai. Here a place different from Sinai is designated. *Law,* that is, proclamation. The prophecy stands that a proclamation shall flow from

Jerusalem into all nations. This was done through the apostles. Let this be the strength of our faith against the Jews. "Their voice has gone out to all the earth" (Rom. 10:18). By the Word alone, therefore, the church is recognized, and in the glory of the Word the reign of Christ is described. The Word draws the people, makes them willing and joyful. Thus the church is exalted and triumphs against tyrants and heretics even in the midst of tribulation, in order that they may be forced to confess that this is true.

4. *He shall judge between the nations.* Ps. 110:6: "He will execute judgment among the nations"; that is, He will perform the office of a judge, will rule through judgment, namely, through the Word. "He," says John 16:8, "will convince the world of sin, etc." This, however, is a description of the kingdom of Christ that is to be extended even among the Gentiles and is not to be confined to the Jews. In like manner, namely, through the Word, He will convict many peoples, that is, everywhere in the world. Although there is but one kingdom, yet it is present in many peoples. But He will convict them so that they acknowledge that they are sinners and are condemned before God because they do not know God, do not fear Him, and do not believe Him.

And they shall beat their swords into plowshares. This is a figurative and periphrastic way of speaking. It means that they will return to complete harmony and peace, and there is no better way to get rid of disagreements than that which Christ uses. In one statement He declares that at the same time all are condemned and that everything is full of sins before God. For those who hear and believe this, for what will they contend? If my property, wisdom, and righteousness are of no avail before God, why should I fight it out for them? In the world there is continual war. The self-righteous fight with one another for their righteousness. The godly condemn their own righteousness and accept the verdict of condemnation; false Christians are altogether carnal and worldly, and for this reason they are the instigators of factions and disagreements. True Christians are in beautiful agreement, because they hold even everything in contempt for the sake of Christ alone.

5. *O house of Jacob, come.* When there is this kind of preaching, the Gentiles will be converted and reduced to nothing, so that their own righteousness is not exalted. Then it will be most of all necessary

for you Jews first to acknowledge that grace. Paul says in Rom. 3[3]: "To the Jew first and also to the Greek." For the promise was given above all to the Jews and was first proclaimed among the Jews. Therefore since they are the first people and the chief part of the church, the prophet properly admonishes them to buy while the market is in front of the door. "In a time of favor," he says below in ch. 49:8, and "at the acceptable time" in 2 Cor. 6:2. "Therefore, O house of Jacob, to you above all this promise applies. Give thanks to God, do not disregard the light but 'while you have the light, believe in the light, etc.' (John 12:36), lest the darkness overtake you and you suffer harm."

6. *For Thou hast rejected Thy people, the house of Jacob.* עֵדֶן מִקֶּדֶם, which the old translation explains with "as of old,"[4] means "arising from before," so far as time and place are concerned. "The Lord God planted a garden in Eden, in the East" (Gen. 2:8). Hence this expression is used ambiguously here to mean from before, that is, before the ages; in the anterior part of a place, or among earlier people, Easterners, or those who are before them. For to the east the Jews have the Persians, the Arabians, and the Chaldeans; to the west they have Palestine with the Mediterranean Sea. This, then, is the meaning: The Jews are more superstitious than the Orientals or the Occidentals, because they are situated between them and know the superstitions of both. They are full of superstitions, more so than the Orient.

7. *They strike hands with foreigners.* This word is found elsewhere in the sense of "to be enough," "to multiply," "to make the number abundant." For example (Is. 40:16), "Lebanon would not suffice for fuel." Likewise (1 Kings 20:10), "If the dust of Samaria shall suffice." They make enough foreign children on earth, as if to say: Behold, God has given the light of the Gospel, truly a great and incomprehensible gift, whereby God is known and all things. But what happens? The Gospel is trampled underfoot and ignored by the hearers. A very small part of them is touched by the Word, and it is this that grieves us ministers of the Word most. Who would not curse the world? Christ says in John 3:19: "This is the judgment, that the light has come into the world, etc." Thus the prophet ad-

[3] The original has "Rom. 3," but such passages as Rom. 1:16 and 2:9 seem more appropriate to the context.

[4] The Vulgate translates *ut olim.*

monishes the Jews here to walk in the Gospel. "But Thou, O Lord," he says, "hast rejected Thy people"; that is, "Thou art compelled to reject them and let them lie prostrate; for they are disdainful, and they despise Thy Word." The emphasis is on the word "Thy people," so renowned and in such great light and grace of the Word. There is a different emphasis on "the house of Jacob." The superstition of the Persians was great. From them came the Magi, of whom Matthew reports (Matt. 2:1). The Egyptians were observers of days. Now even the Turks begin everything at the time of the new moon.[5] But hearts obsessed with such superstitions are exceedingly loath to grant admittance to the Gospel. The same thing is true with regard to the opinions of the scholastics. Those who are wise and arrogant do not want to be reproved; they defend their errors vigorously and learnedly. Therefore they are beyond correction. The Jews do not enter the kingdom of Christ as here in the beginning and elsewhere. They were called children of God – not natural children but foreigners, because of the Word of God which they had. This they have forsaken; they have turned to ungodly doctrine and have become foreign children. There are always many hearers and children of new and ungodly dogmas, as Matt. 24:5 says.

8. *Their land is filled with idols.* He describes their stubbornness. There is always an abundance of ungodly teachers and of those who lead people away from sound doctrine, namely, belly worshipers (Phil. 3:19); and throughout Scripture they are charged with being greedy. Hence He describes not only the prophets who have been alienated from sound doctrine but also those who are addicted to lusts and riches. For whoever is turned away from the Holy Spirit does not seek the things that are above (Col. 3:1). Therefore he has a taste for nothing but earthly things (cf. Matt. 16:23), and they take pains to scrape gold and silver together. What does the pope do? His greed is insatiable. A greedy man lacks what he has as much as what he does not have. He is always a beggar; in spite of all his immense treasures he complains about the loss of an obol. Moreover, there has to be protection for the treasures if they are to be kept. "To protect what has been acquired is no less a virtue than to acquire it."[6] Therefore they provide many horsemen, set forth their opinions frantically and insatiably, scrape money together, condemn

[5] On Luther's knowledge of Islam, see *Luther's Works,* 22, p. 17, n. 14.

[6] Ovid, *Ars amandi,* II, 13.

those who speak against them, etc. And this is what the prophet means, namely, their zeal and greed.

They bow down to the work of their hands. We do not read that the Jews had idols, especially after the return from Babylon, but rather that they waged many wars with the Romans because of images.[7] Therefore the prophet is speaking of his own time or also concerning their various forms of worship, later in groves, on mountains, etc. Then at the time of Christ they were also divided into various kinds of worship, as Matt. 23:20 says, "He who swears by the altar," also Matt. 5:34 ff. An ungodly man shapes his own god, does not have a true knowledge of God, and contrary to the will of God, invents a religion to suit his own opinion. What a person fears, loves, worships, trusts – this is his god.[8] Our God has no regard for our works, but only for the race and for His glory in us. Therefore every ungodly man bows down to the work of his own hands. And the heretics have their own idea, which they themselves have fashioned, and a fictitious Christ. It is not man's business to determine what pleases God; it is the business of God alone.

9. *So man is humbled.* Adam, אִישׁ, that is, man, both common and noble. For Adam means the common man; אִישׁ means the nobleman, the prince, as Ps. 49:2 indicates, all who are born of the earth, common people and princes. Therefore the common people bow down, and the princes are seen in procession; that is, the whole people is given over to idolatry, the bigwigs and the underdogs, etc. Their sin is unforgivable; it is a sin against the Holy Spirit. They seek forgiveness of sins. An acknowledged sin is forgivable. A defended sin is unforgivable. For he who forgives this sin would be in agreement with it and would approve of it. But God does not approve of iniquity. "Evil may not sojourn with Thee, etc.," as Ps. 5:4 says. Thus Moses prayed against Korah (Num. 16), and 1 John 5:16 says: "There is sin which is mortal." Nevertheless, let us pray that he may be freed from sin and from his way of life, that is, that he may acknowledge his sin; for then it becomes forgivable. Paul says in Rom. 7:18: "I know that nothing good dwells within me." But this evil is forgivable, since I acknowledge and confess it.

[7] Luther is referring to such passages as Josephus, *The Jewish War,* II, 10.

[8] Cf. the words of the Large Catechism, I, 1, written shortly after these lectures: "To have a god is nothing else than to trust and believe him with our whole heart," *The Book of Concord,* p. 365.

10. *Enter into the rock and hide.* This is the rich language of the transported prophet, who is eloquent and has at his disposal an abundance of figures of words and thoughts. This is the joy of the Spirit, which makes his eloquence more pleasing and richer. With this eloquence the prophet exults as he sees that Christ's kingdom is higher than all other kingdoms, and as he sees its success. Ardently he pours out the joy of his heart, so that he seems to be singing rather than speaking. This is what he is saying: "There are many gods and lords on earth, as 1 Cor. 8:5 says, many religions and domains. It is for everyone to want his own, etc.; but for us there is only one God and Lord, who by His reign makes the whole world one, not because He will bring everyone into His kingdom, but He distributes His one kingdom throughout the world, namely, a kingdom of the same Spirit and the same people." A great miracle. For this has happened to no monk, to no other region. But by apostrophe the prophet is addressing the whole world, which he embraces with the singular number. It is as if he were saying: "Begone with all your glory, wisdom, and power, which amount to nothing. There will arise glory, power, majesty, and the kind of kingdom from which the greatest kings and the most powerful princes shrink in fear. Therefore hide yourselves, together with all your glory, in a rock and in a cave." But he does not say this to frighten us, whom he invited above, away from Christ, but in comparison with that majesty he pours contempt on all religions and kingdoms.

From before the terror or reverence of the Lord, etc. So greatly, he says, will that glorious king have to be feared and revered that you will hide in a cave and not be able to stand anywhere. This takes place when sin has been proclaimed to the ungodly, and the Gospel to the godly. Of such great splendor is His glory and grandeur that what you have is filthy and worthy of being hidden. This is how the Holy Spirit and faith speak, for they are concealed here. For kings rule, and Christ seems to be dead. Christians are oppressed and killed. That whole majesty is in the Word and in faith. He who has the Holy Spirit sees that all things are under the feet of Christ.

11. *The haughty looks of man shall be brought low.* He explains himself. Whatever is exalted in the eyes of men is cast down; it will be nothing in comparison with the loftiness of Christ, and everything will become worthless. Therefore in brief words he teaches contempt of the world together with all its splendor. In comparison

with Christ, these things are worthy of being hidden in the dust. Luke 16:15 says: "What is exalted among men is an abomination in the sight of God"; and Luke 18:14: "Everyone who exalts himself will be humbled." Therefore by His example and strength Christ humbles whatever is lofty. It behooves all kings to stand in awe if they see the King of kings humbled in this way. No godly king wears a crown in the sight of God. He is not righteous before God. When the glory of Christ is present, he casts off every desirable thing. "If we have food and clothing, etc." (1 Tim. 6:8). But the world is not satisfied with these things but seeks splendor and glory beyond them. Christ says (Luke 12:29): "Do not be of anxious mind."

And the Lord alone will be exalted in that day, namely, through the Word and faith; for it will be proclaimed that in Christ the slightest suffering and the most worthless thing will be nobler than all the crowns of all the kings.

12. *For the Lord has a day.* With true power of another kind the Lord will observe a provincial day and hold an assembly, that is, the day of the New Testament, on which the day of the Last judgment also begins. Then souls will be justified. In the spirit we are righteous, but sins still cling to the flesh. "Although your bodies are dead, etc.," Rom. 8:10 says. It is the day on which it is made manifest that He alone reigns over every proud thing, etc., over all things. This should all be read in the neuter gender. Whether it is wisdom or righteousness or power, there is no majesty in comparison with the majesty of Christ.

The cedars. The figure is clear. Because of Lebanon, which has tall cedars, the prophets frequently use it to describe the striking splendors of the kingdom. The mountains represent kingdoms and principalities. The cedars are the princes of the kingdom, the magistrates, the governors, one higher than the other. Lebanon is toward the north; Bashan is toward the east, in the tribe of Manasseh.

16. *Tarshish . . . of the Mediterranean Sea, beautiful to behold.* This is set forth to serve as pictures of ships or beautiful flags. In sum, whatever seems lofty is filthy to Christ and the Christians. But they make use of temporal goods to sustain life and to help others.

18. *And the idols shall utterly pass away.* In Hebrew: The idols shall be completely changed. "The heavens will perish, but Thou dost endure," as Ps. 102:26 says. And the same King is here. Not only will

that which is lofty in matters of the state, with which he has dealt up to this point, be brought down, but also what is high in the spiritual administration. For the world is divided into these two things even among the Gentiles. For no nation has not had gods. In sum, every form of worship, both of the Jews and of the Gentiles, is dung in comparison with the worship of Christ. Therefore all those forms of worship will be changed and overthrown. Moreover, the idol denotes the culture, the religion, the ultimate witness, what men think and have in mind, etc. And now the idols are changed, that is, monks into laymen,[9] etc., through the Gospel. Even so these spiritual people, will together with their worship, hide themselves in caves; that is, they will confess that everything of theirs, both their righteousness and their religion, are nothing in comparison with the glory of Christ.

19. *To smite the earth.* Better: to terrify the earth. Thus Christ will be preached, because He alone is to be feared.

20. *In that day;* that is, in the day and light of the Gospel every other religion will perish and will be contemptuously consigned to the holes of moles and bats, which shun the light; that is, a man will want his former worship to go into darkness, to be hidden, to perish.

22. *Turn away from the man in whose nostrils is breath, etc.* This is an exclamation. For seeing that at the coming of Christ everything will be thus subjected, trodden underfoot, and will become an abomination and He alone will be the true King and Priest, for this reason do not undertake anything in opposition to Him. Many will certainly try to drive Him out together with those who are His, that is, out of the world, and say (Luke 19:14): "We do not want this King to rule over us." But "Turn away," he says, "stand apart from Him. Beware. There is breath in His nostrils." This means that He can be angry, and powerfully angry at that. And "His wrath is quickly kindled," as Ps. 2:11 says. Thus by threatening He wants to frighten away all who strive against Him. Luke says in Acts 9:1 that "Saul, still breathing threats and murder," was going along like a horse or some other beast revealing wrath with its nostrils. אַף denotes both nostrils and wrath. The word "high" [10] is not in the Hebrew, but

[9] Cf. *Luther's Works,* 45, pp. 169—176, on the laicization of monks as a result of the Reformation.

[10] This is derived from Jerome, who derived it from Aquila; cf. Jerome, *Commentaria,* I, 55—56.

it has "of what account is he?" as if to say: "He is so exalted that no one can understand." This he says against the ungodly majesties who persecute Him, regard Him as a heretic, without knowing how great He is and how great His wrath is. The chief point of this chapter is that Christ will reign through the Gospel over everything lofty on earth, whether external or internal, whether secular or spiritual. All these things will have to yield and be subject to Him, with the result that He alone will remain Lord, King, and Priest forever. Amen.

CHAPTER THREE

1. *For, behold, the Lord, the Lord of hosts, is taking away from Jerusalem, etc.*

THE chief point of the former chapters is this, that the prophet chides the Jews and prepares them to receive Christ, who is to come, just as we are now preparing for the holy Advent.[1] But their preaching was more difficult because they were proclaiming an advent in humility, while we preach a glorious one. Yet, magnificent though this proclamation is, we do not accomplish much with it. The present chapter is directed against these people. It describes the punishment of the ungodly and it is announced to us, who persecute the proclaimed Christ. And it is a historical text for the Jews and a prophecy for our age against princes and bishops.

Behold, the Lord, the Lord of hosts. He describes the desolation of all Judah. But it is a laughable preaching on account of the arrogance of these people, who were haughty because of the magnificent promises of God they had and for this reason did not believe what was being said to them. For this reason they despised the threats of the prophets and said: "We have the promises. The Lord, who said that the kingdom would remain for us, does not lie to us." Thus they now say: "Peter's little bark may move to and fro, but it does not sink. The Lord will not forsake His church." Thus always in the case of false teachers the major premise is true, but the minor premise false, namely, "But we are the church." Therefore it was impossible for the Jews to believe this proclamation.

Is taking away. He Himself, on whom you rely.[2] "Yes," they said, "we are His household, and His temple is among us. All is well."

From Jerusalem. Here he is speaking emphatically against presumption when he mentions the place, the very holy people, and the household.

[1] On the implications of this for the dating of the lectures, cf. Introduction, p. ix.

[2] Luther breaks into German several times at this point.

2. *The mighty man and the soldier.* He describes the desolation of both classes. And both of these two things must be rendered in the neuter gender, as if he were mentioning property and protection. The word denotes that on which they rely, that is, He takes away from Jerusalem everything on which it relies: wise men, rich men, and finally all protection.

The whole stay of bread. The whole supply of food and drink. He will send a famine on you, and this happened during the exile of the people of Jerusalem.

The Soldier, that is, the warrior. Now follows the second part.

The judge and the prophet, the diviner and the elder. In war it is the duty of the generals and the brave men to ward off enemies from the outside. The judge is useful within the walls. For Satan moves against us with wars from without and with rebellions within, but there are more dangers from within than from without. And rebellion is worse than every war. The prophet is mentioned in the proper order, for he assists the judge. But he is a prophet who undeniably has inspiration from God.

The Lord, whose prophet is the teacher. *The diviner.* These are learned men. But the things that are threatened here are very serious.

The elder. The councilman, who has learned by experience, lest Satan constantly stir up new troubles and disturbances in the state. Wise elders escape these troubles and disturbances.

3. *The captain of fifty.* The headman of a guild. He, too, must aid the judge and is the judge's other hand, as it were.

The man of rank. Men holding high office, the powerful, the aristocrats, who can coerce the madding crowd and settle quarrels, men who have the most authority.

The counselors. Now follow the ediles, who look after public buildings, supervise roads and bridges, and have charge of the arsenal. These men must be shrewd.

The architects, or skillful men who design buildings.

And the expert in charms. Hence this means to buzz about. A chancellor who is observant, industrious. This man is discreet and one who would be suitable for legations. He is a syndic or secretary, an orator, and one who could deliberate perspicaciously in difficult situations. He says that He will take away all these aforementioned things from the ungodly, and from this it follows that all these things come from God and are gifts of the Holy Spirit, such as military matters, etc.

4. *And I will make boys their princes.* The one whom He says He will give in the place of elders and teachers He calls a youngster. But adolescents are unskilled, addicted to passions, without experience and youths not only in age but also in judgment.

And babes in conduct and in wisdom.

5. *And the people will oppress.* There will be no lack of elders, and they will be without authority, for the young men will suppress them, and then the statement that secret envy and immature counsel destroyed Troy and Rome will come true.[3] When good men are lost, the law is removed, since there is no one to administer it. Then might makes right.

And every man his fellow. According to the Hebrew this means: "He who has the better of the other person should outwit him."[4]

He will be insolent, as we saw in the revolt of the peasants.[5] Governing is very difficult, yes, also impossible, where there are no laws and magistrates, and where there is no authority.

The base fellow to the honorable. Everybody wants to be wise. Boastfully they say: "I am just as good as you are."

6. *When a man takes hold of his brother.* This is what happens in an insurrection when the best men have been taken away. Everyone wants his own leader, and then the trouble starts, just as happened in Erfurt.[6] This is a description of a city that is disquieted by insurrections, where even if one who would rule were found, yet out of fear of a rebellion no one accepts a governmental office. For in a rebellion to be king is to be in suspense, and everyone strives to raise his own household to a higher level.

You have a mantle. The leader is chosen not according to pru-

[3] On the meaning of this observation, see the parallel comment in *Luther's Works,* 13, p. 208.

[4] Cf. *Some Fables from Aesop* (W, L, 449).

[5] Another reference (see p. 11, n. 12) to the recent upheavals caused by the Peasants' War.

[6] In May 1525, as part of the upheaval that produced the Peasants' War, the council of the city of Erfurt had been presented with an ultimatum by the dissidents and wrote to Luther and Melanchthon for help; Luther seems to be referring to that incident here.

dence, worth, and justice but according to power, whether he is wise or foolish. Only power is considered, while everything honorable is despised.

This heap of ruins shall be under your rule. This is figurative language. "I am far too unimportant for this." It means that he wants to avoid authority. Prudent men do this when the mob rages. When it is out of its mind, nothing but death restrains it, as we saw in the case of the rebellious peasants. For they are without a government when they constantly substitute one for another.

7. *There is no bread.* I do not have so much protection. Thus in the very time of war, even if there are only three in one city, they will disagree; and the rich are most hostile among themselves. The result is that the people remain rebellious and cannot avoid being devastated. There is enough trouble when there is peace, when the subjects obey; but what will happen when there is a rebellion? What are they? All the princes are exceedingly wretched and in a position that is constantly exposed to dangers. But the indolent mob has no regard for their hardships, but sees only the purple and a long array of horses, and I do not think there is another cause for the exploitation of the people than that they do not pray for their princes.

8. *For Jerusalem has stumbled.* He returns to the guilt which he has shown in the second chapter when speaking about the crucifixion of Christ. They are constantly rushing headlong, and the greater the remedy it [Jerusalem] has applied to its civil affairs, the worse off they are. For rebellion is a desperate sickness.

Their speech. This is the ardent endeavor directed against Christ, who was denied and rejected. The speech is the teaching of the Pharisees, the endeavors are hypocrisy and the sin of stubbornness — the sin of refusing to believe the miracles that were performed in such great number. Instead, they persisted in stiff-necked opposition to the Holy Spirit, as they heard from Stephen (Acts 7:51). Thus the speech is a teaching against the Lord. The endeavors are their good works, with which, in opposition to faith, they kept boasting of their holiness, as is the case today too.

Defying His glorious presence. He mentions the battle fought out of wickedness against the Holy Spirit, for they saw the works of God and yet did not believe. This is called defying His presence. This is now the sin in Germany too. They condemn as evil what they nevertheless say is Scripture and cannot in good conscience deny. Such is celibacy; such is Communion under one kind and several other matters.[7] They do not deny that Christ suffered for us, but by stressing their own deeds of satisfaction they do deny what follows from this fact. In the case of this sin there is and can be no repentance, for they are sinning against the Lord and scoffing at acknowledged truth.

9. *Their partiality witnesses against them,* that is, they make no secret of it. The text is obscure; yet I think this is said about the outer surface and mask, which is their manifest appearance. It is as if he were saying that their sin is manifest and that one cannot say that they are going astray and sinning against Christ out of ignorance. Thus our own wickedness is manifest and is exposed to the view of all, so that it would be pure and incorrigible maliciousness for anyone to deny it. One realizes clearly how evil the bishops are. Recognition is taken in a passive sense for what is recognized, and the face shows clearly what they are.

Their sin like Sodom, etc., as if they commanded the people to do things in this way. They defend their sins as the Sodomites did, saying (Gen. 19:9): "This fellow came to sojourn, and he would play the judge!" They themselves wanted to be judges, just as today they command and command again out of pure malice. Therefore we can conclude from this, too, that all the bishops will perish; for they sin openly, and during the former rebellion some saw how they would perish.

They do not hide it, like the Jews in Acts (5:28): "We strictly charged you not to teach in this name." No disgrace is greater than this. Therefore he compares this wickedness with that of Sodom, a passion for sinning. I think the sin of our countrymen is greater than the sin of Sodom was. Who has ever heard more horrible blasphemies, etc?

Woe to them! For they have brought evil upon themselves. There is force in the word "evil." For left in rebellion, they are in a ruinous life. They do not know by what kind of death they will perish.

10. *Tell the righteous that it shall be well with them.* Thus it is stated in the Psalms that it shall be well with them (cf. Ps. 112:5).

[7] For some comments from these years on this issue, cf. *Luther's Works,* 13, p. 352, n. 2 and n. 3.

For when the ungodly have been frightened, the Holy Spirit cannot fail to provide comfort. Abraham says in Gen. 18:23: "Wilt Thou indeed destroy the righteous with the wicked?" The Lord answered: "No." For the Lord knows how to deliver His own "when His wrath is quickly kindled" (Ps. 2:11). He was able to deliver Lot from the midst of Sodom, just as He delivered the apostles from Jerusalem. In this manner Josiah was set free (2 Kings 23). The righteous man will prosper wherever God promises help to those who are righteous and gladdens [8] them with the promise of a reward. For Paul says (1 Cor. 15:58): "Knowing that in the Lord your labor is not in vain." Thus in another place (cf. Is. 40:10): "Say to Judah: 'Your reward has not been taken away.'" Thus here: "Say to the righteous: 'It will go well with him' or 'His work is good.'" Only let him remain certain that he does not sin and that he pleases God. Let the Jews, Pilate, and Herod be afraid. And the angel says (Luke 2:10): "Fear not!" Thus the fainthearted must be buoyed up, for they are terrified and think that they are the first to bring on this disaster. Therefore Scripture says to them: "I will deliver you." But the ungodly are smug; they are not afraid, and they do not believe this prophecy. For this reason He says: "Speak, preach!"

11. *Woe to the wicked!* He will be in a bad way. This can be applied to the punishment and to the guilt.

12. *Oppressors have despoiled.* He describes a subtle and showy sin, the kind the pope and his saints excuse and defend in their own case. Now there is mention of the manifest sins with which they sinned against the laws of the state. The "oppressors" pick off and peel off; they skin and scrape.

And women rule over them. They call them oppressors and tyrants, not princes. Now he calls them women because they are not active in administration, give themselves up to pleasures, and have their minds on dancing, just as women do. They are only junkers. Like our bishops, they know nothing except to count up their ledgers, revenues, and marriage fees,[9] just as women count their garments.

O My people, your leaders mislead you. This is spoken against the

[8] The Weimar text has *lactat,* but we have read *laetat.*

[9] The German word is *Braudtgeld;* despite the suggestion of the Weimar editors that this may be equivalent to *Bruchtgeld,* "penitential offering," we have conjectured the translation given above.

false teachers of whom Jeremiah says (cf. Jer. 8:6 ff.) that they revealed visions to themselves and did not teach repentance. Thus in Micah (2:6) we read: "Evils shall not drop." All the prophets had trouble with this argument: "We are Abraham's children." Likewise Christ in John 8:39. Thus the preachers said to them: "You are God's people," which, of course, is true. But the Lord has not on this account bound Himself to the ungodly, so that He puts up with their wickedness. Therefore the ungodly must be threatened, but the poor in spirit (Matt. 5:3) must have words of comfort proclaimed to them.

And confuse the course of your paths. They bring it about that all your efforts are for nothing. They bring you into wretchedness and trouble, even though you are good to them; for they separate you from My Word. But you have not been excused, for I am warning you. I am frightening you because you belong to the ungodly. But if I saw people who are terrified, I would buoy them up. The majority are always hardened. Few are they who tremble at the judgment of God, and yet on their account the promises of God must be proclaimed.

13. *The Lord stands to judge.* This is directed against those who make people happy by saying: "There is still a great deal of time." These things are said since this is also why sudden destruction will come to you. "They say: 'Peace, peace,' when there is no peace" (Jer. 6:14). But I am not predicting for times far in the future; but the judgment has been determined now, and the resolution has been concluded. He stands to execute judgment like an executioner brandishing a sword in his hand to cut off a criminal's head forthwith, as the psalm says: "He has stretched His bow" (Ps. 7:12). Three times he uses the word judgment, urgently indicating that the time is not far off.

14. *With the elders,* that is, the apostles. They carried out the judgment when they left the Jews. Whether you understand this of the first coming or the second coming makes no difference. For it is true in both cases.

You have devoured My vineyard. You do not desist from guilt. Therefore the punishment cannot be delayed; and here, together with what follows, there is a description of tyranny.

16. *Because the daughters of Zion are haughty.* So far the prophet

has spoken of the men. Now he also speaks of the women, who, since they shared in the guilt, will also share in the punishment. He denounces in particular the impenitence and the smugness with which they boasted that they were descendants of Abraham. *Haughty.* It is a matter of vainglory. Women are haughtier than men. They lift up their necks when they ought to be lowering them.

With outstretched necks. They contort the mouth in mockery. For by nature they have a face created for modesty. But alas, it says the opposite. In men there is dignity.

Glancing wantonly with their eyes. I think that this is said about those who use artificial coloring on their faces, which is a sign of lust and is alluring. He is speaking of the misuse of the eyes, because they certainly would not use the face itself for modesty, but for lust. Therefore he calls them liars.

Mincing along as they go, tinkling with their feet. This word means an ornament for the feet. It is as if he were saying that they have red shoes on their feet, as is the practice among prostitutes. Now, however, he refers to two things, the feet and the eyes, with which they incite to lust.

17. *Will make bald.* First he will uncover their shame. There is a beautiful figure of speech in the statement "He will make bald," that is, He will uncover the disgrace of your unfaithfulness and ungodliness and will take the kingdom and the priesthood away from you. According to history, the other things were done by the Romans, as the psalm (68:1) says: "Let God arise, let His enemies be scattered, etc." The crown of hair is the kingdom.

18. *In that day the Lord will take away the finery of the anklets.* Here again the grammar is difficult and the matter is unkown. I do not know whether we shall express the same idea. *Crescents.* We have translated with "bangles." [10]

19. *Pendants.* This would be easy to translate. Jerome says that "crescents" were pins shaped like the moon[11] (but I do not know).

Necklaces. Ornaments for the neck.

Bracelets are for the arms; *scarfs* are for the head.

[10] In Luther's translation of this passage the German word was *spangen.*

[11] Cf. Jerome, *Commentaria,* II, 70.

20. *Headdresses.* Fillets frequently used on the highest festivals. We do not know what these words mean, for the names of things and herbs are unknown to us, especially in this language.

Perfume boxes are wrapped spices by the scent of which the breath is refreshed.

Amulets, charms for the ears.

21. *Precious stones* on the forehead, frontlets.

22. *Changes of raiment,* festal robes.

Mantles. For they walked along with the breast uncovered.

Linen garments, robes, shawls and veils.

23. *The garments of gauze.* The yellowish shawls, transparent, as in the Netherlands.

The turbans, headbands.

The veils, summer garments.

24. *Instead of perfume there will be rottenness.* There was an amazing use of perfumes among these people. They filled their houses with perfumes. "The scent," He says, "will be rottenness."

Rope. Their garment will flutter.

Well-set hair. It is also remarkable that they used a curling iron.

25. *Your finest men,* that is, whatever is fine in the palaces, not only the common people but also the distinguished and powerful will fall. Princes, generals, and those who ought to be protecting others will fall by the sword. The mighty men, that is, those who ought to be protecting you.

26. *And her gates shall lament.* Everywhere there will be many an image of death,[12] and with these words the haughtiness of the women has been described – the haughtiness which the Lord also threatens through the prophet. There is nothing that God wants less than that we be haughty in connection with these gifts, whether physical or spiritual, which He gives us; but He wants us to humble ourselves in His sight. He does not permit us to claim knowledge for ourselves, but He wants all praise to be given Him. Since He Himself is the Most High, He looks only at the things that are deepest.

[12] Vergil, *Aeneid,* II, 369.

He does not want us (in case He gives us much, as He did to the Jews of old) to be puffed up against others; but He wants us to be humbler, knowing that the more numerous the gifts, the greater the reckoning will be. For "everyone to whom much is given, of him will much be required" (Luke 12:48). Therefore if the Lord bestows much, we must fear rather than be haughty. And there is no other sin that the Lord hates so much as He hates haughtiness, about which the prophet has said many things here. He also uses words of this kind to describe and discredit the smugness which characterized these people, just as it characterizes our braggarts in the church. They say: "We are the church, etc."

CHAPTER FOUR

1. *And seven women shall take hold of one man in that day.*

THE prophet has foretold, as Christ did in the Gospel (cf. Matt. 23:37-39), that there will be punishment for the people of Jerusalem, first for the men, then for the women. He continues to do this. Therefore it seems that this prophecy also belongs to the third chapter. *Seven,* that is, many. There will be such great poverty that without men the women will be left abandoned. There will be widows and many orphans. The only thing they desire is to live with men. It is the duty of the men to support their wives, but it is the duty of the wives to be in charge of the household. Here, however, because of the greatness of the disaster, some give up their duty, which they have from God. They are willing to be servants and to support themselves. Understand, however, that here God is threatening them that He will overthow the order for them.

Only let us be called, that is, be named. Only permit us to be called your wives and to have refuge with you. Here there was also an end to the law (Deut. 25:5) concerning the brother who was under obligation to raise up seed, etc. Here to call means to name. It is a Hebraism just as in Genesis. I want Ephraim and Manasseh to be called by the name of the fathers, to be called sons of Jacob and of Abraham (cf. Gen. 48:16). "Thus there your name was also given to us, that is, let us be called by your name."

We will eat our own bread, which we will prepare. Paul preserves this figure of speech in 2 Thess. 3:12, where he says that they should "eat their own bread."

Take away our reproach. "Woman is the glory of man," we read in 1 Cor. 11:7. Without him she is without head and without offspring, and in the Old Testament, too, the barrenness to which they are compelled here by the scarcity of men was a disgrace. And this is the end of the third chapter, which deals with the punishment that lasts even to the present day. Some, however, have read this prophecy as pertaining to Christ[1]; but they have been mistaken, for here the prophet is speaking of the scarcity of men.

2. *In that day the Branch of the Lord shall be.* Here again he consoles the remnant of the people, as in Jerusalem. Those who are left are only one cluster, yet no matter how much He afflicts them, He preserves and comforts a remnant, because the Lord will be favorably inclined to His servants, and 7,000 do not bend the knee before Baal. Consider the song of Moses (Ex. 15:1 ff.). *In that day,* namely, now, after Jerusalem has been laid waste. The *Branch* is Christ. Yet there is nothing that He seems to do less than grow. The world would rather say that Christ and His Christians are a dried up tree trunk. But they are not regarded as such before God.

Beautiful and glorious. Splendid, excellent, glorious, something superb. The kingdom of the Jews was glorious in a physical way, but the kingdom of Christ is now glorious in the spirit. He says, however, that Christ should be extolled with great majesty.

Glory, which comes from importance in such a way that where there is glory, there something else is close by. But he calls Christ One who comes from the fruit of the land because He was born great from the earth, and it is His greatness that He can prevail over all His enemies and protect all His own; and this is a description of Christ as He defends us. Such a One, he says, Christ will be, but for those who will be from among those who have been snatched out of Jerusalem, as he also says. And here he sets forth the fruit of their riches which He will distribute, because Christ will be such a One not only for Himself but will distribute His benefits to the rest. Thus because of Him and through Him they will be called saints, that is, people set aside for divine purposes, people in whom God dwells and who belong to the employment and service of God.

3. *Those living in Jerusalem,* that is, the elect. For the condemned have perished from the book of life, in which are written the names of the saints in heaven.

4. *When the Lord shall have washed away, etc.* This is also a part of the riches distributed through Christ. He who has begun to believe in Christ departs from evil. For to the faithful is given the Holy Spirit, who cannot be inactive when He is in your hearts. For

[1] "At the coming of the Lord, seven women, that is, the seven gifts of the Holy Spirit," Jerome, *Commentaria,* II, 74.

first He cleanses the flesh from sin in order that the eyes, the hands, the tongue, and the other members may be clean; and indeed He cleanses more every day. Then He fights with death and the devil in order that He may drive them away too. For the most part they stay with us to serve as an exercise for us and as tempters. Otherwise we would not know how much filth there is in us. Likewise that Christ may have something to do in us. And in this way the Holy Spirit is the consuming fire, etc. For this reason we are attacked by many in order that He may always have something to boil away. But he says

Of the daughters, not "of the sons," alluding to the cleanliness of the women.

And cleansed the bloodstains of Jerusalem, that is, the guilt and the old Adam. But at heart we are all thieves, fornicators, murderers, and envious persons. All these are evidences of the filth that must be washed away through the Spirit.

By a spirit of judgment, namely not by eye shadow, purple, and the decorations of robes; that is, the kingdom of Christ does not consist in external works. Refer *a spirit of judgment* to the evidences of filth.

Refer *a spirit of burning* to blood. This is the judgment by which the guilty is condemned. Thus the spirit of judgment executes judgment for the purpose of purging, condemning, and cleansing the old man. Behold, it is a spirit of burning, not sluggish but inflexible and harsh. It penetrates and does not tire; it is relentless and does not flatter. It shows the endurance of the work which Christ performs in His own, of which Paul was aware when he said in Rom. 7:24: "Wretched man that I am! Who will deliver me from this body of death?" First he describes the riches of Christ's kingdom, then the mortification resulting from the fruits of Christ's kingdom. Now comfort in the cross follows.

5. *Then the Lord will create.* He comforts in the way the Holy Spirit usually does. It is as if He were saying: "You will be sheep for the slaughter." This is what we see today. There are no people so wretched as the Christians. They are deprived of honor, riches, life, etc., and they are afflicted with so many evils that they would all fall away from Christ if they did not receive help from God in Christ. What Christ said (John 13:16) must be fulfilled: "A servant is not greater than his master." And Paul says (Rom. 8:17): "Provided we suffer with Him in order that we may also be glorified with Him." And this

fight is very much against the flesh, because it is weak. The flesh has eyes only for present things; it considers good only what turns out advantangeously and concludes that God is favorable only in prosperity. From adversity it concludes that God is hostile. And yet the very opposite is true here, so that it may be strengthened in such experiences. This comfort is here written by the prophet. There follows another passage concerning the cross.

Will create. Above he prophesied that Jerusalem would be destroyed, but now, on the contrary, that it would be made a strong dwelling. These two conflict, and therefore Zion should here be taken for the church, which is the new Zion. Wherever the Word of God is preached, there is Zion.

And over her assemblies a cloud by day. It is well known from where this text was taken. It is as if he were saying: "The old has passed away, behold, the new has come" (2 Cor. 5:17). Now there will be one cloud, when this Branch will have sprung up. And he means nothing else by the pillar, etc., than the reign of faith, that Christ dwells in us through faith. He is our Mediator, Leader, Teacher, Priest; He Himself is the Pillar and the Cloud, that is, the form in which the glory of God appeared, or that in which God became manifest, as He says in John 14:9: "He who has seen Me has seen the Father." He leads us through unknown ways, through torture in the desert, in which He nevertheless protects us *from the storm.* And this is a remarkable way of speaking: That cloud, which is Christ – cling to it, and you will be safe, and yet that cloud will not appear except through the Word which protects and goes before, and we follow.

6. *It will be a pavilion for a shade.* Where the Word of God is preached, there are preaching pavilions. The cloud cools on the right and on the left, let the matter happen as it will, nevertheless that shade covers us.

Fire, which brightly and clearly shines in the night of affliction.

For over all the glory. The glory is that concerning which he had spoken above (v. 2) as the Branch of the Lord, for it is grandeur, and Christ says that the church will be rich in spiritual gifts; it will not be an empty glory but one to shield us from all assaults of conscience. Christ, who is our fire by night and our shade by day, alone wants to be the spirit of burning, both the one to rule over us and the one to protect us; He is the shade and wants to be it entirely and exclusively. Powerfully, by means of a variety of pictures, the prophet sketches for us this work of Christ through the Holy Spirit.

And it will be a pavilion for a shade by day from the heat. There is a double attack: from the heat, that is, from fire, and from the rain, that is, from water. Thus Matt. 7:25 speaks concerning the house built on a rock and says that the strength of the Christians depends entirely on this Rock, which is Christ. The Christian has no other cover than Christ; he does not rely on the arm of flesh, for there is no salvation in man, nor on good works, for they are not good in the presence of God. The Christian should teach and act in such a way that he may dare to stand in the presence of God. But the faithful are supported by the Word alone. The heat is an internal attack, when the conscience is smitten by the wrath of God, an attack which it also feels when the wrath of God is experienced. It is called the lash of God, and that because it is a punishment that God thus inflicts in a fatherly spirit. Yet because our nature feels it with extreme anguish, it is called wrath, even though God is not angry but loves whom He chastises. Satan is added to this anguish, and despair is increased. As a result there is distress within and without, which is the heat, and it is called spiritual. God, however, chastises so that the power of the Word may be shown to us and Satan may see that the Word is invincible and so that thus the power of the Holy Spirit may be glorified. He who has regard for the crowd or tries to gain the good will of princes is deceived, because there is no help in man. Such people cause destruction. Thus God said to Ahaz that he should not fear the king of Syria and promised that He would be his protector, but Ahaz did not believe it (cf. Is. 7:3 ff.). Faintheartedness is not made strong with hands but by the Word of God, which alone heartens and causes to stand. If you trust in men, you will have help neither from them nor from God, who forsakes those who forsake Him. For the Word of God is the exceedingly strong tower of Zion and the pavilion of God offering protection in prosperity and adversity.

Rain. These are the external pressures. In all things Christ is our Defense. But all of these attacks are not perceived and not felt without suffering. The sectarians will someday feel the sun without shade, because they go to meet the naked majesty of God nakedly, casting aside the humanity and flesh of Christ. This is possible only for a time. I have often advised and still advise younger theologians today that they must so study the Holy Scriptures that they refrain from investigating the Divine Majesty and His terrible works. God does not want us to learn to know Him in this way. You cannot nakedly associate with His naked Godhead. But Christ is our way to God. Those who speculate about the majesty are crushed and led to despair by Satan. The reason for this is that they are looking for answers of a kind that they cannot know, such as for the question: Why did God condemn Judas but spare Peter?[2] And such a speculator argues with God as if with some potter. To keep us from striving to observe God in Himself in this matter, He came into the flesh, presenting the flesh to us, in which we might behold God dwelling bodily, as He answered Philip when the latter gazed at Him: "He who has seen Me has seen the Father" (John 14:9). From this, then, you see the madness of those[3] who say that the flesh avails them nothing (cf. John 6:63), though on the contrary God is of no avail without the flesh. Indeed no God will avail for you except the God of Him who sucked the virgin's breasts. On Him fix your eyes. For you cannot grasp God in Himself, unless perchance you want a consuming fire. But in Christ you see nothing but all sweetness, humanity, gentleness, clemency – in short, the forgiveness of sins and every mercy, etc. When you have Him, then good for you; you are a tower of defense with God the Father. Cling to Christ, otherwise you will hear the Father Himself speaking against you when He says (Matt. 17:5): "Listen to Him." The Jews could not listen to Him, etc. And Paul says that the deity dwells bodily in Christ (Col. 2:9). The incarnation of Christ powerfully calls us away from speculating about the divinity. I learned from Staupitz[4] that I had been carried away to the devil by my speculations, for human weakness could not bear these if it did not gain access to God somewhere.[5] This they know by the mercy of God, etc.: The flesh of Christ, like ours, does not strike him down who beholds it.

[2] The question of divine foreknowledge and predestination, as it applied to Judas, was fresh in Luther's mind from his conflict with Erasmus (cf. W, XVIII, 720—722).

[3] On Luther's conflict over the exegesis of John 6:63, see *Luther the Expositor*, pp. 122—126.

[4] John Staupitz had told Luther to "begin with the wounds of Christ" and with the Babe of Bethlehem and to avoid speculation.

[5] The Latin here is obscure: *si quo non daretur accedere, hos sciunt dei misericordia*, etc.

And the man in temptation either will not know God, who created heaven and earth and did other wonderful works, or his knowledge will not give him hope and deliverance from temptation. But Christ (as this text shows in a marvelous way) is useful to us for all things and in all things, and through this very Man we are to come to God. To Him Paul and other disciples of Christ come down; they do not climb up to an observation of the majesty, or Paul was not learned because he was not a sophist.[6] When man looks at Christ, Satan is put to flight, and the conscience of a man in temptation is made happy and free from care. God clearly demands honest and pure righteousness of us, and since no one produces it, He permits no one to approach Him by his own strength. Christ has fulfilled this for us, therefore through Christ alone we have access to the Father. To be sure, it is true that one who has never felt his sin can contemplate God, or better, weave his phantasies about God; he can for a while reach out for the godhead he has invented for himself. But one who feels his sin and becomes fainthearted from fear of God will soon withdraw his foot from his speculations and turn to Christ, and he will be better off. He will have coolness in the shade, protection in the pavilion, banishment of Satan and of evil thoughts, also strength against all the gates of hell (Matt. 16:18), etc. The names applied to Christ in this text should, however, be carefully studied, so that we may know what has been given to us in Christ and that in Him there is victory and light, etc.

[6] As usual, Luther uses "sophist" to mean "scholastic."

CHAPTER FIVE

1. *I will sing to my beloved the canticle of my cousin concerning his vineyard.*

I HAVE said that this passage concerning the pavilion and the shade should be commended to us since in these figures Christ is symbolized and set forth as our Mediator and Preserver. Then I said also that the prophets offer words of comfort after threats, the latter for the sake of the ungodly, the former for the sake of the godly, fainthearted, and troubled. Now, the promises and consolations concerning Christ are repeated so often for this reason, that the flesh cannot believe that anyone is justified by another person's righteousness. Now follows

I will sing, etc. It is a characteristic of the ungodly that no matter how much Scripture is set before them they do not fear God, they are not frightened by His threats nor stirred by His promises. And what is worse, the ungodly, that is, the self-righteous, insist that the promises apply to them, but the threats to the heretics, that is, the truly godly. Thus that word of the psalm [1] is altogether true: "There is no fear of God before their eyes." And even when they experience some suffering in their body, there still is no fear but boasting that they are being punished for righteousness' sake, not for the sake of their sins. Therefore when the prophet saw that neither threats helped them nor promises stirred them, he said: "Well then, we shall sing; maybe they will take my song to heart."

Of my cousin. A cousin, the closest and dearest friend, that is, Christ. It has become usage to employ this word for friends, not for blood-relatives. I like Jerome's translation,[2] because Christ also by blood was a relative of Isaiah, because He, too, was of the tribe of Judah. To His honor he composed and sang this song.

His vineyard. This is the theme of the song, for he would have to explain that the character of this song is that of a vineyard song.

[1] Luther is alluding to Ps. 14:3 in the Septuagint and Vulgate versions, which has been shaped by Ps. 36:1.

[2] Cf. Jerome, *Commentaria,* II, 76.

Had a vineyard. We generally speak in the present tense; the Hebrews speak in the past tense.

On a hill in a fruitful place ("on a mountain horn, the son of oil"). This is the name he gives to the vineyard. They call an elevated and protected place a "horn." Horn is understood to mean the power and kingdom and dominion of the Jews, which under divine protection was sound and strong enough to crush all nations, a land commanding and victorious, a hill towering over all other realms. This hill is also a "son of oil." This is an expression like son of one year, that is, one year old. The hill is given this name because it is rich with oil. A son of perdition, or son of death, is one who has damnation and death; a son of oil, one who has oil and is rich with oil; a son of the right hand, that is, of what your right hand is or has. In Hebrew, a son of oil is one who is described, as to origin or makeup, rather than merely referred to by demonstrative pronoun; thus a son of death, namely, he who belongs to death. A hill of oil is one that has olive oil, that is, one that is fertile. It is as if he were saying: "God gave this land complete fertility, wealth, fatness, etc., but He gave them for a good use and for His own glory."

2. *He fenced it.* שֹׂרֵק. Nothing but top-quality vines. This means he planted it with the choicest vines and should therefore not be interpreted in any other way, and this meaning should be maintained. *He fenced it in,* that is, he built the wall out of stones.

Picked the stones out of it. He grubbed out the rocks, he cleaned it up. All this is said allegorically. In this clause he wants to say: He took good care of the vineyard. Some interpret the fence to refer to the protection of the angels, which is not unacceptable to me.[3] However, it is more satisfactory to construe the fence as being the Law, which Paul explains thus in Eph. 2:14:[4] He has destroyed the wall of hatred through the Law, so that without the Law we might grow together into one body. By the Law the Jews were isolated from all other nations, and this, I say, was their prerogative, that from the Law they were informed regarding the will of God.

Stones are the elect Gentiles. A Canaanite was chosen soon after the Law was given . . .[5] that they might be like all the holy princes,

[3] Jerome, *Commentaria,* II, 77.

[4] The original has "Eph. 3."

[5] There is a small lacuna in the manuscript at this point.

Abraham, Isaac, etc., and judges, kings, and prophets. Thus David was a chosen vine and a noble stem.

Tower. Some refer it to the temple.[6] But I would prefer to interpret it of the entire worship that was held either in the temple or in the tabernacle or wherever they came together to the Word of God. This is the tower, that the name of the Lord was there, the promises, the mercy seat, the Word of God. Solomon also has this in mind: "The name of the Lord is a strong tower" (Prov. 18:10). This was the place of refuge for the Jews, because God dwelt there. Concerning this we read in Deuteronomy (12:5): "You shall seek the place which the Lord your God will choose out of all your tribes to put His name and make His habitation there."

Winepress. If you want to refer this to the altar of burnt offerings, I have no objection.[7] But I myself think it refers to the mortification of the old man, of whom Rom. 12 speaks. Here also our body becomes an altar of burnt offerings, on which we bring the sacrifice of a contrite heart (Ps. 51:17). *Tower* is for the sake of the use of faith, *winepress* for the sake of the use of mortification.

Wild grapes. The grapes are wild, of sour taste. "Are grapes gathered from thorns?" asks Christ (Matt. 7:16). Therefore the grapes represent works, good grapes are good works, bad ones are evil works, the kind the Jews did, who killed not only the prophets but also Christ, and were adulterers, robbers, etc. This song reproves the Jews, who were well built up from the beginning and yet did not produce good fruits. So we turn Christ's best bounties to bad use, while one preaches Christ for his own glory, another for his belly, another to gain many followers, as Paul says (Phil. 3:19). Such acts are not grapes but wild grapes.

3. *Judge between me and my vineyard.* The prophet says these things with great sternness and summons to judgment. He could no longer stand by, he had done everything possible. *Judge.* And now he explains this parable himself.

5. *And now I will tell you.* He prophesies the punishment and perhaps the final destruction of the kingdom of Israel. "I will not hide my judgments, but you will see them openly."

Hedge. He means the administration of the Law, for the Jews

6 Jerome, *Commentaria,* II, 77.

7 Jerome, *Commentaria,* II, 77.

had a twofold kingdom, civil and spiritual. The spiritual kingdom was gone when in Babylon they did not have their temple worship or sacrifice. The political kingdom, too, had been laid waste at that time, though not wiped out. However, both were taken away from them by the Romans after Christ. Of this he is prophesying here. He speaks of things too horrible to be applied to the Babylonian Captivity. The caretakers of the vineyard are the prophets and priests, who cultivate it with the Word and the Holy Spirit; and these God wants to take away from them, namely, the teachers of the truth and of faith and of the proper interpretation of the Law. This is the height of God's wrath.

6. *To prune* is to rebuke, convict, and condemn the unbelieving and to revive faith, namely, to trim off what is unneeded and useless.

To hoe is to plow the land so that it may receive the seed and the rain and not be hindered in bearing fruit either by stones or by the native hardness of the earth. This, then, is the preaching of repentance and of the forgiveness of sins, namely, through the Law and the Gospel. The heretics, Turks, and many nations teach many things, but they do not clear the ground and do not plow, but they trample the ground and burn it up. They appear to be cultivating the land, but in reality they are laying it waste.

Briers shall grow up. Where the Law is not truly preached, unrecognized sins cannot be reproved. Because of the force of the Law, sins are of necessity disregarded, and whatever is thorns and hides sins is of necessity overlooked; thus the cure cannot be applied, and grace cannot be preached. If one preaches man's own merits, when will he preach repentance and grace? What is not evil does not need the Gospel and therefore neither the revealing of sin nor the revealing of the cure. Therefore the thorns are certain excellent men and such as reason calls saints, yet they are without the Spirit and faith, they know neither works nor the goal of faith, and they vex wretched souls. Thereafter they will be deprived not only of prophets and priests of their own nation but also of apostles and their successors, who are the clouds sailing around the world. Paul says, "Behold, we turn to the Gentiles" (Acts 13:46). The wholesome rain is the Gospel. The matter is self-explanatory.

7. *For the vineyard of the Lord.* The Lord had embraced this people as a mother her son. Therefore he calls it a branch and

pleasant planting, attractive and delightful. This is justice, that the Law takes its course, that the innocent are not mistreated and the criminals do not escape punishment. "Gold and silver make the straightest things crooked."[8] "Power, partiality, and money prevent just verdicts."[9] Righteousness is what imparts benefits and renders good to the deserving.

A cry, namely, of those who suffer violence and tyranny, their complaint against tyrants. Here he explains what grapes and wild grapes mean, that is, allegorically.

8. *Woe to those who join house to house.* He now continues with the rest of his discourse in a straightforward manner, in plain words, without allegory. This is a wild grape, the greed of priests and princes. Paul in Eph. 5:3 and Col. 3:5 calls greed a worship of idols. Christ sets Mammon in opposition to God (Matt. 6:24). Greed is an idol in opposition to faith; as if the prophet were saying: "You want to possess the whole city, yes, you buy all the houses, one after the other, without compunction, and you do not regard it as sin. God's justice is different from that of the world, which does not punish greed but rather regards it as a virtue. God, however, does not want the poor to be thrown off their property but that they be helped by a grant or by a loan. But now princes are expelled and deprived of their property, if not by plunder, then by the idol, and thus they do not possess their own things but those of others *until there is no more room,* that is, until there is no home or field left to the poor and no one is permitted to buy anything of theirs ahead of you."

9. *In my hearing.* This is what he wants to stress: You do not want to consider these matters, and you do not regard them as sin, but they touch my ears through the cry of the poor, and because of this cry my ears are constantly ringing.

Surely many houses shall be desolate. These are the words of one taking an oath or of one making a deposition with some pledge. As punishment, he says, for that greed which you consider a virtue, it will happen that very many of those houses will be laid waste. *Large,* that is, grandly and expensively built. *Beautiful,* that is, pleasant. In Luke 12:20 Christ says: "The things you have prepared, whose will they be?" Children must be nurtured, something must be

[8] The Latin of this saying is: *Aurum et argentum faciunt rectissima curva.*

[9] The Latin of this saying is: *Potencia, favor et pecunia praeveniunt iudicia.*

laid aside for them, the family must be cared for, but not with greed. Ill-gotten gains will be ill spent. "Of good ill got, the third heir joyeth not." [10]

10. *For ten acres.* This is the punishment for the unjust acquisition of fields. The names of the measures are different in different areas and uncertain. It is as if the prophet were saying: "You think you will harvest a great quantity of wine and grain, but it will not happen, etc., and hunger is the penalty for greed." Who believes it? The crop does not depend on the extent of the toil or on the acquisition of many fields but on the blessing of the Lord.

11. *Woe to those who rise early in the morning that they may run after strong drink!* More wild grapes. The greedy are very rarely drinkers, very rarely openhanded and spendthrifty, except those who came into their abundance of money by inheritance, not by work or effort. The prophet employs some blazing words. *That they may run after strong drink.* In this he spares Noah and Solomon. Proverbs 31:6 [11] says: "Give wine to those in bitter distress." Misuse and excess are forbidden. The Jews have been dispersed among the nations and have learned carousing, etc. Though they have drunk much in the evening, they get up in the morning and start drinking all over again. And so it is always: Night, Love, and Wine counsel nothing in moderation.[12] Wine inflames to many evils, but especially to thirst and more drinking. What would the prophet have said to the Germans, for whom natural capacity is insufficient to drain so much drink? Theirs are not feasts of joy but feasts of pigs. It is all right to eat and to drink, but to cultivate drunkenness is evil. So also music is a gift of God. Elisha says: (2 Kings 3:15) "Bring me a minstrel, etc." Amos 6:5 says: "Like David [they] invent for themselves instruments of music." Certainly if you make use of music as David did, you will not sin. The work of the Lord is that whatever He commands be done, namely, to believe and to worship God and to serve one's neighbor; or, that there be punishment, which is inflicted on the ungodly, and reward, which is given to the godly. The work here applies to those who were disrespectful, etc., that is, such will be the reward of these men in Job. "Work" is often used in place of "re-

[10] Cf. *Luther's Works,* 21, p. 208, n. 38.

[11] The original has "Prov. 30."

[12] Ovid, *Amores,* I, 6, 59.

ward." The ungodly do not care whether the Lord does or commands good or evil. For that reason they are taken captive. The prophet assigns individual punishments to individual sins.

13. *Want of knowledge,* that is, they will be led away unexpectedly, and that before they know it or think it. A past tense is used instead of the future. A people's glory is its wise men, its scholars, its men of ability, who live off the public treasury in time of peace, but then will die of hunger.

Multitude, that is, the common crowd. They will pay for their drunkenness with thirst.

14. *Therefore Sheol has enlarged its appetite.* He is describing the seriousness of the pestilence and starvation, which became a reality through the Romans above all. Earlier it will appear to have shown so much food, but now it will seem to be gulping it down with an insatiable appetite. שְׁאוֹל, that is, the lower world and sometimes death, more often the grave and the pit. Now, the appetite which he here attributes to Sheol denotes either the excessively large opening or its insatiable hunger, as if the appetite of death could not be sated.

And her nobility go down. The *nobility* are all the best men, noble and common.

Those who exult are the rich and smug, who fear no one and look down on others in comparison with themselves. Hence also the dancers, that is, the lascivious young men.

They go down. O unhappy lot! This is what happens when the Turks or the plague make their destructive inroads; no one is spared!

15. *Man is bowed down.* This is the way they will be taught good behavior; they refuse to be corrected any other way. The fool has to be deloused with a club. The unrepentant are not at all moved by words; with a stiff neck they refuse to believe but prefer to find out for themselves. "Then," says He in Prov. 1:28, 26, "they will call upon Me, but I will not answer" and "I also will laugh at your calamity." The pleasure-bent people despise God and act arrogantly, the prophets are brought low, but finally the little wheel comes full circle.

16. *The Lord is exalted in justice,* that is, justice itself will exalt Him. When He smashes and avenges this ungodliness, then people

will say: "He is the mighty Lord, but meanwhile He also looks after the godly who have been made to suffer by the ungodly, as in the case of Lot, and thus He is hallowed in the godly, whom He raises up to justice, that is, because of their faith. And these are the sheep that have been fed, that is, those who are moved by meditation. And because of the Jews other ungodly people are frightened. The prophet must here be understood as speaking not of something physical, but of wolves, that is, of destroying the ungodly but protecting and nourishing the godly.

17. *Strangers*. Thus Christ says in Matt. 8:11 f.: "Many will come from east and west . . . while the sons of the kingdom will be thrown out." The wealth of the Word of God has become a state of want for the Jews. There is no gain for them, no comfort; but there is for the Gentiles.

18. *Woe to those who draw iniquity with cords of falsehood.* This is the third kind of wild grapes. Not only are you smug in luxury and abandon the Word of God, but you also blaspheme openly, you scoff at both promises and threats, you stubbornly persist in sinning, you are arrogant in the righteousness of the flesh. Just as horses hitched to a wagon always pull even when they are tired, so also we. Hosea 10:11 says: "Ephraim was a trained heifer that loved to thresh." The teachers drive the people as teamsters do, and so they remain in a state of ungodliness. They do not actually question the Lord's power, but they do not believe what is proclaimed through Isaiah. They do not disdain the Lord in Himself but maintain Him in the Word and in preachers and in displays of the Law, yet they proceed from stubbornness to blasphemy. So it is impossible to refute a hypocrite. Therefore they do not draw righteousness but iniquity.

Cords are laws and statutes. Elijah was called father, chariot, and driver (2 Kings 2:12). So the priests and magistrates were chariots and drivers, but such as were empty and void. As a result there were empty cords, empty laws; and the formula of these people is: "Isaiah, let not that which you mention below in chapter 28 come; 'We have made a covenant with death, etc.' (Is. 28:15), we are God's and Abraham's children." So all prophets are judged to be liars. The reason for this is self-righteousness, which puffs up.

19. *Let the purpose of the Holy One of Israel . . . come, that we may know it.* They do not say this to provoke the Lord, because

they regard themselves as thoroughly holy, but they speak up against the prophet and do not fear for themselves. The cry of all the ungodly is: "Peace and safety" (1 Thess. 5:3). They say: We know what the Holy One of Israel has in mind, and we think the devil is speaking out of Isaiah. Disregard of the Word of God is certainly a great enough crime, but to attribute it to the devil, this puts an end to the game, this makes the earth quake, either as about to fall into ruin or as about to be reshaped with great loss of life.

The work and purpose of the Lord is His Word. The blasphemy against Christ is immediately followed by a counterfeit of reality. Solomon says in Prov. 18:3: When the sinner gets into deep water, he becomes defiant, thereupon he blasphemes, and then his destruction is not far off.

20. *Woe to those who call evil good!* This passage depends on the last one, for it refers to blasphemy, and this is the way all ungodly and all men of the flesh act. But the prophet is here speaking not of matters subject to the senses but of the Word, which is good and useful, a light brightening and guiding on all ways, teaching right things, restoring consciences, etc. Therefore he accuses the pestilent teachers through the Word of God; they blaspheme and rail at it but proclaim their own ungodly ideas and the wisdom of the flesh, things which are never good. Creatures are indeed at times put to good use. A lie is always evil. God can put up with sins, and when sins have been acknowledged, God can easily take care of them. God cannot put up with the blasphemer.

21. *Woe to those who are wise!* Solomon says (Prov. 3:5, 7): "Do not rely on your own insight. . . . Be not wise in your own eyes." This, too, refers to blasphemers, and we include both teachers and disciples. Their excessive wisdom makes them oppose the Word of God. Christ performed many miracles, but He never made folly look like wisdom. This unquestionably most difficult work and burdensome task He has left for us to carry out together with those who love themselves, so that they might become wise. Whatever is said to them, this they fight against and disparage. One must certainly walk in fear and humility, and we must first give up our own ideas. Then let us see whether what we have heard conforms to the faith. Let our wisdom be brought low and let us walk in fear.

22. *Woe to those who are heroes.* The same beginning, about

which I have commented above.[13] But this passage seems to me to refer to the common people, the earlier one to the princes, whom the common people imitate. They not only drink to excess, but, like the Greeks,[14] they also brag about their drinking. They are bold soldiers when it comes to draining mugs and glasses (beer knights). They live in smug security and for their own pleasure. Frequently one finds also others in the prophets, because bribes are taken for the purpose of cheating justice. Moses forbade such things. Security gives birth to many evils. There follows the threat of a plague that strikes all, princes and people, at the same time. This so diminishes and weakens them that the tongue, that is, the flame, could not call them less stable.

24. *Therefore, as the tongue of fire devours the stubble.* How quickly stubble is consumed! Yet that is what he calls this powerful nation that is to be laid waste so quickly. *It will be as ashes,* better: "it will be as rottenness."

Root means the leaders; *blossom* denotes the subjects, particularly the young people. Old and young, parents and children, king and people will perish. Nor is their being rather deeply rooted and their rather extensive blossoming something that they might offer as an excuse. He gives the reason:

They have rejected the Law of the Lord. With other sins God can call up grace, and the punishments of other sins can be turned and drawn to repentance. But blasphemy of the Word is usually followed by devastation and desolation.

Word, that is, promises and threats.

25. *The mountains quaked.* So great is the calamity, even before it comes. The mountains represent human beings. They say: A stone could feel sympathetic. *As refuse.* So Ps. 83:9 f. speaks of Sisera and others. This was done to completion by the Romans. After the saints and the wheat had first been taken out, the chaff was scattered, namely, the Jews, who neither are alive nor have they died.

For all this His anger is not turned away. Since they do not stop sinning and do not return to Him who is smiting them but still

13 See p. 62 above.

14 On "to play the Greek" as a term for "to carouse," cf. *Luther's Works,* 29, p. 27, n. 21.

appear wise and just to themselves, therefore God also does not stop being incensed against them and scourging them.

26. *He will raise a signal among the nations.* This should by all means be understood as referring to the Romans, who are to be the scourge of the vine that bears wild grapes. And it will be given, he says, to a people that bears fruit.

He will whistle. He will give them the will to fight against the Jews. To convert this people the prophet employs fiery eloquence, the pressure of an act of war, and a grandeur of words as though he were making a display of a matter of growing importance.

27. *Speedy.* Certainly in this way all the ungodly will unexpectedly perish, even if they delay it for a long time. They do not live out half of their life. See below, chapter 28, and Ps. 55:23: "Men of blood and treachery shall not live out half their days." Next the prophet describes that the Romans are unconquered and persistent. That the Roman name struck great terror everywhere is attested by the Acts of the Apostles, especially chapters 16 and 22. Particularly, when Paul was being scourged, he said, "The Romans will do what they have determined beforehand." [15]

They will break through. They will not be appeased, they will take no leisure, but they will always be at work, the army certainly well trained and drilled.

Not a waistcloth is loose, that is, the sword of that nation will never stop, they will always be under arms, and they will never strip their boots and spurs from their feet, which signifies constant attention to war. Then also, that there will be abundant equipment of the highest quality weapons.

28. *Hoofs like flint.* Strong and hard for trampling. Formerly they fought in chariots.

29. They will be almost *like lions.* They will spare no one. *Young lions* are remarkably agressive and more rapacious than the adults.

30. *Like the roaring of the sea.* This is a description of the sadness and mourning of the Jews. Then they would gladly be covered by the waves, but they will not be able to.

[15] It is not clear whether Luther intends these words as a paraphrase of the words of Paul in Acts 16:37 or whether he is drawing upon legendary material.

Darkness. The terror and commotion of death. The Jews will be seeking caves in the fields in which to hide themselves and will not find them. But the shadow of death will be everywhere. The sun and moon appear to turn black, a symbol of desperation. They have not been able to call upon God. These things have been written down also for us, if we in like manner blaspheme the Word.

CHAPTER SIX

1. *In the year that King Uzziah died I saw the Lord sitting upon a throne, high and lifted up; and His train filled the temple.*

THIS is a remarkable passage, which many have attempted to expound.[1] Isaiah, however, notes the year of the vision, so that he might be more readily believed, as if to say: Up until now I have preached to you what kind of people you are and what will happen to you. Now I add a remarkable vision and one that is very hard for you, but you will be moved not even by this. God was above the temple, the train alone filled the temple, and the temple did not contain the train, much less God Himself. And the seraphim were not in the temple, but they covered the temple round about the Lord. Whether there were only two seraphim or many thousands is not sure. This vision served first of all for the purpose of frightening the people of that time, a people who were presumptuous to an extreme degree, trusting in their kingdom and priesthood. And that surely was no idle reason for boasting. Yet that boasting blinded and hardened the people so that they could not tolerate one prophet. When because of God's blessings men become obstinate, it is not easy to help them. The Jews thought that God was enclosed in the temple and the mercy seat and was held there by their righteousness. This is what the prophet is condemning here, saying that God is not in the temple but outside the temple and far loftier and greater. And he shows that another sacrifice must be made, another kind of worship, another knowledge of God than before. Those forms of worship were not to be relied on, but they were only established with a view to the coming Christ. It is as if he were saying: "Your highest righteousness is hardly the fringe, that is, you have an external and feeble kind of worship of God." As boys are prepared for the manly estate by disciplinary measures, so the outward rites are seeds of a coming power. And the best Jews, who most employed this system of worship, were obviously only a fringe. Again, he shows the Lord

[1] Luther seems to be referring to the materials from the exegetical tradition assembled by Nicholas of Lyra and in the *Glossa ordinaria* on this chapter.

as sitting not among the cherubim, but among seraphim, that is, among flaming ones. Thus Ps. 104:4 says: "Who makest the winds Thy messengers, fire and flame Thy ministers." The cherubim were in darkness.

2. *With two he covered his face* means that the angels worship God with such great reverence that they do not even look at God. The Jews on the contrary stood with head held high and neck stiff, that it would almost be up to God to fear them. Then the angels also covered their feet, because they would not want their walk and their endeavors to appear in the presence of God, as if they were pure before Him. In the Scriptures walking on foot means following some kind of life. John says (Matt. 3:3): "Prepare the way of the Lord," that is, lead a good life. Therefore these seraphim do not wish to boast of their wisdom and zeal of life, but they hide everything. What do we worms have to be proud about?

With two he flew. The angels were borne aloft like birds, that is, they served God not with their own endeavors, but with a confession in which they sing the Trishagion, that is, the thrice holy, whereby they indicate that all holiness in the whole earth must be ascribed to God alone. All the words are grandly put. They shouted. The truest worship of God is a pure and simple confession. God says (Ps. 50:23): "He who brings thanksgiving as his sacrifice honors Me." The other things we have, such as gifts, intellect, good habits, our best endeavors, let these be concealed. We must glory in the Word alone and confess that we have received these gifts from God, we do not bring them along. The ungodly regard God as defiled, though He alone is holy and makes holy. And yet they think that they are hallowing Him with a handful of incense, etc., which is the same as befouling Him. In short: God alone is holy, but the whole people and whatever the people do are completely defiled. To be sure, people agree to this statement according to the sound of the words, but when application is made of it by antithesis, they cannot endure it. Thus we say of ourselves: I am a sinner, unclean, defiled, etc., but we take it exceedingly amiss when others say it about us. It is necessary that God be hallowed and that I be defiled, but in that act of hallowing I must know, believe, praise, and confess that God Himself is alone holy, that He gives and does not receive. The glory be God's; the shame be ours. Cf. Daniel 3 [The Prayer of Azariah, 3-10]. For us to glorify ourselves is to confuse ourselves with God and vice versa. The Jews thought that the glory of God was shut up in a narrow temple and in their worship, and we certainly know God more extensively than our wisdom comprehends. But He Himself fills all things everywhere, wherever He pours out His gifts. The glory is therefore the confession which is due Him and which is paid Him in all the earth.

4. *And the foundations of the thresholds shook.* This points to the shape of true religion, which is confession, praise, the proclamation of God. When this is known, man is terrified and humbled, and he gives up everything in which he formerly trusted and of which he made his boast. The preaching of grace confounds all self-assurance.

Filled with smoke. The same thing happened when Solomon dedicated the temple. We read in 1 Kings 8:10: "A cloud filled the house of the Lord." It signifies that God dwells in faith and that He is not served except by faith which confesses and praises God, who is too lofty to be contained by works. So Paul almost always argues against works of the Law and for faith. And this vision is for faith. Words belong to the Antichristians. Even the miracles of Christ were such as were grasped by the senses. Isaiah saw the Lord sitting, yet not except in the vision. Nevertheless, they are called Lord and seraphim, who were seen and yet cannot be seen. Someone voices the slander that the body of Christ is not in the bread because it cannot be seen and that it cannot be anything else except what is seen.[2] Against those people stands this passage, where the prophet saw what cannot be seen. He saw a form, and yet he says he saw the Lord Himself. One thing is shown, another is hidden. He who eats the bread eats also the body of Christ. Christ's way of speaking, "This is My body," is of the same kind as the Father's, "This is My beloved Son." (Matt. 3:17). Thus in the dove the Holy Spirit was seen.

5. *And I said: Woe is me! For I was silent.* This passage conflicts with the one where God says that He cannot be seen, so that man may live (Ex. 33:20). But here, too, Isaiah grants that he is lost because of the vision (for in Hebrew "I was silent" is used for "I am lost"), so that nothing conflicts with that other passage. דָּמָה, that is, he is likened to, as in Ps. 49:12: "Thus man, for all his splendor, does not abide; he resembles the beasts that perish." This is an explanation with reference to beasts of burden that have perished and are noth-

[2] Cf. the argumentation of *This Is My Body* against this, *Luther's Works*, 37, pp. 76—77.

ing. Thus the prophet says that he was completely reduced to nothing, or reduced to silence, of which let nothing more be said. For דָּמָה means "he was silent," and דּוּמָה means "silence," as in Ps. 94:17: "Almost it would have lived in hell." In Hebrew: "My soul would soon have dwelt in the land of silence." Poets say that ghosts are silent, since there is no memory of them.[3] Therefore this glory is revealed against the stiff necks and against Satan in men's hearts; as if the prophet were saying: "Formerly I, too, used to think that I was holy and that I could teach properly, but now I am found to be like the false prophets, because I have *unclean lips*. This is the distress and trial of conscience than which no other is more dreadful, namely, to be put on trial concerning the Word and doctrine. The ungodly and fanatics can think of everything except this, where they sin most. Isaiah feels this, and his conscience is tormented in final death, and he says that he is unworthy to teach. He confesses not that he has defiled hands, but defiled lips, that is, an unclean mouth, and he says that the entire nation is thus afflicted. No, this seems to be blasphemy, not only because he says he has seen God but also because he confesses that his teaching is useless and he thinks he must teach otherwise. And certainly reason, even when it teaches the Law and the Prophets in the very best way, is defiled. For the Law, as Paul says in Rom. 4:15; Heb. 7:19, justifies no one but rather makes him guilty. Therefore teaching the Law is not the same as cleansing man, neither hearer nor teacher, since also those who teach the true force of the Law are unclean. For by faith, says Peter (Acts 15:9), the hearts are cleansed, not by works or merits. Therefore saintly Isaiah, too, even to the extent that he taught the Law for the purpose of touching consciences, is defiled and dies as a defiled man. Hence the vision has this purpose, that the righteousness of the people may be condemned and they may aspire to the glory which the prophet saw, that is, move from Law to grace. The prophet is saying: We must become holier so that we may go to the Lord sitting on His lofty throne; we must hear the seraphim and the heavenly fires. You see, he brings charges against himself as well as the people. This has been no small reason for a great disagreement. For such things the saintlets do not want to hear, since they regard their own teaching to be most true and most pure.

For my eyes have seen the King, the Lord of hosts. For that rea-

[3] Cf. Vergil, *Aeneid,* VI, 264.

son, he says, "I am lost." But it turned out for the salvation of the prophet that he was thus thrust down to hell, so that he might be led away and lead others away from that uncleanness of the Law to the purity of Christ, so that He alone might reign.

6. *Then flew one to me.* Here now a resurrection from the dead takes place. We see that sinners who acknowledge their sins are not abandoned. The prophet cries out that he is lost, that he is oppressed with the consciousness of a defiled mouth, and that he has felt sin and death. And on that account he obtained forgiveness. "If we confess our sins, etc." says 1 John 1:9; and 1 John 2:1 says: "If anyone does sin, we have an advocate with the Father"; so also 1 John 5:18. God hates the sin of hardening and its being defended. Let them be cleansed and let them confess their uncleanness, especially that of the mouth. For where lips and doctrine are unclean, there unclean works follow. Therefore the seraph approaches to set the prophet free from his sin. But he uses means. So, then, two things are set forth to the prophet, namely, Word and sign. The Lord often acts this way. The lips are cleansed by fire. This is the sign. The Word is: "Your guilt be taken away." Here our sacraments are established. Yet these are disdained and shamefully handled by some who say: Nothing external benefits the soul.[4] But let them criticize as much as they want. What Isaiah experiences here is not a fairy tale, but as there are fearful and serious voices, so there is also absolution, which then is granted through the addition of the sign to the Word. Now, what that sign could do, this our Baptism can also do.

8. *And I heard the voice of the Lord saying.* Now the effect of the vision is shown, which is that the Jews are partly to be received and partly to be hardened. Almost all the prophets were accustomed to contend with these saintlets and wiseacres who always resist the Holy Spirit, blaspheme the Word and grace of God, and boast of their own righteousness, their own works, and their own ideas. And especially when the carnal man begins to learn the things that pertain to faith while his reason has not yet been mortified and has not yet been taught its beliefs, this is a situation to be deplored. The Word of God does not always have humble hearers; on the contrary, the great majority of hearers are proud and presumptuous.

[4] See *Luther the Expositor,* pp. 105—107.

Whom shall I send? That is, many indeed refused the office of teaching, such as Moses and Jeremiah, Jonah and others,[5] especially among the Jews, a most obstinate, blasphemous, and contradicting people, wearying both teacher and teaching with their envy. Here we need courage. Now also our name has a bad reputation; all calamities are traced to us; we are charged with the insurrection that was instigated by others[6]; and whatever explanation we give, whatever we do to ease the situation, there is nobody to hear us. The Lord thinks that hardly anyone is to be found to condemn this nation with its counterfeit righteousness and with teaching that is not sound and does not cleanse hearts, because he would soon have to be killed by that people. Indeed, God Himself will have to employ His glory and majesty and expose His name to blasphemy if He wants us to prevail. So great is the perversity and corruption of nature. But behold, Isaiah was ready. He is very courageous after he has risen from the dead, has been strengthened by the burning coal, and has been made a different man, so that he is ready to hazard his life for God's sake.

9. *Go and say to this people.* The emphasis lies on His saying "this," not "My," as if He were saying "rejected," "accursed." We do not here wish anxiously to torture ourselves regarding the secret will of God,[7] but only to set forth those matters concerning the mood of God and of His preachers. For God is justly angry with the stubborn who please themselves and have no desire to learn to know themselves and to deny themselves. It is to them that this must be said with displeasure:

10. *Hear and hear, but do not understand, etc.*, and they must at last be abandoned. The prophet's words, *make the heart fat, heavy, shut, etc.*, mean that by his preaching the prophet would insult them and inflame them to greater hardness. The evangelists cite this passage in various ways. One cites it in the indicative, another in the imperative; one in the past tense, another in the future, but it does not make any difference.[8] These words can still be ex-

[5] Luther is thinking of Ex. 3:11; Jer. 1:6; and Jonah 1:3.

[6] On the charge of sedition, cf. *Luther's Works,* 26, p. 97.

[7] See p. 55 above.

[8] The passages to which Luther is referring include the following: Matt. 13: 14-15; Mark 8:18; John 12:40; Acts 28:26-28.

plained in an impersonal way, and the meaning briefly is this, that there exists a righteousness different from that of which the Jews boasted, that is to say, not an external but an internal one. But the fact that the Jews would not hear this shows that this is the time when Christ preached and also performed many miracles. The words and deeds of Christ were against the Jews, and they were so embittered against Him that they would not have received Him, even if He had created a new heaven and a new earth, simply because He condemned their works. Solomon says in Prov. 18:2: "A fool receiveth not the words of prudence, unless thou say those things which are in his heart." But if they are unwilling to hear Him, there will nevertheless be those who will hear. He says (Deut. 32:21): "I will stir them to jealousy with those who are no people; I will provoke them with a foolish nation." The ungodly are irked by much preaching, especially by the preaching of faith in opposition to works, but this preaching must nevertheless not be omitted because of them. Here the prophet in no way argues about the will of predestination, but only about God's attitude against the hardened, that they must be forsaken.

11. *Then I said: How long, O Lord? And He said: Until, etc.* This is a clear prophecy of the devastation of the kingdom of the Jews by the Romans, as if to say: The people are obstinate and cannot be healed until they are abandoned. It must not be thought here that their descendants would be healed, but this is a frequent way of speaking in Scripture. Cf. Gen. 8:22; Ps. 110:1; Matt. 1:25. Thus we say: You will not be reformed until death has snatched you away, that is, never.

12. *The Lord removes men far away,* that is, He will scatter them among the nations.

And the forsaken places are many. Better: "What will have been forsaken." The Hebrews have no neuter gender and in its place use the masculine and feminine. And this is the meaning: God does not snatch away after the manner of Satan, who rages in such a way that he tries to uproot everything altogether, but the Lord always preserves a remnant after the evil have been destroyed.

13. *The holy seed.* From this it is clearly seen that the prophet is not speaking about the Babylonian Captivity, from which the same sort of ungodly people returned as they were before, but about the

Roman captivity and about the spiritual remnant, whom he calls the holy seed, men born of God.

And though a tenth remain in it, that is, a tenth part will be saved. Like a little branch from the forest, finally growing and filling the world, so will there be a people. That people will be Mine, the church of Christ. *The holy seed* he calls it, not defiled, as he charges elsewhere. The church, the body of Christ, is the temple of the Holy Spirit, in which there is no ungodly person and sinner, but all are righteous through Christ.

ALLEGORY[9]

The Lord sitting in glory is Christ at the right hand of the Father. The temple is His church or heaven. The fact that He appears in visible form indicates that He is man, for everywhere the appearance of God denotes the humanity of Christ. Now He rules in the church through His humanity, but finally as the glorious God. The seraphim are the apostles and preachers of the Word. Winged angels everywhere signify the ministry of the Word. The two wings are the two Testaments, or the testimonies of the Law and the Prophets. The flying denotes the course of the ministry. "The Lord gives the command; great is the host of those who bore the tidings" (Ps. 68:11). There are many indeed, but all of them with one accord preach the same Christ. Veiling the face and feet means that the life of the godly is hidden in Christ. The feet signify conduct. Faith is not seen and its conduct is not grasped by the ungodly; in fact, it may seem strange and stupid to them. John 3:8 says: "You hear the sound of it, but you do not know whence it comes or whither it goes." Christians certainly live without glory in the world. The seraphim stood ready to serve the Lord. Their cry is a declaration of preaching. "Holy, holy, holy." "No one has ascended into heaven but He who descended from heaven, etc." (John 3:13). And chapter 16: "He will convince the world of sin and of righteousness and of judgment" (John 16:8). Those who boast of their own holiness do not cry, "Holy is the Lord God," but as desecrators of God's name they make their boast in man. The "Sanctus" in the Mass is a song for the boys.[10] But the preacher is the public singer of it. As long as we live, there is never enough singing. When Peter sang this song

[9] Cf. Introduction, p. xi.

[10] It seems that the Sanctus was originally sung by the congregation; then it was turned over to the subdeacons at the Mass; eventually it was assigned to the *schola cantorum.*

in Acts 2:37, "they were cut to the heart and said to Peter and the rest of the apostles, 'Brethren, what shall we do?'" There will never be a lack of fruit and faith for the true preaching of Christ and for His purified holiness. Just as here, too, the lintels of the temple, that is, the house itself, were shaken by their voice, so also those who are in the church are moved by the Gospel and do not belong to the number of the blinded. Paul says, the Gospel "is bearing fruit and growing" "in the whole world" (Col. 1:6). It makes an impression because it is high and exalted. The conscience is terrified when it hears that everything is condemned and Christ alone is holy, and He alone enlightens every man coming into this world (John 1:9). The house was filled with smoke. In other places, such as Ex. 40:34 and 1 Kings 8:10, Scripture says that clouds filled the house and calls the cloud the glory of the Lord. And it denotes a "smoking" faith, one that knows that all our own things are defiled. Here Christ dwells, a light rising and justifying after the old man has been put to death. Confession then follows this hovering smoke, and the confession is: "Holy, holy, holy is the Lord of hosts." Then the severe judgment of God is felt, which forcibly elicits the confession. This is the first part of penitence, namely contrition, which shakes the thresholds and raises the smoke, namely, a feeling of the divine Word condemning the entire human righteousness. Then comes the seraph, that is, the preacher of the Gospel, which is the fiery coal, and promises the forgiveness of sins for Christ's sake and lifts one up to righteousness. Therefore "through the Law comes knowledge of sin" (Rom. 3:20), through the Gospel comes the knowledge and reception of grace and righteousness. The glowing coal is the Word kindled by the Holy Spirit in love, whereby those who have been put to death are revived by the cry of the seraphim. To touch the mouth is to strike the heart with the Gospel, which is sweet to the bitter heart. Then the heart is a fit vessel for honor, because it will go for the Lord, that is, it will be His instrument for teaching others, hearing and breaking through, even though with danger, the last comfort. A remnant will be saved, even though not all hear the Word and many spit it out.

CHAPTER SEVEN

1. *In the days of Ahaz the son of Jotham, son of Uzziah.*

To understand the prophet, one must first of all carefully ponder the historical situation. Jotham was godly; Ahaz, his son, was the most ungodly of all. Under Jotham Isaiah was silent for a while, under Ahaz he began to prophesy again. The latter established many kinds of idolatry and did it with a show of piety, because on every side he was pressed by the worst kind of evils, which he wished to counteract. Let him serve as an example for all people in the world so that they may see what faith in God can accomplish and, on the contrary, how works avail nothing before Him if any one trusts in them. Ahaz certainly did not worship trees but rather a divinity, only he did not do so with the right kind of worship. Idolatry consists in believing someone else rather than God alone. The Christian religion consists in believing in the mercy and goodness of God for Christ's sake. This religion is pure and sincere; everything else is idolatry, even though it uses the name of the true God as a cover. There are as many idols as there are sects. Because of the many new installations for the worship of God, Ahaz was proclaimed by the false prophets to be the holiest of all kings. David was nothing alongside him. The crowd goes after the outward form. And the holier and more zealous anyone is in a strange faith, the more destructive and deplorable he is. Such have they all been. Paul says of the Jews in Rom. 10:2: "They have a zeal for God, but it is not enlightened." They apply the terms God, the name of God, the work of God, and faith in God to that which is not God. They follow a shadow like that well-known dog [1] and lose the truth. Therefore let this example scare us away from every pretense, let it open our eyes so that we may distinguish false religion from the true.

Rezin came up to Jerusalem, better: against Jerusalem. For these wars, see the histories, 2 Kings 16:1 ff.; 2 Chron. 28:1 ff. It was their plan to wipe out the kingdom of Judah. But God says: I have written

[1] Like the earlier reference (p. 42), this allusion to Aesop reflects Luther's work in preparation for the translation of *Some Fables from Aesop* (W, L, 442).

a book which is called "A Remnant Will Be Saved." Again in Zech. 2:8: "He who touches you touches the apple of His eye." The Lord does not allow them to erase the name of His people, even though in His wrath He inflicts a great calamity on them.

But they could not conquer it. Because this was not God's plan but man's.

2. *The house of David* was told, that is, the king of Judah.

Syria is in league, that is, the king of Syria is allied with the king of Israel, and this means war. But this refers to the former section, "came up to Jerusalem, etc." "His heart shook," but it did so because many thousands of the people of Judah had been slain, the kingdom weakened, and cities taken away; and now the enemies were joined together, etc. This is indeed a description of the condition of the ungodly, whom the Word of promise will not help unless despair is already driving them, so that it may be a Word of life providing aid in death, a Word of liberty giving relief in captivity. And indeed it can demonstrate its power in no other way than to come into straits of the kind that befell Ahaz. Here the victory is reported before the fight. The enemies of godliness nevertheless plan how they will desert and that the godly may have no [2] hope of escaping. Here the Lord takes pleasure in casting down the proud and lifting up the lowly. Those two kings were far too sure of themselves; on the other hand, the heart of Ahaz was shaken.

And the heart of his people shook as the trees of the forest shake before the wind. An extraordinary comparison. Where there is no faith, there is no counsel. Now every form of divine worship that Ahaz had dared to set up beyond the Word of God broke down. No one is more scared in trouble than the top hypocrites. In peace they are unyielding and harder than flint; in distress they are shaken like trees at every breeze. But John the Baptist was not like that. The leaves of the trees are exposed to the gusts of wind, for there is no wall surrounding them to ward off the winds. So is the heart that is destitute of the Word of God and wide open to all calamities. Then works try to come to one's assistance instead of the Word, but these provide no protection. But God's wisdom does. Prov. 1:33 says: "He who listens to me will dwell secure and will be at ease, without dread of evil." Likewise (Prov. 28:1): "The wicked flee when

[2] The Weimar text has *ullam*, but we have read *nullam*.

no one pursues, but the righteous are bold as a lion." And in Ps. 112:6 we read: "The righteous will be remembered forever." Let us do the works that God has commanded, but let us not rely on them, but rather on the Word alone, that we may cling to it, letting go of works and all other things.

3. *And the Lord said to Isaiah.* It is uncertain whether שְׁאָר יָשׁוּב is one word or two. Yet it seems to be one and predictive. This is a frequent practice among the Hebrews. Thus it was with the names David, Solomon, Jesus, Peter, etc.[3] So also this name is predictive and signifies the forsaken remnant; the son bore the image of the people, of whom a remnant has always been preserved, for whose sake the king together with the rest of the ungodly experience the mercy of God. The sun rises for the sake of the good, and yet the ungodly also enjoy its light. But so great was the ungodliness at that time that only Isaiah and his son appeared to have survived of the godly, as if God were saying: "I would gladly give you many fellows, but they have all been estranged from Me; only one is left from the bottomless pit of ungodliness, and that one is despised by all. The rest of the people, even of those who believe, do not dare to address Me even in muffled tones."

At the end of the conduit. Jerusalem hung on the side of a mountain and suffered from water shortage, and therefore a water supply was piped into the city in ducts that they closed up in the time of Hezekiah.[4] Perhaps Ahaz was about to make some repairs there.

4. *Take heed, be quiet.* There are four admonitions: *Take heed, be quiet, do not fear, and do not let your heart be faint,* that is, no longer let your heart quake like the trees, but let it be still. Who would not take courage in response to these exhortations? Who would not believe the words of the Supreme Majesty, who thus consoles and so promises? But they were offered to Ahaz in vain. And here you see how a wicked heart and promises agree together. This is an example for us that we may learn. Yet Isaiah believed, as well as his son, if not Ahaz.

Two smoldering stumps of firebrands. A remarkable personification set against the personification above, where the smug and the

[3] David means "beloved"; Solomon means "peace"; Jesus means "the salvation of the Lord"; Peter means "rock."

[4] Luther is referring to the report in 2 Kings 20:20.

presumptuous who do not consider the power of the Word hiding in the small nation of Judah are described. God certainly speaks far more contemptuously of them than the enemies themselves do against us. He does not call them burning firebrands, but stumps of firebrands, that is, the leftovers of coals. They are coals no longer burning but extinguished, although they still smoke a little and are such as little boys play with to the present day. Who would here be afraid when God considers such great kings to be so worthless, if only one would believe it? They are indeed wrathful and raging, but they cannot accomplish what they wish. This is certainly a splendid promise of the kindness and protection of God even for the most ungodly king and idolator, that for him the wrath of those enemies should be minimized and the will of God to protect should be magnified, so that it is a shame that it fell on so unbelieving a heart. To him nevertheless, so that he could and should believe the more quickly and firmly, the prophet recounts the plan and attempt of these two kings.

6. *Let us go up.* The prophet reports this so that Ahaz may have no doubt that the Lord knows what they had in mind.

Let us conquer. So insatiable is the rage of men and demons. God, however, preserves a remnant, as shown above.

For ourselves, that is, so that the kingdom of Judah may be ours.

Tabeel. It appears as though this were a proper name, and yet it seems rather to be a shortened common noun, and it means an agreeable and pleasing fellow, that is, some kind of "Son," as above: "a vineyard on a hill, the son of oil" (5:1), that is, on some hill of oil, in some fertile place. For so the word "son" is used among the Hebrews in place of the specific.

7. *Thus says the Lord God: It shall not stand, and it shall not come to pass.* Now he discloses in what way they are smoldering firebrands, but it is without doubt a detailed and rich promise. Not any one of them will be head of Judah, but the house of David will. They will have to be satisfied with their own realm. Their own bounds have been set for all people. God is the one who transfers kingdoms, etc.

8. *Ephraim . . . will no longer be a people,* that is, Israel will no longer be a people. But if this nation comes to an end, so much more will Syria come to an end, because Ashur will remove them both.

Hence, from this chapter to the thirtieth the prophet always has Assyria in view.

9. *If you will not believe.* This indicates that the king showed signs of disbelief. Therefore he adds a threat to the promise. The king turns up his nose, sends the prophet away, and measures the matter according to the appearance of the flesh, namely, that the two kings are stronger than he, that many thousands of people will be lost, that cities will be lost, etc., as if he were saying: "You call them stumps of firebrands who are forest fires; you are talking contrary to reason and experience and truth." It was exactly as if some one were to say now: "Do not fear the Turks, etc." Therefore the king opposed reality. But the prophet insists that the Word of God is much more powerful than all the kings on earth, for He can also do what He says. The Word of God indeed proclaims things hidden and not manifest, and they are grasped only by faith. In other books and arts you must study and put all things to the test so that you may understand and grasp what is presented. Here it is enough to hear and to believe. Therefore the ancients explained this passage thus: If you do not believe, you do not understand.[5] Certainly a good thought. But the prophet set given works against the Amen, that is, the truth against hypocrisy. He means to say: You will not prevail, and whatever you may have planned otherwise will not endure, it will not continue, it will not succeed. Therefore he condemns every religion, all endeavors, all plans of the king, unless he believes God, not only such things as belong to the external and physical man, but also such as pertain to the spiritual man and the ecclesiastic. Hence faith alone makes certain and has a solid foundation. But the promise becomes useless unless faith is added. Then this passage is also explained Hebraically in this way: If you do not believe, you will not be truthful.[6] For those who believe God make and reckon Him to be true, which is giving glory to God, as Rom. 4:20 says, and they themselves also become truthful through faith. On the contrary, to the unbelieving all things become deceptive, unreliable, and unsure. With this conclusion the prophet said his final farewell to the king. This must be taught everywhere, because he who believes nothing

[5] See, for example, Augustine, *De fide et symbolo,* I, 1, *Patrologia, Series Latina,* XL, 181.

[6] The term "explained Hebraically" seems to refer to the definition of faith as faithfulness and trustworthiness.

accomplishes nothing. But whatever the godly man does will always prosper (Ps. 1:3).

8. *Within sixty-five years.* Israel was carried off under Hezekiah.[7]

10. *Again the Lord spoke.* 11. *Ask a sign of the Lord.* Behold the great and overflowing goodness of God and His sublime patience. For even though disdained in His promise and threat, He still does not stop inciting to faith, as if to say: If you do not want to believe promises and threats, at least believe the signs and choose whatever you wish. Ahaz, in turn, rejects also the sign with the worst blasphemy and ingratitude. God offers a sign; this man cites Scripture.

12. *You shall not put the Lord to the test.* Always the ungodly become more hardened. Now, those are wrong who say that signs avail nothing for faith. God is almost always accustomed to add a sign to the Word, just as here, too, he would have added one, provided that the king would have accepted it. Paul also approves the use of signs in 2 Cor. 12:12.[8] And signs do not make for distinguishing this person from that one.

13. *Hear then, O house of David.* Ahaz pretends religion, as if from fear of God he did not wish to ask for a sign. Such is the nature of hypocrites, who display religiosity where it is not proper; on the other hand, where they should fear, they are most proud and stubborn, as Ps. 36:1 and Ps. 53:5 say. Both are extremely offensive to God and deceptive to the people.

To put God to the test is indeed evil when it is done without a word of God. He who is commanded to put God to the test and does not do so is sinning. God is not being tempted when He Himself orders it. It is not tempting God to believe in Christ, to love the neighbor, because God has commanded these things. However, he who desires to serve God short of His commandment is tempting Him, since he does not know whether it will please Him. Thus Ahaz multiplied the religions of the heathen in Judah, he tempted God and yet did not think he was tempting Him. He thought so, however, when he was ordered to do so. There are many such people, above all the false prophets.

[7] Together with some other portions of these lectures, this explanation of Is. 7:8 disrupts the proper sequence of verses.

[8] The original has "1 Cor. 12."

Is it too little for you, etc. To weary men is certainly evil. But if anyone has sinned against God, who will pray for him? The prophet, however, declares the people guilty of both. He who sins against his neighbor sins against God; but this is the great and unforgivable sin, when someone resists God's Word and work. Other sins are easily recognized and have a form, but this one, with which one dashes against God, is not recognized and is therefore unforgivable, and this is because men are offensive to God.

14. *Therefore the Lord Himself will give you a sign,* that is to say, "Since you refuse to ask a sign of God, He Himself will provide one of His own will." These things are said by a wrathful prophet. And he foretells two signs: The one is hidden, the other open. The latter he explains in chapter 8 in a way not much different from Hosea, chapter 1. But Isaiah includes both signs. The first one does not apply to Ahaz, because he did not live to see it, but the second does. But since he now resists the Word of God and refuses a sign, how can his faith be strengthened? Therefore the prophet speaks of a sign to come, against which they will dash, just as the sign of Jonah was given to the Jews (cf. Matt. 12:39), and those who refuse to believe will perish. Nevertheless, it is a sign of lifting up and building up and strengthening for those who believe (Matt. 12:39; 16:4). And this is the summary of this chapter until the end, because he says that this prediction is already in the process of fulfillment in these unbelievers. עַלְמָה, a young woman capable of giving birth, for an old woman can be a virgin too, but she is not called עַלְמָה.

She shall conceive. In Hebrew it is "has conceived," and that is the indication of a miracle; it is as if the prophet were already seeing it. Again, since he says that it is God's sign, it is necessary that that conception and birth be in a different manner than is commonly and naturally the case, for it would not be a sign if one who today is a virgin would become pregnant after a half year. Therefore she has to be both a virgin and with child. Matthew 1:21 f. clearly explains this.

Immanuel. This describes what kind of person it will be. This is not a proper name. He is indeed the Son of a virgin, and yet He is "God with us," therefore God and man.

15. *He shall eat curds and honey.* This is a description of His

childhood and humanity. As He is said to be born as a true human being, so He will be reared in a true human fashion.

When He knows how to refuse, etc. Thus He will grow up like other boys until He arrives at the judgment of reason. This the prophet explains:

16. *Before the Child knows, etc.* That is to say, You, ungodly man, do not believe anything. But they will be there because of this unbelief, so that those enemies of yours will perish, but nonetheless you too will follow not long afterwards. But this will happen before the Boy has learned to name butter and honey. This is said for the purpose of making the prophecy dark and as an obstacle for the Jews, who to this day do not understand this passage and say that Immanuel is Hezekiah.[9] But this sign was given for the sake of the remnant, that the kingdom of Judah should not be destroyed until Christ would come. It is, however, a hidden sign for the sake of the ungodly.

17. *The Lord will bring upon you, etc.* He says: Because the unbeliever rejects the present sign, he is unworthy also of the future sign. The Assyrians and Egyptians did not wage war against Judah at the same time, but each in turn. And this for the reason that they, having fallen away from God, trusted in men, as will be shown later.

Such days as have not come, etc. Some take this as applying to the removal to Babylon.[10] But the prophecy must be understood in accordance with the matter at hand, for when these things were said here, the Babylonian kingdom did not yet exist. Therefore the prophet attributes to the Assyrians what their successors, the Chaldeans, did, and what belongs to a part is said of the whole. The prophet calls all human dregs Assyrians, namely, Medes, Parthians, Chaldeans, etc., and says in short: You will not live in peace until that sign of offense will come.

18. *The Lord will whistle,* that is He will permeate the spirit, He will arouse the hearts.

He calls the nations of the Gentiles *flies* because of their great number, especially the Egyptians, and *bees* because of their quarrelsomeness and their violent sting and anger.

9 Jerome, *Commentaria,* III, 112.

10 Jerome, *Commentaria,* III, 113—114.

Bees give up their lives with the sting. Ps. 118:12 reads: "They surrounded me like bees." Flies and drones only indulge in eating and contaminate everything. Thus these flies symbolize the greed of the Egyptians. But the bees symbolize the rage and bloodlust of the Assyrians.

At the sources of the streams of Egypt, etc. These are pure figures of speech. He mentions the places where those insects prefer to live. The pleasant pastures near the ravines mean riches; the clefts of the rocks, fortified citadels; the thornbushes, the common people; the water holes, hidden treasures. They will spare none. Here wealth, worth, escape, and hiding will be of no help.

20. *In that day the Lord will shave with a razor.* Here is a new picture. He calls the Assyrians a razor. David says in Ps. 52:2: "Your tongue is like a sharp razor, you worker of treachery." Scripture calls the most destructive men a sharp razor. Among the Jews it was a disgrace to have the hair and beard shaved, as 2 Sam. 10:4 shows. But to shave the head is to drain the realm of nobles and princes, for the head denotes the realm, and the hairs are the aristocracy of the kingdom. Nobility, power, accomplishment, and whatever is of the best quality is to be taken away. Concerning the hired razor see below, chapter 10 [10:5 ff.] and in connection with Hezekiah, chapter 39 [39:4 ff.]. Read how God gives a reward to those through whom He punishes His own people. So also schoolmasters are paid to whip the boys.

Beyond the River. By automatic identification he is thinking of the Euphrates, which is the river nearest to Judea and the largest. *With a razor,* that is, by means of a razor.

The hair of the feet, that is, he means the common people, and the beard is the priestly realm. The beard of Aaron is honored in Ps. 133:2. The mouth is the instrument for teaching, and around it grows the beard, that is, the priesthood. All, he says, will go into captivity, the highest and the lowest. Both earthly and spiritual kingdoms will be made bald, and the feet too, as was done by Nebuchadnezzar, the king of Babylon.

21. *A man will keep alive a young cow.* This is a picture of the desolation after the captivity, when there will be a lack of tillers of the soil. By reason of poverty they will be able to accomplish nothing, and then they will live on milk and honey, they will simply be rustics

and without any government. Thus *in that day,* that is, the day of captivity and deportation, any man who will have remained in the land *will keep alive a young cow,* that is, many cows. For the care of vineyards and all handicrafts will be neglected, and this is what is said in the Books of Moses (Lev. 26:34): "Then the land shall rest and enjoy its sabbaths." By reason of the scarcity of eaters there will be plenty of milk, and this is a description of the desolation that is due to the small number of people. Then he adds a description of it from the point of view of the place.

23. *Every place where there used to be a thousand vines, a thousand shekels of silver.* This was the value of the vines.

24. *With bow and arrows men will come.* In fields once well tended there will be briers and thorns, afterwards wolves and snakes, and robbers will hide there, so that it is not safe to walk through it unarmed. Such is Rome.[11]

As for all the hills. Scripture often calls attention to the fertility of the Judean hills. Judea was hilly, and there were many vineyards there. Where there is no head in the kingdom, there dangers cannot but be present. These are threats against unbelievers. Germany, too, will owe God a razor. God will hire the Turk. These things are surely written for our sakes. Like sins bring like punishments.

11 From the contemporary maps of Bufalini and Cantarius it is evident that at the time of Luther's visit to Rome in 1510 most of the area of Rome was wasteland; its total population is usually estimated at 40,000 persons.

CHAPTER EIGHT

1. *Then the Lord said to me, Take a large tablet.*

THIS is related to the preceding threats against the unbelievers. The Lord had ordered the king to ask for a sign, but when the king declined, the Lord nevertheless promised a future sign with regard to Christ. With this accomplished, the prophet returns to threatening. The devil will contaminate you, he says. To this word he now adds the usual sign, as he also did later, when as a symbol he walked about naked, Is. 20:3. And Jeremiah wore a chain around his neck, Jer. 27:2; 28:10. This sign is almost like Habakkuk's, who says: "For still the vision awaits its time" (Hab. 2:3). The sign is a tablet or large parchment for the purpose of arousing the common people to see that the matter is said and done in earnest, and the common people are more influenced by signs than by words alone.

In common characters, that is, so that they can be read clearly. [The prophet is to write] large letters, such as are commonly used by men, so that no one can excuse himself as though he could not read them.

The spoil speeds.[1] This refers to the Egyptians. *The prey hastes* refers to the Assyrians.

2. *And I got witnesses.* The prophet summoned witnesses to attest the sign. This is much the same as what Hosea did, and he even called in witnesses of his marriage and wedding feast, namely, guests and the fact that he thus named his son. *Reliable witnesses,* sure ones, through whom he could best prove his case and win acceptance.

3. *Prophetess,* that is, one of the daughters of the prophets.

Call his name. Thus the second sign corresponds with the words. The people were quickly to become a prey. The tablet and the son's name have this meaning. It is Christ, however, who most worthily bears this title by His death, for He despoiled hell. But just as the

[1] As the footnote to the Revised Standard Version indicates, this is the translation of the name Maher-shalal-hash-baz.

innocent sons of Hosea are called sons of fornication for the sake of the people who did fornicate, so here Isaiah's son bears his name. However, before the boy could say, "My father, my mother," that is, in a few years, three or four, the king of Assyria came.

4. *Wealth,* that is, the kingdom.

Before the king of Assyria, that is, through the king, who was the true tablet, since this is the sign that was despised both by words and by threats.

6. *Because this people have refused.* The people, void of faith, sought help and counsel everywhere, even among outsiders and enemies, or else of necessity they made agreements with them and hired them at great expense. So you will read below in chapters 30 and 31. But never did they seek help with the Lord. They made treaties which they broke afterwards. "The wicked," He says, "are like the tossing sea" (Is. 57:20). This is therefore a rebuke of their unbelief over against God and their trust over against their enemies. To sum it up: He who trusts in man will go to ruin. Alliances are the cause of two evils. For the minds of some are inflamed, who would otherwise be peaceful; these burden themselves with envy, and when they come to the heart of the matter, nothing happens. Always there are excuses. The Jews, having spurned their own God, even made alliances with strange gods, because they noticed the exceedingly successful military campaigns of the idolaters.

Shiloah was a river in Jerusalem whose waters he describes as still and gently flowing in comparison with waters rushing violently, that is, the people in exile in comparison with a powerful nation, and God despised with God exalted. God, however, is called the true Shiloah, moving silently, that is, favorably, hidden. Below, in 30:15, we read: "In quietness and in trust shall be your strength." He does not do battle with military forces, but His strength is in the weakness of a quiet people, a people that does not rage, in whom at length He will cast down the haughty, after He has first lifted up the lowly. But at that time the kingdom of Judah despised this word, and, desirous of conquering by an uprising, they took refuge in the resources of their enemies. They were conquered by an uprising. God does not want us to be rushing and tempestuous waters but to hope for help from heaven and to prefer a victory won with spiritual weapons. This, then, is the meaning of this passage: The king of

Judah and his princes do not want to uphold by faith the powerful weakness of the people but prefer to act in violence. Therefore they shall have enough violence.

7. *The waters of the River,* that is, the Euphrates. The waters denote people. The little rivers denote walled towns, so also the banks up to the neck, that is, the head, which is Jerusalem. It will remain, it will continue to stand, even though in the midst of waters. Obviously, trusting Hezekiah, of whom the Jews say that he is that Immanuel, was protected in a wonderful way by a clear prophecy. He who puts his trust in men walks on clouds and builds on sand.

9. *Be gathered, you peoples, and be conquered.* It would be better if chapter eight began here. These are threats against the king of Assyria, whose plan was to flood the land of Judah up to its neck, as has already been said, but in order fully to upset and destroy everything, the body together with the head. It was God's plan, however, to preserve a remnant and some grapes from the ruined vineyard. Therefore the prophet scoffs at the plan of that king after he has finished speaking about the blow that would strike the Jews. The word of comfort in the midst of wrath is for the purpose of arousing hope. *Be gathered,* Jerusalem. This is the Hebrew way of saying "Be evil, show what you can do." *Be conquered,* that is, you will not succeed. The repetition shows the intensity of emotion and suggests: "Do whatever you can, and do it as vigorously as possible." The kingdom of Judah refers to the kingdom of Christ, namely, that He would be the one to take the intiative in that kingdom. He provides the aid, they will win the victory. Therefore look for those who are drawn up in battle array with many weapons. Let the strange god first be cast down, and his army will easily be defeated. Let us pray first of all against Satan. Christians fight most effectively when they fight least.

11. *For the Lord spoke thus to me.* He says, "I am forced to contradict those who trust in the flesh and to lead them back to God, because the Lord has commanded me, and He wants it so, for He withdraws me from the people like a hand, a people that wants only to trust in men and to enter into alliances with outsiders, now with this king, now with that one. Yet these kings have plundered them and swallowed them up. Hence I am ultimately forced to set myself against this people and not to speak like them, and I am not afraid

because I am in God's hand. He will protect me. I seek no other protector. But this people thinks, plans, ponders nothing else than that it would be good to form alliances, whereby they deny and anger God. Yet God Himself still deems these people worthy of having their evils and blessings proclaimed to them, if only they would believe."

12. *Do not fear what they fear,* that is, you who are godly, do not be afraid like the ungodly, or do not fear the ungodly who want to frighten you, or do not fear the princes who advise you to forsake God.

13. *The Lord of hosts, Him you shall regard as holy.* Hallow Him who dwells in Jerusalem, in the waters of Shiloah, worship and trust Him, and He will sanctify you and say: "I will be an enemy to your enemies. He who touches you touches the apple of My eye" (Zech. 2:8).

14. *A stone of offense.* Peter (1 Peter 2:8) and Paul (Rom. 9:33) cite this passage and make a general application out of a specific one. Wherever people turn away from faith in God and swerve toward confidence in the flesh, there it will be as is stated here: They take offense, they fall, they are ensnared, they are crushed, etc. Paul says in 1 Cor. 1:23: "We preach Christ crucified, . . . folly to the Gentiles, etc." God's prophets are all regarded as fools. And from the beginning of the world to its end the Word of God is a stumbling block, not indeed by its own fault but by the fault of the depraved flesh which loves darkness rather than God's light (cf. John 3:19), and so that which is given as a cure becomes a poison to the flesh. Life becomes death, salvation becomes destruction, because men attack, blaspheme, reject, and persecute it. Paul says in 2 Cor. 2:15 f.: "We are the aroma of Christ to God among those who are being saved and among those who are perishing, to one a fragrance from death to death, etc."

And a snare. He charges the house of Judah separately with what he has previously attached to the kingdom of Israel in order to fix it the more on Judah once the kingdom of Ephraim has been destroyed. This is something the prophet saw long before it happened.

15. *And many shall stumble thereon.* Because few still believe, others will become hardened; they will regard the Word as folly,

they will fall so that they cannot be lifted up again. They will be dashed in pieces so that they cannot be glued together again.

They shall be snared in errors so that they cannot be rescued; they will remain in everlasting captivity. Therefore we must pray more urgently that the Word may remain, so that cleansed hearts may believe and abide in the light, etc.

16. *Bind up the testimony.* This can be understood as spoken in a general sense, namely, that here Isaiah is speaking as well as Christ, as chapter 2 of Hebrews applies this to Christ. "I will put My trust in Him, etc.," He says (Heb. 2:13). This is, however, praise of the Word of God and an indication what kind of disciples and what kind of stumbling blocks it has. *Bind up!* As a sack is tied up and sealed, so put it out of sight! That is to say: They will take offense, fall, etc., because wisdom and understanding of the Word will be taken away from them because they resist it, as Ps. 109:17 says: "He did not like blessing; may it be far from him!" The testimony, that is, the Word, will be bound up, the Law will be sealed, all things will be concealed. The heart will be veiled, etc. This is not the fault of the Word, because it is plainly preached, but of the hardened heart, which does not want to believe.

Seal the teaching among My disciples, that is, up to My disciples, who believe. To them it will be an open testimony, etc. In Hebrew "disciples" is in the Dative case, and it means that the Word is not hidden for the disciples but that they have the Word which is hidden to others, as Christ says in Luke 8:10: "To you it has been given to know the secrets of the kingdom of God." It remains a sealed and dark word and is nothing but pure parables until the disciples of God, who are of God, hear it. What the wisdom of the flesh does not grasp, because it is spiritual and new, is unsealed and unbound for them as for new and reborn men, as John 8:47 says.

17. *I will wait for the Lord.* He explains how the Word is unlocked, namely, when men keep silent before the Lord, wait, and believe. This the Lord's disciples were taught, to wait for the Lord, not to pat themselves on the back in their works, but to trust the Lord. Ps. 130:6 says: "My soul waits for the Lord more than watchmen for the morning." See Is. 29:18. To one who does not know what faith is, the Word of God is a closed book. Paul says in Gal. 2:20: "It is no longer I who live, but Christ who lives in me," as if

to say, "I lean not on my own righteousness nor on that of the Pharisees but on that of Christ alone." Thus here and in chapter 2 of the Epistle to the Hebrews there is contained the sum of the whole Christian doctrine. "I will put My trust in Him" (Heb. 2:13). This will be my righteousness. He who does not know or do this strikes a blow against the Word of God, even if he makes use of the greatest words of Christ.

Who is hiding His face from the house[2] *of Jacob.* He is hiding because they see the spiritual understanding of the Word, which means to wait for the Lord to be treated as holy, to fear Him. Until they understand this, the Lord's face is hidden from them, as 2 Cor. 3:7, 13 says. The Law is not understood apart from faith, but they do not want to believe, they only want to pat themselves on the back, and therefore God hides His face from them, because they are ungodly and do not want to look upon Him as merciful but as hostile.

18. *Behold, I and the children.* This depicts the course and success of the Word. Though some do not accept it when it is proclaimed, it still is not without disciples. Therefore he rejoices in both the fruit and power of the Word. An honest teacher always has disciples. This is also Christ's word for His faithful ones. "Children." In Hebrew: "Little infants." Peter had this in view when he said in 1 Peter 2:2: "Like newborn babes." They are the least complicated human beings and depend entirely on their mother's breast. So Christians depend entirely on the simplicity of Scripture. They have the "pure milk" without guile, that is, they do nothing but seek the breasts; they do not pass judgment nor argue much about the Word, but they simply accept it as it is given to them, the way babes accept milk.[3]

Whom the Lord has given me, that is, whose hearts the Lord knew. They are not brought forward by their own wisdom.

Signs and portents in Israel. Such babes as simply believe and suck milk eagerly without guile are freaks to the world. "They are men of good omen," says Zech. 3:8. In the presence of God they are the most happy infants, but in the sight of the world nothing is more subversive than they, to the point that men think they have rid the

[2] The Weimar text has *domino,* but we have followed the Biblical text and read *domo.*

[3] During the years of these lectures Luther had occasion to know this from personal experience: Hans Luther was born on June 7, 1526; Elizabeth on December 10, 1527 (she died on August 3, 1528); Magdalena on May 4, 1529.

world of monsters when these have been removed from the scene, and they consider them most unworthy of life. Christ says in Ps. 22:6: "I am scorned by men."

Who dwells on Mount Zion. The prophet is speaking of his own time and his own disciples, Christ of His, Peter of his, we of ours – and yet all are disciples of Christ.

19. *Consult the mediums.* The admonition is of the kind Christ spoke in Matt. 16:6, 11: "Take heed and beware of the leaven of the Pharisees and Sadducees." First comes teaching, then admonition. Such is the custom of prophets and apostles. It is as if he were saying: "Your doctrine will be a stumbling block. You will be an abomination. No harm, only remain constant. False prophets and false brethren, as 2 Cor. 11:13 calls them, will come, trying to pull you away from that state of childhood, but you be wise. They will surround you with flattering words." And yet he does not say: "Consult the priests and the teachers," but he describes them for what they are in the presence of God, even the best of them who discharged the teaching office. He calls them enchanters, soothsayers, etc. This is no small affront to the ecclesiastical administrators. But as many as do not teach the Word of faith are rightly so called. These have the divining spirit, the Pharisaical spirit, the spirit of error and giddiness; they teach their own ideas and dreams.

They chirp and mutter. They are inclined to wordiness, they make a show of wisdom, great knowledge, etc. They want to teach, not hear. They are as full of ideas as dogs are of fleas.[4] Their word bags cannot be emptied. This is the way they talk: "You should consult us and ask us for whatever must be taught. Who gave you the authority to introduce new doctrine without consulting us? Be obedient to your Mosaic masters, the legal experts, of whom you have an ample supply, etc." Let them be answered as follows.

Should not a people consult their God? We have heard nothing but the voice of God. Paul says in Eph. 4:14 that we should not be "carried about with every wind of doctrine, etc." Must we not rather cling to the Word of God than to that of men? Are the dead more properly consulted than the living? God lives, the fanatics are dead, and all of them are likewise blind people and people for whom the

[4] The complete text of the proverb alluded to is: "Fuller [of opinions] than a dog is of fleas on St. John's Day."

testimony is "bound up" (v. 16). There are two sentences here. Our translation combines them into one. Should not a people consult their God? Should they not consult the living rather than the dead?

20. *To the Law rather, and to the testimony,* that is, the Law must be consulted rather than the mediums. The teaching must be sought from God alone, so that one may be your master, Christ, as Matt. 23:10 says. But this takes place through the medium of Scripture and oral preaching. The "Law" is Scripture, and the "testimony" is oral preaching. He who reads Scripture in an unfeigned and humble spirit does not read it without fruit. In this way you have recourse to the Law. That is to say, the Law and the testimony should be consulted.

And if they speak not according to this Word. This is a threat and an outstanding passage about the contradiction of men who do not agree to the Law and the testimony but oppose and condemn those who cling to these alone.

They shall not have the morning light, that is, the Gospel, the Word of God, which is the light that has arisen in Christ: a new sun, a new dawn, as 2 Peter 1:19, Ps. 119:105, and Prov. 6:23 say. Our hearts are the earth, and the morning light is the Word of God. Therefore we must give careful heed to these words, lest we follow strange doctrines, doctrines of the old serpent, of the old man. For to those who will remain in the Law and the testimony the morning light will come up, that is, understanding of the Word. But it will not come up for those who want to be masters before they are disciples or for those who run after another word. Horribly, to be sure, have the Pharisees and Sadducees, the papists and heretics fallen into darkness. See above ch. 5:21: "Woe to those who are wise in their own eyes."

21. *They will pass through it and fall.* This passage can be applied to all conditions of the ungodly. Whenever the Word is present, few assent, many resist. Therefore he says, the people *will pass through it;* that is, the land beyond and outside of the Word will collapse, and the man with a hardened heart will go hungry. Surely the Jews are eagerly waiting for Messiah a long time already, having been led astray by false prophets, meanwhile despising the proclaimed Gospel and becoming hardened. Delay makes restless people. "Hope deferred makes the heart sick," Prov. 13:12 says. Therefore the Jews curse Christ, their own King, because they deny the Word or explain it differently, and they curse us while they deny the Scripture. Hence

their doctrine is full of venomous curses, they could break in pieces when they hear Christ Jesus named. "They have a zeal for God, but it is not enlightened," Rom. 10:2 says. Whoever, then, wishes to avoid the spirit of hardening and blasphemy must humble his heart before that Law and testimony. But what are the forms of blasphemy? In one form a person has the worst kind of thoughts about God and Christ and yet remains committed to the tenet that Christ is true God and that all things contained in Scripture are true. This is a known and familiar spirit of blasphemy. It especially afflicts good minds in monasteries, and this is the last temptation of which the Book of Job speaks in an argument about whether anything God does is unjust. In another form the Word is attacked, as here. It is also called a spirit of remorse, for it is not so well recognized as the former. Hardening and famine follow contempt of the Word, and then blasphemy of Christ and of God. Then their prayer is turned into sin, and they seek in vain for help either from heaven or from earth.

22. *Behold, distress and darkness.* They are without light and peace wherever they turn. Light denotes good fortune anywhere, and darkness misfortune. The repetition shows the violence and the permanence of the calamities. "They go from hardship to hardship," he says, "and even so they do not stop blaspheming." "The future distress," he says, "will not be as light as the last one, when they were captive, suffered hunger, and were molested by their neighbors, etc., but it will bite more sharply, and they will not be afflicted just for a time as formerly." But he mentions two misfortunes sustained before: One through King Tiglathpileser, the other through Shalmaneser. The Zebulonites were neighbors of Syria.

CHAPTER NINE[1]

1. *The way of the sea,* where there was intercourse and trade with the Jews. This is called *Galilee of the nations.* Moreover, Isaiah speaks of the light of happiness and peace. Matthew, however, speaks of Christ (Matt. 4:14 ff.); he quotes the text from the Septuagint, not according to the Hebrew, and he turns the specific prophecy into a general one, as he often does elsewhere.

2. *The people who walked in darkness have seen a great light.*

Matthew (4:16) cites this text with reference to Christ's specific sojourn in Capernaum and Galilee not for the purpose of establishing and strengthening faith but only for the purpose of encouragement.[2] The apostles and evangelists are much accustomed to doing this.

People. So then the people of the whole world, Jews as well as Gentiles, were in darkness, that is, in error, unrighteousness, notions, a false understanding of the Law, etc. *Light* is the Gospel, the gift of the Holy Spirit. It is common for Scriptures to repeat and double the same thing, as is done here, for the purpose of emphasis.

3. *Thou hast multiplied the nation, Thou hast not increased its joy.* Here is pictured the fruit and power of this light which is propagated from day to day, not satisfied with the corner where the Jews live but spread abroad among the nations throughout the world, a thing that irks the Jews. In Deut. 32:21 we read: "I will provoke them with a foolish nation." The Jews, who think that they alone should be God's people, interpret this passage in a distorted way, as if the Gentiles, however numerous, would not come to enjoy God nor rejoice in Him.[3] But this is the true meaning: Many nations are re-

[1] In the Weimar text, following the versification of the Hebrew text, our Is. 9:1 is Is. 8:23, and therefore this heading appears before ch. 8:23; we have placed it here to conform to our arrangement of chapters and verses.

[2] A "general prophecy" was one that did not refer exclusively to one person or event, such as the coming of the Messiah, but could be applied to Him as a particular instance of a broader pattern.

[3] Cf. Lyra *ad* Is. 9:5, regarding the rabbis' exegesis of this passage in relation to the defeat of the armies of Sennacherib.

ceived into the kingdom of God; this makes the Jews sick, by this they are provoked to anger, envy, zeal, and a spirit of stupor (cf. Rom. 11:8). This is what it means to lessen their joy.

The nations rejoice before Thee as with joy at the harvest, as men rejoice when they divide the spoil. The metaphors are taken from agricultural and military life. Christ, too, uses the former in John 4:35. There are many dangers before the harvest, there are many before the war is over. Therefore farmers rejoice in the harvest, and soldiers rejoice when they divide the spoil taken in the war. Read Judges 7, about the Midianites cut down through Gideon. They slaughtered each other with their own swords. In such a manner, says Isaiah, will the nations be redeemed.

4. *The yoke of his burden,* namely, the people's. Better: "their," so that it may be associated with "they rejoice."

Yoke means death, *staff* means a prod, sin. *Rod* is the Law, "the power of sin" (1 Cor. 15:56). This description is certainly contrary to all experience, since all laws ought to be the power and motivation of righteousness. But without the Law sin is dead and weaponless. The Law brings it about that there is sin, that it has power, and that it acts (Rom. 7:8). What does it accomplish? Death. There are therefore three strong tyrants: the Law, sin, and death. Sin is twofold: known and unknown. The latter is original sin, the former the sin of outward acts. This needs to be disclosed by the Holy Spirit through a spiritual understanding of the Law. Then the conscience, frightened by the judgment of God, is alarmed: Even though you may not be an adulterer, a thief, a robber, etc., you are born in sins and you are altogether buried in sins, if you do not have Christ. Paul did not know that desire was sin, as he says in Rom. 7:7. The prophet inverts the order. Paul lists it directly. Therefore there is joy because we have been set free from these tyrants. Joy is a skin-deep tickle, it annoys and is unreliable, for it does not remove death, the fear of death, and sin.

The most oppressive tyrant is the Law, which the prophet here calls our judge and king. It dictates: "You shall love God," etc. But no one is without evil desire. By nature all hate God and the things that are of God. This is not felt except in temptation. The whipped son is angry with his parent. No one likes discipline, not even God's. Natural man would prefer that there be no law, because he is not able to perform what it demands. The sin that has been committed is the second tyrant, and it brings forth the third, namely, death and damnation. Who could be happy when he is answerable to these three? But now they have been vanquished, the Law is fulfilled by Christ and then also by us who have been endowed by the Holy Spirit. He adds the courage so that we may glory even in our sufferings (Rom. 5:3), and thus the Law is no longer outrageous in its dictates but an agreeable companion. The Law itself indeed is not changed, but we are. Obviously this is Christian liberty, when the Law is voluntarily fulfilled, so that it cannot accuse, demand, and render guilty. Where the conscience is not guilty, where there is no sin because it is forgiven, there is no power of death but peace of conscience, the certainty of eternal life. The people of Midian had destroyed everything. So the tyrants condemn all our endeavors and works and wisdom, etc. The torch of Gideon is the light of the Gospel, so is the sound of the trumpet, and the clash of jars is Christ's crucifixion (cf. Judges 7:16). These are the things that overcome those enemies: the Word and the Holy Spirit in the Word preaching Christ as having died for us, etc. We draw no sword, but we only shout, hear, believe, confess: Christ died for us, etc. "Thanks be to God, who gives us the victory, etc." (1 Cor. 15:57). The Law, sin, and death have attacked the sinless Christ, they converged upon Him; but they were themselves made culpable and guilty, they were condemned and rendered powerless by Christ, and this was for us. This is our joy and the reaping of the harvest.

5. *For every violent taking of spoils.*[4] This sheds light and is added for the sake of explanation. For in the kingdom of the church the highest peace and safety will follow after deliverance from sin, the Law, and death. There will be no war. He says (Is. 11:9): "They shall not hurt or destroy in all My holy mountain." The end of righteousness is peace.

Garment mingled with blood, that is, fallen corpses lying in their blood. That is: There will be no war and human carnage, but love, peace, concord. The Holy Spirit will swallow up those evils with the fire of love, so that they will not be called back, because what fire consumes is reduced to nothing. And often in the Scriptures the final destruction is symbolized by fire.

[4] The Weimar text has *praedicacio,* but we have followed the Biblical text and read *praedacio.*

6. *For to us a Child is born.* Here you see the prophet speaking about the kingdom of peace, because he boasts about a Child born and a Son given, who will be the Head and King of this kingdom. And therefore it will be a kingdom of peace, not of strife. All these words are strong and intense. Above he spoke of the greatest affliction, of darkness and the shadow of death. Likewise of the Law, of sin, and of death, the most oppressive tyrants. Against them he now places the King born and given to us, who is to set us free from them and implant us into His peaceful and happy reign. He now proceeds to explain what kind of reign that is.

And the government was made. Verbs of the past tense are to be interpreted in the present tense. Instead of "was made" we shall have "is." Some explain this as meaning that Christ has conquered the world through the cross. Others set this passage over against those above by way of antithesis: On this Child no yoke and rod will be imposed, because He is without sin, but government and freedom will be His.[5] We explain it in this way: The government of Christ are we, whom He carries on His shoulders. Other kings are carried like rods by their subjects. All kingdoms of the world are carried and are burdens on our neck, and they reduce bodies and possessions to slavery. Therefore in the manner of ruling in the kingdom of the world and in that of Christ there is a difference. In the kingdom of the world the prince or king alone is free, all others are servants. But in Christ's kingdom Christ alone is a servant, and we are free. Moses says in Deut. 32:11: "Like an eagle, etc.," and it bore them "on its pinions." So to the present day it is with Christ, once for all, however, in His cross and death. He commanded His ministers and all His members to bear one another. He Himself is the Cornerstone and the Foundation. Thus in the kingdom of Christ those who serve rule, and those who rule serve.

And His name will be called Wonderful. The kingdom of Christ is beyond grasp, reason, and experience. Here the flesh must be put to death with all its wisdom and judgment, and it must be grasped only by faith. We must believe that Christ's righteousness is ours. Reason wants to lean only on its own righteousness, not on someone

[5] On the application of this passage to Christ's conquering through the Cross, cf. Hervais of Bourg-Dieu, *Commentaria in Esaiam,* Book II, *Patrologia, Series Latina,* CLXXXI, 122; Luther probably knew the idea from the comments of Lyra *ad locum.*

else's. We *believe* life, glory, righteousness, and peace but on the contrary *feel* death, shame, sin, and trouble.

Counselor. רוֹעֵץ. Lest we come short in the matter of faith He gives us counsel, that is, the Word, so that we may abide in so wonderful a government of His kingdom. This is truly not a simple word, but it is a word that is able to save in dangers.

God. אֵל, that is, strong, Power. Here it is not the Person or nature of this king that is depicted but only His wonderful government of the kingdom. Therefore He has counsel, He has full power, He can come to the aid of the weary and those spent by trials.

Mighty. גִּבּוֹר or גֶּבֶר, that is, powerful. He gives the strength to triumph through the Word and the Holy Spirit. It also signifies the strength and substance by which we support ourselves. גִּבּוֹר, however, is an active and working force whereby we withstand the enemies and proceed against them and put them to flight through the Word. So Christ both preserves His own and overthrows the enemies, even though the opposite may seem to be the case.

Everlasting Father. This, then, indicates the work and business of this King, not His Person. This name fits no one else. He always increases His reign, He always begets children and rules over them, He always remains the Father, He does not assume the role of tyrant, His children are always His beloved. This is beyond question the most delightful kingdom.

Prince of Peace. In the kingdom of Christ there is grace, comfort, forgiveness of sins, joy, peace. He does not deal with the transgressor in sternness, but as a father. The forgiveness of sins is justification, and peace follows justification. This peace is not only peace of mind but also plenty and soundness of mind and good health of the body. Such is the reign of Christ: It is extended by killing; it is fertilized by the blood of the believers; and the more distress there is, the more peace grows in the heart.

7. *Upon the throne of David.* There will be that abundance of peace and eternity of reign which denotes the resurrection of the dead. David ruled on earth, and his kingdom was no different from others except that it was divinely established over the people of God, and yet the people were mortal men. Therefore David's reign over the Jews was physical, but at length Christ has begun the spiritual reign over the people which will last forever. Hence there will be

a resurrection of the dead. Christ is indeed a King different from David, and the government of His kingdom is different, and yet it is a reign over the same people. To believe in life everlasting is the last article [6] and the greatest. However, Christ prepares, establishes, and strengthens this kingdom in the world through the Word and faith, and He does this in a hidden way.

With justice and with righteousness. Justice is that part of Law which condemns. Righteousness is that part which absolves. In the kingdom of Christ the ungodly are condemned, the godly are justified, saved, and set free from sin and death. A happy reign in which mercy flourishes.

The zeal of the Lord. Zeal is love mixed with hatred, or angry love, or the anger of love. Therefore, while God loves us, He is angry with our enemies, sin, death, Satan, so that He can more abundantly practice His love toward us. Here is nothing but mercy, yet surprising to no one.

8. *The Lord has sent a word.* This is the most important task in the prophets, correctly to connect the preceding with what follows. Until now Isaiah prophesied concerning Christ's kingdom, now he turns back to the kingdom of Israel. So he usually links the physical and the spiritual realms, he prophesies concerning the future good and he reproves the present evil kingdom. So any preacher should stress the Last Day and the life to come and at the same time rebuke current sins. The prophet, then, is saying: "These people have outstanding sermons and very great prophecies concerning the future and the present kingdom, but they despise them in a flagrant way and do not stop their iniquity until their lice are exterminated. In Scripture the arrogance of the kings of Israel is notorious. The people of Ephraim were puffed up against Gideon from the tribe of Manasseh because they had a prophecy that Ephraim would be greater than Manasseh. Pride follows privilege in spiritual as well as in bodily matters. Yet pride in bodily things can be more quickly controlled than in spiritual things, as when one is presumptuous about God. But God does not appear to any but those who fear Him and humble themselves. God is the God of none but the lowly, the oppressed, the groaning, and the sighing. These He commands to be proud, to hope, to be confident, but these are not proud.

[6] Luther is, of course, referring to the closing phrase of the Apostles' Creed.

Against Jacob, that is, against the kingdom of Ephraim, that is to say: Much has been preached to this people, and the Word has fallen on them like a cloud. This is a denunciation of unbelief and praise of divine goodness, which flows with promises and encouragements.

9. *And all the people will know,* that is, they do not want to find out, they do not want to learn and believe. For even though they would know, they would nevertheless not be reformed.

10. *The bricks have fallen, etc.* This is symbolic language, as if to say, "God has flogged the ten tribes. Some cities have been destroyed, etc., but now we shall be better off; it is just as if we had lost a brick. We are God's people, hence we must be a kingdom. Where the king of Syria has destroyed our house, we will erect three others, and these we will build with squared stones, and what was built of sycamore before we will now build with cedar." And so they turn God's blow into glorious martyrdom. Augustine says: "It is the cause of the punishment that makes a martyr, not the punishment itself."[7] Christ says in Matt. 5:11: "On My account, etc." All the preconceived plans of men do not succeed, but on the contrary, since you do not want bricks, you will not have the opportunity to build with dressed stones. But if that chastisement was a comfort, the torment will now follow.

11. *The adversaries of Rezin,* also the hostile army of him against whom he is turned as against enemies.

Against them, namely Ephraim.

Raises, so that they may be the victors.

Stirs up. So that with the several armies assembled there will be a great aggregation.

12. *With open mouth they will devour,* that is, with open and insatiable mouth, as if to say: "I will let you be so despoiled, that neither hide nor hair is left over, so that you may know what you have done in despising the Word."

In all this His anger is not turned away. A hard complaint against the hardness of the people. Hardened by spiritual pride, they do not hear but convince themselves that they are blameless, and whatever

[7] Augustine, *Enarrationes in Psalmos,* XXXIV, 13 (Ps. 35:23), *Corpus Christianorum, Series Latina,* XXXVIII, 320.

they do suffer they draw into the glory of martyrdom. God would gladly stop afflicting them, but they refuse to desist from sin and to turn His anger aside by humiliation and prayer. They prefer simply to die and be destroyed. They do not understand the reason for His promise, which is a mother's rod recalling to repentance, not to destroy but to show forth mercy. God afflicts in order to heal, if we only recognize that. But if we will continue in ungodliness, He, too, will continue with the punishment.

14. *So the Lord will cut off.* "Since you will not be reformed, all of you shall perish at once. I will chop off both head and tail, branch and twig."

"Crooked and bent." Hebrew: *Branch and reed.* Branches are hard, reeds are soft and supple. The prophet himself explains the metaphor of the *head, tail,* and *branches;* he wants to say that great and small will be taken away from the kingdom and that the kingdom will be left as a trunk and bare stump without either hard or soft branches. Yet the root will remain, from which that Flower will blossom of which he speaks below in chapter 11:1. The people, however, the prophet compares to a most showy tree, as one reads also elsewhere.

15. *Elders* are princes, senators, consuls.

Honored men, those who excel by reason of some worth and who are looked up to by the people.

Tail he explains as being a lying prophet, because among the Jews the kingdom was above the priesthood. Therefore, he says, the mighty and the princes of the kingdom and the priesthood, the governors and the teachers, will be carried off. It would truly be proper for the prophets or priests to be the head, that is, the leaders of the people, but now they are the lowest and the last; they do not lead, but are led. This is an expression of the perversity in them, not of guidance.

16. *Those who make this people blessed.* Better: Those who lead the people lead astray, and those who are led are swallowed up; that is, the opposite happens here: Those who ought to be leading others go astray themselves. Ps. 125:5 tells us: "Those who turn aside upon their crooked ways the Lord will lead away with evildoers." Christ asks in Luke 6:39: "Can a blind man lead a blind man?"

17. *The Lord does not rejoice over their young men,* that is, He

will not have or show goodwill. Even though God is the Father of the fatherless and the Judge of widows, He is here compelled to make orphans and widows, namely, because the husbands have been turned over to destruction because of their endless wickedness.

For everyone is a hypocrite and an evildoer. חָנֵף is a hypocrite. According to appearance they brought many sacrifices; nevertheless, they were worthless and deceitful, stupid and godless. No one is more injurious than a hypocrite. Christ calls them "brood of vipers" (Matt. 23:33). For because the hypocrite convinces himself that he is righteous, he wants to be so regarded, and all must believe him. If they refuse, the hypocrites rage and make a show of zeal for God in their tyranny.

Every mouth speaks folly, that is, every man practices folly, that is, consummate injustice, of which one could both sing and speak. Above all, the priests and prophets both say and do such things and deserve extraordinary punishment. He is, however, speaking of ungodly teaching, not of their conversing with each other.

For all this His anger is not turned away. The people do not put an end to their injustice, and neither does God put an end to inflicting punishment.

18. *Wickedness burns like a fire.* 2 Peter 2:3 says they are such because they cannot refrain from sin and therefore their error and their preaching cannot be counteracted. Ungodliness gained the upper hand, it burst forth like a flood. This is the tragic description of error.

It consumes briers and thorns. It consumes and penetrates not only thorns or stubble, that is, not only the lowest, but also the highest, that is to say, the whole nation. Ungodliness, however, embraces both doctrine and life. The thorn bush has a smoother bark than others, but it pricks. Such are the hypocrites. Ungodly teaching inflames, and with great pain do we remove it. But when it is opposed, it burns all the more.

It kindles the thickets of the forest. A forest fire cannot be put out. Therefore all the prophet's preaching is against this ungodliness, and it is just as if he were scattering a spoonful of water on the great fire.

In a column of smoke, that is high smoke. A great and high column of smoke is a sign of a large conflagration. Smoke rises. So the hypocrite is haughty, he tries to fly to heaven without wings; he wants to be a light, but he is only smoke and sham. The Holy Spirit comes down with the true light, etc.

19. *Through the wrath of the Lord of hosts, etc.* "Disordered," better: "hardened." The Word of God is the light, and when it is taken away, men become blind, then they are hardened, they dry up and are destroyed by the fire of ungodliness. Then follows insurrection. For the Word of God is a Word of the Spirit and of charity. A chaos of sects and factions follows departure from Christ. Dissension is the cause of alliances. But where there are alliances, there is not a good reign, but a fragmented and vile one, an allied insurrection.

20. *They snatch on the right.* More correctly, "they will separate," so that it may be a reference to the alliance. They therefore allied themselves on the right, he says, with the king of Judah or on the left with the king of Syria. Both in vain. Or, strangely, the compact on the right means the side where good luck seems to be.

They devour on the left but are not satisfied. To be hungry and not be satisfied is to be disappointed in trust. Man's help is vain. "It is better to take refuge in the Lord" (Ps. 118:9). To eat on the left hand means to remain without an alliance, and yet this turns out badly, seeing that you have forsaken the Lord and are not returning to Him.

Each devours his neighbor's flesh, that is, the treaties will not be reliable, but there will be strife among the allies themselves. The hand will rise up against the head, the members against the body.

21. *Manasseh.* This was the other and smaller tribe of the Israelite kingdom, and although these tribes have been in strife with each other, they will nevertheless plot together against the kingdom of Judah. In the same way various sects plot together against the Gospel now. "Pilate and Herod became friends with each other" over Christ (Luke 23:12).

For all this His anger is not turned away. As long as ungodliness and guilt do not stop, God's wrath and punishment abide. God does not become a dumb idol because of their madness.

CHAPTER TEN

1. *Woe to those who decree iniquitous decrees, and the writers who keep writing oppression!*

When the Jews are not influenced by individual blows, there will finally come a universal one that will destroy everything, as Isaiah now foretells. The same thing we, too, must expect when we are not reformed because of the plague,[1] famine, etc. Moreover, the greatest sin of which the prophet here accuses the Jews is that of the teachers of the people, the experts of the Law, the lawyers, who seek their own advantage with injury to the poor. Personal advantage is the cause of traditions. Solomon says in Eccl. 12:12: "Of making many books there is no end." This is as true now as it was then. Such, however, were the scribes and Levites scattered among the cities; they were not satisfied with the proper books of Moses but distorted Scripture for the purpose of oppressing the people. Laws of "oppression," אָוֶן, they write, and of עָמָל, "injustice, trouble, and toil." Man-made laws then bring forth these evils, both in government and in the worship of God. The Word of God alone makes quiet consciences. Human righteousnesses are fruitless because God has no regard for them. Earlier the prophet spoke of the perverted priesthood, now he complains about the overturned state. Evil morals follow evil teaching, and vice versa. Morals are not helped by evil laws, just as consciences are not helped by evil teaching.

3. *What will you do on the day of punishment?* "Oh," they say, "if only I had money to count until then!"

Where will you leave your glory, that is, the alliances of which you boasted? Likewise, the kingdom, holiness, etc.? Because they had the kingdom and the priesthood from God, the Jews thought that they would remain and not perish, and therefore they did what they wanted. The prophet threatens them with captivity and destruction.

[1] In August 1527 the plague had broken out in Wittenberg, driving the university and most of the clergy to Jena; although he himself had been very ill during the summer, Luther remained in Wittenberg.

5. *Oh, Assyria, the rod of My anger!* There were three Assyrian kings who harassed the Jews: Tiglathpileser, Shalmaneser, and Sennacherib. Here the prophet seems to be speaking about Shalmaneser, who carried off the whole kingdom of Israel (2 Kings 17:3).

6. *Against a deceitful, or hypocritical, nation I shall send him.* Better: "I send him." Scripture points to a twofold punishment: One is a punishment of just measure, which is a fatherly chastisement, not for the purpose of destruction. In Jer. 46:28 He says: "I will chasten you in just measure, and I will by no means leave you unpunished." Again in Jer. 10:24: "Correct me, O Lord, but in just measure." The other is a rod of anger, which causes complete destruction and reduces to nothing.

In his hand is My fury, that is, in the function of these people, namely, the Assyrians. Moreover, lest the kingdom of Judah, consisting of only two tribes, lose hope in the face of the removal of the kingdom of Israel, He here interposes a word of comfort by mocking the arrogance of the Assyrians. And by example this text is also comforting to us.

7. *But he does not so intend, etc.* The king of Assyria does not think as I do, but he wants to attack a people of good will like a people of anger. But I will forbid him, lest he strike the godly. This is an extraordinary personification of the proud heart, and it is to be set forth for the godly as a comfort to them. For such a one does not regard forces against God as too many forces, but he always deems God to be greater. The godly seem like reeds to the ungodly, who regard themselves as forests. Therefore these Scriptural concerns are earnestly heeded in time of trial, as when sin drives to despair, so that hope may be raised. That ungodly Assyrian, afflicting the people of wrath by God's permission, takes an attitude as if he were about to swallow up the whole world, boasting of the power of his princes and then also of the victories he has achieved. "Talk no more so very proudly, let not the old come from your mouth, etc." (1 Sam. 2:3): "the old," that is, that which is sure, as that which is old is strong, especially in trees. We must not look at how many things the ungodly boast of, but what their boasting accomplishes. For this is one thing in the despairing and another in those who trust in God. The ungodly also make fun of the refuge the godly take with God. And this king measures the strength of the gods according to the strength of the

nations. With respect to idols this must here be observed. The nations have many gods, and they worship them in many ways. The well-known God is in Scripture called "God," or "Object of Worship," as in 2 Thess. 2:4; that is, He is not visible to us, nor does He have converse with us in an absolute way, but He is clothed in some form. Thus He was preserved for the Jews in the ark of the covenant. For us He is in the Gospel, in Baptism, and in the Holy Supper. Men deceived by their own idea have therefore worshiped God in one form or another, namely, as they themselves thought Him to be the true One. But God can be had in no other form than the one in which He presents Himself in His Word. Human words and signs are meaningless. So then also this king calls an idol the true God and an object of worship.

12. *When the Lord has finished all His work.* This is comfort for those who remain steadfast in affliction. A wonderful deliverance will come to them, so that their enemies are scattered like dust, no matter how many and how strong they are. All works of the Lord, namely, of chastising His children, are done in judgment and not in wrath. This must not be taken to refer to Sennacherib, of whom it is said in 2 Kings 19:32: "He shall not come to this city, etc."

The arrogant boasting of the king, because he made only the most ambitious plans, namely, from victory to victory, from kingdom to kingdom, and as if he would accomplish all this by his own strength. "God opposes the proud but gives grace to the humble," 1 Peter (5:5) says. That king relied on his strength and his power, as if he had of himself what God gave him. To take credit for what one has received from elsewhere is to annoy God. 13. *Wisdom,* חָכְמָה, is the knowledge of things to be done in order. *Understanding,* בִּינָה, means to beware of ambushes and dangers, that is, to learn about the future from past experiences. Therefore he says, "By my wisdom, for I have understanding." Better: "Because I am experienced."

I have removed the boundaries of the peoples. Or "I have shifted," or "I have changed." "Those who sat on thrones" is in this place to be applied to the boundaries. He says, "I have done with kingdoms what a gardener does with trees. I have placed them according to My will, not as they were before. And I have taken their yield and their value for Myself. I have cast them all down. I have made a servant out of a prince, etc. All this without difficulty. All of them have taken flight at the mere mention of My name, and I have easily taken away all property and wealth. No one has interfered; in fact, every one has run away, as if some one were chasing the hen away from the eggs. Who, then, will withstand Me? If the little birds cannot escape, they rustle with their wings, they chirp, they peep, they even peck, but to no avail."

15. *Shall the ax vaunt itself?* Better: *As if a rod should wield him who lifts it,* inasmuch as he who handles the rod at the same time handles also those who lift it up, that is, God; He also handles both the scepter itself and those who carry it. It is as if the prophet were saying: "Well, proud king, why do you make your boast against God, who wields you as well as those who support you, that is, your people; like a scepter in His hand? And this is as easy for Him as if He should lift up a rod that is made not of wood but of straw." This can perhaps happen when some irascible person is about to strike another and he thinks he has picked up a stick but he has picked up a blade of grass. This king is God's scepter, and the people exalt him, and both are in the Lord's hand. In this way the king who to himself seems made of iron is ridiculed by the prophet because he is not even made of wood and his effort is futile. He is indeed both the saw and the ax of God as long as God uses him as an instrument to chastise a disobedient people. Thereafter he is no longer ax nor saw nor rod, but stubble to be put into the fire. And therefore he can do neither good nor evil, except to the extent that the Lord draws him or cuts and strikes with him. He does not do it himself, and he has neither substance nor work nor fruition of himself. If the saw is not used, it is consumed by rust. Therefore he who made the instrument also performs the operations of drawing and moving. Where, then, is free will? He compares the king's wisdom and power to a dead tool, which cannot move itself. Before God a fly is as much as a man, and vice versa. These words are full of comfort for the godly, but full of threatening for the ungodly and the proud.

16. *Therefore the Lord, the Lord of hosts, will send, etc.* Stoutness denotes wealth and power. Such will be the king. Powerful princes and kings, like pigs, have much fat flesh. But I will soon reduce your fatness and make it lean.

And under his glory. The king's glory is his army, and the Lord threatens to kill the princes and the army.

17. *The light of Israel* (that is, God) *will become.* Earlier the king said that the idols of his kingdom were above the idols of

Jerusalem and Samaria and that other gods were stronger and greater than the God of Israel, who is the Light, that is, the Comforter. When the army of Sennacherib was slain, the corpses were burned, they say. And Christ, who sits in our midst hidden and weak, is now a laughingstock to many, but He will come at last and will have His sport with those who despise Him, as He did with Sennacherib. The God of Israel was scarcely regarded as a lighted candle. But He is the kindling Light Himself, yes, a consuming Fire. Now God again weakens the wisdom and power of the king, who regarded himself as a vast forest. But the prophet says that the king is only a thorn and a brier, which God Himself, a powerful blaze, is about to consume.

18. *The glory of his forest* is the great number of trees, like the glory of the king, above.

Of his fruitful land, that is, the glory of the tilled field is vineyard, grain, olive grove.

In both soul and body will he be destroyed, that is, both the people and supplies, both living and dead, both men and beasts. *Soul* refers to men; *body,* to beasts.

"And he will be a fugitive driven by dread." Better: "He will both waste away and flee." Many will fall, he says; few will escape. Before, there were so many that they could not be counted; now a boy who can hardly count to twenty will count them.

20. *In that day.* This is a word of comfort. He says, the people will not only be set free from the enemies, but they will also be reformed. Trial produces understanding, according to Is. 28:26 and Prov. 22:4. The afflicted are turned to the Lord. The rod will put to flight the folly bound up with a boy's heart. We are not reformed before being chastised. The rod is as necessary for boys as bread is. The rod makes the boys well-behaved.

Lean upon the Lord, etc. Ahaz could not be persuaded by any prophecy to lean upon the Lord, but he rather sought the alliances of men. Those who have been chastened will not do this. This, then, is the fruit of the rod, that they learn to believe God, because they see that the help that comes from men is worthless and trust in them is ruinous. This passage is a warning example against trust in the flesh, whose end is hostility and destruction. They in whom we trust are the more quick to strike us. Gal. 6:8 tells us: "He who sows to his own flesh will from the flesh reap corruption." To trust in the flesh is to trust in one's own assassin. However, the Lord preserves faith: he who trusts in Him will reap salvation. Those who took refuge in the cities of Judah were snatched away.

21. *A remnant will return in truth.* This has reference to the word "lean on" and means that their trust in the Lord will be true; not hypocrisy, but faith without feigning (cf. 1 Tim. 1:5; 2 Tim. 1:5). Up until now they limped on both sides; they trusted partly in God, partly in Baal, partly in their own works, partly in other men. They were carrying on both shoulders, as the saying goes.

A remnant will return. A second fruit of the rod is to be returned to the Lord not only in heart, but also in all affections and external works.

To the mighty God. אֵל, who has the power to save.

22. *Though your people Israel be as the sand of the sea, etc.* Some understand this thus [2]: The Lord will so make a final reckoning with this people that He will bring the reckoning to completion by subtracting, that is, by cutting down the people, forsaking the greater part of them and keeping the lesser. This would be a reckoning of righteousness, and this perfected and small group of people will be *overflowing with righteousness,* that is to say, the apostles will preach this most abundant righteousness, compared with which the righteousness of the Law is like a lie, etc. But the preceding and following context force us to refer the reckoning and diminution to punishment, and the prophet is speaking generally and not only regarding the time of the apostles. This is rather a description of God's goodness, which He exercises in chastising men contrary to the custom of the devil and the world, who do not stop until they have swallowed up everybody. But God will keep the remnant and the dregs.

The consummation therefore is the completion, the completion of the rod, and in the midst of the act of reckoning He cuts short the punishment, that is, by reckoning He does not make the final reckoning. This means: When He smites, it seems as if He wants utterly to swallow up the people because of the attitude of those who suffer the hand of God and appear to themselves to be finished, who see the full end but do not see the shortening. But then the Lord comes and says in Matt. 24:22: "If those days had not been shortened." When we think: This is the end and annihilation, the Lord comes to cut it

[2] Cf. Jerome, *Commentaria,* IV, 143.

short and to draw the pen squarely through the account. Zophar said to Job in Job 11:16 f.: "You will forget your misery; your life will be brighter than the noonday." Thus in poverty and in Satan's onslaughts, in death and disgrace, the Lord always comes and provides a shortening. And this final reckoning began at the time of the apostles, as Paul also cites this passage (Rom. 9:27) and then (Rom. 11:9) another one (Ps. 69:22): "Let their feast become a snare and a trap, a pitfall and a retribution for them." Nevertheless he, too, approves of the shortening that was made. "Has God rejected?" (Rom. 11:1). And this statement of the prophet agrees with his words above (Is. 10:20 f.): "In that day the remnant of Israel, etc.," and "A remnant will return." The king of the Assyrians, he says, is planning a final reckoning also against Jerusalem. But the Lord has a shortening in mind. There faith wrestles violently when it sees that so many know, and it is a most severe temptation that raises the question: Will you alone abide while all others perish? Especially when man ponders his works and endeavors and does not find anything to rely on, then he experiences the reckoning. But he must then fight back and think about the shortening and the preservation of the remnant, not about the number as large as the sand of the sea. Once he understands this, he will also easily understand how great Paul's temptation was when he said in Rom. 9:1: "I am speaking the truth in Christ, I am not lying." The greater the hearts and godly spirits, the more are they assailed. David says in Ps. 118:17: "I shall not die, but I shall live." Again in Ps. 30:5: "For His anger is but for a moment, and His favor is for a lifetime." The meaning is that faith is sorely tried and yet has comfort.

The remnant will be holy and righteous. The rod makes well-behaved boys.

23. *In the midst of all the earth.* In Judea or anywhere, chastisement is necessary, yet not beyond measure. "Blessed are they who hold the middle road." [3]

24. *Be not afraid of the Assyrians.* Because that king carried off some of the cities of Judah. You will nevertheless be preserved as a remnant. The shortening will be made in our midst. King Hezekiah acknowledged this and advised the people of this. He said in 2 Chron. 32:7: "Be strong and of good courage." Moreover, it must be observed

[3] Cf. Ovid, *Metamorphoses*, II, 137.

that Assyria came and was about to besiege Jerusalem, but when they heard that the Egyptians were coming, they turned against them and then returned to Jerusalem to lay it waste. This is what the prophet is talking about here.

And lift up their staff against you on the way of Egypt. That is, on their return from the Egyptians they will take over a certain number of cities, but they will not accomplish what they have in mind. I will shortly avenge also their crime, namely, that of the Assyrians, and I will set Jerusalem free and destroy those people.

26. *The Lord will wield against them,* that is, the Assyrians will be received with such a scourge on their return from Egypt as were the Midianites at the rock of Oreb, when they were destroyed not by any sword of the enemies but by their own and by the slaughter of one another, as Judg. 7 tells us. You will remember this. Again, the Lord will use that rod against Assyria which, as we read in Ex. 14:19 ff., He used against the Egyptians at the Red Sea, or Bull Rush Sea; and He will remove the rule and tyranny of the Assyrian king from you.

27. *Burden* and *yoke.* Taxation and war.

And a yoke will rot from the face of oil. This was a general and proverbial saying among the Jews, just as we have the saying "He has outgrown the rod," namely, when a fatted ox breaks the yoke asunder like a rotting rope. Oil denotes fatness or even mercy. The yoke yields to fatness. Opposite yields to opposite. Thus the Law, sin, and death rot away when Christ, life, and grace are present.

28. *He will come to Aiath,* that is, even if Assyria has come very near and up to the door, do not be afraid. For they will accomplish nothing. Thus when deliverance comes, the trial is very often at its worst.

Migron and *Michmash* are those cities and places which on their passage they were about to seize until they would reach Jerusalem. They are cities in the tribe of Benjamin, in which also Jerusalem was situated. They tried to take Jerusalem not by way of Palestine, nor from the south, but from the east by way of the Jordan. Aiath is elsewhere called Ai (Jer. 49:3).

He stores his baggage. He reviews and disposes the cavalry. Baggage denotes all equipment and weapons. Concerning *Michmash* and *Gibeah* see 1 Sam. 14:2, 5. He is saying these things as though each day a messenger had been coming with the report: "The Assyrians are pitching their camp, now here, now there," thus certainly striking terror into their hearts. Hezekiah had his army in Gibeah. When he heard the rumor about the Assyrians, he fled to Ramah, where Samuel once lived.

30. *Cry aloud.* To cry aloud is to be jubilant and shout for joy. How will you do this in the midst of panic? Perhaps the enemy held that very city, and their jubilation was heard, as though by the citizens of *Gallim* and *Laishah.* Of old, Laishah had been captured by the descendants of Dan and was called Leshem and Paneas and Caesarea Philippi. 31. *Madmenah* is in the tribe of Benjamin and is in flight. The *inhabitants* of Gebim are in confusion and are fleeing.

32. *At Nob* he will halt and stay one day. They will be away from Jerusalem. The enemy will not be able to come closer. Nob is notorious for the slaughter of the priests and the savage cruelty of Saul, described in 1 Sam. 22:11 ff.

He will shake his fist, that is, from different directions he will move in all directions with his hand, he will decide how to deal with Jerusalem. He will dispose his army in a circle in four sections.

At the mount, that is, against the temple.

33. *Behold, the Lord, the Lord of hosts.* This is altogether figurative language. *A small flask* would be better translated "boughs with power," not "with terror." Branches, however, represent the powerful princes, who are the glory of the king as branches are the glory of the tree.

The great in height, that is, what stands up high against the sky. The king of Assyria boasted too much about his princes, whom the Lord will reduce to ashes. "They will be overthrown." Better: "The thickets will be hewn down." Ps. 74:5: "At the upper entrance they hacked the wooden trellis with axes," where there is no distinction of trees.

34. *And Lebanon with its majestic peak.* When the prophets use this word "Lebanon," they point to something great. So here the greatness of the Assyrian king is indicated by the word "majestic." Better: "By the mighty one," that is, the powerful angel. And this is a comfort expressed through figurative language which wonderfully takes hold of men in trouble, and it sounds as if victory were already

there. Ps. 94:19 tells us: "When the cares of my heart are many, Thy consolations cheer my soul." Paul says in 1 Cor. 10:13: "With the temptation He will also provide the way of escape." Weakness overcomes even though the temptation has been in its worst throes. Yet a great and living consolation is at hand. So that king, planning to storm Jerusalem the next day, lost his army that same night. Proverb: When the rope is pulled most tightly, it will snap.

CHAPTER ELEVEN

1. *There shall come forth a Shoot from the stump of Jesse, and a Branch shall grow out of his roots.*

This chapter does not cohere with the preceding ones, as it seems, since it treats of a different subject. But the ability to recognize the coherence of the prophets is important. For the prophets did not speak as drunk and raving men, mixing diverse subjects together. But the Holy Spirit is the best rhetorician and logician, and therefore He speaks most clearly. The first item discussed here is the promise of the spiritual kingdom, which most aptly follows the prophecy concerning the deliverance of the kingdom of Judah and the restoration of external peace, seeing that this promise speaks of a far nobler deliverance, one that is spiritual. This is the way the prophets usually contemplate the connection between the earthly and the spiritual kingdom, as we do too when in our preaching we speak now of faith, now of sight. For this is a proper order, and therefore the prophets, proclaiming either threats or promises with reference to the bodily kingdom, in the second place keep the people of the earthly kingdom in a state of expectation for the coming spiritual kingdom. First comes what is physical, and then what is spiritual. Therefore Isaiah says significantly: *There shall come forth,* as if to say: "This is not the only thing to come true; *There shall come forth,* that is, a nobler deliverance will follow." But he is speaking about Christ, not about Hezekiah, as the Jews quibble.[1]

A Branch shall grow out of his roots. Better: a "Shoot," נֵצֶר, will bear fruit from his root. This is what he called Christ, and such is the beginning of the rising spiritual kingdom. It is obviously different from that of an earthly kingdom, where an assembly of people is provided with a king. In this case the King is born first, and then He gathers a people for Himself. At first there will be a single Sprout risen out of the root, from the old and hopeless trunk, which is nevertheless watered with a divine strength. *The stump of Jesse* is the

[1] The Jewish exegesis of this verse is summarized in Lyra, but he does not refer to Hezekiah by name.

family of David. To him the promise was made in Ps. 132:11: "One of the sons of your body." To this promise the prophet refers here, and he points to the time in which the spiritual kingdom is to have its beginning, namely, when the stump of David will be regarded as lost, so that nothing is less hoped for than that a shoot should sprout up from the root. He says it will not come as long as the kingdom of Judah still continues to stand and is in flower, just as Jacob had said long before this in Gen. 49:10: "The scepter shall not depart from Judah, etc." The stem of Judah had already shriveled up when the Maccabees and the priests ruled. Then the Romans obtained the rule and set up Herod there as king. If these matters are to be applied to all times, it is certainly thus, that God does not help except in the greatest trouble and in the utmost need. He is, Ps. 9:9 says, "a stronghold for the oppressed, a stronghold in times of trouble," so that it may be evident that the matter is managed by the hand of God, not by the plans of men. This is the Christian thing to do, to recognize the acceptable time and the day of salvation (cf. 2 Cor. 6:2), even when it seems to be a day of despair. From a trunk nearly decayed a little Twig will emerge and grow up and make holy, and it will not be prevented by heat or by rain or by all the powers of the air.

2. *And the Spirit of the Lord shall rest upon Him.* Now the prophet describes the forces, weapons, and gear of that King and His kingdom. It is a truly remarkable arsenal. Accordingly, this kingdom will be powerful in goodness and joy, not in weapons, and the protection of the Holy Spirit, who was given to Christ without measure, is certainly strong enough. Read Is. 61:1; John 1:16; Col. 2:9; John 7:16 ff. And here it is plainly indicated that that kingdom will not be physical but spiritual. In that kingdom all affairs will be conducted by the Spirit alone, and the Spirit will be poured out over the whole kingdom.

The Spirit of wisdom. This pertains to the control and conduct of all affairs. But it is a wisdom hidden in a mystery as it is called in 1 Cor. 2:7. The philosophers define wisdom as the understanding of divine matters,[2] how each one should conduct himself before God, namely, that he should know that the Father is gracious, the Son was incarnate by Himself and suffered, how alone he may be justified and saved. It is the Holy Spirit who bestows this wisdom.

[2] Apparently an adaptation of the definition in Cicero, *De officiis*, II, 2, 5.

Of understanding, which some interpret as judgment and assistance against cunning and hindrances.[3] But this pertains to wisdom. For the fool does not regard or consider what will be harmful. Dan. 11:37 says: "He will give no attention to women." Wisdom is therefore an ingenuous and open acknowledgment of Christ, but understanding is the care and concerned endeavor to keep this wisdom unimpaired, so that a person may beware of Satan's cunning. Paul writes in Titus 1:9: ". . . so that he may be able to give instruction in sound doctrine and also to confute those who contradict it." This is understanding. Many have wisdom indeed, but they lack understanding, and this lack perverts the wisdom they do have. Christ is the giver of the Spirit.

Of counsel. So that a person may be able to give good counsel, especially in the time of trouble and the cross, which soon follows the wisdom and understanding given by Christ. Then the Spirit of counsel is needed to provide courage for bearing the tribulations. Ps. 16:7 says: "I bless the Lord who gives me counsel; in the night also my heart instructs me." In the night of affliction counsel is effective. This also applies to the teachers, so that they may teach, admonish, and lift up the despairing. This is the Spirit of Christ, the Paraclete, the Comforter, and the Advocate.

Of might, that is, the forces of power and victory in that counsel, so that comfort may cling in the stricken soul and be triumphant. For the best counsel is indeed given to many, but strength does not follow, comfort does not cling and does not act in the soul. Such people despair, but he who listens to his brother comforting him then by the Word of God and obeys and accepts the Word, forsaking all vain thoughts and speculations, such a one will be saved. To him is added the Spirit of might, and these two brothers are a strong city against Satan. Here Christ is present.

Of knowledge. Paul carefully treated the nature of knowledge in 1 Cor. 8:1 ff. Knowledge, however, pertains to the everyday life among brethren and is the tact and accommodation of one person to another in manner of living, to be weak with the weak, to offend no one, but to edify all, as 1 Cor. 9:22 says. This is the recognition of Christian

[3] In the scholia (W, XXV, 132) this passage is explained: " 'Understanding' is judgment, which arises from that wisdom, so that we pay attention to the things that militate against godliness and are able to judge about false doctrines, about the wiles of Satan, and the like."

liberty and its proper exercise. But if this knowledge exists by itself and love is not added, it puffs up. Therefore the prophet adds:

Of godliness. Although this is not a completely inexpert translation, nevertheless the Hebrew has:

Of the fear of the Lord. To knowledge belongs the fear of the Lord, so that, possessing knowledge, a man may fear to offend God lest he be puffed up. Thus the Christian man is fully equipped and a fit vessel of the Lord if he has wisdom, that is, purity of teaching, if he has understanding, that is, if he guards that doctrine pure and unimpaired, if he has counsel and if victory over temptation follows, if he leads an upright life with his brothers and uses all things to advantage and not as [4] a stumbling block in the fear of the Lord. But where the fear of the Lord has been absent, the rest is easily perverted. This is a picture and description of Christ's kingdom. These are His weapons. In this way that kingdom is extended and the twigs bear fruit.

3. *And the Spirit will fill Him.* This is a new verse and means: He will spiritify, or inspire, or fill with the Spirit. But *in the fear of the Lord Him,*[5] that is Christ, for His kingdom, where things are done in a straightforward manner without respect of persons. No one will be justified by any works whatever, no matter how many, but by faith alone, which comes forth from the fear of the Lord, before whom no one will be able to stand by his own merits, but all these will be denied and will be like masks. There the truth and the mystery will count, not mask and outward appearance. We are dead in alien sin; we must live by alien righteousness. Here no [6] appearance, however imposing, will count, and therefore he adds:

He shall not judge by what His eyes see. We, too, should well learn this, not to permit appearance to impress us, lest we judge a girl reading a book to be better than one who sweeps the house.[7] In his innocence a Christian in no way changes appearance; he only has a heart full of faith. He indeed does harm to no one, but his uprightness is not in a painted form. This single praise is given to the godly, that they fear the Lord. Of the ungodly, on the contrary,

[4] The Weimar text has *ab,* but we have read *ad.*

[5] The Weimar text has *cum,* but we have read *eum.*

[6] We have supplied *nulla,* which seems necessary to make sense.

[7] The Weimar text has *donum,* but we have read *domum.*

it is said in Ps. 36:1: "There is no fear of God before his eyes." The godly make no claims for themselves, but rather whatever they have they acknowledge to be a gift of God's grace; they have nothing to offer God, but they only receive from Him. The ungodly in their desire to influence God by their works despise God and make gods of themselves. David says in 2 Sam. 23:3: "When one rules justly over men, ruling in the fear of God," that is to say, the reign of God is in His fear. Let confidence outside one's own works be feared, and let God be revered as Father, so that He may not be offended. He is, however, offended especially by presumption based on one's own deeds. Moreover, judging and accusing are here taken not in a private but in a public sense, namely, through the Word, whereby the ungodly will be accused and the godly consoled. "The Lord takes pleasure in those who fear Him," Ps. 147:11 says. Sham avails nothing but is an abomination to God. However, the people of Christ's kingdom are the poor, the mean, the insignificant, the faint-hearted, the harassed, the lowly, the fearful. These He will judge; that is, He will make the just cause prevail, He will justify them, He will give them grace, He will forgive the sins of those who acknowledge and confess them and do not rely on themselves. He says in Matt. 5:3: "Blessed are the poor in spirit, etc." Therefore they will be judged with righteousness, that is, they will have righteousness and will increase in it, they will be reproved with equity, which is the righteousness of faith, whereby they are upright before God and men; they do for both God and men what pleases them: glory to God and kindness to men. The ungodly, who regard themselves as holy and defend their sins, are not of Christ's kingdom; they do not enjoy the righteousness and equity of Christ.

4. *He shall smite the earth with the rod of His mouth.* The rod is the spoken Word. Behold, lip and tongue and mouth of Christ are all who sincerely preach the Gospel, as God said in Jer. 15:19: "If you utter what is precious, and not what is worthless (that is, if you distinguish the spirit from the flesh), you shall be as My Mouth."

With the spirit, that is, with the exhalation of His mouth. This is the same spoken Word, and it has power both to save and to destroy. It saves the godly, that is, those who believe and make no claims for themselves, but it destroys the ungodly, that is, those who are proud in their own wisdom and righteousness. But it smites and brings to naught earthly and ungodly men, toward repentance and toward conversion and toward constant enlargement of His reign.

5. *Righteousness shall be the girdle of His waist.* Both Christ and His kingdom have their own weapons, which are not physical, to be sure, as we read in Eph. 6:10 ff., 2 Cor. 10:4, and 1 Thess. 5:8. But righteousness and faith are His sword. By it all trials are overcome, when we believe that Christ is our Protector, in whom we have all things, even though we are sinners. Such, then, is this kingdom, that first the spoken Word of God is proclaimed and then it is believed, the Holy Spirit being active in both cases. This is the righteousness before God and, as 1 John 5:4 calls it, "the victory that overcomes the world" and all evils. This is the difference between this kingdom and all others, which are physical.

6. *The wolf shall dwell with the lamb.* This is the fruit and power of that girdle and armor, the preaching of faith. These are allegories. Then, he says, the tyrants who formerly preened themselves with their power, wisdom, and wealth will shed their feathers and tufts and with bowed neck confess themselves to be sinners, and they will be harmless. And he says, the wolf will associate with the lamb. Not the lamb with the wolf. The tyrant will become a martyr, and the wolf a teacher. The wolves are false teachers according to Matt. 7:15. Paul was a wolf before his conversion. The lambs are the Christians. With the latter the former will be wise in spirit. The young goats are, of course, those that were a clean offering in the Law, not those of whom Matt. 25:32 f. speaks. These are martyrs. Leopards are persecuting tyrants. This is what the Word of God does; it casts down the proud and lifts up the lowly. The calves are the faithful. The lions are the rich. Lion cubs are said to act more fiercely than the adults. That is, those who formerly yielded to no one now obey the Gospel preached to them by the least of the brethren, and they gladly hear the Word. Although the papists abused their power, nevertheless obedience for Christ's sake was freely given to them. Thus in time past the prophets guided the kings. The sheep, in Hebrew מְרִיא, which denotes a fatling; the cow, פָּרָה[8]; the animal that has not calves but whelps; and that which has cubs will be pastured together. That is: Human beings differing extremely

[8] We have corrected both the Hebrew in the Weimar text and the conjecture suggested by the Weimar editor.

among themselves – savage, wild, irascible, hateful, murderous, ungovernable, and the people of the gentle Christ – come to agreement through the preaching of the Gospel. The church will convert the nations not by force but by the goodness of the Word. The lion will fill himself with straw and stubble, that is, he will become tame and adopt a domestic gentleness, just as the ox will submit to the hand.

8. *The sucking child shall play.* This symbolizes the complete harmony of those who were at variance before the Word had been heard. *Child,* that is, the preacher despised before the world will cheerfully drive out the devils residing in men and will not be afraid of them.

Over the hole of the asp. These kill by a look,[9] and so do the heretics with their poisonous ideas and teachings, all of which the preacher draws out with the healing Word. All who are in Christ are called children, and they enjoy dealing with devils. This, then, is the fruit of the Word, to turn men from every error and tyranny. The little boy pulls the snakes out with his hand, that is, the preacher by means of the spoken Word casts out the devils because the Holy Spirit is present.

9. *They shall not hurt, etc.* There will be supreme peace and harmony in Christ's kingdom, and people will neither offend nor destroy one another. They have and make peace. Christians are peacemakers "among those who hate peace," as Ps. 120:6 says, yet in such a way that the church is not changed, but the wolves, leopards, lions, and bears are. Those who hold our teaching have peace. The true knowledge of Christ begets harmony. Later, in chapter 53:11, he says: "By His knowledge He shall make many to be accounted righteous." It is a cause of strife when everyone defends his own opinion. Those who know Christ forsake all human opinions, rely on the Word alone, and on the life and righteousness of Christ alone. In the world and in external affairs there is indeed inequality, but in Christ's kingdom all things are one. Laws cannot bring men into agreement. Faith in Christ creates unity and makes men equal, while every other kind of righteousness is condemned. He says, the knowledge of Christ will pervade and fill all things like a kind of deluge, and human opinions will be overwhelmed in it. Christ is our peace "and has broken down the dividing wall of hostility," as Eph. 2:14 says.

[9] Pliny, *Natural History,* XXIX, 19.

10. *In that day the Root of Jesse. They shall pray for.* More correctly: "they shall seek." In Rom. 15:12 Paul has "they shall hope"; he looked more to the substance of the statement than to the meaning of the individual words. In Hebrew it is: "And His rest shall be glory."[10] This passage shows the Gentiles agreeing and becoming one body with the Jews in Christ and Christ's kingdom spreading throughout the world. This applies properly to us, just as Paul also cites it for the Gentiles. Therefore he hints that all Jewish ceremonies and rites should be abolished and every trust in any other righteousness whatever be given up for the purpose of establishing and erecting Jesse's Root alone, that is, the real David, Christ, whom the Gentiles seek and on whom alone they rely, which is the only righteousness before God. So Christ Himself explains this passage in John 12:32:[11] "And I, when I am lifted up from the earth, will draw all men to Myself," and in Luke 11:23:[12] "He who is not with Me is against Me." But to seek means in sincere faith to cling and to rely and to take care that He alone will be kept.

Stand as an ensign to the peoples. First the root must be made ready and lifted up, so that the nations may then seek it. As 1 Cor. 2:8 says, none of the rulers of this age knew it. But its elevation aroused the nations to seek what the preaching of the Gospel is. Therefore it stands and is lifted up by the Spirit through the Word. But Christ is called נֵס, that is, banner and military ensign, that His reign stands up in the daily battle and its attacks; those who serve God are called the army, and God is called God of hosts. Their enemies are Satan, flesh, sins, world, death. And the Gospel is called the Word of the cross in 1 Cor. 1:18. Therefore the nations look for it, as that merchant spoken of in Matt. 13:45-46 looks for precious pearls. He "went and sold all that he had and bought it." Thus if they repudiate all their own wisdom and righteousness and cling to Christ and His righteousness alone, they are eager to possess Him.

And His rest shall be glory, that is, death, the end of life, the departure from this life. The death of all other kings is the end of their reign. But Christ will reign gloriously from His death forward, and this signifies His resurrection from the dead. In Ps. 8:4 we read: "What is man etc.?" The prophet calls death a rest and cessation

[10] That is, instead of "his sepulcher," as the Vulgate translates.

[11] The original has "John 11."

[12] The original has "Luke 12."

from labors, glory after shame. To the world He seems dead and mute and inglorious. But He lives and reigns in glory. Therefore we have three elements here: (1) the raising of the ensign through the Gospel; (2) the act of seeking, receiving, believing; (3) the object of faith, the Root, that is, Christ, who reigns though dead. When the prophets speak of Christ's reign, they speak of His humanity and of His godhead. The Root of Jesse points to the man. The fact that the nations seek Him shows that He is God. Earlier the prophet wrote (8:19): "Should not a people consult their God?" Glory and faithfulness belong to God alone, who alone helps and saves.

11. *In that day.* The prophet, abounding with spiritual joys, now adorns and enriches the matter which he treats by means of allegories. He is now saying the same thing as before, except that he uses different words and speaks in a different manner. The prophets were the best masters of their own allegories.[13] The meaning of this passage is: With the Jews and Gentiles brought together into one church, there will now be a true exodus from Egypt. In that day, namely when the Ensign is raised up for the nations and they seek the Root of Jesse, that is, Christ.

The Lord will extend His hand, that is, He will bring it to bear.

A second time. Once more, that is, again and in a new and better way, namely, the spiritual. For when Christ was born, the Jewish people had already been assembled and established in physical kingdom. Therefore when He here promises a second exodus after Christ's birth, you must understand it to be a spiritual one.

To recover the remnant which is left of His people. This circumstance distinguishes the second deliverance from the first one from Egypt, where Moses said in Ex. 10:26: "Our cattle also must go with us." All went out at the same time. Ps. 105:37 says: "And there was none among his tribes who stumbled." Here, however, only a remnant is led back, not only those who are in Judea, but also throughout the world from among all the nations under heaven, into which the Jews had been scattered, as we read in Acts 2:9-11. This is therefore an allegory and a mystical explanation of the ancient deliverance. Assyrians, Parthians, Scythians, and Medes constituted one kingdom. The people of Pathros were of the descendants of Ham, who had occupied Palestine or Syria Felix around Cyrene between Egypt and

[13] Cf. Introduction, p. xi.

Africa.[14] The Elamites are the Persians. Shinar is the plain of Babylon. Hamath is Syrian Antioch. The Assyrians are north of Jerusalem; Egypt, Pathros, and Ethiopia are south; and Elam and Shinar are to the east. The isles of Turkey, the Venetians, and the Franks, etc., are to the west. The assembly will not be physical, because the ensign will not be raised in Jerusalem, so that they might come together there, but among the nations of the Gentiles, because both the kingdom of Judah will then be destroyed and the Jews will be scattered in order that they might prepare the way for Christ everywhere.

13. *The jealousy of Ephraim shall depart.* The jealousy of Ephraim is that of the kingdom of Israel against the kingdom of Judah. There will be harmony between both kingdoms. Moreover, the kingdom of Israel will not stand then, and therefore it will be a spiritual restoration. As long as those two kingdoms would flourish, they would toil in constant hatred against each other. But Christ will restore both kingdoms to harmony, and they will be enemies no longer. They will be gathered into one and will have one head.

14. *They shall swoop down upon the shoulder of the Philistines.* All this is allegorical. Formerly there was ruinous war and a meaningless kind of victory, yes, an altogether unhappy victory, but then they will not move forward lazily, they will not be weak but very powerful and very numerous, swooping down on the shoulders of the enemies, who will turn their backs and show their shoulders, not their face. That is: The Gospel will be received with supreme eagerness and obedience, and they will gladly hear and believe it and submit themselves to it.

Along the sea. More correctly: toward the west.

Together they shall plunder the people of the east, that is, those living toward the east. This is an expression of the advance and success of the Gospel. *Together,* that is, cooperatively. Edom, Moab, and Ammon are part of the people of Kedar, that is, Arabians, especially those of Arabia Petra. The Israelites came up from Egypt through the Arabian desert. The Turk has possession of Arabia Felix.

Edom and Moab shall be under the rule of their hand. They will fold their hands in the presence of Israel. In Hebrew it is not "rule"

[14] By "Africa" here Luther means the Roman province of Africa, not the continent.

but "sending," or a casting in of hands, that is, Judah's and Ephraim's; they will thrust in their hands and take the Edomites and Moabites captive. *And the Ammonites shall obey them.* All this by the Spirit and the Word. The apostles and disciples will have favorable results wherever they turn.

15. *The Lord will utterly destroy the tongue of the sea of Egypt,* that is, he will dry up the Nile, which, as it flows into the sea, looks like a tongue toward the sea. We call it an arm. Moreover, in the Scriptures rivers of this kind denote the kingdoms, power, and wisdom of the world. Thus we read in Ps. 42:6: "I remember thee from the land of Jordan," that is, the land of Israel. Therefore the Lord will dry up the Nile, that is, He will humble the kingdom of Egypt and make it ready to yield to the lowly apostles, and they will raise the cross (who before were extremely proud and trod it underfoot) by the Word of God, and the entrance, that is, the office of preaching, will lie open. In Alexandria there was once a very famous school of the Christians.[15] Where "river" is mentioned without qualification, it means the Euphrates, to which the kingdom of the Jews in the time of David once extended, and this river seems to be the deadly end of kingdoms.

"He will divide it," he says, so that it will not be able by virtue of greatness and power to withstand but that it may be passable, and with their remaining strength they will cast themselves down and will submit themselves to those who are to be shod with the Gospel.

16. *And there will be a highway for the remnant,* not for the whole Jewish people. Pay attention to this detail also.

As there was for Israel when they came up from the land of Egypt. As stated above, this denotes an allegory of the earlier exodus from Egypt, that is, wherever there have been seas and rivers, there will be passageways for the Word; the Spirit and Wind of the Lord will accomplish this. Thus the kingdom of Christ is pictured by our prophet first in plain words and then in allegorical words.

[15] Eusebius, *Ecclesiastical History,* VI, 3.

CHAPTER TWELVE

1. *You will say in that day: I will confess to Thee, O Lord, because Thou wast angry with me.*

HERE the prophet depicts the true and lawful worship and sacrifice of the New Testament and sets up, as it were, a certain hidden antithesis over against the Old Testament and its sacrifices, which were many and varied. But in the New Testament there was a single sacrifice of praise and thanksgiving. Thus the Lord's Supper is called Eucharist, that we may gather around it and give thanks to God. However, the best thanksgiving is that public confession before the world, where Christians who confess walk in danger. The prophet foresaw this future preaching and confession of the Gospel, which did not take place in the Old Testament. In the voice of the Gospel God is glorified and preached in Christ. *You will say,* namely, in the church: *I will confess.* This is what will take place in preaching. Nor shall anything else be heard in the church but the voice of praise and proclamation of God's blessings which we have received. This song is in conflict with all human wisdom and righteousness, which are our works and in which we seek our own glory rather than give thanks to God. Hence, to be pleasing to God is simply to acknowledge that we are the recipients of His blessings, not the donors. A Christian confesses that he was condemned and lost and that he has received from Christ everything that belongs to salvation and righteousness; all his own merits he considers worth nothing. This is the fullest and most perfect sacrifice, and it embraces everything in the Old Testament. There animals and cattle were slaughtered; here our own wisdom and righteousness, our endeavors and works.

Because Thou wast angry with me. The church gives thanks not for wrath that is present, but for wrath that has been taken away; for when the yoke of sin and death has been removed, then it will help to remember the evils.[1] Paul says in Rom. 1:18 and 4:15 that

[1] Cf. Vergil, *Aeneid,* I, 203 ; this was one of Luther's favorite quotations from Vergil, as, for example, in *Luther's Works,* 8, p. 97.

"the Law brings wrath," and from this wrath the Gospel frees when it is believed.

Thou didst[2] *comfort me,* that is, Thou didst restore to me the voice of rejoicing. Luke 7:48: "Your sins are forgiven." John 1:29: "Behold, the Lamb of God, who takes away the sin of the world." Rom. 5:1 ff.: For without the forgiveness of sins there is no peace, but the opposite. He is therefore speaking of public, not private, consolation through the Gospel.

2. *Behold, God is my Salvation.* This is a description of the peace that comes after the forgiveness of sins has been received. Thus the heart stands firm, and this is proclaimed. Now I have someone on whom I may rely and in whom I may trust, to whom I may look, namely, God, who no longer is angry and punishes but saves from every danger and evil. Christians are surrounded by countless evils and varieties of death; many are their enemies and detractors, but God provides wings so that they may fly away. Christ is with them and preserves them and does not destroy them.

I will trust. This is the peace and safety of the conscience when it knows God as reconciled and Christ as Savior and Protector. But if it is still afraid of something, this is a temptation of the devil or a residue of the old man.

For the Lord God is my Strength and my Song. This verse is repeated from Moses, Ex. 15:2, who gives thanks for the deliverance from Pharaoh, where the Jews make no boast of their own merits. So now there shall be proclaimed only the blessings of God that make us safe from our enemies. Therefore the *Strength* is *my strength,* that is, my kingdom, my house, the victorious power through which I have my enemies under my feet and shall trample the serpent underfoot, etc. (cf. Ps. 91:13). *My Song,* my psalm, and the subject matter of my psalm and song. I have no one to sing and chant about but Christ, in whom alone I have everything. Him alone I proclaim, in Him alone I glory, for *He has become my Salvation,* that is, my victory. For thus the word "salvation" is often used in the Scriptures for "victory," as in 1 Sam. 14:45. Our Victory is Christ, and when we boast of Christ, we shall win. Satan and the ungodly hear the Word of God not willingly but unwillingly, yet this Word consoles and lifts up the godly who are alarmed either in the hour of death or in

[2] The Weimar text has *est,* but we have followed the Biblical text and read *es.*

want and misfortune. So Elisha, for example, summoned a minstrel in 2 Kings 3:15; see also 9:13. Gideon struck down the enemies with the sound of a trumpet in Judg. 7:22. The evil of the eyes cannot stand the good light but is forced to give in to it. Satan is not thrown out by means of plans made by the flesh, but by means of studying the Word of God.

3. *With joy you will draw water from the wells of salvation.* After the word of the Gospel has been preached and the voice of rejoicing has sounded forth, there follows the discernment of spirits and the distribution of the gifts of the Spirit of which 1 Cor. 12:4 speaks. Christ says in John 7:38: "He who believes in Me, out of his heart shall flow rivers of living water." Waters denote the Holy Spirit, as in John 4:10. In the noonday heat spring water and running water are the most refreshing. So it is in the scorching heat of sin. The comfort of the Holy Spirit through the Word of God is then most sweet. The wells of salvation are the Gospel, sermons about Christ in various places, or even the preachers of the Gospel. In that day, when the waters will have flowed out to many because the Gospel has already been preached, there will follow also in others the praise, that is, the sacrifice which you have.

4. *Call upon His name.* In Hebrew: Proclaim His name, not this or that person's. All good things must be credited to Christ. For a while the name of Christ is not seen, that is, His work is not[3] preached and heard, but then there will of course be His suffering and resurrection for our redemption and salvation.

Make known His deeds among the nations, that is, His works and accomplishments. Recall them, that is, in public proclamation and confession. So also Christ asks for remembrance of Himself in Luke 22:19: "Do this in remembrance of Me." Acts 4:12: There is no other name than the name of Christ.

5. *Sing:* Sing songs, preach, give thanks. *Gloriously,* that is, He has done magnificently, wonderfully; this too, is taken from the song of Moses (Ex. 15:1).

He has done gloriously, that is, He has overcome death, Satan, and sin. He has risen from the dead, etc. And all this for us; this shall be proclaimed not only in Judea but in all the earth.

[3] We have added *non* to conform the second part of the sentence to the first.

6. *Shout and sing:* Sing with jubilation and exultation.

Inhabitant of Zion, that is, church, rejoice, because you already have the forgiveness of sins, peace, the Holy Spirit, salvation, life, God, and all good things. You have been set free from all enemies, you are safe and will not be forsaken. Therefore you have enough reason for rejoicing. This would be true even if you saw damnation and despair in yourself.

For great in your midst is the Holy One of Israel. Have confidence in the Holy One of Israel, that is, Christ, who is great, unconquered, yes, all things for you. Although we are earthen vessels (2 Cor. 4:7), we tread Satan underfoot in Christ; and He who is in us is greater than he who is in the world, as 1 John 4:4 says.

CHAPTER THIRTEEN

1. *The burden concerning Babylon which Isaiah the son of Amoz saw.*

UP UNTIL now Isaiah has preached to the Jewish people both concerning the present physical kingdom and concerning the future spiritual kingdom and the kingdom of Christ. Now he digresses and prophesies against various kingdoms and foreign peoples, and he threatens their destruction as also that of the Jews.

Burden means a prophecy threatening evil, a menacing prediction, and this was a burden, that is,[1] difficult, both for the prophets and for the hearers.

Babylon. The whole area was enclosed with walls. The thickness of the wall was 30 feet, impregnable in appearance; the height was 50 cubits, the towers 60.[2] The walls were of burnt brick, and the greatest number of people were there. The countryside was very fertile and pleasant, etc. Nevertheless, against this seemingly invincible city Isaiah dares to prophesy that it is to be laid waste, and to such an extent as seems impossible, as would scarcely be believed even though God spoke from heaven. But the prophet describes the matter as if it were already being enacted before the eyes, and he uses grand and powerful words so that what seemed impossible might be believed all the more quickly.

2. *Lift up the banners over the highest mountains,* which are near Babylon. It is as if he were saying: "Your enemies are already on the mountains of the neighborhood and will assault you. They have given the signal, they are shouting to terrify the proud, they are raising the hands to show their power, that it is born both of daring and savageness. The towering mountain also denotes dominion, as elsewhere. They, that is, the enemies of the Babylonians, are to enter the gates of the nobles.

3. *I, God, have commanded My consecrated ones,* that is, "My

[1] The Weimar text has *i a.*, but we have read *i. e.*

[2] The source of this information about ancient Babylon seems to be Herodotus, *History*, I, 178—181.

separated, chosen, prepared ones, namely, the Persians and Medes, whom I have prepared for My work and service." Victory is the gift of God.

I have summoned My mighty men, that is, "My giants and heroes to [3] execute to the full My anger against Babylon."

My proudly exulting ones. For I have given them spirit, courage, and daring. They do not rely on their own power.

4. *A tumult on the mountains as of a great multitude.* The repetition shows the fervency and certainty of the matter, and the prophet sets forth what it means to raise a signal. The chariots rumble, the horses neigh, and the men shout, and the number of people is as large as if all the kingdoms of the nations were gathered together. In Hebrew it is "kingdoms" instead of "kings." All this is said for the purpose of striking terror into the Babylonians.

The Lord of hosts is mustering a host for battle. He was so named because of the care with which war was waged for Him. He summoned, reviewed, and arrayed the soldiery and armed host of the Persians and Medes for the war, an army different from that which serves in religious affairs.[4]

5. *They come from a distant land,* from the bounds of heaven. The Hebrews call the sky a dome, or horizon, as much as is seen, and they measure the sky according to the horizons. Likewise, there is the expression "God sits above the heavens of the heavens," that is, above those which divers men inhabit. Here there is one heaven, and elsewhere there is another. Therefore, from the bounds of heaven means as much as the Babylonians can see.

The whole earth, namely, of Babylon.

6. *Wail, for the day of the Lord is near.* And the prophet predicts this as a coming event to the Babylonians, who are now proud. "Woe," says Luke 6:25, "to you that laugh now." *The day of the Lord,* that is, war and devastation from the Almighty. שַׁדַּי is a name of God and means "Almighty," whereby the prophets amplify the matter until it means "One whom no one can resist." Therefore the Babylonians are frightened by the nearness of the time and place and by the un-

[3] The original text has *et,* but we have followed the suggestion of the Weimar editors and read *ad.*

[4] This seems to be a reference to the monks.

conquerable strength and power against them. The hands of the Babylonians will be enfeebled. This is what happens in a war with battle lines drawn up. Soon it is apparent which side is going to win. For the victors are swift, both horses and men. The others are alarmed. God gives courage, and He removes it.

8. *They will be dismayed.* Better: The terrors of distress will seize them. This is a description of the panic-stricken, *like a woman in travail.* This figure of speech is often used in Scripture to denote great anguish, because there life is in doubt and there is more fear than hope.[5] *They will look aghast at one another.* The most wretched lot is not only to be outwardly afraid at seeing the enemies but also inwardly at seeing the blanching fellow soldier. Where one is afraid, he will alarm ten others. Moses said in Deut. 20:8: "What man is there that is fearful and fainthearted?" Moreover, fright makes some turn pale but others flush, as here:

Their faces will be aflame, that is, red like fire. Some redden first before the pallor and then turn pale.

9. *Behold, the day of the Lord comes, cruel.* The prophet is picturing a war that will be altogether cruel and without compassion, and it will be thus by God's design, that the enemies abuse their victory for barbarity. Therefore he calls the day of the Lord cruel. Wrath is a cruel thing, therefore Solomon says in Prov. 27:4: "Wrath has no mercy, or wrath is cruel." It passes through without forbearance. Thus with many words he amplifies and heightens that cruelty.

10. *The stars of the heavens.* Orion is popularly called the staff of Jacob.[6] And among the Hebrews there is often a general term which interpreters have rendered in a specific way. So perhaps it was done here too. Orion stands for many stars.

The sun will be dark. This means that those who are in danger of death think that whatever they see will bring death. The sun, moon, and stars are darkness to their eyes, just as a sky overcast with clouds is called gloomy. But light refreshes. Thus depending on man's eyes, the sun is for him not bright, not cheerful, but gloomy. The prophet is speaking from the point of view of those who are near death, not from the viewpoint of the real cause.

[5] Luther is thinking of such passages as Is. 42:14 and John 16:21.

[6] The Golden Yardarm, the three stars in the belt of Orion, is still referred to as "Jacob's staff."

11. *I will punish the world for its evil.* תֵּבֵל designates the inhabitable earth. Three parts of the earth are inhabitable, Asia, Africa, and Europe.[7] Here he is speaking of Babylon. *I will put an end to the pride of the arrogant,* not "of the unbelieving," *and lay low the haughtiness,* or "victory," *of the ruthless.*

12. *I will make men more rare than fine gold,* that is, "I will reduce the populous region to nothing to such an extent that it will be easier to find gold than a good and noble man, what the Greeks call ὄβρυζον.[8]

13. *I will make the heavens tremble.* "Then," He says, "I will make a marked change in the earth and in the horizon where men live, when I shall have humbled Babylon in such a way that they will have to change their horizon and depart and move elsewhere. Heaven will deny them its bounty, and the earth will cast them out."

14. *Like a hunted gazelle.* Like a terrified gazelle chased by hounds or like a scattered flock, the kingdom will not be able to survive without protection. So contemptuously does the prophet speak of the greatest monarchy. These things are unbelievable to all men except those in whom the Holy Spirit dwells. The Babylonians will not have a king but will run to look for a lord and protector, lest they be killed, and the foreigners in Babylon will flee to their own land, lest they perish with the Babylonians.

17. *Behold, I am stirring up the Medes against them.* Now Isaiah explains himself and names those who are about to demolish Babylon without mercy.

18. *Their bows will slaughter the young men.* They will have no mercy on the fruit of the womb, etc. Babylon, now the ideal and head of kingdoms, famous for its pride, victory, and domination, will be overthrown like Sodom, etc. He is not speaking of the manner of the overthrow but of the overthrow itself, so that nothing will remain, just as in Sodom there was nothing left nor anything restored. The Arabs carry their tents with them, they are a plundering people; espe-

[7] As early as 1522 (W, X-1-1, 21), however, Luther had said that "recently many islands and lands have been discovered, to which this grace [of God] has not appeared for these 1500 years."

[8] Luther seems to have derived this information about ὄβρυζον from Jerome, *Commentaria,* III, 384.

cially the Ishmaelites are herdsmen and shepherds and are most of all occupied with cattle.

20. *It will never be inhabited or dwelt in for all generations,* no, not by men, neither by sojourners nor strangers, but only by beasts that love the deserts, flying creatures of every kind and quadrupeds of every kind, which live by predation and shun the fellowship of men; and by hairy fauns and satyrs, in whose image demons appeared, as we believe, for the purpose of enticing men to idolatry.

22. *Ostriches in the pleasant palaces.* Ostriches live in water, they are not land animals.[9] Therefore one must read "dragons." *Palaces,* that is, castles built for pleasure.[10]

From this passage we can derive what we learn about political affairs from tragedies, namely, that the outcomes of the most exalted affairs are tragic. Great dominions bring great injuries. Although kingdoms and dominions are God's good institution and creation, nevertheless human stupidity cannot make advantageous use of them. It is too limited to be able to manage the best affairs well. It is better, therefore, for everyone to live content with his own lot and not go after high stations. For to whom important matters are entrusted, to him much difficulty and trouble is also added. God, however, gives in order that He Himself be praised and the neighbor be provided for. But human folly turns everything into abuse and its own advantage. This is the cause of destruction and devastation. Kingdoms are governed well not by the rank and file but by capable and suitable persons and magistrates, no doubt by those who rely on God alone and always pray for His help. But rulers should not be uprooted except by outsiders and this only by God's order. This is what we learn about political affairs from this passage.

Let us forewarn here concerning allegory that it may be handled wisely in the Spirit.[11] For playing games with the Sacred Scriptures has the most injurious consequences if the text and its grammar are neglected. From history we must learn well and much, but little from allegory. You use allegory as an embellishment by which the discourse is illustrated but not established. Let history remain honest.

9 The reason for this confusion is that the same Hebrew word is used for "jackals" and for "sea serpents."

10 In the original there follows a passage that belongs on p. 138, where we have transferred it.

11 See Introduction, p. xi.

It teaches, which allegory does not do. But this is what it means to teach: to instruct the conscience about what and how it should know, to nourish faith and the fear of God. In history you have the fulfillment of either promises or threats. Allegory does not pertain to doctrine, but to doctrine already established it can be added as color. The painter's color does not build the house. The human body does not consist of a garland or a beautiful garment. Even so faith is not established by means of allegories. Here you have the threats against Babylon that it would be destroyed, although this seemed impossible to the whole world. You also have the promise that Israel would be liberated, which likewise seemed impossible. Console yourself with this in every trouble. Do not lose hope, consider that God is truthful and that He can accomplish what He has promised, even though there were a hundred Babylons to be destroyed. Israel was held in physical captivity, you in a spiritual one. If you have faith, God will deliver you in the same way and will not forsake you. In this way the histories must be treated, and allegories will be profitable. Then make the application to the pope and the bishops. Formerly there was no hope whatever that the realm of the pope would be laid waste. Rome is the true Babylon, and these things are said of Rome at least in a general way, if not in specific detail. For in general all the ungodly will perish. The defenders of the pope are struck with fear, they do not know how to interpret Scripture. They howl and hiss for the pope, they have become[12] hairy satyrs, ostriches, owls, dragons, etc. They have divested themselves of all humanity and godliness. Furthermore, another allegory can be derived from this passage and from all wars against human and carnal righteousness, which though strong as long as the body is healthy, are nevertheless put in jeopardy in the death struggle. Babylon is carnal righteousness and a conscience priding itself on its reliance on works. The Persians and Medes are the Law of God that touches the heart. All of these, namely, those showy and lofty works, the Law flattens out; it judges them unclean and condemns them. Then follow fear, torments, griefs. The sun is darkened, etc. There is no help. Would that many would successfully get away, because those who are captured are put to death. Here neither gold nor wisdom nor power is of any avail. The Law does not leave any part of the hypocritical righteousness but removes it all like Sodom. This becomes an allegory through the Law and the Gospel.

12 The Weimar text has *facta,* but we have read *facti.*

CHAPTER FOURTEEN

1. *The Lord will have compassion on Jacob,* namely, to lead out of Babylon those who were led there captive, and with them also others, non-Jews, so that Jerusalem will become even larger than before.[1]

2. *And the house of Israel will possess them.* All these things were done under Cyrus, king of the Persians, who permitted the Jews conquered by the Babylonians to return to their own land, etc.

3. *When the Lord has given you rest.* Above, Isaiah predicted the devastation of Babylon and that the time in which it would be destroyed was near, so that the people would all the more quickly and strongly believe the promise of deliverance. Everything aims at the consolation of the godly. In no affliction can there be enough comfort for the human heart because the works of God are great and we are weak. And so the prophet lifts up by means of admonitory threats against our enemies and by means of promises and examples, lest we fall into despair. This chapter is also full of rhetorical figures. The prophet is so sure that he speaks of future events as if they had already happened, although, of course, that kingdom of Babylon was still flourishing and the Jews, on the contrary, were not far removed from despair. Therefore, for the greatness of the impending calamity he uses grand words and powerful figures of speech to strengthen the weakness of faith.

From your pain. The pain of the Israelites in the period of their captivity in Babylon was, as it were, like that of a woman struggling in childbirth and at the point of giving birth, namely, to a kingdom for Christ. For we have the same word here that was spoken to Eve in Gen. 3:16: "In pain (עֶצֶב) you shall bring forth children."

And turmoil, namely, when you will think that everything is about to go to ruin. It will certainly happen that at that time you will have nothing more contemptible than that king who is now extremely dreadful. This is the way of divine deliverance, that whoever is in

[1] See p. 136, n. 10, above.

extreme despair and has nothing more formidable than his own trials will afterwards hold nothing in greater contempt than these. Formerly the pope was more formidable than the highest princes, yet now he is abused with lampoons [2] so that among those who have come to know the truth nothing is more contemptible than he; yes, even the ungodly belittle him.

You will take up this taunt, that is, this mocking triumphal song. There is comfort in vengeance, which is especially sweet to the flesh.

5. *The Lord has broken the staff of the wicked,* that is, his scepter or kingdom, and the violent scepter denotes uprightness, which kings should employ to protect the innocent and punish the guilty. The round apple [3] reminds them that they must rule everywhere without respect of persons. But he bore the staff for the purpose of smiting, not of judging. Since it is the duty of a good prince to serve rather than to exercise lordship, the princes should have their power for constructive rather than destructive purposes, so that they may be loved rather than feared. Wretched is the prince who has lost the common prayer.[4] If the prince grieves over the slaughter of the people and wards off evil from them, this, indeed, is what it means to rule and to shepherd.

That ruled the nations [5] *in anger,* that is without any right, without any judgment, without any laws. This describes the rule of the ungodly and tyrants, who do not fear God and seek only their own advantage. Alas for the detestable reign where the people applaud and dance when the king has been removed!

8. *The cypresses rejoice at you, the cedars of Lebanon,* that is, all the nations surrounding Babylon, especially the Jews, which are alluded to by Lebanon, have rest. Palestine and Judea lie at the foot of Lebanon. The cypresses and cedars are the nobles of the people, the children of Israel and Judah, whom the king of Babylon cut down as he led them into captivity.

[2] Luther had himself been responsible for the publication of such a lampoon, *Passional of Christ and Antichrist,* in 1521 (W, IX, 701—715).

[3] In the scholia on this passage (W, XXV, 143—144) Luther says: "The sign of our kings is the golden apple, symbolizing that justice should be round and absolute, without respect of persons."

[4] To lose the "common prayer" of the people meant to lose their love and devotion.

[5] The Weimar text has *gentis,* but we have read *gentes.*

Sheol beneath is stirred up. Here Isaiah becomes a poet fashioning some sort of theater among the dead and setting up a beautiful contrast. Once, he says, you were sitting proudly on the throne. All were afraid of you, all were bending the knee and saying: My most clement lord! Now you will have the same thing in Sheol, throne, servants, etc. It is an illusion. Sheol is *stirred up,* that is, it has been shaking. The nether regions have become afraid that you will rule there as formerly. Among the Hebrews Sheol very rarely means the place of punishments, but often it means grave, which they also call the pit. This, then, is the meaning: All the dead have been thoroughly terrified at so important an arrival, namely, since you, now dead too, have been lowered into the grave, for they have heard of your cruelty.

Restore[6] "the giants." Restore "the deceased princes."

Goats of the earth. Words having rhetorical force must not be changed.

10. *They will speak,* that is, one after another they all will say: Ah, lord, king, etc., we thought so great a king would never die. 11. *Your pomp,* by which you thought you would fly above the clouds, *is brought down.*

Your corpse has fallen. Better: "With the sound of your harps," that is, your power and pleasure have perished. Formerly you sat in gold, purple, and silk, now your throne will be maggots and your bed worms.

12. *How you are fallen from heaven, Lucifer!* This is not said of the angel who once was thrown out of heaven[7] but of the king of Babylon, and it is figurative language. Isaiah becomes a disciple of Calliope and in like manner laughs at the king. הֵילֵל denotes the morning star, called Lucifer and the son of Dawn. "Heaven" is where we are with our heads, and that is obviously above the ground, just as that most powerful and extremely magnificent king was once above, but now his lamp is extinguished. Formerly he was the light of the earth and thought that at any moment he would rise really high and advance the light toward high noon, but he falls in the very act of rising. Ps. 55:23 says: "Men of blood and treachery shall not live out half their days." *From heaven,* that is, from the highest peak

[6] In the Weimar text this word is printed as though it belonged to the Biblical text.

[7] Luther is thinking of the words of Jesus in Luke 10:18 and of Rev. 12:7-8.

of sovereignty. *Down to the ground,* that is, to the lowest depths. You wanted to tread our God underfoot – this is to rise up above the clouds and heavens, of which He himself is the lord.

13. *I will sit on the mount of assembly.* This is Zion, and Jerusalem is situated on the side of the far north. There God dwelled. This is prophetic interpretation, not that that king was thinking this. It does not matter if you do not say it or think it, as long as you are there in fact. This can also be said of the pope: "I will ascend to heaven."

16. *Those who see you,* namely, among the dead. The prophet persists with his imaginary theater. Diligently, he says, we will stare at you, and they will say: Who is coming here? Who is it?

Is this the man who made the earth tremble? These are the virtues of this king, which are reviewed after his death. After death the ungodly have disgrace together with punishment and damnation.

17. *Who did not let his prisoners go home,* that is, he did not open the prison for the Jews, and now he himself comes down into the prison stretched out, killed like another in war, just as a useless plant is uprooted and thrown away. Wretched is the exit of great lords.

19. *Those who go down to the stones of the Pit,* that is, like a corpse trodden underfoot, that is, you will be found and be counted among the slain lying scattered in the streets, trampled upon, and drenched with blood, and together with these you will be covered with sand or stones. (The Hebrews call all rough, gravelly, and uneven places "stones.") And with their feet they will walk over you, and there will be no sepulcher as glorious as those of the other kings.

20. *You have destroyed your land,* that is, you have raged not only against other kingdoms and other peoples but also against your own. Therefore you have lost the good will of the people, so that there is no one to bury you.

May the descendants of evildoers nevermore be named, that is, not only you will perish but also your descendants, and you will have no name in posterity. Belshazzar, the third grandson of Nebuchadnezzar, was killed at night by the Medes, as we read in Dan. 5:30. The fact that Scripture teaches in Deut. 24:16 that the children shall not "be put to death for the fathers" means that this is commended to human judges. But God, who is the Lord of body and soul, visits "the iniquity of the fathers upon the children to the third and the fourth generation" (Ex. 20:5).

22. *I will rise up against them,* etc. You see that they are not raised up and that they do not remain in the land. For they would not be anything else but greater tyrants if they would rise up living.

I will cut off the name, that is, I will remove whatever is made public and is in everybody's mouth. It is as if He were saying: "Nothing will be said about Babylon, because it will be devastated and devoured. It will no longer be famous, and nothing will remain there of former things." A name indicates the essence of a thing and denotes [8] its nature.

24. *The Lord of hosts has sworn.* Here now he is describing something altogether different from the last. For Isaiah is speaking of Sennacherib, king of Assyria, and by way of a digression he is going out of his way to strengthen the promise to the people of his own time, as if to say, "Do not be afraid. Behold, I shall say something else to you: Not only will the king of Babylon accomplish nothing against you, but neither will Sennacherib, the Assyrian."

In My land, that is, Judea. This is comfort for Hezekiah and the godly people who were weighed down by the yoke of the Assyrian king. The Lord swears – something He would not do if He did not see the extreme need and the wavering hearts and jittery faith of the people over whose neck Assyria was dangling. Therefore He promises them that help has been found.[9]

28. *In the year that King Ahaz died came this oracle.* The last prophecy against Assyria was finished in the fourteenth or fifteenth year of Hezekiah's reign. But what the prophet is dealing with now happened in the king's first year (cf. 2 Kings 18), from which we observe that a strict order was not preserved in the prophetic writings, just as it was not in the Psalms. For that reason we must not be concerned about investigating the plan behind the sequence of the prophecies.[10] It is enough that we have the prophecies. He prophesies against the Philistines, who were the Jews' neighbors, and

[8] There seems to be something missing from the text at this point.

[9] The Weimar text has "Chapter Fifteen" here, but we have moved this heading to p. 146, where the Weimar text has "Chapter Sixteen."

[10] Cf. p. 5, n. 2, above.

from there he goes on to all neighboring nations. "Judgment" is to "begin with the household of God," as we read in 1 Peter 4:17. So he first chastises himself and his people and then the other nations. First the beam must be pulled out of one's own eye (Matt. 7:5). The righteous man is his own accuser first; the ungodly, on the contrary, stick only to the crimes of others and forget their own. The Jews lived in the midst of the nations, and all of the nations hated and persecuted them, for Satan drove them to it because of the Word and works of God which were present among the Jews. But the most hostile of their enemies were the Philistines, so that if misfortune struck the Jews elsewhere, they celebrated. For that reason David said of the violent death of Saul, as we read in 2 Sam. 1:20: "Tell it not in Gath." Grievous and hard to bear is insult added to injury. Against these insulting and dancing Palestinians, therefore, he prophesies a burden, that is, affliction.

29. *Rejoice not,* as if to say: "You should rather be weeping, your rejoicing is untimely. For you are glad and think that the rod about to smite you is broken." Ahaz smote them and Uzziah, the grandfather of Ahaz, over whose death the Philistines rejoiced and thought that they were now going to devour the Jews.

From the serpent's root will come forth an adder. There are certain species of serpents that attack by their breath;[11] those he here calls flying and fiery dragons. And this maxim can be made to fit many places and things. It is easy to make changes, but they are not necessarily improvements. The king is changed in Israel, but not into your protector, O Philistines. Thus in a family the servant, the wife, the maid, etc., are changed, and often it turns out worse. This maxim is spoken against the smugness of human vanity. New things are sought when people disdain what they have. There is no regard for the goodness of what is present, and because of a single little fault many excellent qualities in a man are despised. He who desires to change anything, let him pray that it turns out well. You are happy because the serpent has been removed, but a far more poisonous basilisk will rise up. He compares Hezekiah to an adder, Ahaz to a serpent. The Philistines were harassed more by Hezekiah. That he should be called an adder is not defamatory or dreadful but rather comforting when the ferocity is inflicted on the enemies. So Christ, too, is called

[11] See p. 123, n. 9, above.

death, plague of death, lion, serpent, sin, curse, fire, etc.[12] This is what lifts up the faith of the godly.

30. *And the firstborn of the poor will feed.* These things are said in the interests of the fainthearted against the proud and presumptuous Philistines. If there had been no need of comfort, the prophet would not have spoken in this way. It is, therefore, an indication of the Jews' state of mind; they were in anguish. They must be looked at as a poor man at the crossroads, or as a scattered flock surrounded by many wolves; for their enemies are many. But let them threaten. Let them lie in ambush as much as they want. Those *will feed* who are the firstborn, that is, those beloved and chosen by God. In the regard of their enemies they are few indeed, but in the sight of the great God they are precious, and they will feed and be satisfied while their enemies go hungry, etc. But in view of the circumstances and the condition on both sides it seems impossible that this will happen. There is need here of faith and of hope. These are words of the Spirit. It is therefore not for you to be alarmed at the dreadful appearance of the foes. God, who is greater, is with us; we will sing (cf. Ps. 21:13). For from the serpent's root will come forth an adder; let the enemies be very presumptuous and proud. He says: *I will kill your root with famine, and your remnant I will slay.*

31. *Wail, O gate; cry, O city.* This is the voice of faith and prophetic threatening. Run together into the marketplace; mourn rather and do not rejoice. For your jubilation will not last long.

Prostrate, or better, *melt.* All of Philistia is cowardly. This is the certainty of prophecy, that the prophet speaks of future events as if they were present. He says they are thoroughly terrified in spirit and they pine away in the body. Their heart melts in their belly.

Smoke comes out of the north. Thus Jeremiah says in ch. 1:13: "I see a boiling pot, facing away from the north." Fire denotes adversity and misfortune. In Luke 12:49 we read: "I came to cast fire upon the earth," that is, a separation of men. Here he calls it smoke, which appears before the fire and is a sign of fire close by, and here it denotes the report that is at hand for the evil approaching through the king, namely, the king of Assyria, who would be coming against the Philistines. For Jerusalem is to the south of Palestine.

[12] Luther is referring to the following passages: Hos. 13:14; Hos. 5:14; John 3:14; 2 Cor. 5:21; Gal. 3:13; Heb. 12:29.

There is no one who will flee. Better: "There is no one by himself in his ranks." מוֹעָד[13] denotes a set time or even a definite place. Here it means the set and ordered squadrons of the army. In this smoke, he says, the fire will not be absent, but it will arise in a set place. This is the great force of the king of Assyria.

Everywhere there will be a pronouncement through messengers.[14] In Philistia: You will perish by the smoke. Jerusalem has a protector and therefore will remain. This is the taunt against the taunts of the presumptuous. While all nations round about Jerusalem collapse, Jerusalem stands fast.

The Lord has founded Zion; He protects it. Behold, the promises of God's mercy and protection to a poor and afflicted people as consolation for all the godly who are the Zion of the Lord, and He cannot forsake those who trust in Him. However few I might find among you abiding in humbleness and confidence, this text will remain. And the enemies will die more quickly than you.

[13] We have corrected the Hebrew of the Weimar text.

[14] In the Weimar text this is printed as part of the Biblical text.

CHAPTER FIFTEEN[1]

1. *An oracle*[2] *concerning Moab. Because Ar is laid waste in a night.*

After the Philistines the most hostile enemies of the Jews were the Moabites, who were extraordinarily proud because of the fertility of their country and because it was densely populated, as we read in Jer. 48:1. On the plains of Moab Moses taught his people, as Deut. 1:5 says, and there also he was buried, as Deut. 34:5 f. says. Of a coming event, however, the prophet speaks as if it were present, and he sets it before the eyes as if he saw the event taking place. This is the most effective kind of teaching.

Ar. The chief city of the Moabites was laid waste at night, that is, unexpectedly and by surprise, when they were fearing nothing less and were neither forewarned nor forearmed.[3] In this way the prophet pictures the ease with which they were overcome and despoiled and at the same time the presumption and despair of that people, since by reason of their excessive pride they thought themselves safe from all dangers.

Undone, that is, destroyed, as in chapter 6:5 above. Kir, קִיר, sometimes means a wall or partition. Here it is a proper noun, like Beth, בַּיִת, which otherwise means house. The Moabites named their temple thus because of its outstanding character.

2. *Dibon* was another one of their temples.

Has gone up, namely, the people, in order to weep there, etc., whereas formerly they had been fierce and proud lions in time of peace. So the prophet derides[4] a foolish people in their pride. Even so we usually tremble in trouble and make a wry face, although in our good days we were ready to devour the world. Formerly we were more than men, now we are more than women. Similarly authors

1 See p. 142, n. 9, above.

2 The Weimar text has *Omnes,* but we have followed the Biblical text and read *Onus.*

3 The Latin play on words reads: *nec praemonita nec praemunita.*

4 The word is *eridet,* a Latinization of the German *lacht aus,* "he ridicules."

have written about the insolence of the Gauls.[5] So the Moabites, when they should be making a stand in the battle line and in arms, go off to the idols and weep before them. The worship of the papists is no different from this.

On every head is baldness. These were once a sign of grief, but now they grow beards in time of grief. Behold, those who were fierce lions before will then have neither caution nor strength.

3. *In the streets they gird on sackcloth,* when they ought to be standing on the wall, wearing iron tunics.

On the housetops. There, formerly and especially in Judea, little gatherings and assemblies took place. Therefore, they howl on the rooftops and come down from there weeping. Everywhere there is grief.

4. *Their voice,* that is, wailing and weeping. Not only the common people are wailing, but even the nobles themselves, who ought to give courage to others and protect them with weapons; even their soul is trembling. Those who were iron-eaters[6] are now mostly fugitives. Strong men will behave like sheep. Lions before, they are hares now.

5. *My heart cries out for Moab.* It cries thus: My heart grieves there because of Moab's wretchedness. Or this is prophetic irony, namely: How unjustly you are dealt with!

To Zoar. One of five cities destroyed, in the neighborhood of Arabia. And Moab, "a three-year-old[7] heifer," that is, born three years before. This is the name given to Moab, once wanton and arrogant. In Psalm 68:30 the peoples are called calves. As a cow feeds the calves, so the state calls native citizens and immigrants by name. Thus Moab is pictured as proud, wanton, presumptuous, arrogant, and in full flower, as a three-year-old heifer is especially suited for work and for breeding. Nevertheless, it is about to flee to the end of the country and to a small city.

6. *The waters of Nimrim are a desolation.* It is delightful for a city to be situated beside water. But here the prophet speaks figuratively

[5] Cf. Caesar, *Gallic War,* VII, 22.

[6] An "iron-eater" is apparently a braggart.

[7] The Weimar text has *consternantem,* but we have followed the Biblical text and read *conternantem.*

and thinks of the dried-up waters as being displaced people. The grass withers, and the new growth fails, that is, old and young flee. Otherwise this may also be understood literally. Since there will be no men to do the reaping, the grass itself must wither.

7. *The abundance they have gained.* The meaning is: the riches they have amassed and the people they have assessed.

The brook of the willows. Namely, the Assyrians will lead them captive and shift them beyond their boundaries. Some think the river of Jacob is called the brook of willows.

8. *For a cry has gone round the land of Moab.* Everywhere within all their borders there will be weeping and howling.

9. *I will bring upon Dibon even more,* as if to say: "So I have done to this people, but the end is not yet; because they have not become humble, I will send them a lion." This may be reserved for and applied to Moab and may mean: Some in proud Moab will be spared and not captured nor driven out; yet they will not escape unpunished. There will be no peace for the remnant either. I will surround Moab in such a way that no one can escape.

CHAPTER SIXTEEN

1. *Send a lamb.* He says: "You Moabites, who have withdrawn from the house of Israel and Judah and have stopped obeying it, I urge you: Return to your obedience. Give tribute to the king, and your affairs will prosper." Or, rather, it is prophetic irony, namely: "Send a lamb to Jerusalem now. Up until now you have despised us. Do you now crawl to the cross?[1] Do you now wish to bring a sacrifice in Jerusalem? But it is too late. So you come at long last?

To the mount of the daughter of Zion, that is, to the temple and the worship of God in Jerusalem. Have you proud people finally been humbled? Are you coming now from your great state? Now that your gods do not answer you, do you now seek an answer from the priests of God? After your idols do you now want to worship our God too? He said "lamb" for "lambs" and "ruler" for "rulers."

2. *Like fluttering birds.* These words prove that the preceding words were ironic. "It will be in vain," he says, "you will accomplish nothing. You will be thrown out of your kingdom like a bird out of its nest." He used the same comparison above in chapter 10:14. The daughters of Moab are not only the virgins and girls but entire cities. This is a Hebraism.

Arnon is a huge, rugged, and steep rock, next to which is a vast desert that marks the border of the kingdom of Moab. The city, a walled town, was called Arnon. This place was fit for robbers, and because of them neither entrance nor exit was safe.

3. *Give counsel.* This is pure irony. He says: "This is plainly at hand, that you have to lament. Therefore give yourself counsel, be wise and gather all your sages for counsel. Use your wisdom and counsels so that you can prepare a shade and a preventive against the impending heat and the extremely hot noon, that is, trouble."

Hide the outcasts, just as the birds hide a nest under the branches.

4. *Let my outcasts sojourn among you,* that is, "those whom I have

[1] For another instance of this phrase, see *Luther's Works,* 22, p. 269.

driven and cast out, namely, your people. But you will accomplish nothing." The devastator and expeller, the king of the Assyrians, will be removed and, by antiphrasis,[2] he will have an end.

A throne will be established in steadfast love. The prophet returns to his own people with a pleasant promise, as if to say: "Thus it will happen to you Midianites that you will not have any counsel or help, neither from God nor from men; you will perish, but we will remain." So the ungodly look at the godly as if they would perish in a moment, but the wheel will turn, and against such presumptions we must lay hold of these and like promises with which we may lift up and strengthen our confidence. He says: "Do not look at Moab in its pride, for it will collapse. You, however, although hopeless in the eyes of the world, will be saved." Godly David and his successor, Hezekiah, will be saved, and the throne of David will be established, not in wrath but in steadfast love.

And on it will sit in faithfulness. This is an affront to all foreign kings and princes. Steadfast love is a divine blessing and favor, the remission of sins, and the gift of the Holy Spirit. He says that there will not be a hypocrite there but that pure truth and faithfulness will reign. This King will not only judge for His own Person and in His office deliver the oppressed, the poor, and the widows, but He will also seek justice, that is, He will see to it that the other magistrates of the kingdom will judge in this way, and He will swiftly get justice done and not drag it out for many years. This is the glory and the duty of every prince. But it is a gift of God that is now exceedingly uncommon.

6. *We have heard of the pride of Moab.* This is rhetorical anticipation.[3] "Here," he says, "these things seem foolish to the Moabites who despise us, but don't you become fainthearted. I know the pride of Moab; it is very much advertised (cf. Jer. 48:29). But his pride is bigger than his power; he brags more than he can do." Barking dogs don't bite. Waters that roar a lot are not deep. Where there are extremely many words, there is a lack of substance. In the end one will wail louder than another, and tribe will wail louder than tribe. And this will happen in individual places separately at first, and then together. Not only the common people, but the foundations, too,

[2] Antiphrasis is a rhetorical device in which words are used to mean their opposites.

[3] The Latin term for this device is *occupatio*.

that is, the chiefs in the state. 7. *Kir-hareseth.* The crippled will groan, that is, those who are of the people will ponder words of grief among themselves. They will be unnerved so that they will falter because they do not have the aid of comfort and protection. For even the foundations will be laid waste.

8. *Heshbon.* This state has well-cultivated fields, but it will be as if a paradise of pleasure were directly turned into a desert.

Its branches, that is, the lords of the nations will cut off or shelter the noblest twigs, that is, these foreign possessors from the nations and the disturbers *reached to Jazer.*

They strayed, that is, they roamed about without order, without law and rule, like a frisky bull.

Its shoots spread abroad, that is, scattered. The meaning is that the people will be moved from Heshbon and Sibmah across the sea. Agriculture and wine dressing denote a people equipped with wisdom, wealth, etc. The shoots are the nobles, the sages, the offspring through whom posterity is preserved. They are the youth, men and women, who will be taken away by others.

9. *Therefore I will weep.* He shows that the weeping is to be heard far and wide, namely as far as Jazer. This is putting on an act, for the prophet himself did not weep for this, but he repeats the words of the people of Moab. "I will weep," he says, "for the removal of the choicest youth."

I drench you with my tears, that is, "I will soak and water you."

Upon your fruit and your harvest. The prophet continues in the metaphor. In the time of harvesting and grape-picking men who have something to gather are moved to joy. In the same way parents are happy over their offspring, the state over its young people, the prince over an obedient populace. The prophet, then, indicates that a song different from the song of those rejoicing in the harvest or fruit, namely, the noise and uproar of war, will intervene. Or, the kingdom of Moab was literally laid waste in the time of the harvest. The prophet put summer in place of the summer's crop, that is, the fruits. He is taunting the Moabites by means of irony or sarcasm. That is to say, "I truly think that the voice of people rejoicing has come into your harvest. Those who will be jubilant in your harvest will certainly come. Others will carry off what you have reaped, and they will be jubilant. Ps. 39:6 reads: 'Man heaps up, and knows not who will gather.' The Assyrians will carry off your young people who were trained to till the soil and to manage the affairs of the state." Moreover, this principle extends in its broadest sense to all the misfortunes of the ungodly. When they have scraped many things together, then they depart into hell, and Satan in their death deprives the self-righteous of all righteousness, so that they are compelled to despair.

10. *Joy and gladness are taken away,* namely, yours, Moab.

The enemies will rejoice from Carmel, that is, from the cultivated and fruit-bearing field.

11. *Therefore my belly moans for Moab.* This, too, is imitative. It means the inmost parts. Heart and justice will grieve, groan, and cry out in sadness.

Kir-heres is a proper noun. The prophet means that the kingdom of Moab is to be destroyed altogether; indeed, Moses ridicules both their god and their worship as something empty. "Where," he asks, "are their gods?" (Deut. 32:37). Truly this ungodly practice and this worship of idols is nothing else but weariness and useless toil, and the ungodly and hypocrites have more trouble in their false worship than the godly in the true. The remorse of the ungodly is twofold. On the one hand it is toil and weariness, on the other, destruction and uselessness. The godly always have a joyful conscience and know that they are pleasing to God. They are unconcerned about what may befall them from without, and they will not lack fruit like the ungodly, however great a cross they bear, both from without and from within. The external cross is self-imposed, not of God. The internal cross is of the devil and death. The godly bear only an external cross, not self-imposed but placed by God, and they have no cross within, but they do have peace and a cheerful and serene conscience. Let us, therefore, beware of ungodly doctrines because they are extremely destructive and nothing but toil and grief, yea, a plague of God, as Moses says in Deut. 28:36: "There you shall serve other gods." God can put up with our weakness and our dereliction, if only we will abide in His pure Word. But if the Word is removed, then God Himself and true worship are also removed. In works there are always endless defects, which even the performers themselves always find in them, and among the ungodly satisfaction is never to be made nor any forgiveness of sins. But faith in Christ makes life happy, even though we may fall at times. "Your sins are forgiven," He says (Matt. 9:2). We believe in the forgiveness of sins.

13. *This is the Word which the Lord spoke concerning Moab.* These things were decreed before by God concerning Moab, which always hated the people of God and God Himself dwelling in Jerusalem, and they rejoiced over their misfortune, obviously since they were holy apart from God[4] and devoted to the worship of gods. Now, however, matters will not be drawn out any longer, but "I will set a term of three years," He says, "if perchance they will repent."

14. *The years of a hireling* are such as when some one is hired for a certain job for a specific amount of money and has the right to leave when the job is finished. So "after three years I will release Moab into the hand of the enemies." *Removed,* that is, brought into contempt. Its glory, that is, its kingdom, wisdom, religion, power, population, and wealth will be trifling. Nevertheless, a remnant, though small, will be preserved. Where formerly there was a prince, there will now be a peasant. Summary: By a large number of examples and a cloud of witnesses (cf. Heb. 12:1) we are taught that God does not forsake His own and that He brings the proud low. In the morning the godly will have comfort, though in the evening they must be afflicted and must endure for the testing of their faith, as we read in Ps. 30:5. Always they are troubled by the sins of the inhabitants of hell, always God is with them to comfort them and to visit evil upon those who bother them. Thus He did also to the Moabites.

[4] The meaning of the original is unclear: *cum a deo sancti essent.* Conceivably it could mean either "made holy by God" or "holy apart from God."

CHAPTER SEVENTEEN

1. *An oracle concerning Damascus. Behold, Damascus will cease to be a city.*

In this chapter Isaiah prophesies more and more concerning the destruction of the ten tribes of Israel, rather than concerning Damascus. Above, however, he prophesied against Damascus, which was the capital of the kingdom of Syria. It was often destroyed and often rebuilt. Moreover, in that prophecy against Damascus he devoted himself more to the guilt and captivity of the kingdom of Israel, because the king of Israel had made a covenant with Syria against the kingdom of Judah, that is, was thus more closely joined to Gentiles than to Jews, yes, put more confidence in ungodly men than in God, and Judah suffered harm at the hands of its brothers, so to say. Therefore Israel, a partner in Syria's guilt, will become a partner in Syria's punishment. In the end, however, there is added consolation for the calamity.

And will become a heap of ruins. The prophet does not describe the war or the enemies, but he embraces the matter in its broadest scope in the simplest and shortest statement.

2. *Aroer* is a city in the land assigned to the tribe of Reuben, formerly in the kingdom of Sihon, king of the Amorites (cf. Josh. 13:16). But that is not the one spoken of here. This one is in Syria and is a metropolis, under which were other cities. But some interpret it as referring to all of Syria.[1] *Aroer*, however, means a plain where tamarisks grow, a place uncultivated and sandy. The prophet wants to say that Syria will be a desert after its people have been driven out, so that herds can safely recline there.

3. *The fortress will disappear from Ephraim.* Here the prophet applies the punishment to the guilt. Damascus was Israel's reliance. He says that this will be laid in ruins and the kingdom will for that time cease to be.

[1] Jerome, *Commentaria,* V, 178—179.

And the remnant of Syria, that is, both kingdoms will be laid waste, just as glory seems to be spoken of in irony.

4. *And in that day the glory of Jacob,* power, wealth, justice, wisdom, the worship of God, the cultivation of the land, wives, and many children.

The fat, that is, the large and powerful kingdom will be feeble, sparse, and powerless. With the removal of the powerful and the nobles, only the dregs of the people, the poor and the peasants, worthless cobs will be left. The Assyrians will be the harvesters and grape-pickers.

5. *In the Valley of Rephaim,* which was a pleasant meadow and plain opposite Jerusalem toward the west, where there was much grain. In short: Lowliness is saved, pride perishes.

7. *In that day men will regard.* Above in chapter 10:22: "The consummation is cut short and will overflow."[2] This is what happens when the Lord rebukes the ungodly and the proud. The remnant learn righteousness; they are upright. Certainly, then, the man who will have been left and who will have survived the punishment will be turned to the Lord, and the idols and their empty worship will be forsaken. The works of their hands are also the ark and the temple, etc. But here only this is considered, where the Word of God is and where it is not. The Word puts its stamp of approval on the work, so that it may be called divine. A work apart from the Word of God is to be abhorred.

Their eyes will look to the Holy One of Israel. It is He who truly makes holy. Not so other gods and works. The hypocrites, on the contrary, desire to make God holy. 9. *Strong cities* was the name for the cities in which there were idols. In the Scriptures God is called Rock, Confidence, Strength, Power, etc. But there were golden calves at Bethel and Dan, just as among us cathedral churches are called episcopal sees. In short: When the children of Israel moved into the land of Canaan, there was nothing to do but to abandon everything and to flee. The aristocrats were killed, and the branches and bushes, that is, the lowest classes, were left. Hence, just as they did to the Canaanites, so it will be done to them.

[2] The Weimar text has *mundabit,* but we have followed the Biblical text and read *inundabit.*

And there will be desolation. Having described the punishment, the prophet now points out the guilt also. Behold, that here (v. 10), too, God is called a *strong Helper,* or, better from the Hebrew, "a Rock of strength."

10. *Therefore you will plant a forsaken planting.* He is describing the emptiness of the religion invented by man and the plantings not of an earthly kingdom but of religion. The plants denote disciples instructed in the worship of idols, disciples who are unassuming, orderly, and compliant. Also, this righteousness has its own reward, namely, wealth, favor, peace, and therefore they are called "faithful" plantings, or rather, "pleasant." "These," he says, "you will prepare not for yourself but for a foreign king, namely, the king of the Assyrians." He describes the zeal and the diligence of the ungodly, which is nevertheless in vain. So they are also in a hurry to have arise and come to pass what they have planned. Yet its end and fruit is the devil. "He who sows to his own flesh," says Gal. 6:8, "will from the flesh reap corruption." They sow honey and it comes up mustard.

12. *Woe to the multitude of peoples.* This is the comfort for the king and the people of the Jews, that Assyria, about to lay waste the plantings and about to attempt to destroy the kingdom of Judah, will not achieve it but will itself perish. Yet it will come with an incalculable number of people, just like the sea, which cannot be contained at all when it breaks through, and it will come with great turbulence and noise, as of rampaging waters. The sea, rivers, mountains, trees symbolize kings, princes, aristocrats. Just as the sea devours the land, so the army overruns the people. But the Lord will thunder at them, the Assyrians and the roaring of the waters, and it will be very easy for Him to drive them off, just as the wind easily chases the chaff on the mountains exposed to the wind. In the valley the chaff is safer. But the prophet makes use of such grand words and poetic figures in order to strengthen faith. For a fearful heart cannot be lifted up enough, while, on the contrary, a hardened heart cannot be terrified enough. Then he also consoles the former so that they may be forearmed and may not despair when the disaster strikes.

14. *At evening time.* He is alluding to the statement in Psalm 30:5: "Weeping may tarry for the night." This means that that disaster will be of short duration. One bad night before the morning breaks,

and the matter with the afflicting Assyrians will be disposed of. But every trial seems permanent to our mind, and our reason does not see the end of the trial. Therefore divine mercy appoints an end for it which we cannot grasp. With God our trial is but of an evening's duration. The flesh, however, does not know how to reckon this but judges according to the senses. Therefore we must rather cling by faith to the Word of God. But these promises apply to us by way of example. For although we have the Word, we must expect all the troubles that others have sustained. Therefore, for the same affliction we make use of the same promise and comfort. Trials seem long lasting, but they are short before God, who provides the outcome and will indeed permit us to be afflicted but not overcome. For we are founded on the solid Rock, which is Christ.

CHAPTER EIGHTEEN

1. *Woe to the land that rides on the wings of the shades, which is beyond the rivers.*

THE prophet now turns to the south, an area noted especially for shipping. First of all, however, he prophesies against those who are beside the Red Sea, which is stagnant and has many papyrus reeds, from which ships were constructed, and these people are called Arabian or lower Egyptians. *Woe,* he says, *to the land* that has the shades of wings, that is, of ships. These only fly with sails as birds do with wings, that is, as a people very active in commerce puts its trust in ships. For in the Scriptures a shade denotes protection. The prophets hated and rebuked nothing so much as a trust placed "elsewhere" and not in God. *Beyond* instead of "this side of" *the rivers.*

2. *Which sends ambassadors by sea.* He is describing the mania of those people, namely, truly a plundering and thievish people, a pursuit which they think is lawful for them. And most of their operation is on the Red Sea, by which merchandise comes to Alexandria and from there to other places.

In vessels of papyrus. The Hebrews called all utensils vessels. Here they mean ships.

Go, angels, that is, messengers, so that the report may reach that land, namely, that the king of the Assyrians and war and disaster are coming.

Tortured and torn. These words can be explained either in an active or in a passive sense to depict a land rebellious and full of robbers, so that they are not safe among themselves.

Awaiting. In Hebrew: Measured with a rope.

Whose land the rivers divide, that is, where each one is cut off so as to be isolated, where there is no social intercourse, and they live in the midst of waterways. A people without laws. According to the authors,[1] they can be named Troglodytes, Ishmaelites, etc.

[1] Cf. Herodotus, *History,* IV, 183; Pliny, *Natural History,* VI, 34.

3. *All you inhabitants of the world.* Isaiah first prophesies war against them and then starvation. The inhabitants of this world, that is, the neighbors and inhabited areas. Concerning the banner on the mountains see Is. 13:4 above.

4. *The Lord said to me.* Namely, when very hopefully the earth will have brought forth its sprouts, then I will destroy them with an intense heat so that they will not reach maturity. Even so it often happens now too. Among the Hebrews rain is called light, because they call all sad experiences darkness and all joys light. He says, "I will keep the clouds from raining. Then I will add an intense heat, which is more harmful after a rain, because with the rain it draws out the juice of the crops so that they cannot grow."

Cloud of dew, or dewy cloud. Mildew. This is indeed harmful when the dew falls at the same time the sun is shining. For it shrivels and consumes in such a manner that worms and caterpillars are born from it. Men, he says, will receive no fruit from them, but birds and beasts will use them as best they can. Allegorically, however, this means that it will be with the people just as with the fruits of the field. The *heat* is the king of Assyria, who will devour that blooming, that is, enlarged, people and the young and the handsome and the strong, so that they will be booty for the birds and beasts, and thus the spoilers will be despoiled.

7. *At that time.* At last, he says, also those Troglodytes and Arabians will bring gifts to the Lord in Jerusalem; that is, trouble will give understanding, and the rod will make well-behaved children. A wild people will be changed and will become devout to the Lord. Thus Luke says in Acts 2:5: "Now there were dwelling in Jerusalem Jews, devout men from every nation under heaven." Again, there was the Ethiopian eunuch in Acts 8:27 ff. But in this way the prophet shows that a remnant of this people is to be saved, that from among the worst will come the holiest, but on the contrary, the holiest in Jerusalem will be the most depraved. Thus God will perplex the devil. At Rome is the head and the seat of the devil. The cross is the bier of Saint Robber, as the ancient line puts it.[2] *Amor* read backwards is the capital of the world and the beast of the earth.[3]

[2] This seems to be part of a sequence hymn for "St. Dismas," the thief on the cross.

[3] According to a comment made at table, perhaps around this same time (W, *Tischreden,* II, 284, No. 1971), Luther had found this verse while at Erfurt.

CHAPTER NINETEEN

1. *An oracle concerning Egypt. Behold, the Lord will ride on a swift cloud.*

OUR God, he says, dwells in Jerusalem; He will undertake something new and stir up rebellion in Egypt. Thus He does both to the queen and to the province that He wants to devastate and destroy. *He will ride on a swift cloud.* He will not delay; swiftly the disaster will strike them.

The idols of Egypt will tremble, that is, worship and religion will quake. Their nothingness is indicated, because in time of danger they provide neither help nor counsel. The king of Assyria, on the contrary, was the scourge of all nations around Jerusalem, something that is to be expected in the whole world concerning the Turk.[1] Therefore he here calls the Assyrians a light and swift cloud, who will easily overcome Egypt, an extremely powerful kingdom. Because of images and idolatry human thinking is perverted; it fashions a god for itself and does so according to its own whim and the suggestion of Satan. A knowledge of God is implanted in all men, and therefore they think that God is to be worshiped. In this they certainly make no mistake, but they do err in the manner of their worship if they worship Him not simply according to His Word and will but rather according to their own ideas.

The idols will tremble. The meaning is: Hypocrisy does not bear up under the scourge of God; true godliness does. As long as ungodliness fares well, the hypocrites are proud and fierce beyond measure, but nothing is more terrible to them than an onrushing calamity. They become foolish, and because they have neither the Word nor the true understanding of God, they falter and stagger.

The heart of the Egyptians will melt. When confidence in one's own righteousness falls away, fear and contradictory ideas and counsels arise. For nowhere but in the Word of God does my own quaking find firm footing. God is the counselor and the wisdom of the godly,

[1] In 1526 the Turks had been defeated in the battle of Mohács, but in 1529 they laid siege to Vienna.

who believe in Him. Disunity is the beginning of a kingdom's overthrow, as we read in Luke 11:17. This results from the collapse of confidence in religion, for then some urge this, others argue against it. When God is about to fight against men, He first takes their heart away, He deprives them of courage and daring, He causes them to disagree among themselves, He undermines their every counsel. Where there are religions, there are a variety of prophets. The Egyptians, however, were more superstitious than others.

5. *The waters will be dried up.* These are allegorical expressions. They say that formerly the Nile flooded all of Egypt with the waters rising 16 ells in height.[2] From this the land was made extremely fertile, but they say this has now ceased. The Nile receives seven rivers into itself.[3] Therefore Egypt was rich in waters and fish. For this reason the prophet uses the picture of the fishermen to depict Egypt's calamity.

The waters of the sea, namely, those that flow into the sea, will be drained, that is, those living beside the sea will be despoiled. So it is in Job (Job 14:11). Tyrants empty out, that is, plunder, the house; the river will be deserted, that is, the wealth will be destroyed.

The waters of the ramparts, that is, the canals around the cities.

6. *Reeds and rushes:* wealthy citizens.

7. *All that is sown will be driven away,* that is, all people, even the country people and the lowest classes, will be exposed to plunder and will be put to flight.

8. *The fishermen,* that is, the businessmen; 9. *The workers in combed flax,* that is, the skilled craftsmen. No disaster is alone, nor does it strike only one. When the fishermen become inactive, the work of those who weave nets and those who dig fishponds and liveboxes is destroyed. Thus far the prophet has spoken of the war and poverty and plunder of the Egyptians. Now, the use we are to make of a prophecy of this kind, which is made against all the nations encircling Jerusalem, is this, that we may learn that our enemies will not escape punishment, that God is the avenger of the godly, and

[2] Cf. Herodotus, *History*, II, 19-27.

[3] The sources of the Nile were a puzzle both to antiquity and to the Middle Ages; Luther seems here to reflect the explanation found on the maps of Ptolemy, as revised by later writers.

that none of the ungodly are more powerful than God. Again, we should learn that the godly are to be preserved, even though they should go down to the depths of hell.

11. *Foolish princes.* Now there follows a mockery against the Egyptians' boast of wisdom and antiquity, for the purpose of praising the true and only wise God. But Isaiah taunts them thus: Since you are so very wise and of so ancient a race, why do you not understand how to escape the danger? You think you know more than the Jews, but you are truly foolish. There was the counsel of the princes, but something else was decreed by God, namely, that Egypt was to be made subject to Assyria. This is the way of a doomed empire; it is hardened and puffed up, and the more the evil threatens, the prouder and more inflexible it becomes, just as the impenitent do not fear God and do not hear the voice of the Lord. Thus Paul says in 1 Thess. 5:3: "When people say, 'There is peace and security,' then sudden destruction will come upon them." For this reason the heathen invented the wheel of fortune.[4] But the ungodly, on the contrary, do not believe that evil will come to them, and so they always predict the good for themselves. So here the king of Egypt, no matter what is said against him, sings:

I am a son of the wise, that is, you have wise men. The Hebrew way of saying it is "I am a son of the wise." And today the papists boast of wisdom and antiquity; these two harden the minds, and the prophets pursue and reprove this especially.

13. *The princes of Memphis are deluded.* "The princes of Noph," as if to say, their counsels indeed had an impressive appearance, but they deceived them, and nothing came of it. The counsels of the ungodly seem to have hand and foot and are not far distant from the act, but nothing is more contemptible among them than the counsels of the godly and of doctrine.

The corner of the people, or rather, the cornerstone of the tribes, that is, the king with the people. Corners denote heads, princes, kings. Our cornerstone is Christ, as we read in Eph. 2:20. *Of her people,* that is, of Egypt.

14. *The Lord has mingled within her a spirit of confusion,* that is, He has poured it in. This is the course of their deception by the Lord, namely, it has been done. The picture of the drunken man is

[4] Cf. Tibullus, *Corpus Tibullianum,* I, 5, 70.

frequent in the Scriptures, as in Psalm 107:27: "They reeled and staggered like drunken men." In time of peace the ungodly are very sure of the spirit and of wisdom, but in trials they do not stand fast. They turn from this to that. Where there are many divergent recommendations, there is sure disaster. But where many recommendations are in harmony, there is safety. "A cart is never drawn well by unmatched oxen."

The drunken man goes astray on the road, he weaves hither and thither. So does the ungodly when he is weighed down with trouble. In the Scriptures the cup may denote misfortune that is assigned; Christ had His cup, and every godly man bears a cross. Some become drunk from the cup, some who are not ungodly will drink so that they waver and stagger, and they will not have the sense to avoid it. The godly man is a strong counselor who upholds them with his word and consoles them when they take the cup, so that they do not become drunk. Every trial apart from the Word of God makes a man drunk, that is, uncertain and desperate, so that he does not know where he is going. The godly have learned that the scourge is a reward of the Lord that will turn out for their benefit. They know that it is the Lord's good will that they be put to the test and not be destroyed. The ungodly, staggering as they do, even vomit. Their counsels are sheer vomit and filth, food for pigs.

15. *And there will be nothing for Egypt which head or tail, palm branch or reed, may do.*

Above in Is. 9:14 the same thing is said of tail, branch, and reed. The prophet who speaks a lie is a tail. The meaning is: In time of disaster the Egyptians will not have a prince or a judge, both in spiritual and in civil affairs. Both government and priesthood will be destroyed for them, both realms will fall into ruin. Then they will not have any branches, either large or small, and the people will perish together with the perishing state and religion. The government will be without people and the priesthood without disciples. The laws and worship will perish together with the devastated kingdom. This is the punishment for contempt of the Word of God.

16. *In that day the Egyptians will be like women.* Concerning this also the historians write that in Egypt the men do the work of women and vice versa.[5] The female sex is weak, they lack courage

[5] Herodotus, *History,* II, 35.

and judgment, they are timid and slow of mind. Sometimes even the timid find good judgment, but in doubtful matters no one can give counsel. *The hand,* namely, of the Assyrians which the Lord will shake over Egypt this way and that way, that is, the Assyrians will move through the whole kingdom and lay everything waste, and the Egyptians will find neither help nor counsel.

17. *And the land of Judah will be,* that is, then the Egyptians will remember the word spoken to them which they now despise and ridicule as a lie. "But," he says, "I shall live when those things happen and they will be afraid at the memory of the land of Judah because of the prophecy that was foretold there, so that to the present disaster there is added fear and dread of the future, and they will fear things more cruel than they are now experiencing."

They will fear because of the purpose of the Lord, namely, "what I have intimated to them and what they ridiculed. But when it will come to pass, there will be no end of terror." So it happens with the Word that it is not believed but despised when it is proclaimed, but is feared the more when it is fulfilled.

18. *In that day there will be five cities.* After the prophet's prediction of disaster and the spoken taunt there now follows a salutary and blessed promise for the Egyptians who will receive the Lord, who always preserves the remnant. And though Egypt was an ungodly land and more superstitious than others, it will then have greater praise than the rest of the nations. Egypt troubled the Jews after their exodus less than others and therefore will have more moderate punishment.

The language of Canaan, that is, Hebrew.

19. *There will be an altar to the Lord in the midst of the land of Egypt.* This must be understood as referring to the time after Christ, not before. "In the place which the Lord your God will choose," Deut. 12:18 says, and above in Is. 2:3: "Out of Zion shall go forth the Law." Before Christ no other place was to be established for the worship of God beside Jerusalem. Therefore the prophet is speaking of the time when the Gospel was spread. He puts five cities in place of many, a definite number for an indefinite one. In the Gospel there were ten virgins, five foolish, etc. Also there were five talents, etc. (Matt. 25:1 ff., 15). Hence "five cities" means that several, not all,

but some, will follow the Word. This is what we could now say regarding Samaria. Five cities speak the holy language. The number five has its mysteries.[6] The language of Canaan, Hebrew and Syriac, is the mother and fount of all languages and is common in the East, and perhaps Adam lived there, too. The Chaldean language is a corrupted Hebrew.[7] In this way, then, the Egyptians will be honored, that those who now not only do not speak our language but also hate us, that those who alone want to be the wisest and the best and consider their own language to be the best, will take refuge with us and assume our ways, forsaking and renouncing everything of their own that they now hold dear, both in wisdom and in eloquence. And in our language they will learn the hidden mysteries of God.

18. *They will swear allegiance to the Lord of hosts,* that is, they will worship as God Him whom the Jews worship in the land of Canaan. To vow and to swear are Hebrew ways of speaking and mean to bind oneself to God and have Him as one's God and worship Him. This pertains properly to swearing. One who confesses God is called one who swears by God. The psalm says (Ps. 63:11): "All who swear by Him shall glory," that is, all who confess Him. Those who now boast of their idols will boast and glory in the Lord of hosts. "In all their disputes an oath is final for confirmation," we read in Heb. 6:16. This is what it means to worship, to confess the Lord: rightly to use His name, namely, for the confirmation of the truth, as is done by an oath and by calling upon Him through faith in His promises and His truth.

City of the Sun, הַהֶרֶס, Haheres. From the certainty of the prophecy he mentions one city by its proper name. In ancient days there was at Alexandria an outstanding school of Christians. Heliopolis.

An altar to the Lord. The name of Christ will be raised far and wide in Egypt. *Altar* instead of "altars." The name is the same as altar in Heb. 13:10: "We have an altar from which those who serve the tent have no right to eat." Because he mentions one altar, he preserves one Lord and one worship of Him. The spiritual altar in different places is one. Christ is our altar on which we place our bodies, the bodies of sins to be slaughtered and consumed. For He

[6] The use of the numeral 5 as a mystic number appears to be reflected in such passages as Matt. 25:2 and Gen. 43:34, as well as in the designation of the Five Books of Moses.

[7] By "Chaldaean" here Luther presumably means Aramaic.

is an altar of burnt offering and of incense. Through Him we bring our prayers to God the Father.

20. *It will be a sign and a witness,* that is, the Word will be preached there, and they will flow to it as to a banner, and it will be a witness as of the Lord's presence. It will not be an altar for display as in Judea, but there will be other sacrifices and other incense, by which he cuts off the sacrifice and incense of the Jews and suggests that they will come to an end. The witness was present among the Jews in the individual cities where the Scripture was read. But the rites and sacrifices were only in the temple. That spiritual altar will be a sign of finding the Lord and a witness of teaching the people.

They will cry to the Lord. Where the doctrine is sound, there is prayer and the Spirit of prayers. And where the Word of grace is, there follows cross and affliction. Therefore the Egyptians will cry, that is, they will be true Christians and will have the Word of grace and the work of grace, that is, prayer.

He will deliver them.[8] This should be understood as referring to spiritual deliverance.

"Defender," or, better, "master," who will teach them and have authority over others and save them by the Word. The true Master is Christ. However, those who proclaim Christ are masters also.

21. *The Lord will make Himself known.* This is the main thing for us, because "by His knowledge He shall make many to be accounted righteous," as we read in Is. 53:11. *He will make Himself known,* that is, He will be revealed through the Gospel. They will worship Him with sacrifices.

In any conflict, the superior position of Scripture must always be kept in mind. The Word once given by the Lord must be held fast if trial should come and the situation would appear to be otherwise. Know, Moses says, that "the Lord your God is testing you" (Deut. 13:3). Therefore God wants us to abide by His prior Word. When, therefore, it is said here that the Egyptians would speak the language of Canaan, swear by the Lord, cry to the Lord, and pray and do everything that is characteristic of Christians, it means that those sacrifices and gifts will be sacrifices of praise and thanksgiving and not ceremonies of the Law for the purpose of obtaining righteousness;

[8] The Weimar text has *liberatos,* but we have followed the Biblical text and read *liberat eos.*

for otherwise Christ would have died in vain and would be preached in vain. Also the sacrifices of the Christians are the mortification of their own bodies. Vows are the giving of thanks and praise, faith and clinging to Christ, and telling His wonderful works. The words of Ps. 18:49, "I will extol Thee, O Lord, among the nations," were a vow of Christ. The vows of the Old Testament concerned themselves with external and temporal things, such as were in their power. The vows of the New Testament are to commit oneself to Christ, to worship Him by faith, praise, and confession and praise. For God is not worshiped except by faith. Thus the field is cultivated for the sake of the produce. The believers humble and condemn themselves, but they proclaim and glorify Christ and His works. These are the vows of the New Testament. Civil vows have the emperor and the laws in view. Vows made in impossible things are ungodly and devilish, as are those made even in possible things for the purpose of being made righteous by means of their performance.[9]

22. *And the Lord will smite,* that is, chastise them. Paul says (1 Cor. 11:32): "When we are judged by the Lord, etc." "The Lord reproves him whom He loves" (Prov. 3:12; cf. Heb. 12:6; Rev. 3:19). Therefore also the Egyptians will be God's chosen children, but He will not turn them over to death. The Lord does not judge and afflict in order to destroy but in order to test and to help, and so that we may not become listless and lazy. The blow is therefore one of healing and conversion. When the ungodly are struck, they turn away.

23. *There will be a highway from Egypt.* This should be understood as referring to the publishing of the Gospel. There will be peace between those nations and agreement in faith and doctrine. It will be public. In unity of faith they will agree with Israel, and Israel with them.

24. *A blessing* of the seed of Abraham will be in the land.

25. *People, work of My hands, heritage* mean the same thing. This is the prophet's effusiveness. This is, however, a very clear passage showing that the Jews will be equal to the Gentiles and vice versa. With the abolition of the Law, therefore, the Gospel concerning the grace of Christ will be preached to the heart for Gentiles as well as Jews, "and there will be one fold" (John 10:16).

[9] Cf. *The Judgment of Martin Luther on Monastic Vows, Luther's Works,* 44, pp. 251—400.

CHAPTER TWENTY

1. *In the year that Thartan came to Ashdod.*

In the last chapter Isaiah foretold the calamity of Egypt together with a promise of grace to come through Christ. Now he goes on to foretell misfortune in that appointed time for their neighbors, the Ethiopians, with whom they had made a treaty to withstand the king of Assyria. And the prophet points out that that trust is worthless, and they will be put to shame in it. The fear of God and faith in God, as all histories teach, have no room in us, unless reliance on ourselves and our flesh will first have been cast out. But the Gospel is at war with all the exalted things of the world, which are an abomination in the sight of God.

Thartan. He was a prince and military leader.

2. *Loose the sackcloth.* Thus God is wont to add a sign to His Word, not of mutual love and recognition, because love itself and the other fruits of faith and the Spirit are stronger. The deceivers, too, can be baptized and can participate in the Lord's Supper. And the miracles of Christ are signs, not that the Christians might recognize each other by them[1] but that faith might be strengthened by them. God, however, adds signs to the Word to arouse faith and fear and because He does not wish to give His Spirit except through some outward means. For that reason He has instituted the ministry of the Word and the signs, through which the Spirit may be given. Thus, too, He was first given in the strong wind and fiery tongues, as we read in Acts 2:3. The external thing, unless divinely ordained, of course accomplishes nothing. But what is divinely instituted cannot fail to produce results. Here the sign is added as if it were the Word, concrete and before the eyes, so that the sign might teach the same thing that the Word teaches.

3. *For three years as a sign.* The duration of this sign is three years, and then it will be fulfilled indeed. In Jeremiah there is the

[1] This is an attack on Zwingli; cf. *Luther's Works,* 37, p. 141.

sign of a chain around the prophet's neck, summoning the people to fear and repentance (Jer. 27:2).

To make Egypt *naked* is to deprive and rob the kingdom of its men, young and old.

"To be shod" means to hold fast to the government of the kingdom. To Idumea, he says, I will extend My shoe, that is, I will make it subject to myself. The subjects and disciples sit at the feet. Above, in chapter 7:20, we read: "The Lord will shave . . . the hair of the feet," that is, the subjects.

"To walk and move in" is to reign and rule. "He whose testicles are crushed or whose male member is cut off shall not enter the assembly of the Lord," as we read in Deut. 23:1; that is, he shall not hold public office.

"To have a garment" means to have wealth and power. To reveal the private parts is to remove confidence and glory. The glory of a prince is in the great number of his people. *Shame* means a small number.

5. *They shall be dismayed and confounded,* that is, they shall cease their undertaking. Egypt will be deterred from Ethiopia out of fear, seeing itself put to shame in its confidence, which it had toward that country to which it looked as to a sure help. And Ethiopia has boasted of Egypt in vain. We ought to boast in the Lord alone, for He punishes those who deny Him. This, then, is the goal of all histories, namely, to teach and to learn faith, fear, and humility and to reprove pride, presumption, and trust in the flesh.

6. *The inhabitants of the islands,* namely, of Egypt and of Ethiopia.

In these is our hope. Hope, or refuge. God more readily puts up with anything else than with presumption and trust in the flesh. He crushes the serpent's head (cf. Gen. 3:15), He derides trust in the flesh. "It's splendid, the way we have been set free!" they say. This is sarcasm. From the rain we have plunged into the river. "The Lord takes pleasure in those who fear Him, in those who hope in His steadfast love" (Ps. 147:11).

CHAPTER TWENTY-ONE

1. *The oracle concerning the wilderness of the sea. As whirlwinds from Africa sweep on.*

THE worst hatred of the Jewish people and the prophets is directed against Babylon, because the Babylonians even laid waste the remnant of that people, that is, the tribe of Judah and the temple. Therefore Isaiah foretells their destruction and the deliverance of the Jews, which was accomplished by Cyrus, the king of the Persians. The prophet cannot forget Babylon even when he begins to speak mainly concerning Christ. Meanwhile, however, many and diverse events intervene. The Jews are harassed by many people against whom he prophesies while his discourse concerning Christ is interrupted. Thus he again speaks about the Babylonians, who perhaps again troubled the Jews after that first prophecy, or else the prophecy is broken up, or the sequence of the prophecies is interrupted. So we in our preaching concerning our worst enemies, sin, death, and Satan, testify as much as possible also against our enemies and persecutors close by. The prophet refers to Babylon by a new name, "the wilderness of the sea," because of its work, namely, because of its position, not because of its location. He calls it a wilderness, however, in an active sense because it does not lay waste on a small scale but as the sea does, which cannot be resisted. He does not say "of the river" but "of the sea," whereby he calls attention to cruelty, savagery, and tyranny. Against this wilderness, he says, there will come another wilderness destined to lay it waste. God does not long put up with presumption and reliance placed outside Himself. Just like the whirlwinds in the South that overturn everything, He comes from the desert, from a terrible land. He means the armies of the Persians and Medes, and He also calls them a desert in an active sense, a desert, however, of a terrible land, not of the sea. It is as if the prophet were saying: "The Lord punishes cruelty with cruelty, and out of that land He will deal in a terrible way with the Babylonians." In Ps. 137:8 we read: "O daughter of Babylon, you devastator! Happy shall he be who requites you with what you have done to us!" The

wind from the west is moderate, from the east it is dry and harmful, but from the south it overturns everything. Vergil says: "He brings the south wind to bear on his flowers." [1]

2. The one who is unbelieving deals faithlessly. More correctly thus: The despiser comes against the despiser, the plunderer against the plunderer. בֹּגֵד is the word for one who despises and is brazenly indifferent to everything, and with overbearing contempt refuses to listen to others. Thus in Ps. 25:3, בּוֹגְדִים. Such was Babylon, and such are the self-righteous now, the papists. David says (Ps. 25:3): "Let them be ashamed who are wantonly treacherous," בּוֹגְדִים, that is, the despisers. Babylon was בֹּגֵד, treacherous, in its confidence. But the king of the Persians put his confidence in God, by whom he was called and sent against Babylon.

Go up, O Elam. These are the words of God. Elam was a son of Shem. From him came the Persians.

All the sighing she has caused, namely, Babylon, by which she caused many people, especially the Jews, to sigh. This is a Hebrew way of speaking, just as this statement, "they are justified through the faith of Christ," means not the faith by which Christ believes, but the faith by which men believe in Christ; as if he were saying, "All sigh and cry over Babylon, so that I can no longer bear it."

3. *My loins are filled with anguish.* The prophet is speaking imitatively. For these are words or feelings or gestures of the afflicted Babylonians, whom the prophet thus ridicules. The power of propagation is in the loins.

The pangs of a woman in travail, that is, of death. Joy dilates and relaxes skin, flesh, and bones. Sadness, however, contracts them. The twilight and the night are longed for by the fatigued workmen. Sleep refreshes the fatigued and revives the strength. The most satisfying sleep is in the twilight, whether in the morning or in the evening. Of this sweet sleep, of twilight he says, the horrors and tremblings deprive me.

5. *Prepare the table.* This is pure irony and fancy. So it is also in Vergil: "They invade the city that is buried in wine and sleep." [2] Thus the king of Babylon had banquets in supreme security. Nothing

[1] Vergil, *Eclogues,* II, 58—59.

[2] Vergil, *Aeneid,* II, 265.

was done there except carousing and drinking, etc. It is as if he were saying: "When you say, 'Slaughter, O cook, etc.,' then the shout comes: 'Take the shield,' that is, suddenly Babylon will be captured. Then first put on the shield; only then, as the secure and idle usually do, get ready [3] what you need to protect yourself."

6. *Thus the Lord said to me: Go, set a watchman.* This was added as a sign to confirm the prophecy, so that he might well and sufficiently deride them.

7. *A chariot of two horsemen* instead of "two-man chariots," to indicate many teams of horses, asses, and camels. The prophet is himself the watchman, however, seeing what will come to pass, and already setting those events before the eyes and proclaiming them daily. But the smug people have made light of it. Yet the prophet uses such grand and powerful words in order to make the Jews more courageous, because in time of affliction no amount of consolation is enough. The man in the chariot is Cyrus, the king of the Persians.

9. *Fallen, fallen is Babylon.* All these things are said for the consolation of the Jews, but the weak cannot believe it.

10. *Daughter of the threshing-floor.* This is the Hebrew way of saying whatever grain the threshing-floor has, namely, what is to be threshed on the threshing-floor. It can be explained as referring to the Jews, whom the Lord threshed through the king of Babylon, not for destruction but for the purpose of separating the grain from the chaff. Or it can be made to refer to the Babylonians, who were to be threshed by the Medes and Persians at the Lord's command. The world is the Lord's threshing and the daughter of His threshing-floor. For us the Turk and other tyrants are the threshers.

What I have heard from the Lord, as if to say, "Do not consider me a fool, for what I say will surely come to pass. The Lord has said so."

11. *The oracle concerning Dumah.* Dumah was one of the sons of Ishmael, as we read in Gen. 25:14, who gave names to these regions. Thus also this region was part of the land of the Ishmaelites, or Arabians, and almost all of these Arabians were born of the seed of Abraham by his wife Keturah, and of Ishmael, the son of the

[3] The Weimar text has *parati,* but *parate* seems to fit the context better.

slave girl. It is to this region and the people of Dumah, then, that the prophet threatens a calamity that is to come from Idumea.

One is calling to me from Seir. This is mimicry on the part of the prophet, imitating the feelings of either the conquered or the conquerors. To me, that is Dumah, there is borne the report of a disaster from Seir, which is Idumea. Edom was called Seir because of hairiness.

Watchman, what of the night? This is ridicule, as if to say, "How are you doing, night watchmen? How much of the night is left? Is the day near?" The repetition denotes the vehemence of the emotions. The prophet, however, rolls allegory and history together into one. Of the natural night he makes an allegory, which is calamity; as if he were saying, "You people of Dumah, are you still pretending? Have you been afflicted enough?" The watchman answers: "The night will not be over even if the day comes," that is, the trouble remains and we must be on guard, even though we hopefully look to the coming day. These are the thoughts of the ungodly, who even then can have hope of deliverance. And yet they do not hope but are anxious and cannot foresee the light. The godly, on the contrary, say: "The night will pass away, and a permanent day will follow." So these people of Dumah despair, even though they may think of peace to come, for they do not believe.

12. *If you will inquire, inquire; come back again.* These are the words of the despairing and those who refuse to accept comfort. This is not the end of the questioning, they say. The meaning is this: "You ungodly are looking for comfort, and yet you do not believe that you will obtain it." They say, "We have looked for peace and, behold, there is trouble and disturbance." The ungodly seek nothing more ardently than peace, but they do not dare to believe that they will have peace; and when they are truly perturbed, they do not have the capacity to expect consolation. The godly, on the contrary, stand fast in the sure Word, which promises peace and consolation.

13. *The oracle concerning Arabia.* Among the sons of Ishmael there is also Kedar (Gen. 25:13), who gave his name to the greater part of Arabia. Against this land Isaiah prophesies here. Dedan was one of the grandsons of Abraham, whose territory extended to Kedar. But the prophet wishes to point out the flight of the Arabians from their cities and homes because they have heard the report of their

devastating conquerors and because they will not consider offering resistance or taking up arms.

14. *To the thirsty bring water.* This is mockery.

The inhabitants of the land of Tema were neighbors of Kedar. He says: "Come to the aid of those who are fleeing from the sword already unsheathed and bare, those who formerly were powerful but are now beggars and exiles, those who are being repaid for what they did to others. The Lord, who never deceives, has said this: 'Glory, wealth, power, people, etc.,' that is, these Arabians are famous in the valor of war and they prevail with arrows and brave men. But the Lord wishes to destroy and enfeeble them. It is the Lord who does not lie. This is most certain."

CHAPTER TWENTY-TWO

1. *The oracle concerning the valley of vision. What do you mean that you have gone up?*

THIS is a prophecy of calamity against Jerusalem and above all against its chief and governor, who is here called Shebaniah. And it has to do with the first Babylonian captivity, for Jerusalem was captured twice. In a remarkable way the prophet here speaks figuratively. Up until now he has been foretelling the calamities of the neighboring nations, calamities they enjoyed hearing about, just as we are wont to flatter ourselves and consider all others fit to be afflicted and think that we can lawfully sin under cover of God's name. This Isaiah is repudiating. "I will not spare you," he says. "Because you are afflicted with similar vices, you will also be struck with similar punishment." But as in the last chapter he called Babylon the wilderness of the sea, so he also calls Jerusalem by a new name, "the valley of vision." There is an antiphrasis [1] in the word "valley," because Jerusalem is elsewhere called a mountain. It hangs on a kind of slope, which has Mount Zion on the south, the temple in the middle on an elevation, and on the downgrade the valley of Kidron, by which name he named the whole city. It is as if he were saying: "Until now you were the most famous mountain on earth, that is, when godliness and holy men flourished in you, but now you will be brought low, and yet you will not be a level plain but a valley. Your glory and fame will be reduced to nothing." But by a Hebraic figure of speech the prophet calls it "valley of vision," because it has had many seers, that is, prophets, as if it were called "valley of prophets." And at the same time he reproves the ingratitude of the people of Jerusalem, because they have not believed so many prophecies.

2. *You are full of shoutings.* "Full" – the situation of a former time, just like "tumultuous" and "exultant." Shouting, that is, outcry, jubilation, rejoicing, because of the large population. This is dramatization and visualization of the calamity, as if to say: "I have pre-

[1] See p. 150, n. 2.

dicted devastation for others; why do you, too, Jerusalem, head for the rooftops [2]? Rich and poor, you run for refuge and hide yourselves on the rooftops, or you want to protect yourselves from the roofs. There is the rumor of war terrifying you, so that you wander hither and yon, you go up to the housetops to watch for the approaching enemies and to seek counsel."

Not slain with the sword, but with pestilence and starvation. The princes have avoided the bow of Nebuchadnezzar, the only one he aimed, and he did not engage in battle. They have not withstood him but have permitted him to bind them and lead them away.

3. *Far away,* that is, to Babylon.

4. *Therefore I said.* The prophet assumes the role and the attitude of the people lamenting that calamity, as if to say, "Then you will mourn without consolation."

The daughter of my people, that is, of the city of Jerusalem. The city indeed was not laid waste or destroyed, but the leaders and the people were led away.

5. *A day of killing.* When the people will be killed and crushed and will be destitute of counsel, then there will be nothing but weeping and wailing in Jerusalem. And this will happen according to God's plan to recall their sins and offenses to their memory. The king of Babylon would not have had so much power if God had not promised it and had not withdrawn His hand from the Jews.

From the battering down of walls and from the noise of the enemies will come the killing and the crushing. At that time there was one kingdom of the Chaldeans and Persians. These are Elam. Kir was an outstanding city of Assyria. The men of Kir, he says, brandish their shields so that the sun glitters and gleams in them.

7. *Your choicest valleys.* Fruitful fields, orchards, superbly cultivated vineyards, they will have them all, and there will be chariots instead of crops. No one will be permitted to go in or out, because the horsemen have surrounded everything.

8. *He has taken away the covering of Judah,* that is, every concealment of holy vessels and of gold, of silver and of weapons.

House of the Forest, which Solomon built.

[2] The Weimar text has *terra,* but we have read *tecta.*

9. *The breaches of the city* both in the walls and in houses, and the forcible entrances of the enemies. In this way the prophet depicts the desperate situation of the city.

You gathered the waters. All this is said of the pillaging of Jerusalem, where there were two pools to alleviate the water shortage, the upper one farther away from the city, the lower one closer by.[3] It is as if he were saying: "The enemies will take possession of the upper pool; therefore you must draw water from the lower one."

10. *You counted,* that is, you will take stock. Because the king of Babylon will carry everything away, you will collect money from house to house, you will construct a pool and a ditch and lead the water into the city.

11. *But you did not look to Him.* O hardened hearts, that do not acknowledge their guilt and in time of punishment do not return to Him who is afflicting them, but meanwhile soothe themselves by saying: "The temple of the Lord is with us, we are the seed of Abraham, the people of the just and holy God." What they suffer they will more quickly ascribe to the devil than to God, and to the sins of others more readily than to their own. They want to be martyrs without God, and they strut along in their own presumption.

12. *And the Lord will call,* that is, a sad time will be proclaimed, not one in which you will repent of sins, but in which you will grieve over the present disaster. So it happens today also, but that prediction is despised and ridiculed just as it was then. No matter how much unhappy events were foretold by which these people ought to have been summoned to weeping, they were happy, indulged themselves, etc., in contempt of the prophets, against whom they said ironically:

13. *Let us eat and drink, for tomorrow we die.* In 1 Cor. 15:32 Paul cited these words against the Corinthians, who in like manner were mocking at the resurrection of the dead.

14. *Revealed in my ears.* Revile the revilers through the Lord, as if to say: "You will certainly not indulge in that mockery with impunity, because the Lord sees, hears, and knows you completely. For our nature relies on things present and despises things absent.

[3] The "lower pool" is spoken of here in Is. 22:8-11; the "upper pool" is mentioned in 2 Kings 18:17.

It cannot do otherwise unless it is threatened by the Word and Spirit of God from heaven. Again, our nature is arrogant in good times and broken up and despairing in bad times.

15. *Come, go to him who dwells, etc.*, that is, to the treasurer or overseer of the temple or the princely court. The priests were close associates of kings and princes, and some also belonged to their councils.

To Shebna, who is over the household.[4] Here is an example for all presumptuous men. But since he was in the court of King Hezekiah, it is certain that he was a good man. Else Hezekiah would not have upheld him. Such a man, then, is assailed with threats? Perhaps he was secretly unfaithful, or surely irreverent toward God. Otherwise he was a man both honorable and hypocritical, whom no one could judge except Isaiah. Thus this man, who had the fine reputation, is attacked, so that others who saw this say: "What will happen to us?" Or, through this the prophet intensified the people's wrath not a little against himself, so that they said: "Not only does he attack us but also that excellent man who dwells in the king's court with honor, is loved by the king, etc. To the devil with that prophet!" Behold, how the Holy Spirit must judge those whom the world cannot judge. Note, however, what He reproves in him, nothing but that he would carve a tomb for himself.

16. *What have you to do here?* That is, what possessions and persons do you have? The prophet indeed speaks contemptuously with that magnate who thought he had all things and people in his power there, namely, as master in the king's house, as chief over the food and finances, as friend of the king, of the princes, and of all the people. But Isaiah is speaking of the future and is visualizing how that man would have nothing, and in very brief words he shatters his presumption and confidence.

You have hewn here a tomb for yourself. Was that so great a sin? Is it a sin to have possessions? And to take care of them? Certainly there had to be some other vice in him, namely, security and neglect, in which he committed some secret sin or presumed that what Isaiah had foretold would not take place. A slip in faith is easy. So Moses, Aaron, David, Peter, all the apostles, Jerome, Augustine, and others

[4] We have reversed the order of these two paragraphs to conform them to the sequence of the Biblical text.

fell. There has always been some remnant of the flesh in the saints, as we see from 1 Cor. 10:12. Therefore let no one be presumptuous. Shebna, then, sinned in not believing the prophet and in calling others away from faith by his example. He was the instigator in despising the Word of God and of His prophet. Therefore the prophet asks him so confidently, "Who are you?" Altogether: "You will be nothing, you will keep nothing, in vain have you prepared for yourself so regal a tomb either in the house or in the garden, or in the rock or on the mountain.

To construct a tomb for oneself denotes security, to desire to stay in that land and therefore to despise whatever the prophet said. It is not evil to make use of creatures, unless it be done in contempt of the Word of God. There is nothing so good, nothing so trivial that does not become evil and destructive when contempt of the Lord is added, and building a tomb for oneself is more serious in this way than is adultery or murder.

17. *Behold, the Lord will hurl you away violently.* It is as if he were saying: "You will not remain in this land but will be snatched away just as if some strong man were with a strong hand throwing something that could not withstand the throw. The hand of the Lord is the king of the Chaldeans. The opposite of what you planned will happen to you. You will not remain but be cast out. You will not be buried here nor with honors but out in the open, and you will be brought to a strange and ignoble land. You will not live at ease as you think, but you will be driven round and round, you will be thrown like a ball in a wide land, from disaster to disaster.

18. *Like a ball into a wide land.* This simile can be used to describe spiritual as well as physical trouble. For thus a terrified conscience is whirled about. It can come to rest nowhere, and nowhere has it peace. It seems that Shebna lived also under King Manasseh and perhaps became a tyrant when Manasseh was led into captivity. For that reason the prophet adds here:

Shame of your master's house, or "of your masters'." It seems that he had confidence both in his masters and in his own power.

20. *I will call My servant Eliakim.* He was a supporter of the Word; Shebna opposed him.

21. *I will clothe him with your robe.* A garment denotes the

priestly ministry, a girdle the service at court. Here in short words are described the qualities of a good prince, qualities from which prince Shebna deteriorated. The prince should be a father of his country. Thus the servants of Naaman called him father in 2 Kings 5:13. Here the prophet speaks of one who shall be a father "to the house of Judah," that is, to the whole kingdom.

22. *And I will place the key of the house of David, etc.* In the Book of Revelation (Rev. 3:7) these words are cited as applying to Christ. It was customary for this people to carry keys around the neck and on the shoulder. "I will give him the keys" means he will be the treasurer, the overseer of provisions and money, who will receive and disburse and without whose authority no one will receive or expend anything. This is what it means to close and to open.

23. *I will fasten him like a peg.* After you, Shebna, have been thrown away, I will establish him and make his authority secure. The peg signifies the administration of the house. For thus we, too, call our house "the four pegs." [5] A fence signifies possession of the field.

And he will become a throne of honor to his father's house. Solomon said: "A wise son makes a glad father" (Prov. 10:1; cf. 13:1; 15:20). He is the crown and glory of his father. A man wise in public administration is a great gift of God, and he is called a safe peg, or rather a rare gem, and through that one good man many good things come to be. The opposite is also true. He is called a *peg* because all cling to him, all business falls on him.

In a sure place, that is, holding strongly, so that nothing can fall off it. A nail thrust into a ruin is easily moved. He says he will be firm and will uphold those whom he will govern, and he will faithfully rule over them. He will not be a reed shaken by the wind (Matt. 11:7), that is, he will not be influenced by either fear or favor. It is not enough to be a wise, useful, and honorable prince, if he is not also firm and serious. For there are many assaults on him who desires to govern well. *A throne of honor,* that is, he will have a glorious throne. A good man is pleasing to God and useful in the state. Naaman the Syrian, of whom we read in 2 Kings 5:1, is an example. He was the source of more safety than the king of

[5] The original has *palus,* but we have followed the suggestion of the Weimar editor and read *palos.*

Syria. This man will have a throne, powerful and effective, which will then produce glory and adornment for the family and the tribe.

24. *They will hang on him the whole glory.* This he says because he has called him a peg and then he shows whom he should govern.

Various kinds of vessels. Offspring, descendants, vessels, mixing bowls, and musical instruments I will hang on him. Solomon said (Prov. 20:12): "The hearing ear and the seeing eye, the Lord has made them both." What should a good man do against rebels? What would an obedient people be without a good magistrate? I will make him, he says, not be idle but govern his children, both those of the flesh and those of honor. He is the father, which is also an honorary name. Both old men and young men. *Vessels,* that is, other officials in various public positions. And he does not haughtily despise those who are less than he, neither the small nor the poor, but, on the contrary, these will come to him for refuge. *Cups:* the skilled craftsmen necessary for the state. *Musical instruments:* Those who are in charge of such things as pertain to adornment and elegance, not to necessity. He says that he will have an obedient people in all the orders and offices, and he himself will faithfully carry out his government. Here, then, let us acknowledge that a good ruler is a gift of God, and let the people be attracted to peace. To those who confess their sins and pray, the Lord will give good rulers; their own willing and choosing will do nothing. The devil is more interested in having foolish rulers and rebellious people; if the opposite obtains, it is evidence of God's blessing.

25. *In that day the peg will give way.* Namely, because of the sins of the people, because of which the prophet threatens also the foregoing disaster.

It will be cut down and fall, that is, it will be split in two. The ruler will perish, he will be led away [6] by the Chaldeans.

[6] The Weimar text has *adducetur,* but *abducetur* would seem to fit the context better.

CHAPTER TWENTY-THREE

1. *The oracle concerning Tyre. Wail, O ships of Tarshish, for Tyre is laid waste.*

Tyre and Sidon are famous in the Scriptures and are outstanding cities. Tyre was twice taken: first by Nebuchadnezzar, and then by Alexander the Great, concerning whom Isaiah is speaking here. Tarshish is the ocean sea. The prophet summons to wailing, as if the devastation had already been accomplished, as is his custom. The "Chittim" are the Macedonians.

2. *They are still,* that is, they are nothing. There is no business there, and there is no noise of workers there. Tyre was an island which Alexander joined to the mainland and made into a peninsula.[1] *They replenished you,* namely, with merchandise.

3. *Seed,* that is, grain, wine, and fruits. Shihor was the mouth of the Nile in Egypt adjacent to Judea. *On many waters,* that is, on the sea.

Merchant of the nations: trade center, market. Here the prophet reproves the greed and pride in good times, which are often followed by many other kinds of vices. Tyre is here called the sea and the strength of the sea; for it was a thoroughly fortified city on the seacoast, and its commerce was on the sea.

4. *I have neither travailed nor given birth.* A city is called woman and mother because she has many children, that is, citizens, and daily increases their number. But Tyre complains that she is without people and bereft of citizens.

Virgins. He is speaking of their youth, not their virginity. Rather, of the hope of producing offspring. That is, "I will no longer be a city, and therefore you, O Sidon, will not be able to be enriched by me. And you and Egypt, who rejoiced with me, will grieve with me."

[1] When Alexander the Great besieged Tyre in 333 B. C., he constructed a mole connecting it with the mainland, a distance of about half a mile.

7. *Is this your city?* Isaiah mocks at the confidence of the people of Tyre, who are proud and contemptuous of the prophets and esteemed the prophets as dregs in comparison with themselves. But, he says, when you have been deprived of kingdom and people, then they will ridicule you and say: "Is this your exultant city? Where is now your pomp?" The cause of Tyre's arrogance was its great age and the fact that it was so strongly fortified and so very rich. Trust in the flesh and pride against God in God's house are the worst.

Whose feet carried her. How contemptuously the prophet speaks of Tyre, which now sails in royal ships and whose citizens are the equal of kings and princes in wealth. This supreme wealth, he says, will be changed into extreme poverty. They will not remain nearby but will go far away to be able to find a home. Africa has inhabitants from Tyre and Sidon, and there is the same language.

Is this your city, which boasted of its origin from days of old? Tyre, a most ancient and fortified city, exposed to capture, here makes her boast against the admonishing prophet and is never penitent. It is, however, the nature of the Word of God to place before us all things beyond our grasp, things impossible and clearly desperate, so that we might cast all things aside and believe in God. Is not this beyond the grasp of nature that so great and so powerful and wealthy a city should be taken? Thus by Scripture we are led to believe things that are absurd, impossible, and contrary to our reason. For this is the work of God to humble the proud and exalt the humbled, to make something great of the least and vice versa. Just so he does here with the wealthy city of Tyre. Let this be an example to our arrogant tyrants!

Whose feet carried her to settle afar, that is, those who once were like the most exalted princes are now rustics and settlers. Therefore the text says:

8. *Who has purposed this against Tyre, which once was crowned? The Lord of hosts has purposed it.* All those things are designed to befall you by God Himself, who earlier had set similar evils in motion against His enemies, who is so powerful that He stretches His hands over the sea and confounds kingdoms. Him you should justly fear.

Crowned, that is, glorious and full of pomp. They thought a destruction of Tyre was impossible, and therefore they did not fear nor repent.[2]

10. *Overflow*[3] *your land like the Nile, O daughter of the sea.* By reason of exceedingly great certainty he mocks at unbelieving Tyre, as if to say, "Sail on, sail on, run over your land, naked and plundered by enemies, just as the river overflows and bears nothing of the bridge or of the land with it."

There is no girth for you anymore. A girth denotes government, as if to say: "You will not have an ordered government but a confused reign." *Anymore.* For He who stretched out His hand, He is the Lord who gave command against Canaan and who did other great things in the Red Sea, who also commanded Joshua to wage war against kings. This God spoke to me against these things.

12. *You will no more exult,* that is, you are no longer to glory.

Oppressed virgin daughter of Sidon, pass over to Chittim. Chittim is the land of Macedonia, to which Alexander will carry you captive.

13. *Behold the land of the Chaldeans,* that is, Tyre was disturbed not only in connection with the Macedonians but also in connection with the Chaldeans. "There, too, you will have no rest."

The Assyrian laid the foundation of the land. The king of Assyria founded the city of Babylon and governed it. The Tigris and Euphrates watered its site, its towers and fortifications were built on the banks of streams and were accessible to ships, and yet it fell into ruin. This will happen also to you unless you repent.

In that day Tyre will be forgotten. The prophet hints at Israel's 70-year captivity, of which Jeremiah speaks clearly (cf. Jer. 29:10). To be forgotten means not that it will not be remembered but that it will always be remembered in a bad sense. They will have no praise.

16. *Remembered.* In the Scriptures remembrance is high praise. To be recalled is to be commended. "This do in remembrance of Me" (1 Cor. 11:24-25) means "to My praise."

[2] The manuscript contains the following marginal comment: "Up to this point I have copied this from George Schmalzing. The rest I have gathered from the Doctor [Luther]"; cf. Introduction, p. ix. Here again we have reversed two paragraphs to conform them to the sequence of the Biblical text.

[3] The Weimar text has *Transit,* but we have followed the Biblical text and read *Transi.*

As in the song, that is, a good and new remembrance will again be observed after the oblivion is past. He calls it the song of a harlot, however, not because a harlot but rather some excellent matron seems to be singing. For all forms of idolatry have the semblance of piety.

Take a harp, that is, get braggarts for yourself and poets as companions to promote your praise.

Make sweet melody, that is, be earnestly concerned about publishing your praise.

17. *At the end of seventy years.* The text says:

"And he will lead her back to her wages." It ought to be like this: *She will return to her harlotry for hire.* He calls idolatry and zeal for ungodliness a harlot's hire.

18. *Supply abundant food.* He is describing the true nature of the food and clothing of wealthy Tyre. The people of Tyre are to have food to the point of satiety and a constant supply of clothing. Now that the kingdom of Christ has come, they have made efforts to allocate and distribute all their goods for the use of the poor. They allow themselves not huge outlays and sumptuous meals but moderate ones in keeping with the needs of the body, and they distribute the rest to the poor. Would that the bishops and popes of our time would desist from their display and luxury and not try to be like kings, as when abbots of monks have been made barons.[4] In this way the whole kingdom of Christ will perish because of their arrogance, as they neglect the duties of their office and the works of love and withhold their goods from the use of the poor. But this is a disease common to all the ungodly, who are unworthy to come to the aid of the needs of the poor with their goods, because a good work above all requires the initiative and dignity of a person. For not all are worthy to share with the poor; meanwhile they abuse their gifts in a spiritual and a physical way. The godly indeed, satisfied with food and clothing and their lot, bless God and come to the aid of the other brethren. Note the example in the early church, and here the prophet says that they eat to satiety and are clothed "even to old age." In Hebrew old age is that which endures a long time, long-lasting. They partook of the common food and wore ordinary clothing and did not indulge to excess as our ungodly bishops do.

[4] The involvement of the medieval monasteries in the feudal system compelled many abbots to assume baronial authority and sometimes even to wage war.

CHAPTER TWENTY-FOUR

In the following chapters he describes the devastation of the land of Judea and of the synagog that does not accept the Gospel. Until now he digressed from there and reproved alien cities. Now he returns to his own people, whose prophet he was and to whom he is prophesying. This passage speaks of the devastation which, around the time of the Tyre which has become subject to the reign of Christ, threatens many regions that have not been converted. Thus the devastation was threatening them, just as disaster comes upon the ungodly everywhere when the Word has gone out. So also here devastation has come upon the land of Judea and upon the synagog. This might be the summary of the four following chapters.

1. *The Lord will lay waste,* that is, He will destroy it,[1] He will demolish its hedges. Just as a vineyard entirely stripped of posts and hedges lies open to all wild beasts for destruction, so he speaks of it as denuded[2] of hedges, that is, of apostles and teachers. It will be deprived of good counselors and excellent men, and He will reduce it to total destruction.

Its surface. Every tower and building is called the surface of the land. Princes, magnates, aristocrats, and whatever has an appearance in the world is called the surface. And so God will humiliate this surface and twist it and distort its whole aspect and appearance.

2. *And it shall be, as with the people, so with the priest, etc.* It is as if he were saying: "While the land of Judea stands, it is the best state, it has the best government and the best men. There there will be the greatest distinction of persons, because the priest is other than the people, and the master is other than the slave. But with the destruction of the land everything will perish without order. There will be no distinction of persons, all will be equally despoiled and scattered, and they will perish. This will take place in such a way

[1] The Weimar text has *iam,* but we have read *eam.*

[2] The Weimar text has *nudatum,* but we have read *nudatam.*

that you will see all the good things of the cities perish in disharmony and confusion."

3. *The earth shall be utterly laid waste and utterly despoiled.* Nothing will be safe in the land. It will be exposed to all for damage.

For the Lord has spoken this Word. The historians write that Jerusalem was captured by a special divine command of God.[3] So the prophet here says that this will take place because the Lord has spoken this Word. For if a united Jerusalem had set itself against the Romans, it could not have been laid waste. Thus also Titus was amazed that he had taken so great a city, so well fortified, and he ascribed it not to his own army but to the divine will.

4. *The earth mourns and withers, the world languishes.* These are Hebrew modes of speech, to say that the earth mourns and the vineyard mourns when there is nothing fertile and pleasant in them. In German: It is miserable and deplorable, just as the best and pleasant fields are called gay and pretty. *Falling off,* that is, pining away, withering. The leaves are said to fall off when the sap and native fluid in the tree ceases, when there is no hope of sprouting again. *Languishing,* that is, diseased; when its strength is removed, it has no reserve left to be rekindled. It is completely worn out, so that it cannot recuperate. As we say of something quite hopeless, it is altogether spoiled.

Height, that is, whatever is high, splendid, and outstanding in this people, its priesthood and royalty, this is entirely sapped of strength and destroyed, and a few paupers have remained in Jerusalem who have accepted the Gospel. Thus it will be for the people of Jerusalem in the last destruction. All things will be made to languish.

5. *The earth lies polluted.* To profane is to play the hypocrite, because they have profaned the earth by their ungodly hypocrisy and impiety. For the earth cannot be more polluted than by hypocrisy and profanation, counterfeit justice and hypocritical holiness, and therefore long hardened hypocrites submit to no correction but act insolently toward all.

Under its inhabitants, that is, the earth groans under the weight

[3] Cf. Josephus, *The Jewish War,* VI, 9.

of these hypocrites, because burning[4] with an evil zeal they consigned God's apostles to death.

For they have transgressed the laws, violated the statutes, etc. All hypocrites refuse to obey the law and words of God, as the Garden Brothers do.[5] The fanatics and ungodly instigators of sects transgress the law of God and change it in the interest of their own wanton desire and luxury. This is what our hypocrites are doing.

Broken the ancient (or everlasting) covenant, that is, they have invalidated God's promises concerning Christ in that they did not accept them by faith. Thus you see here that the greatest sins threaten the teachers and rulers, not the common people, who do not break God's commands and promises, but the leaders are addicted to this sin. Just so at this time we see the pope addicted to this sin, and we dare in no wise agree with him, though otherwise we might wish to approve his gross sins, if only he would not attack the Word.

6. *Therefore a curse devours the earth, and its inhabitants suffer for their guilt.* This is the reason why this land will be so wretchedly laid waste, alluding to Deut. 28:15 ff., concerning the curse upon the disobedient. *Devours,* that is, destroys it utterly.

"And its inhabitants are irreconcilable," that is, they transgress and remain in guilt and are damnable and irreconcilable. Just so the pope with all his righteousness does nothing more than transgress and remain in his guilt.

Few men are left, that is, the apostles and godly believers. These alone have been preserved by God from this devastation.

7. *The wine mourns.* The devastation and desolation of all animate and inanimate creatures follows upon the destruction of men.

All the merry-hearted reapers, who otherwise are joyful, will be sad.

8. *The mirth is stilled,* that is, bridegroom and bride and all the happy people become sad.

9. *No more do they drink wine with singing,* that is, the joyful do not drink together in the taverns.

Strong drink is bitter to those who drink it, not that the wine itself

[4] The Weimar text has *urens,* but *urentes* would seem to fit the context better.

[5] A reference to the Anabaptists, whom Luther calls "Garden Brothers" elsewhere.

is bitter, but because of sadness and grief it does not taste sweet to them, however sweet it was.

10. *The city of chaos is broken down.* Chaos denotes lack of cultivation, ravage, and ruin. Just so it is with Jerusalem today. Scarcely traces of it are found.

Shut up. This is the usual condition of ruined cities. They are altogether bereft of use by men, and there are no inhabitants there.

11. *There is an outcry,* that is, lamentation, in the streets *for lack of wine.* There is the lamentation of those who complain in public, as if to say, "O God, how well off we were formerly in this street and in this house!"

The gladness of the earth is banished, that is, all things are mixed up and have no distinctive features, just as it is now in Rome.

Desolation is left, that is, there is nothing left in the entire city but desolation.

The gates are battered into ruins, that is, the meeting places of the senate and the larger buildings of the courts are referred to. That is to say, there is no court to dispense justice.

13. *For thus it shall be in the midst.* Following prophetic custom, he compares the devastation of the earth to a vineyard whose grape gatherers are enemies, whose grapes and fruits are the best men of the city, as if to say: "The city is so thoroughly laid waste that hardly a few remnants remain, or as if the enemies out of oversight had unwillingly left these items behind."

As when a few olive trees, that is, as in the gleaning and beating after the grape harvest is over.

14. *They,* that is, the ones remaining, *will lift up their voices.* This text clearly speaks of the apostles proclaiming the Gospel and openly praising the mercy of Christ. *They will neigh,* that is, boast of the majesty and victory of the Lord; they will glory over Christ's victory, whereby He conquered Satan, the flesh, and the world. St. Paul very beautifully depicts this exultation and triumph when he writes in Col. 2:13 ff. So the prophet writes: *over the majesty of the Lord,* and he describes Christ's total power and especially His resurrection, whereby He has justified us and in which all the godly must trust above all.

They will neigh in the sea. This signifies the far-reaching course of the Gospel which was set forth by Christ and the apostles, especially around the seas and their shores, as may be read in the Gospels and the Acts.

15. *Therefore in the valleys they will give glory to the Lord, and because of this they will call upon the name of the Lord in the islands of the sea.* It is as if he were saying: "The word of the apostles will not be empty, but by it the name of the Lord will be glorified, not only on the mountains but also in the valleys and in the lowest places, and by men everywhere His name will be glorified," that is, the "voice" of the apostles "has gone out to all the earth" (Rom. 10:18) to the glory of the Lord.

16. *From the ends of the earth songs of praise,* that is, glory and song. *The glory of the Righteous One,* of the Lord our God. The prophet imagines himself to be a participant in the devastation of Judea and saying: "Hitherto the praise of God was sung only in temples and other places and by few people. Now, however, it is published in all parts of the earth." Therefore he speaks of the pleasantness and the glory of the righteous Lord, namely, Christ, which we have heard everywhere *from the ends of the earth.* Even so after Christ's death all things done by Christ are very fully rehearsed, that is, the most joyful righteousness of Christ, the Righteous One, will be taught, whereby He justified and sanctified all His righteous ones.

But I said My leanness to me, that is, meagerness. The prophet laments that he is impoverished by the fall of the Jews, who have not accepted this loveliness of the Gospel; while the Gentiles run to it from all directions, the hardened Jews do not savor it. He shows that this evil torments him and his body, so that he repeats these words, *I pine away, I pine away.* "O how emaciated I have become for your sakes because of the damage that has been done! Paul, too, has this intense concern, as expressed in Rom. 9:2 and 10:1. Whence comes this leanness to me?

The treacherous deal treacherously. Those are the liars and despisers who rely on their own ungodliness to such an extent that they are not softened by any admonitions, even though they do not have any just cause. Our papists are like that now.

And despise with the contempt of the despisers, that is, they spurn the Word of truth so much that they hold it beneath any contempt.

17. *Terror, and the pit, etc.,* that is, those despisers will be given up to a reprobate mind (Rom. 1:28), they will fall into various dangers of doctrine and disaster, so that the blind will lead the blind into a pit,[6] and their ungodly doctrines accomplish nothing else than that they are terrified and remain in their errors and snares, forever captive and in subjection. These things follow the despisers of the Word.

18. *He who flees at the sound of terror,* that is, if someone escapes one snare, he will fall into the pit; if he has escaped the pit, he will fall into the raging streams, that is, the clear punishment of God coming from heaven and from the sky like a flood. These are things which the punishment of God's total wrath brings on, and those who have escaped some drops of punishments will fall into the deluge of divine wrath and rage.

The foundations of the earth. The nobles and princes, who are the foundations of the earth and leaders of the people; they themselves stray about on uncertain standards and doctrines and are wavering foundations, retreating from here and from there. As it happened to the Jews, so it will also happen to our papists, God willing, because they cannot sustain themselves by their ephemeral jokes unless protected by the secular arm.

19. *Utterly broken.* It is the prophet's nature to grieve over the punishment of the ungodly as much as he rejoices over the proclamation of the Gospel.

Broken. It will be torn apart like the branches of a tree.

20. *It will be stirred up mightily,* that is, it will be constantly in turmoil, as we see in the synagog of the Jews. Because the Jews devised altogether invalid and futile counsels, nothing will help them, although they have sought many remedies. Not only will their counsels come to naught, but these plans will be conceived also to their own destruction. They will make a bad thing worse. First he says the earth is shaken; second, it is vexed by their counsels; third, by a breakdown; fourth, by a swaying and trembling, just as drunks usually stagger and are carried along. It will stagger and fall down, and they will have no happiness, strength, counsel, or help, but nothing except fear remains for them. In the manner of Cain they will be fugitives and vagabonds, like the gypsies and Jews in our time.

6 Although the Weimar editor identifies this as a proverb, it seems to have come from Matt. 15:14.

It sways like a hut. As the shepherds' huts and night shelters are moved from day to day.

Its transgression lies heavy upon it. He gives the reason why that land wanders so much, namely, because the promises and covenants of God have been violated. This transgression is a burden and a hardening for them, so that they are compelled to fall, as Christ says (Luke 19:44): "You did not know the time of your visitation."

21. *On that day the Lord will punish.* He is here speaking of the kingdom of the Jewish people, which had been lifted up even to heaven and had the most excellent princes, who did everything in the Lord's name, and they boasted that it was God who did everything they accomplished. For that reason they were called princes of this star of heaven and heavenly princes and people of heaven, because they gloried in the Word of God. He ridicules these people, who with unbelievable pride and pretense gloried in themselves, listening to no prophet, at all events relying on their own outward boasting and sham, and refused to be either rebuked or accused by them.

Above the host of heaven. Some read "exalted," [7] that is, above the Jewish people, who were proud of the title "host of heaven," a title no people ever had.

In heaven with the splendor of God.

And the kings of Rama, that is, of Judea.

22. *They will be gathered together.* When they have sinned for a long time and filled up the measure of their fathers and slain all the prophets and apostles and Christ, then God will settle their account all at once, as Christ threatens them in the Gospel.

In a gathering of one bundle, of one judgment and condemnation. The dead as well as the living will be prepared, and the living will be shut up in prisons; and thus the Lord will punish all the past and present sins of the fathers and the children.

After many days, of the destruction of Jerusalem.

23. *The sun will be ashamed.* The ruined and still living Jews will not see the brightness of the sun and the moon when Christ, the Lord of hosts, will reign spiritually on the mountain in full view.

[7] That is, they read *miliciam celsi* rather than *miliciam celi.*

His elders, his apostles and bishops. Even though they have the outward brightness of the sun like other living beings, yet since they have much sadness because of their sinful transgression and the threatening punishment, even the sun and the moon will not seem to shine for them, because they have an empty heart. For all things are as we are in spirit; so the sun, moon, bells, drums, and songs sound and shine sad to the sad, but are joyful to the happy and rejoicing. The sad and gloomy at heart see and hear nothing but sad and gloomy things, as we learn by experience. As a result, those who have hitherto wickedly boasted of the name of the Lord are now unable genuinely to enjoy all creatures, however delightful. Just so our papists boastfully claim the name of church for themselves but cannot honestly use its smallest benefit. God will punish also those ungodly crowds of papists with such a disaster that they will not be able to boast of themselves in any way. This prophecy expresses the disastrous destruction of the Jews.

CHAPTER TWENTY-FIVE

1. *O Lord, Thou art my God; I will exalt Thee, I will praise Thy name.*

THIS whole chapter belongs to the preceding, because it deals in like manner with the devastation of Judea. However, it starts out with praise and exaltation of God, in that the prophet rejoices in the Jews' hardening and ungodliness. So the godly may deservedly rejoice over the destruction of the ungodly, just as we would rejoice over a devastation of Rome, and do it piously. Therefore he says here: *O Lord, Thou art my God.* God be praised. *I will exalt Thee,* that is, I will magnify and proclaim Thee.

Wonderful things, namely because of the apostles and the Word. What wonderful things? He answers:

Plans formed of old, "plans which Thou didst form, faithfully and surely, because Thou didst promise these things to Abraham and his descendants. These promises are faithful and true, that is, they are fulfilled and brought to completion." It is as if he were saying: "Thou hast paid up in full, because there is nothing untrue, but Thou hast most generously fulfilled all promises." This is the prophet's joy with regard to the promises carried out and fulfilled by the mercy of God. So we, too, are joyful in the treasure of the Gospel.

2. *For thou hast made the city a heap,* that is, a pile.

The fortified city, that is, armed. Thus, in the second place, he rejoices over the boastful glory of those who put their trust in the fortified city, boasting that Jerusalem was the strong city of God and therefore impregnable.

The palace of aliens, as if to say: "Hitherto Jerusalem was fortified with palaces, but those have been razed, so that it is not a city, for the very citizens of Jerusalem are false and outsiders, and none are genuine citizens."

It will never be rebuilt. In its last destruction Jerusalem will be so thoroughly laid waste that it is never ever to be rebuilt. This is a great text against the Jews.

3. *Will glorify,* that is to say: "From having lost one city, Thou wilt gain a great and strong people, namely, the Gentiles. Until now Thou hast had a small people in a city, but now Thou wilt have a large and numerous nation of Gentiles."

Strong people, cities of ruthless nations, that is, "They will bring sacrifices to Thee in all places. Not only in temples but everywhere they will worship Thee."

4. *For Thou hast become a stronghold to the poor.* This people is large in size; but as for their spirit, they are a poor, afflicted people.

A stronghold to the needy in his distress. Here he describes the kingdom of Christ, which receives the poor, the needy, the afflicted, the weak, and the weary. Of Christ, their King, this is said. When He says that He has been sent to preach the Good News to them, He is exalted (Luke 4:18). To them He says (Matt. 11:28): "Come to Me." To them He is gentle and merciful, but to kings and to the wise He is a terror.

A shelter from the storm. Protection and trust. To Him alone we must flee for refuge. Hurricane, wind storm, and rain storm designate persecuting tyrants. In this storm we shall flee to Christ for refuge and for shade against the burning heat of the sun.

The blast of the ruthless is like a storm against a wall. This is a simile. It is as if he were saying: "Thou art the refuge in a time when the rage and blast of the tyrants makes its assault, as when a storm is borne in upon a wall." Thus in every calamity that befalls us he assures us that the restoration will follow promptly. For we [1] are hardly a hedge and a shaky wall that could set itself against a great swirl of waters and winds. So also we are nothing against the tyrants, we are extremely helpless against their power; but then it follows that we may be comforted in this refuge, Christ, our Asylum.

5. *Like heat in a dry place.* Thou wilt subdue the noise of the aliens like the fiery heat in the desert under a burning cloud. He wants to say: "Thou wilt deliver Thine own from the tyrants as heat does in the desert without rain, drying up all the seeds of the earth."

The shade of a cloud. Mildew and honey dew, which destroys everything, as if to say: "He will withdraw the rain from them and dry them up with heat and give them an altogether poisonous shade and fog."

[1] The Weimar text has *Non,* but we have read *Nos.*

"And Thou wilt cause the branch of the tyrants to waste away." This means: "Thou alone art the helper of Thine own, so that they overcome all tyrants purely by patience since Thou, O Lord, dost overcome and destroy them. As that heat and destructive cloud creates barrenness, so Thou dost destroy them." So the Lord confounds all kingdoms. We do not need swords and weapons but patience. They will die among themselves. "Thy people will endure in bloom, but they will be dried up like seeds." Their song is: It wastes away, it is dried up. Just so we see that all the greatest kingdoms have perished, from whom He first removed the rain, that is, those whose wise men and kings He took away; then they collapsed by themselves. We see this happening to the fields when the cloud is gone. Thus God will suppress our tyrants if He withdraws the cloud from them. In other words: "I will deprive them of wise men, so that they will be finished one after another." As I heard at Erfurt, there would be no lack of money but of men.[2] Therefore by this picture the prophet most aptly describes the ruin of the ungodly. For just as in the springtime, when the grainlands are sprouting beautifully and progressing most hopefully and then come heat, drought, and harmful clouds, or mildew, so it will be for the tyrants who are flourishing supremely and moving along in their best effort. They will perish on the spot, and so will our tyrants, Ferdinand, the emperor, etc.[3] However much they may thrive at present, they will fall on the spot. The springtime is there now, but the drought will get them. They will not succeed in what they are scheming in their councils, but rather they themselves will become good for nothing when it pleases God.

6. *The Lord of hosts will make a feast.* Here the prophet is speaking of the abundance of the Gospel. This is Martin Luther's thought: In that time when the Gospel will be preached, God will prepare *a feast of fat things;* that is, Jerusalem, fat with great and many people, will be laid waste, and God will prepare this feast, namely, of the rich and powerful Jews. *For all peoples,* for the Romans and others. *A feast of lees,* not of grapes. He says that it will be a fat

[2] Luther seems to be referring to his student days at Erfurt, beginning in 1501.

[3] Ferdinand (1503—1564), who became emperor in 1558, was at this time king of Bohemia and of Hungary; the emperor was his brother, Charles V (1500—1558).

feast. All the fat animals will be devoured, and all the wine must be drawn out down to the lees. This means that this people of Judea is to be altogether exhausted and destroyed.

A feast of fat things full of marrow. He repeats what he has already said above. The inner and choicest part of the barley is called marrow; it is also called fat. He has fed them with the fat of the grain. Thus among this people He has oppressed princes, kings, and nobles, not just the common people.

Wine on the lees well refined for "grapes squeezed out." This means that everything is devoured and drained to the last dregs and remnants. Thus by this comparison he most aptly pictures the total reduction of Judea.

7. *And He will destroy on this mountain the covering that is cast over all the peoples, the veil that is spread over all nations.* He wants to say: "This will be the fruit of the Gospel, that He will remove from us every appearance of chains. And we rise with Christ. 'We have passed out of death into life'" (1 John 3:14). But he speaks of death and the things that pertain to death figuratively.

The appearance of coverings, which means that all nations are wrapped up in death. From this appearance of death and from death itself and from all evils we are set free by faith in the Word and through the Spirit. "The appearance of the covering" refers to death and all its evils. However, he calls it "the appearance of the covering" and shows that its appearance and bonds have easily been made subject to Christ.

8. *He will swallow up death forever.* He follows Hosea's word (Hos. 13:14): "O Death, I will be your plagues. O Sheol, I will be your destruction." For He says that He will soon extinguish death, but that he will always swallow it up little by little, just as our old man day by day ought to swallow up death through the Spirit. So also Christ destroys death. As a plague consumes the body little by little, so Christ is the pestilence of our death and of our old Adam.

And the Lord God will wipe away tears from all faces, that is, from all faces, miseries, disasters, griefs, and tears Christ frees us and consoles us in our spirit.

And the reproach of His people He will take away. Since the godly are nothing but the cast-offs and offscourings and the reproach of the whole world who are rejected by all, so that nothing remains for them but sufferings without and within inflicted by the devil, O that these consolations of Christ may by all means find a place in us, so that He can console us in our wretchedness and affliction and we may daily come to a better knowledge of Him. Our King, Christ, who has such an afflicted people, is such that He always comforts them.

9. *It will be said on that day: Lo, this is our God.* This is the preaching concerning Christ, and he is describing the worship of the New Testament, because the prophets always distinguish between the worship of the New Testament and that of the Old Testament. The worship of the New Testament is to believe, to trust, to hope in God's mercy. No one has this kind of faith and hope except those who have been thoroughly afflicted both inwardly and outwardly. The prophet says not only that He will save us, but he adds:

Let us be glad and rejoice, that is, let us give thanks to God in various forms of praise even in all afflictions, for if we have been set free from one evil, we arrive at another one. This is the exercise of the godly and the worship of the New Testament.

10. *The hand,* that is, the strength of the Lord. *Will rest,* that is, it is in the church, although it may not be openly apparent. His power is there, because He frees us from all evils.

Moab shall be trodden down. Moab denotes the ungodly synagog that is to be laid waste, a synagog that is unbelieving in the time of the Gospel. It will be trodden down like a dung-pit and like chaff on the ground, because that synagog will be utterly worthless; we see this by experience among the Jews, who have no kingdom and neither priesthood nor government. This is a most apt illustration. John also used it to depict devastation most particularly and to show the people to be worthless (Matt. 3:12), as straw is a mere nothing for the dung-pit.

11. *And He will spread out His hands in the midst of it,* namely, of Moab and the ungodly synagog. That is, Christ will spread out His hand and His power over the Jewish exiles *as a swimmer spreads his hands out.*

The Lord will lay low his pride together with the artifices of his hands. That is, wherever the Jews try to escape, Christ will be there and will pursue them.

[W, XXXI-2, 140]

12. *The high fortifications.* No matter how well fortified Jerusalem is, it will be made equal to the dust of the earth, and not one stone will remain on another (Matt. 24:2). These two chapters have in a figurative way described the devastation of the ungodly synagog. But the prophet intersperses them with references to the kingdom of Christ, who does not forsake His own afflicted but at length frees those who by faith have been well exercised in these things.

CHAPTER TWENTY-SIX

1. *In that day this song will be sung in the land of Judah.*

THIS is the song:

We have a strong city. We have a firm and powerful city. This is the praise and preaching of the church, against which the gates of hell shall not prevail (Matt. 16:18), because the city is strong in government and priesthood.

He sets up salvation as walls and bulwarks. Wall and dungeon are well guarded, not with wood and iron, but with salvation and victory and triumph. These are the fortifications of this new city, that is, the church, which is unconquered, whose salvation is Christ, its Fortification.

2. *Open the gates, that the righteous nation may enter in.* This is not a city that is accessible to the few but one that is open to all who enter and is full of people. Thus all should have access to the church.

The righteous nation which preserves faithful things. This nation is righteous in that it preserves faithful things, that is, the promises of God. The righteous, by faith indeed, these are the inhabitants of this city. Thus there will be sung in that city what the city is, what kind of people it has, who is its governor, etc.

3. *Upholding counsel.* Thou art upholding Thy plan, which Thou didst promise of old. This plan is called a counsel in Scripture, because God established it and promised it to the fathers. He does not invalidate those promises, and therefore he says: "Thou dost uphold counsel."

Thou shalt keep perfect peace. We have the best fortified city and holy citizens, not rebellious and restless but kindly, good, and harmonious. Therefore we shall have peace everywhere.

Because he trusts in Thee. This is the origin of peace, namely, hope and faith, as Paul says in Rom. 5:1: "Since we are justified by faith, we have peace with God," that is, we shall be harmonious, of one mind. That which you perform does not happen to those who seek peace in various things. What we have, namely, Christ and His grace, is not an ordinary good. No one has more than the other, and therefore there cannot be discord, but peace, because in the Lord we are all equal in the likeness of hope and confidence, but not of customs, as some have thought.[1]

4. *Trust in the Lord forever.* If you love peace and wish to have a quiet heart, *trust in the Lord,* because there is no other way to genuine peace than to trust in the Lord, to hear the Word from which hope and faith arise. *Forever:* Do not withdraw, but keep trusting always in all afflictions and trials. If He wished me to be forever poor and hungry, I would not wish to abandon faith.

The Lord God is an everlasting rock. Hope should be everlasting, because the foundation is everlasting, because our God does not ever get weary of helping, and so we should also not cease hoping. But this is true preaching, which disagrees a great deal with our preaching.

5. *For He has brought low the inhabitants of the height,* namely those who are confident, who live on the heights, just as Judea is situated on a height. These He brings low, that is, He casts them down to the ground and the dust. As he had said above in the prophecy concerning Moab and its destruction, so he says it here in the song. The Christian is daily attacked by Satan, and therefore he must keep on trusting forever. Since the battle and struggle to keep the faith is very great, Satan is so wicked that he plots how to sap the strength of him who stands in the Word by making him tired. Satan devises this plan in order to weary those who endure in the Word. So Cyprian describes his wickedness in that he did not want some martyrs, who were most eager to die, to be killed before he had wearied them for a long time.[2] Therefore we must keep on trusting, not for one hour, but always, from the morning watch even to the night. Because the Lord is *an everlasting rock,* that is, greater

[1] For example, the Confutation of the Augsburg Confession, VII, 4, asserted: "They are praised also in that they do not regard variety of rites as separating unity of faith, if they speak of special rites. . . . But if they extend this part of the Confession to universal Church rites, this also must be utterly rejected, and we must say with St. Paul: 'We have no such custom,' 1 Cor. 11:16." M. Reu (ed.), *The Augsburg Confession* (Chicago, 1930), II, 353—354.

[2] Luther may be thinking of such a passage as Pseudo-Cyprian, *De duplici martyrio,* 30—35, *Patrologia, Series Latina,* IV, 979—982.

than the whole world, for that reason Satan attacks us. *He has brought low the inhabitants of the height.* These things combat the presumption of those who presume upon their own resources, like the superbly situated city that was brought low nevertheless. No one is so fortified and so safe that he cannot fall, and therefore we dare not trust in ourselves. But, on the contrary, even the weak must trust in the Lord.

6. *The foot will trample it.* This is a description of the destruction of Jerusalem, as if to say: "That city, together with its walls and impregnable structures, will be so thoroughly leveled that it will lie under the feet and steps of the poor. Cripples will be able to walk over it."

7. *The way of the righteous is level.* He erects another building in place of the former city that was razed. *Of the righteous,* that is, of the church, which marches along evenly everywhere.

Thou wilt make smooth the path of the righteous. Your paths move in a straight line. To make smooth means to move straight ahead, for there will be an easy way and a level road for the godly without offense and scandal; it will be smoothed and preserved by the Lord, lest they withdraw from the Word and deviate toward the ungodly teaching of the heretics. All these are promises concerning the preservation of the doctrine and Word of Christ on earth. These things result: they have an even peace, an unencumbered life, and they do not proceed differently with works and merits. Then they are safe, because the Lord will guide them in this way and rule of life, as Paul says in Gal. 6:16.

8. *In the path of Thy judgments we wait for Thee.* It is as if he were saying: "To remain on the true way and path is a course nothing short of a constant exercise in the Word, because once the Word has ceased, sects and schisms soon arise." Therefore we must diligently and from the heart desire God's *memorial name.* But when we habitually and daily disdain the Word, as the Corinthians did, Satan soon leads us astray. Therefore he says here: *We wait for Thee,* "we abide in Thy Word, not looking to another but listening to faithful shepherds, we walk in faith, we wait for Thee, though we do not see Thee." The prophet goes more fully into this thought in what follows.

Thy memorial name is the desire of our soul. This desire of the soul is not directed to works and other laws, but it is a spiritual and inner desire *to Thy memorial name.* This is the level and right way, not in the direction of our name and our memorial. This is the name of the Lord, that Christ died and rose again for our redemption and justification. "He who did not spare His own Son" (Rom. 8:32). This is the sweet name and our way. In this memorial of Christ we walk by faith as if on the way with the desires of our soul. The papists, the work-righteous, and the hypocrites lay obstacles in this way by means of their traditions, drawing us away from Christ to our own name and thus on another way.

9. *My soul yearns for Thee in the night, my spirit within me seeks Thee in the watches of the morning.* The thought is the same. God, my God, I watch for Thee from the dawn. This describes how the soul is constantly and daily on the alert, as also Paul exhorts in Colossians that we should diligently consider and exercise ourselves in the Word of God by means of songs, hymns, and psalms (Col. 3:16).

In the morning, that is, first, or before all, thus: "Seek first the kingdom of God" (Matt. 6:33). Or, "early" in the sense in the morning hours, which is always the most appropriate time for hearing the Word. So also *in the night.* Here the morning hours are indicated, as if to say that we must take earnest care to hear the Word early every day, although all men must consider it.

And with the desire of the soul, that is, with all squeamishness put aside. Even in the greatest abundance of the Word we need to be watchful and not moved by squeamishness, as is now the case with nearly everybody, so that the abundant preaching of the Gospel produces an aversion. They are hardly petty wiseacres, but they all pass judgment and say: "Now we know just as much about Christ as any doctor." They look for nothing else but to say much about holy things [3] elegantly but frivolously, nevertheless. The Holy Scriptures do not want such people, but rather such as are fervent and full of burning desire. The Scriptures do not want people given to tiresome speech and talk, people who prate about many things but teach nothing, who firmly make up their mind about something and produce an effect, as Erasmus does in all commentaries.[4]

[3] We have followed the suggestion of the Weimar editor and inserted the word *sacris.*

[4] This was Luther's consistent criticism of Erasmus; see, for example, *Luther's Works,* 30, p. 248.

In my spirit I have dawned, that is, I have come in the morning. I have "earlied" myself to Thee. With thirst and joy of heart I have come to Thee.

When Thy judgments are in the earth, etc. We are exhorted to preach the Word, because the Word of God will not go out and return empty (Is. 55:11). So it is here. When Thy Word has been in the earth, then the inhabitants will learn righteousness. Then by the gleam of the Gospel they learn true righteousness, because they learn hypocrisy and ungodliness when the Gospel is lacking. For since such fruit of the Word is to learn righteousness from it, therefore we must earnestly see to it that the Word is heard everywhere for the progress of righteousness and for a warning against presumptuousness and self-glorification. So this has hitherto been our experience: Since the Word was lacking, we fell into every ungodliness and hit upon different ways. There was no instruction in sure righteousness, and therefore we must with extreme diligence watch for that Word by which we get so great a treasure. Therefore Paul admonishes Timothy (2 Tim. 4:2): "Be urgent in season and out of season." This advice must be given to those who at any time become delinquent, as also the prophets complain (Jer. 20:8): "The Word of the Lord has become for me a reproach and derision all day long." So it seems and happens to our preachers that by their earnest preaching they apparently accomplish nothing in the people. This text comforts those preachers and assures them that they are not preaching into a void, even though barely two were listening to it.

10. *Though we show favor to the wicked, etc.* You see that all the saints and prophets complain about the ingratitude shown to the Word. This is not only our experience. For the enemies say: You see here how much carnal license has sprung from your Word, so that no life is more vicious.[5] I reply that this is not the fault of the Gospel.

Favor is shown to the wicked. Grace, mercy, and the Word are offered to the ungodly, God gives His own Word, God performs His own service; but the ungodly despise it and do not want to learn righteousness. Some persecute, some despise, but few profit.

In the land of uprightness he deals perversely, that is, the ungodly are in the land and on the way of uprightness, where uprightness,

[5] This was a frequent theme of anti-Reformation polemics; see, for example, *Luther's Works,* 23, pp. 407—408.

sincerity, and good behavior are learned through the Word, and yet they have no taste for it. The church is the land of uprightness, of good and true behavior, the daughter of the true Word. In this church there are also many ungodly people. It is not surprising if the church in our time has many ungodly people. For the church must needs be attacked from without by tyrants and from within by false brethren, sects, heresies, and schisms. Let no one hope for a church that is without ungodly people, openly or under cover. Therefore the body of the church and the Word are unfairly accused of harboring ungodly people. By no means. For the human body is not blamed if it defecates, spits, and vomits, since these are its acts of purification. The body is not therefore unsound though it has festering eyes and a scabby skin, because these are purged out with the excrement. Even so the ungodly heretics are not members of the church, but refuse. Therefore the ungodly papists are unjustly slandering our church. They are stirring up the dirt.

And does not see the majesty of the Lord, that is, His loftiness and victory. What belongs to the exalted Lord, namely all the gifts of the Spirit, the ungodly do not see. Although they are in the church, the ungodly are not to see the internal gifts of the Spirit. When meanwhile they look at the weakness of faith, of morals, and of affections, when they see others in the church slipping, they are to wallow in the dirt and say: "You see that in their church there is no one honorable; they are carnal, they are licentious, etc." With these things they slander the church. This is all they see, but they are not to see the majesty of the Lord and the sublime gifts of the church. They are not to see Christ's head but look at His rear. They are not worthy to see and to praise a single good feature of the church, but to find fault with everything in the church of God. They have no eye for the great things of the Lord, for the fact that our consciences have been set free from all the elements of the world, from the pope, from purgatory, from poltergeists. These things the ungodly do not notice, but they must see only the excrement of the church. They do not see the majesty of the Lord, only our disgrace.

11. *O Lord, Thy hand is lifted up, but they see it not.* O Lord, thy hand is always over us to protect us even in the greatest possible dangers. We are rich, though we are poor; we make others rich, though we are spiritually poor. These things the ungodly do not see, since they look at us according to the outward appearance.

Let them see and be ashamed, when it will be revealed. They see that the church endures in the midst of disaster because the hand of the Lord is over it when they see its perseverance.

Let them see Thy zeal for Thy people, and be ashamed. They have a zeal above and against God's people, as the Jews are confounded and provoked to become a foolish people and nation, according to Deut. 28:33 ff. The adversaries are provoked because another people has been accepted. The indignant ones will themselves perish.

The fire for Thy adversaries, by which Thou art wont to destroy them. With it Thou wilt devour also them. This denotes destruction. As fire reduces everything to ashes, so Thou wilt utterly devour them, as we see in the Jews today with their scepter and book removed, of which also Moses says (Deut. 32:22): "It devours the earth and its increase," and they will be consumed by the last fire. This will be the fate of our tyrants, who will be put to shame by the zeal for the people. They will go to the devil, and we shall remain.

12. *O Lord, Thou wilt give peace.* This is the comfort of the godly against the insults of the adversaries. We have peace within, nevertheless.

Thou hast wrought for us all our works. This is our solid boast, because all works of the church in word and act are not [6] its own, but those of God Himself. Therefore they will endure, because the church trusts in God and not in itself, let the devil assail it as he will. For all the gifts of the Spirit — the Word, faith, love, power, righteousness — this wealth is not the church's own; it is divine and of God Himself. Which of the ungodly will fight against them? You see, these are not our works, but God's.

13. *O Lord our God, other lords beside Thee have ruled over us,* that is, in the eyes of the world tyrants oppress us completely, but they only kill us outwardly according to the body.

But Thy name alone we acknowledge. "Although outwardly tyrants and papists rule over us, we nevertheless acknowledge Thy name. Let Caesar subjugate us. Thou, O Lord, wilt be our savior and protector, and we shall not forget Thee. This is the way it looks in the church, which is surely persecuted outwardly; yet in Thee our

[6] We have followed the suggestion of the Weimar editor and added the word *non* here.

remembrance of Thee always flourishes within." Thus you see the Christian people subjugated by tyrants, but under their tyranny we men of peace are finally set free, and the confidence of the tyrants is destroyed. "The more we are oppressed, the more we acknowledge Thee."

14. *They are dead, let them not live.* It is Martin Luther's opinion that these are the words of the godly, who comfort themselves with the thought that they live though they are dying. But this is what the text says: "The dead shall not live, and the tyrants shall not rise again," that is, our oppressors will die while they live and have no hope of life. We, however, live even when we are dying.

"Giants," in Hebrew, רְפָאִים.[7] In Hebrew this is a word with a double meaning. It is used for physicians and for the dead, and most often it is used for the departed. Perhaps by some figure of speech he calls the living giants the dead because they are already in death among the Christians and extremely close to death, since they have no savior as do the godly, who are alive in the midst of death.[8]

To that end Thou hast visited them with destruction. The reason why the tyrants are dead is that they are completely destroyed when the Lord visits them even with thunder. The same thought is expressed in Ps. 10:1 ff. and Ps. 36:1 ff. This is because they will never live nor rise again.

Thou hast increased the nation; Thou art glorified. That is, what is unknown not only among the giants but also in their synagog is published among the nations, because the Gospel is preached[9] since the Jews refuse to accept it.

Thou hast enlarged. "Thou art proclaimed far and wide in the whole world."

16. *O Lord, in distress, etc.* He contrasts the godly and the ungodly, when the Gospel passes beneath the life of both, and another set of tyrants arises after one set has been destroyed. There can be no Abel without a Cain.

[7] Luther seems to have confused three similar, but unrelated, Hebrew words.

[8] An allusion to the antiphonal hymn, *Media vita,* which Luther had rendered into German in 1524.

[9] There appears to be something missing from this clause: *quia recusantibus Iudeis praedicari euangelium.* Perhaps *praedicari* should be *praedicatur.*

They sought Thee, they poured out a prayer when Thy chastening was upon them, that is, "When Thy chastening touches them, then there is the murmur of their cry. The rod produces good children. So good is trouble for the godly that they cannot trust and live properly without harassment. The spirit of the godly rusts away, as it were, unless they are well exercised by tribulations. Thus when the godly are touched by them, they murmur, they groan in an unutterable spirit (cf. Rom. 8:26) to Thee, they sigh softly to God and do not make a horrible racket. And thus the Christian should do in every trouble; he should not shout or blaspheme, yet he should flee for refuge to the Lord in murmuring and distress with the sighs of his heart and his mouth. This is 'the chastening of the Lord.' For there is no danger, either external or internal, except Thy chastening." There follows the likeness of the pregnant woman.

17. *Like a woman with child.* Christ uses the same thought and almost the same words and employs the likeness of the woman in travail to show the grief of His own followers (John 16:21). Soon after the labor, when the child has been born, the woman no longer remembers her pain. Even so the godly cannot escape dangers and tribulations and are as troubled as a woman in travail, who has no way out but must bring forth. So, in every trouble, when the godly are thoroughly harassed and exercised, then they are almost reborn and borne up, and thus delivered, they grow in faith. Note this. Any tribulation of the godly is as it were the birth and renewal of a man. Therefore the godly man is like a woman in travail, who is hard pressed by unremitting dangers.

18. *So were we because of Thee, O Lord; we were with child, we have as it were brought forth wind.* This is the application of the comparison. As the woman is in distress, so we conceive the new man through tribulations and give birth, that is, we strain and are in distress with pains and affliction. These are the pains of childbirth in such great distress that we hardly draw a breath. This indicates that the affliction of the godly is so great that they can hardly inhale or exhale. We are governed by these pains and reborn through faith.

We have wrought no deliverance in the earth. And still there is no help for the land, that is to say, the ungodly are shaken by no teaching, admonition, and distress, they remain ungodly. This is the cry which the godly have for the ungodly.

19. *Thy dead shall live.* He is speaking antithetically. Above he said that the living giants were dead and would not rise again, but that the godly lived in the midst of death, as Paul said that he was often dead (2 Cor. 6:9). This is the comfort of the godly, that in the midst of dangers they live by faith and hope.

O dwellers in the dust, awake and sing for joy! To dwell in the dust is to be in the lowest kind of death and in distress because of all the persecutions. This is the promise to the godly that they may comfort themselves when they are in the midst of slaughter like sheep led to the slaughter without any hope. Bestir yourselves in faith and peace and praise the Lord.

For Thy dew is a dew of light, and Thou wilt draw the land of the shades into ruin. "Thy dew is a dew of fields and meadows," and by this poetic metaphor he calls our dew the dew of the meadows. For just as the dew falls from heaven without human assistance, so Christians come into being and are multiplied by an act of God; and if meanwhile we are oppressed by all earthly afflictions, nothing else happens than that we are refreshed with the blood. Just so the church always receives growth from the refreshment of the blood, as the meadows are cheered by the dew.

20. *Come, My people, enter your chambers.* He admonishes the people as in Ps. 4:4. Do not complain and cry out in times of persecution but *enter your chambers,* keep quiet, do not be angry and impetuous. But pray to the Lord in secret and make your complaint to Him, as Peter says of Christ: "When He was reviled, He did not revile in return" (1 Peter 2:23), but kept silent, that is, He entered into His chamber.

Hide yourselves for a little while, that is, "Wait a little and endure, because My wrath and your persecution are sudden and last only a moment. Therefore see to it that you bear it for a little while. Do not erupt, because none of our troubles in the world are everlasting but only transitory." These are the riches of divine consolation that support us in every kind of trouble.

21. *For behold, the Lord is coming,* that is, the Lord will punish His persecutors and will not permit much blood of His saints to be

shed. Thus the tyrants who hoped that John Hus was dead saw him still alive; they dug out his ashes with the earth more than a cubit deep and threw them into the water.[10]

[10] Luther's associate, Johann Agricola, collaborated with Nicholas Krumbacher in the publication, at Hagenau in 1529, of documents dealing with the death of John Hus; thus Luther had an opportunity to become acquainted in detail with the events of 1415.

CHAPTER TWENTY-SEVEN

1. *In that day the Lord with His hard and great and strong sword.*

ALMOST all exegetes[1] interpret this passage as referring to the devil, whom they call serpent and Leviathan and whom Christ called the prince of this world (John 14:30). It seems to me the prophet is speaking about the kings of Syria, of the Egyptians and others, and about the kings and princes of the Jews at the time of Christ, all of whose kingdoms were to be made subject to the Roman rule. When Christ's kingdom and the Gospel were already imminent, the Roman rule came first and established peace throughout the world, so that the Gospel could be preached by the apostles everywhere on safe roads.

In that day the Lord will punish with His hard sword, that is, with a harsh sword. For the Roman rule was harsh and was quick to use the sword. This sword is great and grand, that is, powerful, strong, and made of iron. It is invincible, because it brought all into submission. With this sword, I say, the Lord will punish.

Leviathan the serpent. Here he mentions two serpents, signifying the kings ruling over the world, as Scripture frequently calls kings serpents and as the prophet calls the king of the Egyptians the dragon of the Nile who lives beside the Nile.[2]

The bar serpent, that is, the straight one, a serpent that swims with a straight body, which symbolizes the kings that rule uprightly and in an orderly way.

The twisting serpent, that is, curved, which swims coiled and in a circle. This represents the kings whose rule is restless and disorderly.

He calls the serpent *Leviathan* allegorically. Leviathan properly speaking is a sea monster. These two serpents, the straight one and the twisted one, fought with each other until the Romans swallowed them both. Therefore he allegorically calls the serpent Leviathan and refers to all the kings who sport about on the sea and the princes

[1] Jerome, *Commentaria,* VIII, 316.

[2] Luther is probably thinking of Ezek. 29:3.

who directly and indirectly make a game of ruling the people. *Leviathan* is an addition, that is, some insatiable thing. Thus the ambitious princes cannot be satisfied with kingdoms but are eager to add kingdom to kingdom, and so also an insatiable demon is called Leviathan.

2. *In that day.* At the time of the Roman rule, when those kings have been subjugated.

A pleasant vineyard, sing to it! In Hebrew: a vineyard of חֶמֶר. חֶמֶר denotes quality, the best wine, such as red wine is with us. Therefore it is called pure wine, which is the best, and it denotes the godly church, which will be a vineyard of pure wine, not bearing wild vines, but a vineyard of pure wine. The church will bear good wine, not like the synagog. This song follows.

3. *I, the Lord, am its keeper.* This is the glory of the church, that it has no teacher and bishop but Christ, who alone rules over His church through His Spirit and His Gospel, as Paul writes of it in an excellent manner in Eph. 4:15. Here the Lord says: "I am its guardian, bishop, keeper, and teacher, not as the old Law was administered by Moses and through the service of angels.

Every moment I water it, that is, My church. I myself will quickly revive it, exhausted as it is by all deceptions and errors. I will be with it; I will not forsake it. I will give it to drink. "Come to Me, all you who thirst" (John 7:37). Such promises Christ makes to His church, and we should promptly believe them.

Every moment I water it. Lest anyone harm it, I guard it night and day. In this way the text coheres, as if to say, "Lest anyone harm it," that is, "lest any leaf fall off suddenly, I will water it thus in heat and drought, because a dry vineyard is altogether ruined." In this way He expresses the greatness and power of His promises to the church, that He will care for it in this way. *Night and day,* in time of peace and in time of trouble He will preserve it, so that not one leaf wither and fall off. Night and day Christ is concerned for our welfare, that is, at all times He can easily turn day into night and night into day and adapt all things to the benefit of His church.

4. *I have no wrath.* This is strengthening for the fearful church. He says: "I cannot be enraged. I appear to be enraged, but it is not true." We feel it as wrath, but it is not wrath, just as parents are not wrathful when they chastise their children. Let this be a gloss re-

garding all the tribulations of Christians, which should be inscribed for the godly in all persecutions: *I have no wrath.* Note this.

Who will give me thorns and briers! This is said in opposition to our evil and carnal thoughts and the designs of the devil, which turn one so kind into one enraged and harsh as a thorn and brier. For Satan and the flesh act thus that when the kindly Lord thrusts us into dangers, they argue impatiently: "The Lord has forgotten me, He is angry with me, He has thorns, etc."

I would set out to battle against them. It is as if He were saying: "My Christian is indeed in difficulties, but I will go to war and battle for him and defend him. Therefore he must not believe that I have thorns and briers, but much more that I am a waterer and defender and that 'a bruised reed I will not break, and a dimly burning wick I will not quench'" (Is. 42:3). Therefore with these words He here reproves those who make Him out to be hard as a thorn, and He comforts His own, so that they might take refuge with Him in all tribulations, knowing that there is no wrath in Him.

I would burn them up together. These are still the words of God, who is chiding our notion which conceives of God as wrathful and as a severe and incendiary destroyer. When He chastens us out of His goodness, then our reason argues that God is drawing us into the lowest hell. The godly and the church have this temptation in tribulations, a temptation which He reproves. They should not harbor such thoughts but rather believe that in these divine trials they are protected and never destroyed, because He Himself is their guardian and bishop. Thus the afflicted Paul prayed the Lord thrice, but God did not remove the affliction, saying: "My grace is sufficient for you, etc." (2 Cor. 12:9). Let this teach the weak and faint brothers to be consoled, because they may be persuaded by Satan that God is angry when they experience tribulations.

5. *Or who will lay hold of My protection?* Here follows the second part to console us in time of temptation, when we despair that Christ is not able to preserve us. Therefore he says: "Who will lay hold of My protection? "Who is so strong that he can prevent Me from saving My church and from smiting the adversaries?"

Let them make peace with Me, let them make peace with Me, that is, "Let no one make Me out to be thorny and severe when it comes to consoling. Let no one make Me out to be weak when it comes to defending. I will make peace, nevertheless, and I will be a king of peace, whether you have thought Me to be hard or powerless." It is as if He were saying: "Let no one despair of Me, but let him have peace in Me, though in the world he may have distress. I want peace." In this way He brings the words of comfort to an end.

6. *In days to come Jacob shall take root, Israel shall blossom.* "The days will come when I will defend My vineyard, so that Jacob may take root, that is, produce sap," and *Israel shall blossom,* that is, "the church, thoroughly harassed by the cross, will put forth shoots, germinate, and grow verdant through the apostles and the godly.

And fill the whole world with seed. It is as if He were saying: "Far from being hard, since I could not be wrathful, I will rather be a king of peace in such a way that My vineyard will germinate and spread itself abroad."

7. *Have I smitten him with the blow of a smiter, or killed you with the killing of a killer?* "I will not smite My church the way someone is smitten by enemies. I will not allow it to be thus smitten, but I chasten and chastise it. I do not smite with the blow of a smiter, I do not kill in the manner of killing, but in the manner of making alive." "The Lord brings down to Sheol and raises up" (1 Sam. 2:6). Let every Christian know, therefore, that his tribulation is not evil but good, imposed by a good God. It is not as reason and Satan argue: "You are poor, cast off, and thoroughly afflicted. God is hard and unmerciful, He has forgotten you, He is your enemy and adversary." Such afflicted consciences can be abundantly consoled by this chapter. For from it we can draw plentiful arguments for a letter of comfort: (1) Trust, child. (2) I, the Lord, am your keeper. (3) I will instantly water day and night. (4) I have no wrath. (5) Who thinks that I am thorn and brier and exceedingly hard? (6) I am so powerful. No one will hold back My strength. (7) I will have such a peace that My vineyard will take root and flourish. I smite and chasten you not with the smiting of the smiter, but in the manner of a keeper and a father.

8. *Measure by measure, by exile Thou didst contend with them.* Jerome seems to have doubled the first word.[3] This describes[4] the

[3] The Hebrew word, whose meaning is obscure, itself involves a duplication of sounds and is therefore translated (with the aid of other versions) "measure for measure."

[4] The Weimar text has *describat,* but we have read *describit.*

spirit and manner of judging, the spirit in which the Lord chastises His church, namely, that it be a chastening with moderation, which He may take away in His own time, not as the enemies do.

He removed them with His fierce blast in the day of the east wind. The east wind dries up and burns, especially at Easter time,[5] and destroys the blossoms. So God grants that His church is chastised with a burning wind and very great persecution, yet He chastises it by measure.

9. *Therefore by this the guilt of Jacob will be expiated.* It will be chastised in this so that the remission of sins may be exercised, as Paul says to the Hebrews concerning the heavenly Father (Heb. 12:6 f.). With supreme benefit He chastises His own with much greater love than earthly fathers. Thus you see that the Lord's chastening is distinguished by many features, namely, that it is paternal, that it is applied in moderation, and that it is for the purpose of implementing the remission of sins, because it leads a man to call upon God. "Call upon Me in the day of trouble; I will deliver you" (Ps. 50:15). He speaks thus so that we may more easily forgive others. We groan and sigh to God always, and thus spirit, faith, and love grow. Thus the forgiveness of sins follows and is put into effect. Thus you see how noble and necessary God's chastening is. For through the Word the forgiveness of sins is proclaimed, through faith it is received, and through the cross it is put into effect.

And this will be the full fruit. This is the effect of the cross, that every sin and the whole body of sin may be destroyed by believing in forgiveness, lest we fall either into presumption or into despair, but it keeps us in the middle way, that we acknowledge our sin and call upon God.

When He has leveled all the stones, so that no groves or idols remain standing. In the very cleansing from sin he says that all altars and stones will be crushed and destroyed, so that there will be and remain no idolatry whatever, but be destroyed to such an extent that even the stones of the altars will utterly be reduced to ashes, that no idolatry will be practiced in groves and with images. An idol, however, is both the source of all sins and our presumption, and is clearly against God's First Commandment. The cross and the chastening of God casts this idol down that we may abide in God's First Command-

[5] Luther is thinking of such passages as Jer. 18:17; Ezek. 19:12; 27:26.

ment, that we may fear and dread and love God. If we have remained in this commandment, they easily perform the works of the remaining commandments in the original righteousness. Thus those who in their presumption trust in their own power, wisdom, and wealth, these choose their own things as divine worship and spurn God, as we see in tyrants, heretics, and hypocrites. These rely on their own power, wisdom, and wealth contrary to God's First Commandment. This is what it means to commit idolatry. The saints and godly, however, are kept by the cross and chastening in the fear of God and are estranged from trust in themselves. This is the fruit of the chastisement of God, that it teaches us not to flee but to approach God and, what is greatest, that it kills that supreme idolatry, trust in oneself. This killing is much greater than the outward mortification of the flesh, of lust, and of other outward things that cannot be compared with this killing. But the cross casts out this idol so that we do not rely on ourselves. Even so all hypocrites on the basis of a little good (as it seems) have such confidence in themselves that it knows no bounds, as happened to me once upon a time. How much pride came over me when I correctly celebrated one Mass![6] Shame on you! So it happens also to all other hypocrites with their glittering works. They defend their idolatry with their works. This idolatry God's unique chastisement casts out.

All the stones of the altars, namely, of the ungodly worship. All these stones, that is, all our self-trust, He casts out.

Like chalkstones crushed to pieces, that is, "I will by My chastisement so destroy that idolatry that not another will grow, just as there is no hope in altars and stones that have been completely returned to ashes. Thus with the chief presumption of the heart removed, we will not easily fall into another kind of idolatry. All the prophets who were active against this idolatry were slain because of it, since the flesh cannot bear to have its own opinion cast aside. Therefore the Lord's chastening is necessary.

10. *The fortified city* of the Lord. This again refers to Jerusalem, which did not take up the cross but relied on itself as a fortified city relies on itself.

A habitation deserted, that is, they did not want to be comforted but to rely on themselves, and therefore it will remain deserted. So

[6] At the celebration of his first Mass, Luther, like many other young priests, had been overwhelmed by awe and by the fear of making a mistake in the ritual.

Jerusalem relied on its worship, its temple, its Law, its fortifications. This was entirely taken away from the people, therefore the city is desolate and forsaken. Our papists have the same experience. *Habitation,* that is, splendid palaces and the splendid and constant building of the temple.

Forsaken, fallen into ruin. This will befall our tyrants.

Like the wilderness. It will have neither kingdom nor priesthood nor any government, as befell the Jews, as we see from experience: Although they seriously try many things, they remain forsaken and wandering, and no plan of theirs is successful.

There the calf grazes. Jerusalem will be reduced to such a state of destruction and devastation that the cattle will graze there.

And strips its branches. Even the branches and shoots will be stripped off by the cattle. In this roundabout way the prophet shows that pride and presumption will be destroyed from the ground up, like a city where grass and bramble bushes grow.

11. *When its boughs are dry, they are broken; women come and make a fire of them.* This is what he wants to say: Thus it will happen to the area that all fruits of the earth will dry up and the crop will be stubble that is good for nothing but that poor women gather that crop in the fields to make fire. This denotes the empty attempt and endeavor of the Jews, just like that of the farmer. A harvest for the stubble of the furrows. This describes the punishment of the ungodly and the presumptuous. Therefore the godly need chastisement lest they fall into presumption. For the presumptuous ungodly are moved by nothing, neither threats nor promises. They regard their punishment as martyrdom, they ascribe their well-being to their own works and never truly give God credit. All of these people who rely on their own holiness find out that with all their efforts they are always laboring in vain, gathering a harvest without fruit, as it will be with the farmers. The prophet gives the following reason.

This is a people without discernment, that is, it does not care and take heed. This is a nation without purpose. The prophet follows Moses, who threatens a people that does not understand and give heed to God, people who spurn everything they hear and care nothing for the words of Christ and the prophets and apostles. And because of this contempt of theirs they are punished in this way that their harvest is withered.

Therefore He will not have compassion on them, He will not spare them. He will show them no favor. Because they spurn the proffered grace God will subsequently have no compassion on them.

12. *In that day from the channel the Lord will thresh out.* Because the people spewed out the proffered grace, they have not been spared.

And you will be gathered one by one, O people of Israel. Thus he declares that by a gathering some, namely, the gathered remnant of Israel, those who come to their senses, will be converted to God, as Paul points out to the Romans (Rom. 11:5). These the Lord will by his Word shake out and winnow from the unfaithful. For the preaching of the Gospel is the Lord's winnowing-fork. *From the channel,* that is, from the bank of the Euphrates river.

To the Brook of Egypt, which is an arm of the Nile, for between these two rivers the exceedingly powerful Word of God was put to use, namely between Syria, Samaria, and Egypt. *You will be gathered,* namely, by faith. *One by one,* that is, they will come as individuals and in small groups, not in companies.

13. *In that day a great trumpet will be blown.* He does not say that the Gospel will be trumpeted forth and the people will be gathered one by one in some places, but that even the lost and the outcasts in the land of Syria and Egypt and Assyria are to be gathered, so that the Gospel is to be preached not only between these two rivers, but it is to be preached beyond and outside this area for the assembly of many brothers to call upon the Lord *on the holy mountain at Jerusalem,* that is, the church.

CHAPTER TWENTY-EIGHT

THE beginning of this chapter is obscure. Some apply it to Israel, some to Jerusalem and Judah.[1] If we wish it to be referred to Jerusalem, then by metonymy Ephraim must be made to refer to Jerusalem.

1. *Woe to the proud crown of the drunkards of Ephraim, and to the fading flower.* These words are difficult for us who do not understand the Hebrew idiom. It is necessary, in the first place, to inquire of which people this text is speaking. Some think it refers to the ten tribes of Israel. I myself take this chapter to mean specifically Jerusalem and the tribe of Judah; I am influenced by the following word, Ephraim. We leave it to the judgment of the hearers, relying on their own judgment, whether they take it to mean the kingdom of Israel or the kingdom of Judah. *Woe to the proud crown of the drunkards.* By circumlocution he describes the kingdom of Judah, as if to say, "The kingdom of Ephraim has great confidence and pride in its own kingdom, righteousness, and worship, and glories in them as a girl glories in her crown." *Drunkards.* Yet it is drunk, nevertheless, that is, wealthy, since as a result of the glory, power, and worship in which they trust they are more than drunk. Just as the physically drunk hear nothing but their own words, so the kingdom of Ephraim relied on its splendid cities, governments, righteousness, and glories and heard nothing beyond these.

Which is on the head of the rich valley. Historians report that the land of Samaria was outstandingly fertile and was second to none in fruitfulness.[2]

Overcome with wine. When one's head aches after a drinking bout, as the Germans say, "He bumped into the beer and fell under the bench," because they themselves are drunkards and live like beasts of the belly in a fat land. This is a picture of the kingdom of Judah, and by these images the prophet censures their presumption,

[1] Jerome, *Commentaria,* IX, 325—326, refers these verses to the ten tribes.

[2] Luther may be referring to such passages as Josephus, *Antiquities of the Jews,* XVI, 5, 2; Pliny, *Natural History,* V, 15.

confidence, and smugness in riches and resources and glories, in which they felt excessively smug and made their boast against the most godly admonitions and threats of all the prophets.

Woe to the fading flower of its glorious beauty, that is, of its costly pomp. As above, he compares the kingdom of Israel to a glorious crown and perishable flowers and very costly pomp, all of which are perishable and frail. Yet they are so smug and presumptuous in their glories and righteousnesses that they seem to themselves to be in command and to flourish. However, they are flourishing like a fading flower. Thus it is with our pope, the proud crown, relying on himself.

2. *Behold, the Lord has one who is mighty and strong.* He is speaking about the king of the Assyrians, who will be made mighty and strong by the Lord and whose strength will be like the thrust of a hailstorm, etc. He compares his power by means of these illustrations and shows what it is like. For just as no one can repel hailstorm and tempest, so no one can withstand his power. By means of these three comparisons he describes his exceedingly powerful army and strength, as if to say: "This is the kingdom of Israel, confident and proud of its crown, its flower, and its boasting, all of which are transitory, especially, in the time of hailstorm and tempest, of lightning and flood." In other words, "You Israelites are vainly confident against the Assyrians, like a flower against flood and hail."

3. *Trodden underfoot,* that is, the kingdom of Israel will be like a wreath that is trodden underfoot.

4. *Like the premature,* that is, that kingdom is as stable as fields that want to blossom and bear fruit before the accustomed time. They will most certainly perish, because the fruit is devoured when it is still in the stem and branch, and it perishes before it is plucked off by the hand. So all premature fruits very quickly die away. Thus destruction comes promptly to the ungodly. They will be "like the grass on the housetops, which withers before it grows up" (Ps. 129:6). And the ungodly are like thorns on a branch, because the thorn dies when it is still in fresh sap. These comparisons show that the ungodly come to naught in the midst of a plan, when they are absorbed in their supreme and most eager endeavor, just like premature fruits that are very promising but dry up before the harvest comes. So

you, Israel, will be oppressed by the kingdom of the Assyrians as by a storm. Therefore note well that the ungodly always boast of themselves, for they are the proud crowns, the flowers *of glorious beauty, etc.* In that boasting they persist, they put forth much effort, they plan diligently for the future, but they shall not live out half their days" (Ps. 55:23), that is, they will not accomplish half of what they boast with excessive certainty. On the contrary, they will perish in the midst of their effort. So you see our tyrants still self-confidently trying much but always fading out as they rely on their own ideas. For those, however, who hold fast to Christ and His Word every undertaking and plan will happily endure.

5. *In that day the Lord of hosts will be a crown of glory and a diadem of beauty.* That clause supports the second interpretation,[3] namely, that this chapter must be understood as referring to the kingdom of Judah. For when Israel was laid waste, the remnant remained in the kingdom of Judah. This remnant no longer will boast in itself but in the Lord, who will be crown, flower, and glory to them when through sufficient discipline in dangers they have learned to fear God. The remnant of the people, not the whole people, but the few who remained – these had God as their crown and glory, that is, they trusted in Him as their God.

6. *The Lord will be a spirit of justice to him who sits in judgment.* As formerly they were insatiable drunks having a spirit of laziness and disorder, now having the Lord by faith, they learn the spirit of justice, they will speak and do justice, that which is just, and this they have been taught by the Lord's chastening. Such men were Ezra, Zerubbabel, Haggai, Nehemiah, a very few so disciplined by it that they not only did justice but also taught it to others.

And strength, that is, the Lord will give them strength; they will have a spirit of justice to arrange and set up excellent laws, but they must also have power and authority, and the vigor and strength to execute the laws.

To those who turn back the battle at the gate, that is, the residue that was restored from the Babylonian captivity for the purpose of rebuilding the city of Jerusalem. He calls every disaster of Israel a war. *Gate* surely is peace, law, and the establishment of peace

[3] Jerome, *Commentaria,* IX, 327—328, interprets these verses as being addressed to the two tribes.

when the war was over. By allegory this devastation inflicted on worldly boasting can be shifted to Christ, who has devastated all the glory of the world.

7. *These also are ignorant because of wine.* There he makes a division, having made his speech. Now he speaks of the future under the reign of Christ. Here he describes the very strength of the hypocrites and ungodly, who in no wise come to their senses by the admonition of the prophets. It is as if he were saying: "Also our people, who are with us and stand with us, are in no respect better than those who in the past were ruined in the destruction of Israel, for they also stagger with drunkenness and presumption." The words "drunk" and "drunkenness" are used in Scripture particularly for those who presumptuously trust and boast in themselves.[4] These reel and walk staggering in their own glory. Thus the princes and priests do not know how to govern and teach; they stagger in their own errors, they are called drunks and are worse than the drunk peasants, who do not exercise any reasonable control but draw everything to their own pleasure. Thus, then, by this most apt comparison he describes the wicked princes and bishops, who are not sober in the Word and wisdom of God but are drunk with their own schemes and ideas and stagger hither and yon, unsure, teaching nothing certain and being uncertain themselves. Thus they stagger back and forth like drunkards. They are not sure of their own ideas but always say: "Perhaps this will please God; perhaps, perhaps thus it is established and ordained by the church."

The priest and the prophet know nothing because of drunkenness. The prophet has nothing but rebuke. Here he thunders against the aristocrats, the prophets who were lawfully appointed and called to the seat and office of teachers – against these he inveighs so vehemently as drunkards and staggerers and "know-nothings." No wonder that they could have torn him to pieces.

They are ignorant, that is, they do not have the Word. *They are confused with wine,* that is, they are flung headlong. They did not drink wine but were swallowed by wine, because they in no wise stopped their boasting and meanwhile listened to none of those who admonished them, always going astray in their set opinions.

They err in vision, that is, they know nothing of prophesying.

[4] Luther is thinking of such passages as Jer. 51:7 and Rev. 17:2.

They do not know the Word of God, which they should be teaching. They do not know what they say, as Paul says,[5] where they teach everything in reverse order. They teach faith where they should teach works, and works where they should teach faith. They are coarse asses who preach nothing certainly and distinguish neither Law nor Gospel.

And they vomit judgments, that is, when they ought to speak, they vomit and belch; when they ought to put forth a wise judgment, they belch forth what is their own.

8. *All tables are full of vomit, no place is without filthiness,* that is, it is in all places. Wherever the Word is not taught, there is nothing but ignorance, drunkenness. And the more ignorant they are, the wiser they appear to themselves; they are in a frenzy with teaching so that they may fill every place with their vomit. For the one who can't carry a tune always wants to sing. *All tables,* that is, all places where the Word is taught by which the conscience is fed, in those places they themselves want to be everywhere. Note, then, that human traditions are nothing else than the vomit of a drunken peasant, a food for which you need swine, not the consciences of the godly. For this reason the prophet here rails at them so much. Who in our time would dare thus to slander the pope and the bishops? Would they not be insane? And even if it is completely true, they would rave, because their traditions are the vomit of drunkards, and the monks are devouring sows. Thus you see the prophet vehemently attacking the drunken priests, and with extreme intensity he says that they do not speak but belch; thus we can properly call all human tradition and glittering hypocrisy vomit. If I should today call the pope a drunkard and a belcher, what hope have I of living? That is what this passage does.[6] A drunkard adopts a thirsty man, a drunkard seeks a sober man. It seems clear that by antithesis he is contrasting drunkenness with zeal to hear.

9. *Whom will he teach knowledge?* That is, where shall we teach, whom shall we teach, since these take up every place with their ideas? *Knowledge* in the Scriptures denotes the recognition of the truth and the ray of light. Wisdom indeed is faith itself, teaching us how to believe, trust, and fear God. For he who has knowledge of the truth

[5] This may be a reference to 1 Cor. 14:9.

[6] There is a lacuna in the manuscript at this point.

is not hindered by empty traditions, by the observance of days, places, vestments, and appearances. From that knowledge and understanding comes wisdom, that is, true faith. Our drunken bishops and tyrants do not see this knowledge.

And to whom will he explain the message? The message and knowledge denote the Word and the report concerning God, as Paul writes in Rom. 10:16: "Who has believed what he has heard from us?" that is, the word and the report. Therefore what is heard is the Word, as far as it is strewn into the ears. That is to say, "We indeed preach the Word, but hardly any accept it." He replies:

Those who are weaned from the milk, those taken from the breast. The Word of God is grasped particularly by the little ones and the simple. In Ps. 131:2 we read: "I have calmed and quieted my soul, like a child quieted at its mother's breast." As a child that is weaned cries and wails and wants its mother, so, etc. And in summary: "The poor have good news preached to them" (Matt. 11:5), because the Word of the Gospel is appropriate to none but the afflicted, such as a weaned child, while the drunken and gluttons spurn it. Note, then, that the Word of God is proclaimed throughout the world, that it is received only by the poor and afflicted, and meanwhile it is met with hostility by others. For it is the Word of life, of hope, of strength, of joy, and of grace. Therefore it is accepted by none but the dying, the despairing, the weak sinners, and those weaned entirely from the flesh. The unweaned tyrants, who rely on their own resources, do not accept it but rather persecute it. Only the poor accept it.

10. *For it is precept upon precept, line upon line, etc.* In Hebrew "precept upon precept" means, "command here, command there," as if the Jews were saying: Wherever we turn, there is nothing but *precept upon precept, line upon line.* By this name the prophet designates those who make sport of the Word. But this is the summary: All prophets teach three things: The command and precept of God. *Precept.* Secondly, they teach the promises of God. Thirdly: But because the flesh always wavers and falters when the fulfillment of those promises is delayed, the prophet encourages all to persevere in the promises.

Here a little, that is, wait for it a little at a time, do not lose hope, our salvation will soon come. This is what is meant in the Scriptures by teaching and admonishing. But the prophet says these things against the ungodly in an imitative and mocking way, because the ungodly said that the prophets did nothing but issue commands and precepts, as if all our endeavors were futile. So today our papists say: "Creed, creed, Decalog, Decalog; these heretics can do nothing but teach these things, and not the doctrine of the church." In these words the prophet rebukes such ungodly people, who neither obeyed the commands nor looked to the promises but always made fun of the prophets for promising so much, and who experienced no comfort. So it befalls the preachers of the Word who promise much comfort but meanwhile live in extreme persecution and affliction and poverty, while at the same time Satan, the king of Bashan, supports his servants in the height of luxury. The ungodly see this, and those living in such outward peace continue in their ungodliness, as if to say, "Go away with your *precept* and *line*, you beggar, who are always saying: *A little here;* we have waited, and nothing has happened." The flesh cannot bear the cross for one hour, but hates it. Therefore the Word that brings the cross is turned away, and thus such a man accepts neither teaching nor admonition. See the passage in Jeremiah,[7] where the ungodly say, "But since we turned away from the queen of heaven, we have lacked everything" (Jer. 44:18). So today they say: "If I leave off performing my worship, I shall die of want; if I fail to read Masses, how shall I nourish myself? Then Satan mocks us and says: *Precept upon precept, line upon line, here a little, there a little.* So today the ungodly says: Believe till a roasted goose flies into your mouth.

11. *Since with mocking lips He will speak to this people.* It is as if he were saying: "The Lord will also speak to you, to you with mocking lips, and will deride you, as Ps. 2:4 says: 'The Lord has them in derision.'" This is a theological passage and fitting for the New Testament. It is as if he were saying: "The Lord will speak to you not with lips but with derisive gestures. For you deride your prophets who say in your tongue: 'The time will come when I will deride you in an alien tongue.' Summary: I will teach you My Gospel through My apostles; and when this is ridiculed, I will speak to you in another tongue and will deride you, reject your whole righteousness, reject you, and in your place I will receive the foolish Gentiles. That will be a serious joke for you." You see that the Jews know this from experience. Those who in every way had their sport with, and laughed

[7] There is another lacuna in the manuscript at this point.

at, the predictions of the prophets, *precept upon precept, line upon line,* now experience this in earnest, since they burden themselves in vain with nothing except commandments for their own hands and they wait in vain and always hope to no purpose. Just so our ungodly sophists, who laugh at the purity of the Word, are derided by God with various lies and errors. This, then, is the punishment of the ungodly, that they ridicule themselves with their own ridicule and are ridiculed by God. Thus the best life and tongue, the Gospel, is for the ungodly a derided rock of offense, though it should be saving and a fragrance of life (2 Cor. 2:16). But the ungodly only deride themselves as they mock us. To which people will He speak in a mocking language? To that people:

12. *To whom He has said: This is rest; give rest to the weary,* that is, this people deserves derision. Why? Because it rejects the doctrine of peace and comfort, because to this people the Word of grace is preached day by day, and yet they spurn it. Then they will have many false teachers who make them restless with various labors and works. *Give rest to the weary.* They have preachers who have the divine command to revive and comfort the afflicted with the Word of consolation, because God wants His preachers to be comforters, and they should always preach the forgiveness of sins to troubled consciences.

And this is repose; yet they would not hear, that is, "They have the Word of the prophets in which there is rest, quiet, and repose, yet because of their ungodliness they have refused to hear it. Therefore I will give them over to lies and speak to them in mockery and derision." As it happened to the Jews, so it is today happening to the papists. And here the prophet is speaking of the disposition and punishment of the ungodly, as those who have rejected the Word of true hope and trust and are therefore wrapped up in the word of false hope and lying. They are given over to a base mind (Rom. 1:28). With them there is no end of commanding, of awaiting, and of admonishing; and yet everything is futile, as is the case with the papist hypocrites today, who have spurned God's mercy and Word and fall into various futile works and mock themselves with their uncertain opinions, which they prefer to the divine Word. Therefore he says:

13. *The Word of the Lord, etc., that they may go and fall back-*

ward and be broken. This is a most dreadful punishment that ought to press the ungodly down even to ashes. Yet the smug papists do not listen to it. Here, then, you see their punishment. *That they may go,* that is, not in the Word, but in errors, because they spurned the light of the Word. *And fall backward:* They make no progress; they go, but they run from one error to another, because they have lost the way of truth, and therefore they constantly fall into fictions and errors, as I myself experienced with the most learned Jews.[8] These remained in their own opinions alone, even though they were refuted by me. Thus the papists, having abandoned faith, have venerated sects, works designed to gain righteousness, vigils, cowls, and even their own lice,[9] invoking the aid of unknown saints, and have fallen not only away from God but in opposition to God. This is what it means to "fall backward," not forward. Therefore we must be admonished to pray to God in a most watchful manner. *And be broken.* Jeremiah states that they are afflicted with a twofold grief (Jer. 17:18): (1) of the heart, where the heart, wearied and disquieted by all works, has no inward peace, and the more it labors, the more it is disturbed; (2) of the body, namely, they cheat themselves and nature by vigils and foods which the body needs, as Paul says in Col. 2:23. Although they live in riches without sweat, they cannot use their riches freely and pleasantly so that the body may have enough. Thus the Jews and papists have no inward peace, and they cannot freely make use of any creatures outwardly.

And snared, as birds are captured by fowlers. This is a most wretched punishment, that when they go astray, fall, and are broken, they have no one to lead them back, but are snared even worse, as we saw in the case of the papists and monks who said: "The more burdensome the monastic order becomes, the happier I am." Thus they cannot be called away from their own ungodly ways, but they interpret their punishments as a cross and their successes as merits. So Thomas Aquinas says: "One who enters a monastery undertakes a Baptism, and as often as he renews his daily vow he is renewed in his Baptism." [10] These are the snares in which they ought to remain with their orders and errors. Thus you see that those who are without

[8] This seems to be a reflection of Luther's discussions with rabbis while he was translating the Bible.

[9] For a fuller statement, cf. *Luther's Works,* 21, pp. 281—283.

[10] Thomas Aquinas, *Summa Theologica,* II-2, Q. 189, art. 3.

the Word walk in darkness, fall backward, are bruised without and within, and finally are snared as captives. This is the punishment of the ungodly.

14. *Therefore hear the word of the Lord, you scoffers.* Here follows a most vehement admonition of the prophet to hear the Word diligently. A *scoffer* is most accurately one who not only is himself evil but also ridicules all the things of God, His Word, wisdom, and righteousness and also has his sport with the prophets and their word and relies on his own righteousness and uprightness, as we see in the Pharisees and scribes in Christ's day.

Who rule. Such ungodly and scoffers rule and tyrannize over the consciences of the people. It is as if He were saying: "You scoffers are not ungodly for yourselves alone, but with your traditions you also oppress and tyrannize this most wretched people, who should be made subject to My Word."

15. *Because you have said: We have made a covenant.* In the plainest terms he pictures the nature and whole body of the ungodly, who are so exceedingly uncertain, and yet most secure in their own presumption, that they can be diverted from their ungodliness neither by promises nor by threats nor by admonitions, but they say: *We have made a covenant with death.* Thus the monk says: "If I have kept my vow, I cannot possibly be lost," and he draws the conclusion: "Everyone who has kept this rule, has eternal life." There faith, fear, and the Word of God are neglected, and they rely on their traditions, convinced that if they keep these, neither death nor hell can harm them. We see this covenant very plainly in the rules and monastic orders of the papists, and such were the Jews. Trusting in their own righteousness, they rejected Christ.

And with Sheol we have made a vision. The word חֹזֶה in Hebrew means vision, prophecy, and agreement. This is what Paul says to the Colossians.[11] It is always peace, peace for you, because the ungodly construe all their worst deeds, passions, and persecutions as obedience to God, and this is their peace and covenant with death. They say: "Why should God punish us who serve Him with works, affections, and even with murder? How God ought to cater to us obedient ones!"

[11] Despite the reference to "Colossians," such a passage as Eph. 2:11-18 would seem to fit the context better.

When the overwhelming scourge passes through, it will not come to us, that is, "we are free not only from death and hell, but from every scourge and evil." At all events, they do come to the ungodly, and yet they live in such smugness.

For we have made lies our refuge, and in falsehood we have taken shelter. Not that they themselves call their plans lies and falsehood; they rather call them righteousness and truth. But the prophet calls them that. For the ungodly claim to call a spade a spade [12]; so here they call a lie righteousness and falsehood truth. A lie and falsehood are nothing else than the appearance and pretense of godliness, something that Paul assails. On this idol the ungodly place their trust and revere the works of their hands, as we see the Jews and papists multiply all their efforts in the pretense and appearance of godliness. This is a lie and falsehood, because they live in externals and behind a mask and rely on them and cling to them.

16. *Therefore thus says the Lord God: Behold I am laying.* This passage is treated more fully by the two apostles Peter (1 Peter 2:6) and Paul (Rom. 10:11). I understand this chapter as referring to all Israel and Ephraim. By metonymy I take it to mean "all Israel." Before the prophet threatens them with destruction, he first sets forth promises to strengthen the believers, as if to say, "You ungodly people do not come to your senses. Know this: I will delay punishing you, I will first pick out the chosen men from your midst."

Behold, I am laying in Zion for a foundation a stone. The text must be carefully considered on the basis of its explanation by the apostles, namely, that Christ is the stone, not sand, so that we may be most solidly built on Christ. *Foundation:* not something thrown down, not easily overthrown, but firmly established through the preaching of the apostles, as Paul says in 1 Cor. 3:10 and Heb. 2:2. This stone, thus established, is built upon by one who has confidence in the true Word of God. This stone will render its superstructure sure and strong, because it is excellently established against every attack.

A tested stone. The Hebrew word בֹּחַן means a tester, so that Christ is a tested stone, that is, distressed and afflicted, or He is a testing stone, that is, a stone by whose shape all other stones are tested, so that we may be conformed to the image of the Son of God (Rom. 8:29). As Christ was polished, hewn, and squared by the promise,

12 On the meaning of this, see also *Luther's Works,* 1, p. 5; 26, p. 147.

by death and the cross, so we, in His image, should become well polished by such suffering and such a cross. Therefore it behooves all the godly to be thoroughly tested by cross and persecution. For this reason the flesh which shrinks from the cross remains unpolished in its desires and unsuited to this stone. *Cornerstone.* Paul says in Eph. 2:14 that Christ has broken down the dividing wall between two people and was made the cornerstone of the two walls, uniting them in one building, that is, the church. *Precious.* 1 Peter 2:7-8: "To you therefore who believe, He is precious, but for those who do not believe . . . a stone that will make men stumble." Thus we see in the Jews that they did not accept Christ as the cornerstone, that is, as the assembler, and therefore He is not precious to them but a stone of stumbling and offense. Meanwhile, Christ is, nevertheless, the cornerstone in the fullest sense; He is the precious stone, supremely to be revered by the believers, though He be rejected by the ungodly Jews and papists and though He be called heresy and error.

Of a sure foundation. In Hebrew מוּסָד מוּסָּד, "grounded in the foundation," as if to say: "Let all the storms of the tyrants and of the heavenly spirits and all dangers rush in, I will construct a sure foundation against their violence. I will see to it that this stone and building will remain firm." This is our comfort for those who believe in Christ: By no power, either of tyrants on earth, or in the nether regions, or in the air, can you be jarred loose. This is our defense in Christ against them.

He who believes will not be in haste. The promise follows the description of the stone. Paul explains this passage thus: "He will not be put to shame" (Rom. 10:11). Therefore let us inscribe this passage in golden letters, as if to say: "All other works, rites, kinds of righteousness and piety are put to shame and are in a hurry. Only *he who believes will not be in haste* and will not be put to shame. Hence, apart from faith there is nothing but confusion. *To be in haste* and to put to shame mean the same thing. For to be in haste and to flee are the precise characteristics of a terrified conscience that hastily flees the rustling of a leaf (Lev. 26:36). Most aptly therefore he attributes "being in haste" to an alarmed conscience. *He will not be in haste is* for the godly, who do not flee but have Christ as their stone and mediator. It follows, then, that a Christian must not believe that we are justified by another righteousness. Let all works by which we aim to gain righteousness and all our own merits depart, because we are built upon the foundation not by doing works but by believing. Therefore let every godly man, terrified by sin, run to Christ as the Mediator and Propitiator, and let him leave all his own works behind.

17. *And I will put justice on the scale.* A threat to the ungodly follows upon the promise of the godly to the godly, as if to say: "I will weigh out justice with a balance, that is, I will make a distinction between the good and the bad. I will not be so rash that I will destroy the good with the bad, nor so good that I will not punish the bad for the sake of the good, but I will first separate the good from the bad. As a carpenter, who marks off with the plummet what must be cut off, so I will put the measure and rule around this stone to determine who is to be saved and who is to be cast off." The measuring line is: "He who believes and is baptized" (Mark 16:16). This faith is the norm of saving with reference to this stone. The believers will remain with the carpenter's wood. The unbelievers must be chopped off like kindling.[13]

Hail, that is, the wrath of God. *Waters,* that is, the flood. Those who have not believed, even though they had the intercession of all the saints, will not abide. "As the blades of straw cannot stand the hail and the flood, so they will not endure My wrath, because they put their hope and confidence not in Me but in a lie, and for that reason they will very easily be crushed." For all kinds of self-righteousness, even if practiced for a thousand years, have made all toil futile, and are therefore carried away by the water and the hail and the wrath of God.

18. *Then your covenant will be annulled.* The ungodly man completely rejects this admonition until he has learned by experience.

When the overwhelming scourge passes through. These are threats to the ungodly, who do not escape the wrath of God. Although they feel very sure of themselves and are always presumptuous about everything in opposition to the warnings of the godly, when the flood and the wrath of God come, they go completely to pieces, as we experienced in the Peasants' Revolt.[14] We saw how much the papists

13 The Weimar editor suggests that *spreue* in the manuscript be emended to *spene.*

14 As Luther indicates, the panic evoked by the Peasants' War of 1525 pervaded all the classes of society.

trembled, how in all the princes and bishops there was nothing but fear. They spoke softly to the peasants, so that they might remain in power, but they never approached God in prayer. Thus you see that the ungodly are elated and exalted in good times but despair in bad times. Christians, on the other hand, fear God and are safe both in good times and in bad times.

19. *As often as it passes through it will take you.* By this amplified description he wants to impress upon them that the prophet, too, is concerned about depriving them of every bit of courage, so that they might put their hope in one hour of deliverance. But disaster has its doors open to them every hour, because they do not have the Foundation and Rock, Christ, and therefore they are very quickly flung down by every wind, as the parable in Matt. 7:27 shows.

If *in the morning,* namely, the flood comes, it will take you in the morning; if *by day,* it will take you by day, and likewise *by night;* that is, always you are exposed to disasters unprepared. *In the morning* can also mean "quickly," as it is understood frequently in the Scriptures.[15] So here *in the morning* is "very quickly," when you have not expected it, in the midst of peace. This has often happened and will happen to presumptuous hypocrites, who live presumptuously within and without and are very easily put to shame. And take note: The more a hypocrite has accustomed himself to his own righteousness, the more he is driven to despair; and the more a man falls outwardly and is wounded in his conscience, the more he lets go of himself and is driven to Christ. Therefore it is true that many more people go to heaven from the gallows than from the church cemetery. And Christ says (Matt. 21:31): "The tax collectors and the harlots go into the kingdom of God before you." Therefore all hypocrites, trusting in their own resources, are unprepared, since they do not look for God, and for that reason they are very easily and very quickly deprived of all hope, as the prophet states here.

And it will be sheer terror to understand the message. Fools must be deloused with clubs. For fools who are without the Word are influenced by no admonitions and always sing their stale old songs, "Lamb, lamb."[16] And as Solomon says (Prov. 27:22): "Crush a fool in a mortar with a pestle along with crushed grain, yet his folly will

15 Luther is thinking of such passages as Ps. 90:5.

16 The phrase is obscure.

not depart from him." They never give up, and therefore the prophet says, *It will be sheer terror to understand the message.* They do not want to be instructed, therefore they must be driven with whips. For this reason the fools need to have a club on the shoulders; thus in distress and terror they depart from their presumption, and it makes them understand the message of the Word. So, then, the message of the Word is not received in peace and presumption; but when affliction and trouble come, then the power of the Word exerts itself both with the godly and with the ungodly. For you see that in the most important matters and in good times even the godly do not give heed to the Word but do receive it in affliction. How much more in the case of the ungodly.

20. *For the bed is too short.* Two proverbial comparisons are used: The bed is short, the cover is narrow; and so one has to adjust to the situation. Therefore also by affliction we are driven to the Word away from our presumption. Jerome applies this to marriage, where the husband says to his wife: The bed is narrow, it cannot hold both me, your husband, and an adulterer. Either I or the adulterer has to fall out of it."[17] Thus Christ, our Husband, cannot be there at the same time with our presumption. One has to fall. But this thought of Jerome's is allegorical. Let us understand it literally concerning distress. For just as the shortness of the bed keeps us from stretching our limbs but makes us pull them up so that we do not fall out and get cold, so distress holds us together so that we do not fall away from the Word of God, neither in good times or in affliction, but by faith abide in it. The cross teaches us how to snuggle up, since in good times we sometimes stroll and stray, inwardly by presumption and outwardly by our endeavors, our lusts and luxuries, and other evils.

21. *As on Mount Perazim, etc.* It is as if he were saying: "Because you scoff at the Word, the Lord is forced to do a strange work, namely, to judge and to destroy." For the proper work and nature of God is to save. But when our flesh is so evil that it cannot be saved by God's proper work, it is necessary for it to be saved by His alien work. Because in good times we stroll and stray from the Word, our covers have to be made narrow, and we must be disciplined by various afflictions so that we may be saved by God's alien work; the ungodly are altogether driven by God's proper and foreign work because they

[17] Jerome, *Commentaria,* IX, 335.

do not want to get under these narrow covers but want to stretch out in their own. Meanwhile God keeps His own by means of the cross and narrow covers and thus separates them from the ungodly. This is God's alien work, by which He condemns the ungodly, so that we may be saved. So you see that our flesh is outwardly indulgent when it is without the cross, and therefore various afflictions are necessary to control that flesh. I Chronicles 14 reports the story of Perazim, where the king did not want to do battle unless he had signs of the winds. In Hebrew פָּרִיץ means robber, or one who breaks through, one who separates and divides, one who does not walk on the king's highway but like robbers goes on untrodden roads through hedges and bushes. So the heretic forsakes the true way and walks in his own ways. Here he stands on Mount Perazim, because he is separated from the true way, from the righteousness of God and the Word, and goes his own way. He will be a divider who stands on Mount Perazim. This is what Christ did: He divided the ungodly from the godly by His Word in order to save His own. And so he does with our flesh, in order to preserve us through various afflictions. There God, too, stands on Mount Perazim.

In the valley of Gibeon. Read this story in Joshua 9, where God freed his own from the enemies by means of a hail storm. So Christ defends His own by His Word, which to the ungodly is nothing but hail and hailstones, while to the godly it is rain. To the ungodly the Word is scandal, pestilence, and death; but to the godly it is righteousness, refreshment, life, and sweet aroma. This is not the fault of the Gospel but of the ungodly, who by their unfaithfulness turn all good things into evil for themselves. Therefore this work is called God's alien work, to cast down the ungodly, who are themselves to blame, and to save His own godly people, who accept the Word and all the things of God. "These, then, I keep and defend by means of My proper work." But by their ungodliness the ungodly turn God into Satan, light into darkness, and righteousness into offense, and these are, therefore, lost by their own fault through God's alien work.

"Strange is His cultivation to produce a strange culture," that is, God must act by means of an alien work. For if He wants to sow the seed, He [18] must get rid of the weeds. Thus this is done by God's own proper work, in which He plants and raises His own, and uproots, drives out, and casts away the ungodly; and this same work becomes

[18] The Weimar text has *pellam,* but we have read *pellat.*

a strange work for the ungodly. We may very easily experience this in the rose, which is of one and the same nature, but the bees and spiders have different matter in it.[19] This is pertinent, because the righteousness of the Gospel had to be established, and for that reason it was necessary to condemn man's own righteousness and works. So it was necessary for God to do a strange deed and to conclude all under sin in order finally to justify them. He condemns and expels righteousness and the people clinging to their righteousness in order to raise up His own righteousness. He kills the flesh in order to make the spirit alive. This is, therefore, a most joyful thought which shows that every flower and splendor of the flesh must fall away so that the spiritual flower may bloom.

22. *Now therefore do not scoff.* He is addressing those who laugh at the words of God, saying: "You will not cause damage to the Word, but rather you will bring harm upon yourselves," namely:

Lest your bonds be made strong, that is, you are falling into a greater error. This is an excellent illustration, touching the power of the Law and of consciences, because the conscience is held captive by the Law. These are the bonds, namely, the Law, as we read in the Gospel: "Bind him hand and foot" (Matt. 22:13). Thus bound, they are unfit for anything. Such are those who live in the Law without faith.

For I have heard a decree of destruction. This passage is treated above in chapter 10:23. The prophet is saying: "I have heard a shortened decree from the Lord, which will come upon the whole earth and which admonishes them to come to their senses."

Shortened, that is, He will not destroy all. But He threatens the ungodly, lest they be totally consumed and destroyed; yet He preserves for Himself the remnant of the godly. This is the "shortened destruction."

23. *Give ear and hearken.* It is surprising that the prophet calls the people to repentance with so many words. He says: "Give ear, hear, hearken. Listen to me, I have something to say to you."

Does he who plows for sowing plow continually? This whole text to the end is comfort for the godly who see this destruction. Paul uses this argument in Romans 9–11, where he takes issue with the arguments of the Jews, who boasted that a truthful God will certainly perform what He has promised them, that they are God's people and

[19] On this saying, cf. *Luther's Works,* 26, p. 422, n. 48.

have many promises. Paul sweated much over these boasts of the Jews, lashing out at their empty boasting and showing that they have been rejected. So here the prophet says that the Gentiles are to be accepted and the Jews forsaken, and yet God remains truthful, even though it may seem otherwise. So today destruction looms up for the church under the pope and everywhere, yet it will not be so. Many people will nevertheless be preserved in the papacy and elsewhere, yet a very small part is saved. So it was among the boastful Jews who were rejected. We see them boasting: "We are God's children because we have God's promise; even if many of our people are evil and worthless, God's promise will not be void." So our papists boast of their number, their traditional right, the continuity of centuries, the apostolic sees. We must answer them: "God is truthful. Those who believe in Him are the church and the godly, even though they are the least and the fewest. 'Does the plower plow all day long?' " So it seems in the case of the plowman. When he breaks and turns the soil, he appears to be destroying the soil altogether, and yet he is preparing it for sowing.

24. *Plow, open, harrow, level.* It is as if he were saying: "Does the plowman always set out to plow and always to cut a furrow, and does he do it day after day? Is not such a plowman irritated by the hard work that accomplishes nothing?" But he does his work in its order much more for the purpose of sowing the seed. So it is necessary that our trust and righteousness be plowed and broken up, that the green sod be turned over, that we clearly despair of it and prepare ourselves for a better seed. Thus *when he has leveled its surface, does he not scatter dill,* or coriander, or vetches? He says: "Thus the plowman must not be viewed in his plowing and breaking, where he first destroys and lays waste the earth; for this is his alien work and it looks like a destruction of the earth, yet a fruitful harvest follows this." By this comparison he points also to God's reproof, which is to condemn the ungodly as by an alien work, but to receive the godly, who will put God's varied gifts to use in the field. The different kinds of seed designate the variety of God's gifts, as in 1 Cor. 14:1 ff. This parable of the plowman is, then, an indication of the work of God. When He appears to be destroying everything with devastation, destruction, and killing, then at last He lifts up His own, who have been well desciplined by these dangers and miseries. Thus this plowing on the part of God will apply itself to the seeds. The application follows.

26. *For he is instructed aright,* that is, the ending turns out this way, that "God will teach His own."

God will teach His own. Note. In the end the plowman tears up the soil for the purpose of seeding it, for it would be futile to sow the seed in untilled ground. So Christ plows His church and His own with extreme persecution and affliction, namely, so that He may sow a body to our flesh and that an imperishable body may sprout and rise up.

Aright, God will make everything turn out right.

Instruct, that is, plow and kill. *Teach,* that is, sow the seed and raise up. There follows another comparison about threshing.

27. *Dill is not threshed with a threshing sledge, nor is a cart wheel rolled over cummin.* We do not know the customs of these people, and therefore we cannot properly explain the comparison. *Stick, cart wheel, rod, staff.* But note this: So it is in threshing, that it has different kinds of operation, and each fruit has its own threshing implement. And fruits and grasses are not threshed and beaten in order to discard them altogether but to separate the grain from the husks and make it available for man's use. So also God threshes His people with condemnation, killing, and various dangers in this way, that it looks like total destruction to us, as it looks in threshing; but then it is finally prepared for use. So the Christian is consumed and afflicted, not to despair altogether, but to be killed. Therefore every plowman, sower, and thresher is a picture of God; the earth and the seed are pictures of the people, so that we are thus plowed and threshed by God to get rid of the coarse husks. As He does not always thresh just to be constantly threshing, but to look for bread; so we are not always afflicted, but only for a time, so that we may come to eternal life. The conclusion follows.

29. *This also comes from the Lord God.* Two things are required for a good undertaking: excellent counsel and a thoroughly happy ending. So here God in His excellent counsel plows and threshes us so that the plowman might have grain and bread, so that He Himself might have His own people. Therefore God's counsel is wonderful: He condemns our own endeavors in order to bring us to the goal; and though to our reason and flesh the situation in that condemnation appears to be completely hopeless, yet it will finally come out at a happy ending. He begins in wisdom and wisely sees it through.

CHAPTER TWENTY-NINE

1. *Ho, Ariel, Ariel, the city where David encamped!*

WE SAW in the last chapter how the cross of the godly is depicted with consoling comparisons. In this chapter the prophet goes on to describe the end of the remaining part that is willing to come to its senses and that is not thus plowed and threshed.

Ho, Ariel. He himself explains which city this is, lest someone speculate that because of the name Ariel it is a city other than Jerusalem.

The city where David encamped. He calls this city by the double name, *Ariel, Ariel,* that is, lion. By this name he rebukes the arrogance, presumption, and boasting of those who put much confidence in their temporal kingdom, saying: "Our kingdom is the kingdom of David, it is not like other kingdoms. We have the worship of God, the priesthood, on account of which we are not only not [1] overcome, but we are the conquerors of all others." Because that people has the most pregnant reasons for its presumption to boast, as I have said above,[2] where Paul went to a great deal of trouble to empty that glory, it is here presented as boasting *Ariel, Ariel,* "lion of God, lion of God."

Add year to year. The prophet laughs at their presumption, as if to say: "This is our greatest boast, that you have the highest festivals, sacrifices, ceremonies; you are holy, confident, and undismayed because you rely greatly on these ceremonies and rites of yours." Thus it is reported that they brought sacrifices in the midst of the destruction of Jerusalem.[3] To such an extent did they rely on their own ceremonies and deeds of righteousness.

2. *I will distress Ariel, etc. And she shall be to Me like an Ariel.* A very brief word showing their devastation, as if to say: "My Ariel, My saints in Jerusalem do not want to hear My Word. Therefore

[1] We have followed the suggestion of the Weimar editor and inserted *non* here.

[2] See pp. 235—236 above.

[3] Cf. Josephus, *The Jewish War,* V, 1.

there will be *moaning and lamentation,* that is, Jerusalem will be laid waste and neglected. *And you shall be to me a true Ariel.* This is paronomasia,[4] as if to say, "I will regard you as a real Ariel." At first Ariel is used in an active sense, because it belongs to God. Here it is used in a passive sense: separated from God, that is, one against whom God is fighting. So today we see the papists, who boasted that they were God's Ariel, for whom God would fight. They are God's Ariel all right, against whom God fights, even though they always rely on their own boasting. Therefore he most aptly describes the ungodly with the word "Ariel," as if to say: "I will surround you with a rampart and deal with you as with a lion."

3. *And I will encamp against you round about.* These are very plain words about the destruction of Jerusalem, and it seems that Christ in the Gospel quoted these words from this passage (Luke 19: 43). *And I will besiege you with towers.* He is speaking of the wall and the ramparts of the enemies who are besieging the city. He mentions three disasters: (1) the encirclement; (2) the outer siege-works; (3) the fortification of the enemies, so that they cannot escape in any way.

4. *You shall be humbled.* It is as if he were saying: "You who are so proudly elated over your kingdom and raise your mouth toward the sky and speak into heaven, that is, so have your own righteousness and your kingdom lifted you up, this will throw you down so low that you will mutter *from the earth.*" So it happens to all the ungodly who refuse to receive the Word but rely on their own resources. These are at last crushed into the dust and the earth, that is, having been deprived of the Word of God, they are submerged in their own traditions. They do not have the seat of Moses (cf. Matt. 23:2) but a pestilential and earthly and exceedingly wretched one. Thus we today see the most foolish and earthbound ideas among the Jews and papists.

You will speak: you will teach. *From the earth:* your doctrines.

And your voice will be like the voice of a ghost. It is as if he were saying: "They will be completely without the Word of the Lord but will be belly teachers the way a magical spirit is a ventriloquist, who speaks out of his head and for the sake of his stomach."

And from your dust, that is, your preaching will be low and earthly, as we see the Jewish refugees scarcely whisper their laws. This

[4] The Latin term used here for this play on words is *agnominacio.*

is the clearest and most dreadful punishment of the ungodly – the destruction of their kingdom and their priesthood, the reduction and destruction of their city, the loss of the Word, and the preaching of their own inventions and dreams. This is a prophecy of the destruction of Jerusalem, in what manner it is to be deprived of its kingdom, priesthood, etc.

5. *Like small dust.* This is an ambiguous and dark passage, because there seems to be no proper sequence. For if we take it to refer to the destruction of Jerusalem, the rage against the destroyers of Jerusalem follows badly. Jerome thinks that this dust does not refer to destruction but to the abundance and number of the enemies, who are as numerous as dust.[5] This appeals to me too. The meaning would then be: The Jews should not by any chance rely on their number, because they will be crushed by the Romans in far greater numbers, like the countless grains of sand by the sea. Here the multitude denotes the abundance of the Romans who will scatter them.

The ruthless. Hence this comparison speaks of the multitude of those who scatter but not of those who are ground down. It refers to the forces of the enemies that cannot be resisted, as we similarly speak of the Turk today, who advances with his army like clouds.

And in an instant, suddenly. It will happen soon and suddenly, at that moment "when they say: 'Peace and security'" (1 Thess. 5:3). When they have stood in their supreme boasting, then the destruction of the enemies will come. So the ungodly are always hopelessly lost. Suddenly, "unexpectedly," "immediately," not in time, but hopelessly, as all evils threaten their safety, as we read in Job (Job 1:13 f.).

6. *You will be visited by the Lord of hosts with thunder.* This is an exclamation. In sum: The Lord will visit you with all dangers, thunder, whirlwind, earthquake, great noise, and the flame of a devouring fire. There are different kinds of divine visitation, and God will once visit us with them all.

7. *It shall be like a dream.* This text seems to be threatening the Romans, who will have devastated the Jews. I think thus: The prophet is foretelling future disasters of the kingdoms; he is prophesying concerning the rod of Him who strikes: When He has struck the ungodly with this rod, He destroys these people too, as we read in Daniel

[5] Jerome, *Commentaria,* IX, 341.

(Dan. 2:35 ff.). From the iron that crushes all things comes that which is itself finally crushed. Balaam ruined the Jews and was then ruined too. So Rome, though called the eternal city, was at last laid waste also. From these examples it is clear that no rule prevails for long, but God despoils one kingdom by another. He scourges one rascal by another and then throws the whip into the fire. *It shall be like a dream.* All powers, kings, and kingdoms pass away and are unstable. Christ alone endures, and He uses them like a rod.

8. *As when a hungry man dreams.* This can be understood in a good sense, as the preceding was understood in a bad sense concerning the assaults on Ariel. But those who want to conquer Mount Zion, Christ and His own, will perish utterly. As the Romans later presumed to drive out the Christians, so also our tyrants are hungry and thirsty and try to swallow Christ and His own. They want to devour and guzzle everything; but when they think they have swallowed them all in martyrdom and they themselves are glutted, then the Christians will survive so much more. The adversaries stay hungry and thirsty, because their plot against the godly is nothing but dreams; for when they think or dream that the heresy has now been driven out, then the Word comes up all the more, and the godly are raised up all the more. So these gluttons always remain hungry, because they hatch every plot and scheme as if in a dream. So today we observe this in the tyrants and schismatics, who are in a dream dreaming that the Lutherans have been driven out and destroyed, but they will see when they have been awakened. For since they still live in a dream, they are not able to pass judgment. Thus to a natural dreamer this illusion seems like nothing but the real thing, for a dreamer cannot judge otherwise. So it is with our arrogant carnal people. They are very properly called dreamers, and this comparison fits them most aptly; for such men taken up with such visions cannot distinguish truth, as our schismatics dream and snore in the matter of divine bread [6] and boast of their victory. They are real dreamers. Thus the tyrants presume and dream that the godly are very easily destroyed, but Christ leaves them in their dream, and when they awake from it they will find out, just as the hungry dreamer experiences.

9. *Stupefy yourselves and be in a stupor!* The most careful distinc-

[6] This seems to be an attack *en passant* on the claim of Zwingli that the true doctrine of the Lord's Supper had been substantiated for him in a dream; cf. *Luther's Works,* 37, p. 52, n. 85.

tion of the prophets would be necessary, because here there should almost be a new chapter or a very large initial letter. "Be stupefied." Here he speaks about that most wretched blindness of the Jews, who could not read in spite of open books, whose blindness far surpassed the dreams of the Gentiles. *Stupefy yourselves and be in a stupor* should be one word: Be dismayed. Paul seems to have quoted this passage, or rather the Habakkuk passage (Hab. 1:5; Acts 13:41; cf. Acts 28:26 f.) "Be astounded and wonder" – stand aghast!

Blind yourselves: Become blind. Become mad, foolish, blind, raving, and besotted. This is a bitter concession. On your way in the devil's name! This is what will happen to you. These words of the prophet are fitting attributes of all apostates and hardened, ungodly people.

Stagger. As drunkards stagger, so the ungodly teachers waver hither and yon, ignorant and unsure. The translators put down six verbs: "Be stupefied, be amazed, waver, stumble, be drunk, stagger." But there are only four in Hebrew: (1) *Stupefy yourselves and be in a stupor:* They are stupid, they stare at you like cows. (2) "Waver,"[7] or as in chapter six above (Is. 6:10). Be blind,[8] like the dreamers with closed eyes. They see like a chicken. (3) *Be drunk.* (4) "Stagger like totterers." With these four words he pictures the unfitness of the ungodly for the Word. They are stupid, blinded, bereft of hearing and sight; they are intoxicated with their own ideas. As we say, "It is useless to tell a story to a man who is stone-deaf,"[9] and, "It is useless to philosophize before an ass,"[10] so it is when the ungodly hear the Word. "Be stupefied." This is not an imperative but a bitter concession, as if to say: "If you will not hear the Word, then be stupid, etc. Go to the devil if you will not have it otherwise." Why?

10. *For the Lord has poured out upon you a spirit of deep sleep.* This is their drunkenness, that the Lord pours into them not wine but a spirit, not the Holy Spirit but a spirit of deep sleep. To *pour out* is to give over to a base spirit. Not that God infuses such a spirit,

[7] The Weimar text has *Fluctuat,* but we have followed the Biblical text and read *Fluctuate.*

[8] The Weimar text has *Excecat,* but we have followed the Biblical text and read *Excecate.*

[9] Cf. *Luther's Works,* 2, p. 22, n. 34; 4, p. 400, n. 90.

[10] Cf. Cicero, *Oratio in Pisonem,* 30.

since His Word is good, but that, since the ungodly will not hear it, they are given up to a base mind, as we read in Rom. 1:28.

And has closed your eyes, and covered your prophets, and princes who see visions, that is, "When the Lord has poured *a spirit of deep sleep* upon you, then He will close your eyes, so that you cannot see the Word set forth and, because the light has been put out, you can see nothing" – so that they do not see the Gospel, grace, and wonders, and what is most dreadful of all, that the *prophets,* the rulers and spiritual heads, and the *princes,* the temporal lords, see nothing. These two realms have to be nothing but darkness and seductions, as we see in our time how we are under the blindest kings and bishops, who in their blindness oppose us and say: "Do you think that so many princes, prophets, and so great a world have been in error?" The prophet answers: "Yes, indeed, because the princes and prophets have been blinded and overcome by a spirit of deep sleep."

11. *And the vision of all this will become to you.* It is as if he were saying: "I will demonstrate by an example that you are blind, that by your ungodliness you are closing the Scripture for yourselves," as we observe with regard to the Jews, who do not see the very clearest prophecies of all the prophets. So today we see that the papists do not recognize the plainest testimonies of Scripture. This is the fault not of the prophecy but of their blindness and ungodliness. As it is not the fault of the book and the letters that a peasant cannot read, but the peasant's, so it is not the fault of the Bible, which is very clear so that even boys understand it, but it is the fault of the ideas and darkness of the papists, who love darkness rather than light (John 3:19). This passage in general has all the ungodly in view who in all the universities, monasteries, and fraternities cannot in a godly manner explain one chapter or article of faith. Let us pray the Lord to preserve us from such *a spirit of deep sleep.*

Of a book that is sealed, that is, of a closed one.

12. *When men give it to one who can read* or *one who cannot read.* There are two comparisons. This sealed and closed book benefits neither the reader nor the nonreader. This shows that the fruit of ungodliness is that neither readers nor nonreaders can understand. Paul attacks this in 2 Cor. 3:7 and 4:3, where he speaks of Moses' veil, which is not on Moses but on the face of the people and on their heart.

This is that veil and sealed book. Thus it happens to our bishops who do not know the Scriptures. The book is closed, they can read, they are ungodly, they despise the Word. This, then, is the punishment of those who despise the Word, those whom He often wanted to gather together and they refused: "Remain forsaken and ignorant now," as we see in the monastic and papistic orders, who are frustrated with much striving, as the following text says.

13. *Because this people draw near.* Christ cites this passage in Matt. 15:8, where He adds the word "in vain." With this single word He embraces this whole chapter and every attempt of the ungodly, who have zealously crucified themselves with their labors, who exercise themselves with vigils, "who draw near to Me in order to obtain Me," and yet they are blinded. Why? Because they are hypocrites and self-righteous. *Draw near* properly refers to the state of mind of those who are externally zealous and glittering in appearance and boast that they are next to Christ. But they "draw near to Me" in this way that "they honor Me with their mouth and lips." Is not this most terrible that the pope, the bishops, and all the papists, sweating with strenuous efforts, even with the Word of God, are in position nearest to God, but with their heart least of all? Thus we make a concession to the adversaries, who boast that they are nearest to God. I say: "It's true. With your mouth and lips you are closest to God, preaching that Christ suffered, was born, and died for us." This is what the papists have said with their mouth. This is the approach of the mouth. But when I say: "If Christ died for us, we toil in vain with our endeavors," there they oppose us while they rely on their own boasting, and therefore in their heart they are far from God.

And their fear of Me is through a commandment of human teaching. This is what the Hebrew says. "What they practice toward Me is called *fear,* that is, worship of God, or piety, and religion, and that has gone directly off into manmade teachings, so that they are more afraid of, and have more respect for, the teachings of men than of God." This we see in the Decretal, where there is such stern adherence to this teaching that they lift their own rules above the commandments of God, where fornication, robbery, usury, and murder are far less important than the eating of meats and eggs on a fast day. We saw this in the monasteries, where pride reigns in the highest degree, where the hood, scapulars, and other observances are defended much more quickly than the commandment of God.[11] They pay no attention to God and His Word in setting up their own rules. In this they decree the greatest sins and merits. But when they thus turn things upside down, God upsets and rejects them by a just judgment. For God wants His worship to surpass all others. The pope, however, extols his worship over all; he does not permit anyone to whisper one little word against him, but meanwhile he himself overlooks more than enough against Christ and His Word and, worst of all, he himself persecutes Christ, as we have hitherto seen by experience and still see. To listen to anyone saying anything against the pope was a greater sin than if it were against God; so has the fear of human traditions taken possession of us. This is indicated by these words, "with the mouth and lips they honor Me." For the ungodly seducers proceed in this way that they always come praising God with the mouth and the lips. For all evils and seductions are done under the guise of godliness. Every calamity begins in God's name. He says, moreover: They *honor Me*. What is this, that they even *honor Me?* The ungodly invent such a god for themselves as has regard for them and saves them on the basis of their works and merits, as our papists all believe in God and glorify Him, yet nevertheless everyone relies on Francis or Dominic and their respective party. He does not worship the true God, but by his perverted practice he thinks and boasts that he is worshiping God; yet he lies shamelessly and, as Paul says (2 Tim. 3:5), they indeed glorify God in appearance and words, but not at all in deed and in power.

Through commandments of human teaching. Where people have once forsaken the Word, it is inevitable that tradition will soon follow; or there is opinion, that is, error, on the part of those who erect their own idols according to their own ideas, and then error soon follows. Meanwhile, however, they always have their supreme boasting, also for these; for he says here "their fear." We experienced this among the papists, who were terribly afraid where there was nothing to fear and were not afraid where they should have been afraid. This, then, is the nature of human traditions: They bring very great fear

[11] The scholia on this passage say: "The same thing happens in the monasteries. When pride, hatred, laziness, lust, etc. reigned there to an extreme degree, they were regarded as trivial sins. But to go out of one's cell without a scapular, to violate the Lenten fast, etc. was an unforgivable sin. (W, XXV, 197).

with them, but it is altogether perverted and opposed to God. Therefore he says: *Their fear of Me, etc.*

14. *Therefore, behold, I will again do marvelous things with this people.* In Hebrew the word *marvelous* is doubled, that is, "Everywhere I will deal marvelously with this people, here, there, and everywhere." How will He deal marvelously with this people? Thus:

The wisdom of their wise men shall perish, and the discernment. This is the marvel of divine wrath, that these ungodly people believe nothing and are not persuaded by us, accepting nothing beyond their own security and replying to our admonitions: "If you get to heaven before me, do not dust out my eyes." Thus you see that they have no wisdom, no faith and understanding, no discernment of Scripture and the Word. The wise men are those who know the rule and analogy of faith. The understanding ones are those who test doctrines and adjudicate them by a keen judgment, those who in fear test all things according to the analogy of faith. The ungodly lack these gifts and have no understanding or faith but always snore away in their own smugness. Such are the Jews and especially the papists, who in their security and traditions have boasted only of their church against the whole Scripture and the doctrine of faith and love, and very, very few shine with outward mortification, with which they tire the body for a little while as is their pleasure. However, there has been nothing in them of the Word, of faith, of conscience, and of love. Always the heart has remained the same. Therefore they remain in their dream, possessing nothing of faith or of love, because they are neither wise nor understanding. And when they will be most wise, they will be most ungodly; and when they want to be most understanding, they are the most stupid. This is so because they do not have the Word but their own traditions.

15. *Woe to those who hide deep from the Lord!* We have already heard about the ungodliness of these people and about the punishment for it, once the pretense of wisdom and understanding has been left behind and the truth of the matter has been brought in. Now such people begin to defend themselves and hide from the Lord. How can they hide from the Lord? I answer: He is speaking in the manner and from the point of view of the ungodly, who say: "I am not afraid of your Lord, whom you preach, for He does not see me." In other words, "Dear Isaiah, I have no fear of your God; He will not

scald a finger for me." Psalm 14:1 describes it more fully: "The fool says in his heart, 'There is no God.'" "As for us, let us do our works; God will not notice those people." Psalm 10:11 reports: "He thinks in his heart, 'God has forgotten, He has hidden His face, He will never see it.'" Just so our adversaries all say that there is a God; but when we proclaim the true God to them, they do not want to accept Him but prefer to worship their own. They do not want the evangelical God, and so they have their own God and keep our true God hidden. They hide Him with their teaching, their good intention, and their divine obedience, in whatever manner a man can cheat.

Whose deeds are in the dark. They think they are not seen by God, because they do everything in the pretense and appearance of godliness in the opinion that God does not see. They are censured by the prophets, who reject their hypocrisy.

Who sees us? Who knows us? It is as if he were saying: "Who told you that our works are evil? How do you know? Who has shown you anything more upright than us? You think that you alone are wiser than we are."

16. *You turn things upside down!* I tell you that this your mask and godliness is perverted and prove it by the following comparisons: O you fools, do you think you are deceiving God? No, no, as the product cannot hide from the potter, so you cannot hide from God the Maker. He will see your ungodliness, however much you may do it with the appearance of godliness.

17. *Is it not yet a very little?* He is making a threat, as if to say, "No teaching, admonition, or threat avails for you. In the name of God, the situation must be changed."

In a very little while Lebanon shall be turned into a fruitful field, and the fruitful field into a forest, that is: "I will change things by a wonderful change, so that the Jewish people is not a people and the Gentiles, who are not a people, are a people, as a field is physically changed into a forest and a forest into a field."

Carmel. A region completely given to agriculture is used figuratively to denote a *fruitful field. Lebanon,* that is Jerusalem, which was built with materials from Lebanon, as also the whole temple was constructed out of wood from Lebanon. "This city is to become 'Carmel,' that is, a *fruitful field,* and I will change 'Carmel,' or the fruitful field, into a city." Thus by means of this simile he indicates the fall of the Jews and the reception of the Gentiles. So your papistic church will be changed into a field; and the field, that is, where there is no appearance of a church, there will be the church. As these papists, the most ignorant braggarts of the church, could not explain one little verse of a psalm, so these Lebanese braggarts of love are now Carmel, and we are Carmel. We Lebanese have attained to glory before God, although this is not apparent to the world.

18. *In that day the deaf shall hear,* that is, the nations that seem deaf *shall hear the words of a book,* a book that is sealed to the blind Jews. "As Christ says in John 9:39: 'For judgment I came into this world, that those who do not see may see, and that those who see may become blind,' so you, presumptuous hearers, will be deaf; and the deaf and ignorant, who do not think that they hear, these will hear. Thus the prophet fights against the stubbornness of the ignorant, as the Jews, who boast of their wisdom and of the fact that they hear a great deal, do not hear. The deaf Gentiles, however, who claim nothing for themselves, these hear *the words of a book,* that is, the Scripture. So in our time the Gospel is heard by those who acknowledge their error.

Out of their gloom, that is, blindness. *And darkness,* that is, their traditions. *The eyes of the blind,* the Gentiles, see.

19. *The meek shall obtain fresh joy in the Lord.* The Hebrew word עֲנָוִים means wretched, afflicted, and extremely unfortunate. It does not, strictly, mean *meek.* From such all boasting and bragging about works and merits has been removed, and they boast only in the Lord. These very people accept the Gospel, saying: "Although I am poor, wretched, and lost, Christ is nevertheless my rich man and my Savior." So it always follows that such people have tribulation in the world, but they have peace before God the Father. These are the עֲנָוִים, that is, the poor. The afflicted in spirit, those who upon self-examination cry out that they are poor and afflicted – these alone boast of the glory, power, and riches of the Lord, not of their own resources, as Is. 9:3 says, that the ungodly do not rejoice in the Lord, but only the wretched and afflicted glory in Him. Therefore this text drives out all merits and every reliance on our righteousness.

20. *The ruthless shall come to naught.* When the tyrant will have come to naught, etc. By the light of the Gospel men learn to trust in Christ alone, when they have been liberated from the tyrants of their

souls and have been made subject to their Shepherd, Christ. This was done in the time of the apostles when the synagog was repudiated and the church came into being. עָרַץ properly means to be terrible, and from it is derived the verbal noun עָרִיץ, which means tyrant. Thus Ps. 10:15 and Ps. 37:35 refer to the ungodly man who is exalted. He calls the pope and the bishops עָרִיץ, because they harass the consciences of the lowly with snares. Christ promises that these will bring oppression and that He will set His own people free.

The scoffer, that is, the mockers and despisers of the Word continue, smug in their tyranny; they *watch to do evil.* In Hebrew אָוֶן means toil and hard effort and fittingly is applied to our deeds of righteousness, toil that only makes those who rely on it sad and annoyed. Summary: "I will root out all tyrants, teachers, pastors, and scribes who are nothing but 'watchers for evil.'" *They watch,* that is, they are zealous, they are wiser than the torches of light. For the flesh devotes more care and zeal to its deceptions and schemes than the godly do to the godliness of the Word. So we observe in our schismatics, who remain extremely alert. These are descriptions of the ungodly teachers, who do nothing else all day than lead astray and increase sin by the idol of our righteousness.

21. *Who make a man out to be an offender by the Word,* that is, through the preaching of a Word, as if the ungodly were saying: "Do you, prophet, say that we are the authors of sin though we zealously preach God's Law to the people?" He answers: "It is through the Word that you lead the people astray."

And lay a snare for him who reproves in the gate. They are unwilling to put up with one who rebukes them, but they kill the godly prophets; yes, they establish their own traditions and defend them against true preaching. *In the gate,* that is, in a public place, as we say, in the church or at the town hall. That is to say, like fowlers and hunters they sneak up on those who publicly denounce them to their face. Thereby he indicates that these people make their attempts on those who reprove in the gate, not by violence but by ambushes and false accusations to have the title of piety and to kill the prophet as a heretic. This is what it means to be hunted and waylaid by our adversaries.

And turn aside. If they cannot kill them, they then turn away from them for the weightiest reasons as from a most pestilential heretic. For they call the just preacher a heretic.

In vain: for nothing, without cause, although they muster the weightiest reasons. "If we let him go, then all the people will turn to him and overthrow the church." Thus they insult Christ and us. For in vain, without cause, they turn away from the righteous, they avoid them and with a loud hue and cry they denounce them as heretics. All these tyrants the Lord will root out and cause them to fail, so that the lowly may come to the true and sincere Word.

22. *Therefore thus says the Lord, who redeemed Abraham, concerning the house of Jacob.* When those tyrants have been rooted out, you will see the lowly and the poor rejoice and dance for joy, then you will see them sanctified. For Jacob will have the same God as Abraham, while those ungodly people set up a god different from the God of Abraham, as our sects invent another god for themselves. The Franciscan fashions for himself a god who is hooded and girded with a rope and one who has regard for our works.

Jacob shall no more be ashamed. This is the greatest comfort of the godly. It is as if he were saying: "Until now, while the ungodly teachers were in control, there was nothing but confusion, sadness, and constant fear. But now that Christ the Shepherd and the Gospel have been revealed and the ungodly have been rooted out, we stand justified and have peace with God in our hearts through Him, as Paul exquisitely depicts that glory and joy in Rom. 5:1.

23. *When they see their children.* When they have seen many deriving benefit and edification from this very fruit of the Gospel, they will see many becoming children of Jacob, who are *the work of My hands.* For faith is God's work alone and is given to those whom God draws and teaches. Thus when they see children growing through the Word and faith, then they will give thanks to God the Savior, who brings many to the faith of Jacob.

They will sanctify My name, that is, they will proclaim not their own name and merits, as our papists do, but will extol the name of God alone, who gives the increase. *They will sanctify the Holy One of Jacob. My name* and *the Holy One of Jacob* are the same.

And will stand in awe of the God of Israel, who will be their true עָרִיץ. This is the worship of the New Testament: to worship, to sanctify, to fear, to love, etc.

24. *And those who err in spirit will come to understanding,* that is, although the ungodly always resist, yet some of them, too, will be

seized, who will yield to the Gospel. So today there are some who break away from the papists and schismatics, people who *err in spirit* and are immersed in a spirit of error, but they will learn understanding at last together with the ability to judge doctrine, after they have forsaken their error. Above, the prophet spoke of wisdom and understanding. Wisdom is the very knowledge of God, of which also the ungodly boast. But they do not possess understanding, they do not promote darkness in spite of spiritual discernment.[12] They do not have a prompt insight since they lack understanding. To understand means to have a clear insight. And lest they fall into all kinds of doctrine without understanding, the Word is preached to them so long as they need understanding.

And those who murmur will accept instruction. לֶקַח means instruction and knowledge. From this is derived the name Luke, that is, "teacher."[13] Here he calls them "murmurers." Those who appear to be the wisest teachers will become murmurers. Because they speak earthly things out of their own head, they freely accept teaching. So you see the fruit of the Word, that teachers who were puffed up by their own opinions become disciples and hearers. For such people are רוֹגֵן, talkative, more inclined to speaking than to listening. The Gospel will convert some of them.

12 The original Latin is somewhat obscure: "non spiritus iudicio obscurant."

13 According to Eusebius, *Ecclesiastical History,* III, 4, 6, Luke was an Antiochene by race; Luther may be reflecting that tradition here.

CHAPTER THIRTY

1. *"Woe to the rebellious children," says the Lord, "who carry out a plan."*

This chapter has been variously torn apart and maltreated in the commentaries.[1] As for me, because I see the prophet being extremely severe in his reproof, I believe that we must apply to his own time what he preached to the people of his day and for his own times. And from this chapter to chapter 36 he deals with a new word, as it were, by means of which he teaches a variety of things, but especially two. First he is concerned about keeping the people loyal in the faith and arousing them to their common danger from the king of the Assyrians, who was harassing the people. But the people, on the contrary, were always looking for alliances, and it is against this attempt of theirs that the prophet is constantly speaking. For they were planning to ally themselves with the king of the Egyptians against the king of the Assyrians and, turning their backs on God, the supreme Protector, they sought refuge with men. It is all these things that the prophet assails so violently. So it would be with me; if I should be obliged constantly to take care of the Word and the building of the church and pilgrimages to St. James [2] and other matters, I, too, would inveigh against them. Thus I also think that this was written in the time of Hezekiah, the best of kings, who had the worst rascals around him as senators and counselors, who obstructed the king's most godly decrees. This can happen with our prince too.[3] It is these counselors of Hezekiah whom the prophet rebukes most sharply.

Woe to the rebellious children. The Hebrew word סוֹרֵר means disobedient and self-willed and describes those who have turned their heart away from the decree of their excellent king. It is as if he were

[1] Luther seems to be referring to the material assembled in Lyra's comments; among the earlier exegetes who dealt with the chapter were Haimo of Auxerre, *Commentaria in Esaiam*, Book I, *Patrologia, Series Latina*, CXVI, 862; also Hervais of Bourg-Dieu, *Commentaria in Esaiam*, Book IV, *Patrologia, Series Latina*, CLXXXI, 282.

[2] Cf. *Luther's Works*, 4, p. 130, n. 41.

[3] See Luther's remarks of 1534, *Luther's Works*, 13, pp. 170—173.

saying: "You renegade children, who ought to be children but are apostates." You may well believe that they found it very difficult to put up with this scathing rebuke.

Who carry out a plan, but not Mine; and who make a league, but not of My spirit. This is the deliberation of those who do not want to believe and obey the prophet and Hezekiah but say: "Our king is a fool who does not want to protect us, and that prophet will lead us astray. Let us look for outside help from the king of Egypt." Therefore the prophet replies: "You carry out *a plan, but not Mine,* and you seek protection, *but not of My spirit,* but rather in opposition to Me."

That they may add sin to sin, that is, "in this your plan fails; you will not be saved but aggravate preceding sins by following sins." By that harshness of reproof he desires to terrify them.

2. *Who set out to go down to Egypt.* This is the argument and burden of this chapter, as if they were saying: "We do not want to listen to Isaiah nor obey the king, because they are fools. Let us go down to Egypt to look for help. Isaiah is a beggar, he does not have much to lose." Dr. Martin does have much to lose.[4] He can be quite daring, but not we." *To take refuge.* This was their intention.

3. *Therefore shall the protection of Pharaoh turn to your shame.* This is the prophecy of the prophet against the plans of those who put their confidence in men and forsook God. We see this in our time, that the favor of kings is not reliable. Therefore the courtiers have this proverb: The favor of princes is like April weather.[5] Thus we see in our time that all the princes and the whole world are perverse, and this is our plaint: the world is unfaithful. Therefore learn to trust in God alone and not in man, because man deceives. Either he is unable to help you, though he wants to; or, if he wants to, he cannot. Hence we must not rely on any man, be he ever so good. Thus he says here:

The protection of Pharaoh shall turn to your shame, that is, "Do not rely on man, else you will be deceived. Do not rely on any man; you will know by example and from experience that, unless you call upon God alone, the world plays you false and deceives you. But speak thus: 'Dear God, Thou alone wilt provide and accomplish every-

[4] This seems to be a reflection of the political conflicts of the time, e. g., at the Diet of Speyer in 1529.

[5] Cf. *Luther's Works,* 14, p. 232, n. 11.

thing.' And if you do wish to rely on man, do not do so absolutely, but rely absolutely on God." *The protection of Pharaoh* represents all human confidence.

4. *Though his envoys reach Hanes, etc.* It is as if he were saying: "I tell you that you are exerting yourself in vain." They called the city "Hanes." In Hebrew we call it Zoan and in Greek, Hanes. This is a royal city. Another city is Cannis. Perhaps we are dealing with just one city which had two names because of the different languages, as the Hungarians give the name of Belgrade to a city which we call Weissenburg on the basis of the Greek.[6]

5. *Everyone comes to shame through a people that cannot profit them, etc.* This is what they have accomplished: nothing but shame. They have received no help but only what leads to shame and disgrace. They have procured no help and achieved nothing more than that people who were disappointed by the king of the Egyptians, who could have helped them, were ridiculed all the more by the king of the Assyrians. So it might happen to us when we boast of anyone, in whom we might be disappointed if we needed him.

6. *An oracle on the beasts of the Southland.* He has already prophesied against their plans. Now he attacks their costly treasures which they take to the king of Egypt on beasts of burden and at very great expense, and all for nothing. These are threats against asses and elephants that were carrying the gifts down to the king of the Egyptians. He calls them "beasts of the southland," because they are to carry these gifts there. These most wretched pack animals go into a land of trouble which was to be laid waste by the king of Assyria. This is a land of anguish because the people do not rely on God.

The words *from where comes the lioness and the lion, the viper and the flying serpent* should be placed in parentheses. This road to Egypt is a desolate one through the desert, where the lions and vipers are. It is as though the prophet were saying: "They travel by dangerous routes, because there really are lions and lionesses there. Since they have departed from God, they walk the lions' way and follow the serpents' path." For the ungodly are themselves lions and vipers, as Christ calls them a brood of vipers (Matt. 23:33). Those who refuse to hear the Word of God from the prophet Isaiah are following dan-

[6] "Belgrade" means "white fortress."

gerous routes. *Flying serpent,* that is, fiery serpent with a poisonous breath, as in the desert. Summary: This prophecy is directed against the wretched pack animals that carry riches on their backs over extremely dangerous routes as presents for the king. Thus the prophet rebukes their greatest plans and expenses, which are in vain after all.

7. *Therefore I cry out over this,* that is, I cry out over the ungodliness and lack of foresight on the part of those who have forsaken God and are looking for human help.

Rahab, רַהַב: Egypt sits still, that is, it will completely ignore you and will not protect you. Therefore you must give up relying on men and on Egypt, because Egypt will certainly do nothing to protect you. Egypt will surely not bother to preserve you. In the Scriptures Egypt is quite often referred to as *Rahab,* that is, "pride" (cf. Ps. 87:4).

8. *And now, go, write it before them on a tablet, etc.* Here again the interpreters are toiling and disagreeing.[7] There was a similar command in chapter 8:11 above. This is customary procedure with the prophets: When the ungodly refuse to believe the bare Word, the prophets add an external sign. So Jeremiah, getting no results when he predicted the Babylonian captivity, wore a chain around his neck as an external sign (Jer. 27:2). So here the writing drawn on the tablet is a sign. Thus in our time the Word is read and taught by means of the tongue, the pen, songs, and paintings as a witness to the ungodly.[8] So he says here: *Write it on a tablet,* or "slate." *In a book,* that is, "on a sheet." *Inscribe,* "engrave." *That it may be for the time to come,* that is, "the future," so that this may be a prophecy. So you should openly write it before their eyes, so that their descendants might inherit the warning of their parents, who were cut off because of their unbelief, and this might serve them as a perpetual witness to frighten all descendants. By means of this alarm he wants to deter the ungodly from their malice. Thus in our time today we wonder at the great darkness in which we have lived apart from the Word of God in our own ideas. There follows what was written on the tablet:

9. *For they are a rebellious people, lying sons, sons who will not hear the instruction of the Lord.* In this way the descendants will see

[7] Luther may be referring here to the comments of Lyra *ad* Is. 30:8.

[8] Luther seems to be referring to the work of Lucas Cranach the Elder (1472—1553) and of Albrecht Dürer (1471—1528), whom he regarded as artistic interpreters of his Reformation.

the ungodliness of their forefathers, who nevertheless believed themselves to be very godly. Here, too, you have a general characterization of the ungodly. *Disobedient, lying children,* not true children but such as contradict the Word and refuse to hear it.

10. *Who say to the seers,* that is, the prophets, רֹאִים. "To see" is to prophesy. *See not,* that is, "We command you on pain of excommunication, on pain of the wrath of the apostles Peter and Paul, not to speak that message of yours to us." Just as they spurned the clearest and truest articles of John Hus, so these people said: *See not.*

"And to the observers," that is, the preachers. "To see" and "to observe" is to preach. *What is right,* as if to say: "Speak, but only what pleases us." So the papists say: "We would gladly hear them. But they do not have the Word, only heresy." And this false teaching the prophet calls true. *What is right,* as if the prophet were saying: "I preach to you what is right, namely, faith and upright conduct. They, however, want to hear their own ideas from us, and they want to go off to the right or to the left.

Speak to us smooth things, because the flesh thoroughly detests the Word of faith, which kills the flesh, presumption, and all things hypocritical. Thus the papists would be more than ready to permit the preaching of the Word, if only it were smooth. But since it is bitter and conflicts with their rites and ceremonies and abuses, they are unwilling to hear it.

Prophesy illusions, "fraud, that which deceives." The ungodly do not say this, that these things are illusions. On the contrary, they call it truth. But the prophet uses this word "illusions," which they do not want to hear, to agree with their way of looking at it. They actually say: "Teach us the truth."

11. *Turn aside from the path,* that is, "Lead us off the true way." And yet as far as their public image is concerned, they say that they are on the true path.

Let us hear no more of the Holy One of Israel. "Do not tell us about the Holy One of Israel, our Protector, but speak to us about the well-armed king of Egypt, who will help us. Dear sir, shut up about your God." So our papists, as soon as they have heard the Gospel mentioned, cry out: "Be quiet! This is Lutheran and ungodly." Our descendants, too, will see this their ungodliness as though it were written on a tablet. Under a pretense they order us to preach the Gospel, and yet they in fact bring action against it.

12. *Therefore thus says the Holy One of Israel:* Because you *despise this Word.* He threatens them with a punishment which applies to all the ungodly, that suddenly and unexpectedly destruction will come upon them and that their solace will vanish ever so quickly. It is as if he were saying: "This is your iniquity, that you have despised the Word and that you put your hope in chicanery. Your fate will be like that of a man who stands on top of a wall to look out for the enemy when the walls collapse under him and crush him." That will be the fate of those who trust in chicanery. The very thing in which they trust will be their downfall, just as he who depends on the wall is struck down by it.

And trust in oppression and perverseness. To resort to oppression is to put the worst construction on everything. Oppressors and perverse men, such people the Gospel has with it. Those who call our Gospel heresy interpret our truth as a lie and our truth and all good things as evil and false. They declare their own falsehoods to be entirely true, as is the case, in fact, with all opponents of the Gospel. The ungodly put their hope and trust in such people, and they take consolation in this slanderous and perverse teaching of theirs.

13. *Like a break in a high wall, bulging out, and about to collapse.* For the collapse of walls is a crashing fall. As some waters flow and boil up, so a wall in its final collapse crashes down irresistibly – crash, bang, like a river.

Whose crash comes suddenly, in an instant. This is an additional thought regarding the sudden and irretrievable collapse, because the ruin of these people is similar to the wall about to crash and to the unexpected evil. As one does not try to repair a wall when it is at the point of crashing but gets out of its way as fast as possible, so there will be no help for them.

14. *Its breaking is like that of a potter's vessel.* As a vessel of a potter is shattered in such a way that not a sherd remains, so also the ungodly will be so utterly crushed that not a fragment or anything else will remain of them. Such is the collapse of the ungodly. By means of this illustration he takes the offensive against the ungodly despisers of the Word, and by this most dreadful parable he attempts

to turn them away from disaster. There follows an exhortation and a promise and a golden text.

15. *In returning and rest you shall be saved.* We translate it thus: "If you will sit down and be quiet, you shall be saved." "Do not lose heart and do not lose your temper. Wait till the storm blows over and keep still." Now that is a marvelous victory, to conquer by sitting and waiting! Meanwhile the flesh runs and toils and looks for help.

In quietness and in trust shall be your strength. Trust in God, be patient, and commit everything to Him. In a wonderful way you will see God as your protector. So a former bishop of Mainz was obliged to wage war against the duke of Saxony.[9] The bishop kept on with his duties and gave no thought to the implements of war. He hoped for victory in silence and trust. And this we must believe and do in our time, so that against the emperor, against Ferdinand, and against Duke George[10] and the strongest foes, who could grind us under their feet – against them, I say, let us use the most patient victory both of silence and of trust, as success has hitherto come to us. This passage is, therefore, an outstanding, golden, and magnificent promise: "In sitting quietly you shall be saved." All the experience of the nations bears this out. For the Romans boasted of Fabius that he restored their cause by delaying.[11] "Patience conquers all things," and Paul says to the Romans (Rom. 12:21): "Overcome evil with good." We must most certainly believe that the evil man will not remain unpunished and that the godly man will not remain unavenged. In this we sin, however, that we cannot wait for the time of divine vengeance, or when God delays with His vengeance. For God does not leave any sin unavenged, but either punishes one kingdom by another, or one person by another, and protects the upright and true, as the heathen say: "Truth can be opposed but not deposed." So the godly, protected by the truth of God, are opposed but not driven out. So here, the ungodly are unwilling to wait out the king's silence and the prophet's admonitions. Therefore, up to chapter 36, the prophet toils

[9] It is not clear which bishop (or archbishop) of Mainz Luther has in mind, but it may be the most distinguished recent incumbent, Berthold of Henneberg (1484—1504), who had engaged in several political struggles for the dignity of his see.

[10] Charles V was the emperor; Ferdinand I, his brother, was at this time king of Bohemia; George was duke of Albertine Saxony.

[11] Luther is referring to Quintus Fabius Maximus, who died in 203 B. C.; his caution in the Punic Wars earned him the nickname *Cunctator*, "Delayer."

with threats, intimidations, and promises to lead them to silence thereby, saying: "The king is ungodly, he cannot possibly escape punishment. We are the godly, God is our zealot, He will not allow us to go unavenged. Therefore *in quietness and in trust shall be our strength.*" This alone you have. Be calm, wait, wait, commit your cause to God, He will make it succeed. Psalm 37:35 has to do with this thought and exhortation: "I have seen a wicked man overbearing." Look for Him a little at a time; wait, wait. But since this waiting seems long to the flesh and appears like death, the flesh always wavers. But keep faith. Patience will overcome wickedness. And the philosophers say: "Evil defeats itself." [12]

And you would not. You were disobedient to the king and the prophet. *No!* "By no means, because we would be fools [13] in our expectation." *But we will speed upon horses,* that is, we will in no wise escape this evil except with the help of horsemen. *Upon swift steeds,* that is, "Let us use dromedaries to seek refuge for our safety with the king of Egypt, who will set us free with his army." Thus they rely not on the invisible God but on the visible presence of horses, gold, and their own power. *We will go up,* that is, with horsemen.

Therefore your pursuers shall be swifter. I swear to you by all that is holy that you will not escape. This is a related threat.

17. *A thousand shall flee at the threat of one, etc.* The punishment of the ungodly is described in a remarkable way. Granted that you are a thousandfold stronger than the Assyrians. Yet the Lord will bring it about that one of the Assyrians will be stronger than a thousand of your men. For it is not number and resources but a brave and strong spirit that will win, and quite frequently a very small army defeats a large one. Thus Maximilian with a small force crushed countless Venetians.[14] And I have heard from some of his soldiers, who said that at first sight of the armies they saw victory before the battle, because in a defeat both soldiers and horses are extremely listless before the battle, so that the size of the army in no way helps to gain the victory. This is so because all resources are for nothing where there is no courageous spirit (something that God gives to all,

[12] The Latin form of this widely used epigram was: *Malum vincit seipsum.*

[13] The Weimar text has *moreremur,* but we have read *moraremur.*

[14] Between 1508 and 1516 Maximilian I had intermittently waged war against Venice.

to the godly as well as to the Gentiles). For the greater the army, the more abominable the flight when panic comes over them. Therefore victory depends on the courageous spirit which God supplies, as we read in the Scriptures. *A thousand shall flee at the threat of one,* that is, he makes matters worse: At one small voice and at the word of one man a thousand will flee. What would happen if he were to unsheath a sword? "At the threat of five a hundred thousand of you will flee." Granted, then, that you may be very well equipped by comparison, yet victory and conquest consists in trust and in fear. And God alone gives them. Look at brave and victorious Julius Caesar.[15]

Like a flagstaff, that is, you will be so completely overcome that there will hardly appear to be anything left, as when a fleeing army leaves a solitary banner behind, so that scarcely one sign of your army is to be seen. *Like a signal,* that is, a military banner. This is a threat to the ungodly. Though exceedingly numerous, they will be defeated to such an extent that hardly any remnants may be found. So you see that when panic comes over the enemies, a hundred thousand can be crushed and twenty can capture a city. What is a scared army? Nothing. It is as if it were dead. Therefore God alone is the proper general and soldier, who gives heart and confidence to His own and takes the heart away from His enemies and gives them fear.

18. *Therefore the Lord waits.* See how earnestly the prophet impresses upon the people that they should wait, as if to say: "Repent of your plan. God is still waiting to be gracious and not to destroy; for He is long-suffering, though He would have every reason to be angry because of your flight into Egypt."

Therefore He exalts Himself to show mercy to you, that is, He magnifies Himself, and in the greatest patience He promises you mercy and is not injured by your sin.

For the Lord is a God of justice, and therefore He is a God of mercy, because He chastises you by measure. He is not a raging and destroying God but a God of justice and of mercy.

Blessed are all those who wait for Him, that is to say, they who wait for God are the holy, the good, and the godly. No ungodly man can have this experience and this delay. They always fix time and place for God beforehand, and, beyond that, they forsake God. They

[15] Cf. *Luther's Works,* 13, pp. 198—200.

depend on what they can feel and hear, not on faith. But the godly wait for God, even when He takes His time. Therefore the blessed are saved. Everything would turn out alright, if you could only wait. Therefore, in all trouble let us wait for God, and we shall be blessed.

19. *The people in Zion will live at Jerusalem.* These are golden promises. It is a shame to have to mention them in the presence of the ungodly.

You shall weep no more, because "however quickly you will call on Me, I will hear you and have mercy on you; I will protect you from the king of Assyria, so that you may be the people who will dwell in Jerusalem." With these words He indirectly hurls insults at the king of Assyria, as if to say: "You, king, though you rage and persecute people, you will accomplish nothing. They will remain in Jerusalem in spite of everything."

At the sound of your cry. "Just pray and cry. At the first cry I will hear you and I will answer you." Who, I ask, believed these magnificent promises of the prophet? The king, no one else.

20. *And the Lord will give you the bread of adversity and the water of affliction,* that is, the king of Assyria will think that you are about to succumb [16] to hunger and thirst, but the Lord will give you the bread of adversity, that is, in adversity. The bread is not a bread of adversity, but it is given to people who are in adversity. This is an exceedingly rich promise. The enemy outside thinks that they will perish from hunger. God, however, blesses and multiplies their bread so that they do not suffer hunger. So God protects His own and nourishes them too. "And the Lord will give bread in affliction and water in adversity."

"And He will not cause your Teacher to flee." What more can God do? God loves you so. If you believe and wait, He will give you bodily abundance and spiritual abundance besides; He will give you prophets who will make you sure and steadfast. He will not give you a fleeing prophet, who will make you unsure and wavering.

21. *And your ears shall hear a word behind you,* that is, the Lord will give you the prophet Isaiah, whom you shall hear. For this is an excellent virtue, when a people can remain loyal to a true teacher

[16] The Weimar text has *victurum,* but we have read *victum;* perhaps the correct reading would be *vincendum.*

so as not to be stirred up by all the imposters to waver this way and that. These promises are rich, because when they will dwell in Jerusalem against the will of the Assyrian king, God will also fill them with bread and water during the siege and, best of all, He will preserve them in the true doctrine and set them free from false and ungodly teachers. *Your ears shall hear a word behind you,* that is, first the Word is heard, and then peace is given. The teacher and the Word are first seen and heard from the front and face to face; but when it is received, a man then feels the power of the Word of grace. I understand this simply by the analogy of a shepherd who, as he tends the sheep, follows the flock and shouts behind it. It is as if he were saying: "You will have the most faithful shepherds. They will always follow you and keep their eye on you, because they do not precede you but constantly follow you and keep their mind on you."

This is the way, walk in it, that is, with every effort they will lead you on the right way, namely, the way of God's commandments; they will lead you away from impassable places. You will not land on some byway, and they keep on shouting, "Beware of false prophets" (Matt. 7:15). These are very powerful promises, to have such shepherds as will lead their own on the king's highway. It is supreme grace to hear this voice, to hear: "This is the way."

22. *Then you will defile your silver-covered graven images.* After you have had holy teachers, this result follows, that you will cast away all idols, because the cover is narrow and the bed is short [17] and will not at the same time bear Christ and Belial, light and darkness (2 Cor. 6:14-15), the righteousness of God and man's righteousness, etc. Such contradictions cannot exist in the godly. Therefore they cast away all idols in whom they trusted outside of God. Just so we observe in our time that in the midst of the godly all traditions vanish. Thus he says here: "After you have been instructed in the faith, you will condemn all idols, regard them as nothing, and consider them unclean." So today we despise the hood and other things that we formerly revered. For the Jews of Isaiah's time were not so foolish that they wished to worship silver and gold, but by these they wanted to worship God, as our papists claim to be worshiping God through the creatures.[18] *You will scatter them,* as though we were saying to the

[17] See p. 233 above.

[18] This had been the standard defense of the liturgical use of images since the iconoclastic controversy of the eighth century.

idols: "Go away, get out of my sight!" With this confidence in our pastors and in our faith, let us say most emphatically to the idols: "Begone! Get out of here!" So Paul says in Phil. 3:8 that his own righteousness and uprightness became refuse when he learned to know Christ. In this certainty and confidence let us cast away our idols. Let us not hesitate and say: "Perhaps there is still some good in them, I want to see." Rather say, "Begone! Get away from here!"

Your gold-plated molten images. "It is your gold out of which you make a god for yourself. Shame on you, that out of a creature that is subject to you you make a god for yourself, when you should have placed it under your control. Thus the hypocrites put the very idol that is under them above them, because they want to be justified by it, they fear it, they rely on it, and therefore they treat it as their god. For that reason he says here by way of shame: "The covering of your gold," or garment, that is, this gold and silver have so great an appearance of piety that this gold seems to be much more distinguished than other gold. So our pictures, bells, and organs may appear more distinguished because of our worship. With this guise of piety the ungodly cover and adorn everyone of their idols. As the heathen adorn their idols with pearls, with gold and silver, so our ungodly people cover their ungodliness and idols with a show of supreme piety. As also the ungodly teachers themselves walk around in sheep's clothing, so all kinds of ungodliness are offered for sale under the cover and appearance of piety. On the other hand, Satan conceals the ungodliness of our fanatics with their humility, as they walk about in shabby clothes, call themselves brothers and friends of the cross.[19] In this form they cover up their ungodliness, and thus Satan moves in on us from the right and from the left. If he cannot capture us by means of supreme splendor, he captures us with humility.

23. *And He will give rain for the seed with which you sow the ground,* that is, not only will you have this, that you are nourished and that you grow rich in the city alone, but with the king dead and slain you will succeed out in the fields, as Moses said (Deut. 28:6): "Blessed shall you be when you come in, and blessed shall you be when you go out."

And grain, the produce of the ground, that is, in seedtime He will

19 It is not clear whether Luther is referring to a monastic title or to the late medieval fraternity called *Gottesfreunde.*

give rain and in harvesttime good fortune. He will grant you good seedtime and harvest. Therefore he says: *rich and plenteous.*

In that day your cattle will graze in large pastures, in the meadow. Your work of seeding and harvesting will be blessed, and your cattle will be so blessed that they graze in the richest and most fertile fields. Most abundantly and amply He will give you everything. These are very great promises of God. *And the oxen etc.* This is a symbol of the exceeding abundance and fruitfulness of your harvest. Your cattle will eat mixed barley and wheat where formerly they had eaten stubble. Now in that fruitfulness you will give them everything, and He will air out their fodder with winnowing forks and fan, with a winnowing fork and a winnowing basket. It belongs to the granary and to the barn.

25. *And upon every lofty mountain and every high hill.* Here you see the supreme abundance for the stomach and for the conscience of those who believe God. So he says here: "I will see to it that even on the highest mountains, which are otherwise barren, there will be the highest fertility, as could be said of the Fleming mountains here in front of Wittenberg.[20]

Brooks running with water, that is, rain and irrigation. When will this fruitfulness be? He answers:

In the day of the great slaughter. When you were besieged, you did not believe that such fertility was present because you thought Jerusalem was being laid waste. So faith sees God's gifts instead of the impossible. As here, with the devastation leading the way, no one could be persuaded that such fertility would follow, so faith draws its conclusion from the impossible. My flesh, however, could never be persuaded by the impossible. I would say: "Why do you speak to me about such richness? I would believe you if you spoke to me of hunger. Why do you speak about brooks running with water? If you spoke about rivers of blood, I would believe you." So our fanatics argue from the impossible: "What we have here is bread. Christ is in heaven, therefore bread is bread."[21] *In the day of the great slaughter.* He wants to instill faith in them, as if to say: "God will

[20] This hilly area near Wittenberg was so called because Albert the Bear (d. 1170) had established some Flemish settlers there.

[21] On this argument, see, for example, *Luther's Works,* 37, pp. 46—49.

bring about a great slaughter of the enemies *when the towers fall,* that is, the tyrants and important persons." For in this time countless troops perished, something that no one saw except the prophet Isaiah. In the accustomed manner of Scripture [22] he calls all important and leading men *towers,* since they stand like towers among the buildings.

26. *Moreover the light of the moon will be as the light of the sun.* This passage has been butchered in different ways.[23] Some apply it to Judgment Day, others to the time of the New Testament. The latter interpretations happens because it sees the need of a context in which everything coheres nicely and is clearly distinguished. Otherwise they create confusion, and just anyone explains the text according to his own brain. The former interpretation is the work of insane preachers. We stay with what is established in the beginning of the chapter. The prophet is speaking of the treachery of the people who forsake God and turn to man's counsels. The succeeding text ridicules this idea in the light of history. Therefore this whole chapter has a reciprocal unity. Calling the emperors "towers," that is, important people, this will come to pass in that day of the great slaughter. It follows: In that very day of slaughter, when the king of Assyria will have been killed, then *the light of the moon will be as the light of the sun,* that is, in that time the day and the night will be exceedingly bright, much brighter than before, six times brighter. Now everything that was gloomy hitherto becomes clear, as we see that in times of danger our emotions and fears sap the strength of our body and they are in the dark, as it were. So you see it in the story in Judges 5:31, in the song after victory. So all things are sad and cloudy and dark for those who are in danger. Again, in happy times, when the heart is enlarged, all things become bright and joyful and it appears that one day is seven days. This is an exaggeration of the emotions of the joyful, who are surrounded by supreme joy and nightly vigils. Hence we must believe that on the day that the king of Assyria was defeated a great joy arose, so that one day was brighter than seven days strung together and the night seems like the day.

In the day when the Lord binds up, etc., in that day when the Lord

[22] Luther is apparently referring to such passages as Micah 4:8 and Zeph. 3:6.

[23] Cf. Haimo of Auxerre, *Commentaria in Esaiam,* Book II, *Patrologia, Series Latina,* CXVI, 869; Hervais of Bourg-Dieu, *Commentaria in Esaiam,* Book IV, *Patrologia, Series Latina,* CLXXXI, 295.

has set them free from the bonds and blows of the king, then this will happen to them. This is an example of exalted faith in the prophet, which in extreme peril does not forsake men, but consoles them to trust in God.

27. *Behold, the name of the Lord comes from far.* Now he describes the coming slaughter of the king, as if to say: "Look, the king is already drawing near; he is besieging you." Our King, namely, *the name of the Lord,* is coming too, but *from far,* because you think He is coming from a distance, when He will most certainly be coming, nonetheless.

Burning with anger, that is, this our God will not only [24] fight for us, but with supreme wrath and anger He will also devour the king. These are extremely vehement words. *Burning with anger,* not simply wrath; it is as if he were saying: "You will see, He will fight a severe battle." *And heavy to bear.* This anger may not be endured. *His lips are full,* that is, He comes forth with the most serious threats on His lips and His countenance. I think that this depicts God's wrath from our point of view. He who would believe God to be such a protector of His own would not easily forsake Him when the adversaries are in pursuit. *His tongue.*

His breath is like an overflowing stream. He snorts as Paul is said in Acts 9:1 to have breathed threats. These are all signs of anger and of the wrathful God against our enemies, as if to say, "Who will destroy them with snorting?" *Like an overflowing stream that reaches up to the neck.* This is a comparison. As no one can escape from the stream as high as the neck, so no one will escape God's anger. *To sift the nations with the sieve of destruction.* As a flood scatters everything so that one may be flung here, another there, so God's wrath shatters all their strength and power. This happened when the angel killed one hundred eighty-five thousand for that king (2 Kings 19:35).

A bridle that leads astray. Thus I shall lead the king of Assyria on no sure way. It is called a *bridle that leads astray* when one person comes one way, and another a different way.

29. *You shall have a song as in the night when a holy feast is kept.* God will deal in a very tragic way with the enemies. Thus in dramatic words the prophet here describes the victory of his own and the

[24] We have followed the suggestion of the Weimar editor and added *solum.*

slaying of the king of Assyria, as if to say: "On that day of victory through the angel you will go through the city rejoicing and singing, as you are wont to sing in the nights of the feasts of Passover, Pentecost, and Trumpets."

30. *And the Lord will cause His majestic voice to be heard.* He copiously describes the Lord's anger against the enemies, and he blends the gladness of God's people with the "majesty," or splendor of victory, His majestic voice. Perhaps He hurled them down in thunder and lightning.

And the descending blow of His arm, namely through flashes of lightning and bolts of thunder. *In the threatening.* As He killed the kings of the Egyptians and the nations in the Book of Joshua, and Sodom and Gomorrah, so He will slay them with thunder. He will destroy with a storm, that is, with a cloudburst. In this way we will attack the king with thunder, lightning, hail, and rain. This is the divine victory of God.

31. *The Assyrians will be terror-stricken at the voice of the Lord,* that is, the thunder of the Lord.

32. *And the impact of the rod will be thorough.* He insults them as if with some dance. God will strike them in such a way that the strokes of the rod will be felt for some time. *It will be thorough,* that is, it will press through to the foundation. *Timbrels and lyres.* He is mocking them, as if to say: "Just wait, God will fight too and beat the timbrels and blow the horns." I think this refers to thunder and lightning.

Battling with brandished arm. The Hebrew word תְּנוּפָה means "scattered," where an army is driven to flight in various places. These are different forms of fighting, when the thunder strikes down a group here, the lightning there, and the hail at a third place.

33. *For Topheth was prepared yesterday for the king.* All say that here the punishment of hell is set forth.[25] I believe this to be true allegorically, but historically he is speaking concerning the manner in which the king is to be punished, as if to say: "Our Lord God will prepare a shambles for the king when He comes." *Deep and wide,* which they will not be able to avoid.

[25] Jerome, *Commentaria,* X, 366.

With fire and wood in abundance. He will prepare a holocaust for him, and for this He will supply sufficient wood by means of thunder and lightning. *The breath of the Lord, like a stream of brimstone.* He alludes to the destruction of Sodom and Gomorrha, cities which He destroyed by His breath and with fire and brimstone.

CHAPTER THIRTY-ONE

1. *Woe to those who go down to Egypt for help and rely on horses!*

IN THE last chapter we heard in clear words the prophet's prophecy concerning victory over the king of the Assyrians. He proclaimed it to keep a fearful people in faith and steadfastness toward God. Here, then, the prophet continues exhorting the people by means of a similar persuasion, because he encourages them not once but many times, since the kings very frequently made alliances with each other. Besides, the chief task is to lead the frightened common people to faith and to keep them in it. Without having experienced them we do not know such fears as the people in the prophet's time experienced. Therefore the common people always began again to be afraid and to flee to men for refuge, and the prophet had an incessant concern for them. In this chapter he again threatens them not to seek foreign aid. Secondly, he offers the most beautiful promises. Thirdly, he threatens the downfall of the enemies. This is the gist of this chapter. Since everything is subject to change and daily rocks back and forth, there is need for encouragements.

On horses, of the Egyptians, which are abundant and numerous. This is rebuke. "You are sinning against the First Commandment. You do not trust in God." They have confidence in creatures.

But do not look to the Holy One of Israel, as if to say: "You are sinning against the First Commandment. You can rely on horse and chariot but you cannot rely on God, who made you and the horse and the chariot and can destroy them. *Or consult the Lord,* that is, the ungodly are not influenced by any threats or promises.

2. *And yet He is wise and brings disaster.* This is a threat. "In vain they rely on creatures, but they consider Me, God, a simpleton who has no help to offer." So they cry out against the admonition of the prophet, and to them he replies, as if to say: "Listen and observe, your God is not a fool, but in a little while He will be wise enough for you." Thus we could say to our tyrants: "We are heretics to you, but you will see a little later whether we will be heretics to you." *He*

brings disaster, that is, to the unbelievers. "When disaster comes, then you will know from experience with danger how wise I was. Then you will see Him whom you once called a simpleton."

He does not call back His words. This is ambiguous. It may have been said concerning the prophet's words then and there, because he said, "Stay with God and do not look for foreign aid." And this Word of God spoken by the prophet is not set aside, he says. The same point is made in Jer. 23:14 ff.: "See now, whether I am right or whether you are right." Or, this passage can be understood as referring to the First Commandment: "You shall have no other gods before Me." "I the Lord your God am a jealous God, visiting the iniquity, etc." (Ex. 20:3, 5). It is as if he were saying: "If you have not kept my Word, the anger of the jealous Lord will come, because He will not call back His Word." I prefer the former interpretation.

But will arise against the house of the evildoers. "Because they are not only unbelievers but also evildoers and blasphemers of the Word, I will destroy them." *And against the helpers,* in a passive sense, *of those who work iniquity,* helpers because they sought out those who work iniquity.

3. *The Egyptians are men, and not God.* This is a highly significant axiom, which must be applied to all the sundry forms of confidence in creatures. Thus we must say to the papists: "Why is it that you papists rely on princes? They are men and flesh." This is so because all human and fleshly things are condemned by Scripture when it comes to relying on them. We should make use of them, not rely on them. Thus this proverb is opposed to every form of reliance on men, and it seeks to arouse faith in us in the greatest dangers. What are all dangers? They are vain and transitory. Why should you, a holy man, want to rely on them or fear them? Do not do it at all but trust only in God. What is an Egyptian? A man. What is man? A bubble that quickly bursts. "When his breath departs, he returns to his earth" (Ps. 146:4).

When the Lord stretches out His hand. That is, when the Lord will bring the king of the Assyrians, He will destroy both the helper and the helped. "Cursed is the man who trusts in man" (Jer. 17:5), because he will tumble down. All Scripture speaks against this innermost ungodliness of the flesh because it is the source of every evil and most frequently takes us captive. You see that the whole world is nothing but a ruin because it goes about in this ungodliness and relies not on God but on men.

And they will all perish together, on both sides. Now follows a promise by way of a threat that rouses them from sleep.

4. *For thus the Lord said to me,* that I might comfort you.

As a lion growls. These are magnificent promises for the godly. The Lord God compares Himself to a lion in protecting His own. For as a lion growls over his prey even in the midst of the shepherds and walks boldly about, so God says: "Strong and roaring in the midst of the prey (which you are), I will protect you." For the lion does not flee, as if to say, "Just come and touch me with one finger. I am only one, you are many. Come and touch me. I defy you." So our God, though He is all alone, withstands all tyrants. *So the Lord of hosts will come down to fight upon Mount Zion,* that is, He will wage the battle in the city against the king.

5. *Like birds hovering.* Another promise, in which God promises that He will protect them. *Hovering,* that is, with spread wings, as a hen protects her chicks with spread wings and menacing beak, so God will protect you, deliver you, and pass over you. This is a glorious promise: To protect and to deliver, to spare and to rescue. "Protecting and delivering you in the city, passing over you in the army of the Assyrians and scattering them, I will rescue you. I will pass among them as on the street."

6. *Turn to Him from whom you have deeply revolted.* This is the conclusion. Turn from your presumption to the Lord Himself, who promises to protect you, because *you have deeply revolted,* as if to say: "In your desperation you have departed altogether too far from the Lord. Stay, trust in Him, because He will protect you."

7. *In that day.* After this lion has protected you and you have learned by experience, you will then see that you did well to put your hope in the Lord. Then you will say: "Now I see that my endeavor was of no avail; only God helped me." These things are idols that we cast away. For such presumptions as we depended on are idols like those of our work-righteous people. There follows a threat concerning the king that is to be made to fall.

8. *And the Assyrian shall fall,* as above by thunder through an

angel, the Assyrian is struck down, a flash of lightning. *And he shall not escape from the face of the sword,* because the ungodly are terrified by a leaf in the wind, as by an army and they flee "when none pursues" (Lev. 26:36). *And his young men shall be put to forced labor.* This he says derisively to the Assyrians, as if to say: "Their young men are now proud and think that they will get away by running to their generals and their comrades, but I will prevent them from doing so. I will make them slaves that must pay tribute. They will not be jobless and victors but slaves and conquered."

9. *His rock.* Not only will the army itself run away, but even Sennacherib, the king himself, who is the rock and strength of the region, will flee.

Says the Lord, whose fire is in Zion, and whose furnace is in Jerusalem. The Jews interpret this as referring to the temple, where the fire and the furnace are.[1] I understand it simply thus: "I am the father of the family and I live in Jerusalem." Both in the Hebrew and in the German idiom [2] the furnace, or hearth, points to the family and the domestic life, because houses are reckoned on the basis of hearths.

[1] This comes apparently from Lyra *ad* Is. 31:9; the *Glossa ordinaria* applies the passage to the church.

[2] The same is, of course, true of English usage.

CHAPTER THIRTY-TWO

1. *Behold, a king will reign in righteousness, and princes will rule in justice.*

SOME treat this chapter as referring to the reign of Christ.[1] We say that this part of the prophecy together with the foregoing is a promise of the future kingdom, which will stand in fullest flower against the schemes of the king of the Assyrians. It is therefore a description of a kingdom in the most flourishing condition and a reformation of the former kingdom. And though in appearance the kingdom seems to be headed for destruction, nevertheless, since I believe the divine promises, it will stand.

Behold, a king will reign in righteousness, namely, Hezekiah and other upright kings. *In righteousness.* It is necessary above all that the king and head be righteous, discreet, and upright. Then the body will be governed most excellently by such a head. And though there are some counselors and citizens, these are members, and they cannot do as much damage as when the king is a fool and a dolt. Therefore great care must be taken to put an excellent king or ruler into office. When the head is in good condition, the body is very well governed. *And princes will rule in justice,* that is, you will not only have a just king but also good princes, who will rule well. Although in all kingdoms there may also be some good-for-nothings, yet the heads themselves are just. For the kingdoms of this world are all weak and therefore have weak members too, since no body is so sound that it does not have some defective member. Care should at least be taken that the head is good.

2. *And a man shall be as when one is hid from the wind.* The first requirement is to have a good ruler, then good administration of the laws will follow. For good laws are no good if there is not first a good executive. Therefore the psalm calls upon the "rulers of the earth" (Ps. 2:10) to love justice. For to have good laws means nothing in itself; but if they are administered by a good executive, the state will

[1] Cf. Jerome, *Commentaria,* X, 371.

then prosper. Here, then, you see the institutions and office of a ruler who has been established by God against the devil and his members, who plot all manner of ungodliness against the godly by means of theft, murder, adultery, all kinds of trickery, the exposing of boys, and the ravishing of virgins. Against these the ruler has been set up as an umbrella, so that he may chastise them and protect the good, as Paul describes it very well in Rom. 13:4. Here, then, you see depicted the highest praise of the institution of the ruler who comes to the aid of the poor, the orphaned, and the needy with good things. As for you, observe whether the ruling office is not an estate of abundant mercy and of good works, which protects us against Satan and his members, the thief, the adulterer, etc. And when the ruler arrests them, he is doing a divine work.

A covert from the tempest, that is, he cannot be hurt by any evil because he lives under the good protection of a good prince.

Like streams of water in a dry place. This is a very apt illustration. Nowhere is water treasured more highly than in dry and parched places. So the good rulers are compared to rivers and fountains that provide moisture, that bring relief to the weary and to those spent with toil. They are as pleasant as a refreshing drink is to a thirsty man. Another comparison:

Like the shade of a great rock in a weary land. They are not like the shade of a thin reed, but great and exceedingly solid rocks, which are not moved by any person or by fees but are a most dependable shade to the wearied pauper and to the just man. See how much that is holy and excellent there is in a good prince and ruler. In truth, a pious prince and burgomaster is a great saint. He must be a solid rock against all the schemes of the disobedient, against all the plots of the subjects, against all the feelings of his friends, so that he will not have greater regard for his acquaintances and friends than for the strangers. It is a difficult task for a man to stand in such a way as to be the shade of a rock to all the just. So you see how difficult an office he holds, to be hardhearted and heavy as a rock, so that he cannot be moved by either threats or promises. Thus a woman boasted about king David (2 Sam. 14:17): "My lord the king is like the angel of God," who cannot be turned aside by either terrors or rewards. Let him who aspires to a ruling office be courageous; let him not rely on his own resources, but let him pray to God on bended knees. For he has been established not only against the world but also against

Satan and his members. Therefore the ancients said: "The office reveals the man."[2] For there we see who is a courageous spirit and who is not among those who take possession of the office.

3. *And the eyes of those who see will not be closed.* When such a king reigns, the teachers and preachers will also be righteous, and false prophets will be rooted out. *And the ears of those who hear will hearken.* They will have fine preachers and students. There you see that the ruler is installed for the promotion[3] of the Gospel. For the Roman empire in its role of peacemaker surely must have been of help[4] to the apostles, so that the Gospel might be preached throughout the world. Political peace is a great thing and is of a great benefit for the spread of the Word. Where there has been an ungodly prince, however, there will be ungodly teachers and hearers because he permits nothing but lies to be preached. There is something great about a good ruler. Therefore good doctrine, excellent hearers and preachers will thrive under a good ruler.

4. *The mind of the rash will have good judgment.* The rash are most properly called fools who soon reveal what is in their heart. A wise man will first deliberate in his heart whether a thing is useful. Therefore Solomon puts the heart of a fool into his mouth, but he puts the wise man's mouth into his heart (Ecclus. 21:26). Such rash fools soon rush into public statements to give the impression of knowing something; they do not stop to think what good their speech and council might do, they do not have "speech seasoned with salt" (Col. 4:8). In sum: The state will thrive best when justice thrives. Then excellent teaching and teachers and hearers will follow, then also a thorough reformation of the fools will follow.

And the tongue of the stammerers. He properly calls the ungodly teachers stammerers in the metaphorical sense. They do not speak when they speak, they stutter pa pa pa, they perform the act of speaking and yet say nothing. Vain babblers, who took the stage and raised one question after another, in fact, countless questions, they

[2] See *Luther's Works,* 9, p. 17.

[3] The Weimar text has *promocione,* but we have read *promocioni.*

[4] The Latin verb is *profuisset,* a pluperfect subjunctive, suggesting a "condition contrary to fact"; but the sense seems clearly to be the one given in the translation, as the parallel passage in the scholia (W, XXV, 210) also indicates.

filled the church with empty words: Whether, whether, question, question,[5] but they accomplished nothing.

They will speak readily and distinctly. In few and perfectly clear words they will teach the hearers and enjoy doing it, as you see today, where formerly nothing was accomplished by the aimless preaching of the stammerers.

5. *The fool will no more be called Nabib.* נָדִיב properly means generous, as is stated in Luke: He does good to many, doing good to all and protecting them with the greatest generosity.[6] Such is the title of a good prince, נָדִיב, a benefactor. The foolish prince, however, who does not discharge his office, is not called נָדִיב. He is called a fool. Scripture calls those נָבָל who are unsuitable and are of no benefit to anyone except to themselves and their own insatiable belly. These are properly the greedy, who seek nothing but their own advantage.

6. *For the fool speaks folly.* This is proverbial in Latin, in Greek, and in German.[7] Although those who are in the courts deem themselves to be very wise, make many words, and are always the first to speak, they are very foolish and greedy and not good for anything even to one man, only to themselves. Hence there is need of a wise prince who will not be flattered or provoked by the showy words of the fools who crowd the court.

And his mind plots iniquity, that is, these people look out for nothing but their own affairs and the advantage of their own belly, and they skin the people, so that in this way they achieve nothing but grief among the people.

To practice hypocrisy. The Hebrew word חֹנֶף means hypocrisy. For under the guise of wisdom and hypocrisy they produce nothing but corruption. Yet, as a cover for that corruption they present the greatest appearance of wisdom. All of our princes suffer such corruption.

To utter error concerning the Lord, that is, in the name of God and of the Gospel and with a good front they sow evil while they say: "This is what the Gospel says, this is what Christ says," and

[5] A *Quaestio* was a proposition for discussion or debate in scholastic theology; it frequently began with *Utrum.*

[6] The reference to Luke is unclear; the Weimar editors suggest Luke 6:27.

[7] Luther quotes this saying in Latin, Greek, and German.

thus under cover of the Lord's name they speak errors. They say nothing but what will line their own purses. They say only what will serve them in their kitchen.

To leave the craving of the hungry unsatisfied. As good princes achieve a good government, a good state, and the success of the Word, etc., as indicated above, so these נְבָלִים, these foolish princes, who scheme to achieve the opposite, hinder and prohibit all these good things. This is what it means to leave the craving of the hungry unsatisfied. This is the worst use that is made of an evil ruler.

7. *The vessels of the greedy are the worst.* The proverb says: The stingy man's purse does no one any good. We freely explain by means of German proverbs, so that the text may be made clear, lest anyone ridicule us for not having interpreted in the usual manner. Now the prophet wishes to show that all that belongs to the greedy – their pantries, their kitchen, and their purse – is of no use to others and, as the Greeks say it in their proverb: It is like hay in the dogs' manger.[8] For the hay in the manger is of no use to the dogs, and yet they do not want other beasts to come to the manger and eat. The greedy are affected in the same way. They have no use for these goods, yet they keep others from using them, and thus they offer no one anything and do no one any good. Therefore the prince must be a נָדִיב, generous and gracious. He must not be a נָבָל, that is, foolish and greedy; otherwise he will be no use to anyone, just as a greedy citizen helps no one, robs everybody, gives nobody anything, is of no use to anybody. Therefore the prince and the teacher should not be greedy but be concerned about others as their office demands. *Vessel* denotes all kinds of bags.[9] For the type of man who looks out for his own interests cannot judge and teach correctly, but out of the true doctrine he makes a moneybag for himself.

He devises wicked devices to ruin the poor with lying words. Here the prophet is speaking especially about the ruler and about teachers, whom also Peter describes (2 Peter 2:3). "In their greed they will exploit you with false words." By lying words they devise ways and means of deceiving you. Because they are greedy, they look out for their own gain and are out after yours, both physical and spiritual. This is what we experienced with the pope. He calls him זִמָּה in Hebrew, which means one who intentionally plans crimes. *To*

[8] Cf. p. 78, n. 1 above.

[9] The Weimar text has *retinacula,* but we have read *retiacula.*

ruin the poor with lying words, that is, with words he has made up. Not that these people call them lies, but that the spirit of the prophet does so.

Even when the plea of the needy is right, that is, he speaks lying words even to the poor, whom he ought to train and instruct, inform and comfort. The ungodly teachers who seek their own gain do all this for the sake of filthy lucre.

8. *But he who is noble devises noble things.* The truly generous prince plans and considers how he might help soul and body and be of use to all, recognizing that he is there for that purpose. The noble prince devises noble things, that is, he is eager to be of service to all. These are properly noble princes and bishops. In the masculine the word נָדִיב means a nobleman. In the feminine it denotes a princely and noble thing.

And by noble things he stands. First he says that the prince devises noble things. Here he says that his steadfastness abides and that he stands by his nobility. It is not broken by vexation and ingratitude but always stands firm, whereas the greedy fall in the meantime when they do receive thanks for it.[10] This, however, is praise for the constancy of the princes and teachers who in gratitude and ingratitude, in the kindness and the vexation of their subjects and hearers always continue in their generosity and sincerity. Thus in this time a large group of courtiers around Hezekiah have withdrawn from the king and fawned on the young prince Manasseh. The prophet sees this and therefore rebukes them with this indirect reproach and berates them as ingrates.

9. *Women who are at ease.* This should be a new chapter. The prophet sees the destruction coming after this joy, he sees the darkness coming after this light which the prophets gave. So today we must admonish our overconfident people, lest in a little while they again fall into darkness. He calls them women metaphorically, that is, wealthy cities furnished with a good government, or people who after their victory have fallen into supreme confidence and complacency, just as we become complacent upon acquiring one good preacher and at last fall into the dangers of darkness again. By this general admonition he declares that this error will be in them even

[10] The Latin phrase is *non graciam habent ex illa,* which may be a literal translation of the German *und kein danck dazu haben* (W, XXXV, 457).

to the time of Christ, just as there is no end of sinning on our part. *At ease,* that is, self-confident and complacent cities, despisers of God.

Rise up, that is, from your self-reliance. *You complacent daughters,* that is, you cities, I say to you that because of your excessive complacency you have come to forget God, just as today we who have been enlightened after liberation from the bonds of the pope do not give thanks to God because of our excessive complacency.

10. *In a little more than a year,* that is, there will be some time. It is a matter of a day and a year. He mentions a specific time for an indefinite time. The time will come, believe me, and this time has not passed in vain. None of your merits and strength would help you.

You will shudder, you complacent women. He is speaking against their confidence. "You who are sleeping in supreme confidence and peace, that peace will be shattered by the Babylonian captivity." *The vintage will fail, etc.* There will be neither vintage nor fruit harvest, which now make you happy. In other words, disaster will come upon you.

11. *Tremble.* This is an admonition whereby he would scare them away from their self-reliance, as if to say: "You who are now complacent, tremble and shudder, 'because it is time to strip and gird your loins,' that is, the king of Babylon is at hand, who will strip you, despoil you, and divest you of your kingdom, government, cities, and riches." They will be made bare to the point of shame, they will be despoiled and reduced to the most horrible devastation. To despoil does not sound as strong as to make naked, to plunder thoroughly. *Gird sackcloth upon your loins,* that is, "You who once wore the master's purple now, as slaves, will put on sackcloth."

12. *Beat upon your breasts for the pleasant fields, for the fruitful vine.* This explains the nakedness, namely, that the fields and vineyards will be forsaken, since there will be no one to cultivate them.

13. *For the soil of my people growing up in thorns and briers.* They will grow up, that is, there will be no fruitfulness in their fields, but there will be extreme devastation.

Yea, for all the joyous houses in the joyful city. Where there are very spacious and very highly decorated houses, which are now secure in supreme joy, there will be a thorny field.

14. *For the palace will be forsaken, solitary.* With the inhabitants

taken away and the people removed, there will be no activity. *The hill and the watchtower will become dens forever,* as you see that in ruined cities the remnants of towers become dens for wild beasts. *A joy of wild asses.* That is, grass will grow around those towers, where wild asses and flocks will graze. In other words, there will be a most desolate loneliness, as Vergil says: "Where Troy once was, there is now an open field.[11] *Wild ass.* I think that this name refers to all wild beasts of the forest in general.

15. *Until the Spirit is poured upon us from on high.* This very short verse consoles us by its ending, as if to say, "Under King Hezekiah all things will flourish, but then days will come again when you will be made desolate by the Babylonian king, until at one time the end of all ends and the Savior Christ will come. Thus by a leap the prophet rises up to Christ Himself, the King of kings. The Holy Spirit has come from on high on the day of Pentecost, where He has begun the new reign and former kingdoms have been abolished, the flesh in us has been transformed, and our desires have been put to death.

And the wilderness becomes a fruitful field, that is, the blind will see, and the seeing will be blinded. The wilderness will become a thoroughly cultivated field through the Word and the church, and those who seem to be cultivated, namely the synagogs, will be turned into deserts by the Word and the church. There righteousness will be found where there is now no righteousness, and vice versa.

17. *And the effect of righteousness will be peace, and the result of righteousness, quietness.* The effect, or reward, is suitable to the counterpromise. For the effect and reward of the righteousness of faith is peace. This is by analogy of the fields whose result or fruit is wheat and corn. Thus you see here the fruit of the righteousness of faith.

And safety forever. These are words of praise for the righteousness of the New Testament, namely, peace, quietness, and safety, as Paul points out in Rom. 5:1 ff. In vain do we say (Ps. 38:3): "There is no health in my bones because of my sin."

18. *My people will abide in peaceful habitation,* that is, my people will live in habitations of peace and dwellings of safety and in the tranquility of plenty. These are the fruits of faith, of justification,

[11] Vergil, *Aeneid,* II, 325—326.

and of grace. For such trust in the flesh does not exist, but it is by faith alone and by the grace of God. The accent is on the words *My people.* "My, My people," because this is a new people renewed by the Spirit, a people set free from the demanding Law, from biting sin, and from gloating death. These foes are vanquished, and therefore we have great confidence.

19. *And it will hail when the forest comes down.* My people will have the above-mentioned blessings; but Jerusalem and the ungodly will not have these benefits and this rest but will be in the hail, in the storm, "and in lowliness," that is, in the lowest depths, at the nethermost place. He calls Jerusalem a city going down an incline, a city lying on the slope. By this location he refers figuratively to the city's fall, and by means of the site itself he refers to the city's destruction, as if to say: "This city is hanging on the edge of the abyss, yea, it is hanging over too far and is headed for destruction." *Forest.* He is thinking of Lebanon, out of whose forests Jerusalem was constructed. *Hail.* That destruction will come by hail, that is, by the storm and turmoil of consciences. These things will remain *in the descent of the forest;* that is, they will lie prostrate in Jerusalem. *Hail,* that is, disquiet and disaster. So it will be in the presence of the ungodly, who rely on themselves.

20. *Happy are you who sow beside all waters,* that is, here and there and everywhere among the nations. *Who let the feet of the ox and the ass range free.* He refers to the farmers who sow the seed around the overflowing waters. Thus the apostles sow the seed around the waters, that is, among the nations. There the "oxen," that is, the preachers, and the "asses," the godly burden-bearers of Christ, yet sluggish in the flesh, are permitted to range free. So you see, the Gospel provides "oxen," that is, priests and teachers, and "asses," that is, godly men. Thus in this chapter the prophet very briefly passes through various disasters after the reign of Hezekiah to the reign of Christ. In the following chapter he returns to the king of Assyria.

CHAPTER THIRTY-THREE

1. *Woe to you, destroyer, will you yourself not be destroyed?*

THE prophet refers to the downfall of the king of the Assyrians, of which he has spoken above. He is, however, seething with various emotions: with teaching, admonishing, scolding, threatening, because Isaiah is working among a rebellious and treacherous people, who opposed King Hezekiah sitting on the throne and rejected his admonitions. This is a new speech; he drops the former subjects. In direct address he turns his face toward the king of the Assyrians, and in this way he makes his own people strong.

Woe to you, destroyer, will you yourself not be destroyed? It is as if he were saying: "I grant that the king of the Assyrians is about to devastate you. I know it very well, because you have little courage, since you indeed see the devastator but not Him who will destroy him." This is the people's objection to the prophet. *He who despises.* That is, not only will he ravage you, but he will also despise you and disregard you, the way a king despises some citizen or unruly peasant. In Hebrew the word is בֹּגֵד, which signifies those who in their excessive pride have no concern for others and regard them all as stubble and nothing. Thus the king of the Assyrians was the most arrogant despiser of Israel's God and of all His dominion. So it is with the Turk today. He is a terror to all, he fears no one. He causes such great commotion and fright that the common people say: We see the devastator and that no one withstands him. To these the prophet acknowledges: "Yes, I see it all right, just as much as you do." Now he proceeds to answer them.

When you have ceased to destroy, you will be destroyed; and when you have made an end of despising, you will be despised. This is an outstanding passage. This is the way things are. When the ungodly have climbed up on the wheel of fortune [1] they soon tumble down, because at their very ascent they stand in confidence and pride, thinking that God is asleep. They sing their praises before the victory.

[1] See p. 150 and p. 162 above.

They shout hurrah before they are up the hill. Read about the supreme disdain and arrogance of the king in 2 Kings 18:19; 19:10 ff. In such self-reliant arrogance they tumble down very quickly. For God permits them to rise to a pinnacle of confidence so that they seem to be completely safe. God Himself alone knows how the ungodly rise and fall. It is then that, as Ps. 9:9 says, "the Lord is a stronghold for the oppressed, a stronghold in times of trouble." This is the method of our God, that He permits our enemies to climb up to the highest level so that they become altogether presumptuous, and then He throws them down. When the godless man stretches the rope most tightly, it breaks. Therefore, let us not tremble and run away when we hear about them. Let us draw an example of faith and comfort from this text. When the devil climbs the highest, he falls down. So it happened to the pope, who reached the highest heights in the death of John Hus but then and there began to decline.

2. *O Lord, be gracious to us.* From the above-mentioned admonition to the people the prophet turns to prayer. Since the victories of the Christians are won by the Word, whereby we are consoled and made strong against the enemies, we then turn to God: *O Lord, be gracious to us.* "We are desolate and afflicted; the king of the Assyrians with his rage and power can overwhelm us in one moment. Thou, O Lord, protect us. Be not angry with us, then we shall very easily bear the king's rage."

We wait for Thee, that is, "We shall prescribe no time or place for Thee. Only protect Thou us according to Thy will."

Be our arm. "For we will not rely on our bow and our strength, but we ask Thee to be our strength." *In the morning,* quickly. The Scriptures very often use this to mean "quickly." This is, however, the attitude of a trembling faith, for which delay is difficult. The prophet feels like this too. *Be our arm in the morning,* that is, quickly, like those who hurry in the morning to take a quick look. *In the morning.*

Our salvation in the time of trouble. This prayer linked to a strong admonition has kept many in the faith. We do not feel it unless we are in such dangers.

3. *At the voice of the angel.* As a brief prayer consists of one statement, so here the brief sermon is contained in one verse. Therefore we must not strive for βαττολογία (cf. Matt. 6:7), because a true prayer consists of a sigh, of very short words, as we see here by ex-

ample. A brief and well-prepared prayer begs for mercy alone. It has no regard for one's own merits, but a man's own need drives him to pray. Now a prophecy follows.

At the voice of the angel people flee. It is as if he were saying: "You, king of the Assyrians, by the voice of your lofty eminence and by your power have scattered all nations and killed the fugitives, because you have vaunted your dreadful name. Take note, however, that no matter how long you have done this, you are approaching the end." *At the lifting up of Thyself.* It is as if he were saying: "Why do you look at the king as he puts all people to flight? I will set before your eyes that he himself will flee from the exaltation of our God, as I said above, by means of lightning, thunder, war, and dispersion (תְּנוּפָה).[2] He will flee while we are safe, because we have been heard in our confident prayer to God and we have been set free." In this prophecy he places the king's flight before their eyes in order to comfort them, as if to say, "Although he planned to strike and to stab, he will be glad to give leg bail."

4. *And spoil is gathered.* "You proud enemies, you will not be in a position to carry your weapons away, but you will leave them behind as spoil."

As the caterpillar gathers; as locusts leap, men leap upon it. He makes two comparisons. They are like men putting carterpillars and locusts to flight, and like some man who chased away sparrows and little birds, so that the poor little creatures barely got away. Thus he compares the army of the king of Assyria to caterpillars and locusts ravaging the earth. This army the angel routed where those who lived in self-confidence did not expect it. He will ravage and destroy you with lightning, thunder, etc. This is wonderful consolation. "My dear fellow, hold on, take it easy, the king will be properly dealt with, as one should chase away a flock of birds."

5. *The Lord is exalted, for He dwells in Zion.* We have a Lord in Zion, who dwells with us and is our fellow citizen in Zion. He is exalted. *He will fill Zion with justice,* that is, He made the city upright by His Word, He cleansed us by His Word before He protected us. We are now godly.

6. *And there is faith in your times.* "You think that He will blot

[2] Cf. p. 267 above.

us out too, since all others are already blotted out. By no means. But we have the Word and faith, which you will not conquer."

Abundance of salvation. Here lies the emphasis. "Not only will faith be yours, but abundance, חֹסֶן, is yours also, that is, rule and government, while you think that all things are thrown into confusion." We have lordship and salvation. We will surely keep our lordship in your presence. *Wisdom and knowledge,* that is, we shall also have a spiritual kingdom and good preachers, and thus by a supreme triumph we shall withstand you in both a temporal and a spiritual kingdom.

The fear of the Lord is His treasure. We are rich in lordship and salvation, in wisdom and knowledge, yet we do not rely on them, but He Himself is our treasure. *The fear of the Lord.* Through it we shall overcome all your most extensive treasures, we who externally are of no reputation.

7. *Behold the valiant ones cry without.* The prophet becomes more emotional as he makes his refutation, saying: "There are others who did not believe who were frightened by the king of the Assyrians and withdrew from king Hezekiah." These provide the greatest terror for the prophet and the greatest comfort for the enemies. It is just as if some intimate companion would forsake our prince and go over to his enemy. *Behold, the valiant ones cry without.* Imagine scouts returning and saying before the city: "Alas, we are done for." Thus they stir up the people in their gates, sad to the point of despair. *The envoys of peace,* who would normally bring good news, *weep bitterly* while speaking their unfortunate message. The words of the envoys are:

8. *The highways lie waste.* "The streets are completely laid waste, that is, the king of the Assyrians is in control of everything, so that no goods and no help can get through to you." *Covenants are broken.* "There is no treaty because the king is angry with you; you need not hope that he will make another covenant with you." So they announce the hopelessness of help and alliance. *He despises cities,* "he has no regard for cities, he cares for no men, he receives none graciously." These are excellent examples of hopelessness and the most fiery darts of the flesh in time of persecution. We, too, ought to take note of them in our dangers. Isaiah is bitter here.

9. *The land mourns and languishes*, that is, "it is most wretchedly

laid waste, and there is no longer any hope for the buildings and fields." *Lebanon is confounded and withers away.* "This Lebanon, how shamefully chopped up it stands!" These, then, are the words of the messengers who were accustomed to bringing good and joyful news. Now there is nothing but despair together with the worst exaggeration on the part of the messengers.

Sharon is like a desert. These are all words the prophet refutes as the messengers speak and walk around with outstretched hands, torn clothes, extreme lamentations, and despair. *Lebanon is confounded and Sharon is like a desert.* Some like to take this to mean that even these two extremely fruitful mountains were laid waste by the enemies, just as they think that Carmel is the southern mountain in Judea.[3] I myself think simply that it refers to Jerusalem, which by metonymy is called Lebanon, Bashan, Sharon, or Carmel. It is as if he were saying: "What do you think? I seem to be seeing Jerusalem about to be reduced to ashes." So the prophet makes use of various names to call forth tears of despair, as if I would describe this city thus: "Here is Wittenberg, the true Jerusalem, the true Rome, the true Venice." We would use such words to increase our praise. So here the prophet, who is himself near despair because of the report of the envoys, is occupied with such a task. It is as we read in Moses (Num. 13:32-33), where the spies brought the message: "All the people that we saw in it are men of great stature. . . . And we seemed to ourselves like grasshoppers, and so we seemed to them." So here, too, they are out to confound Isaiah by saying: "Yes, we see Jerusalem totally destroyed, and Isaiah is responsible for this." Such useless words Isaiah had to put up with from the common people.

10. *Now I will arise, says the Lord.* Accumulation against accumulation. *Now I will lift Myself up; now I will be exalted.* "I, too, will lift Myself up." It is pride against pride. He promises to confront them in proper style.

11. *You conceive chaff, you bring forth stubble.* See in what a humble way Christ's plan is described, as in Ps. 2:2, 4 we first read: "The kings . . . and the rulers take counsel together," and then in great words, yet most simply, the text depicts God's plan: "He who sits in the heavens laughs; the Lord has them in derision."

Here he presents a comparison of the proud who attempt great

[3] Jerome, *Commentaria*, X, 378.

things. They have huge bellies and appeared about to give birth to twins, but, instead, have produced grief. It is as Horace says, "The mountains are in travail, but a ridiculous mouse will be born." [4] So here: He is pregnant with straw and gives birth to stubble. With wonderful irony the prophet compares all their force, power, pride, victory, and presumption to stubble and straw, which are good only for the fire. This should greatly strengthen us against the insolence of the ungodly, who flaunt their arrogance as they rejoice in their victory.

Your breath is a fire that will consume you. That is, "I will consume by fire your self-inflation and pride and the very army in which you trust." Let us, then, be strengthened by the fact that all our enemies with all their forces, their pride and inflation, if we only pray to God, will be stubble and straw, even though externally we appear in their sight as stubble. They are pregnant indeed; but while they have conceived a swelling and grandiose plans, they bring forth stubble. They attempt great things day by day but accomplish nothing. All shrewdness, power, and strength, which is like an iron mountain before our eyes, is in fact like stubble that is to be consumed by fire. This is a rhetorical device to belittle great things and to magnify small things. In the prophet you therefore see the most abundant rhetorical and poetic figures of speech by means of which he can magnify or diminish. Thus we should stand fast in the midst of all tribulations and such great increase of enemies, even though we have been in extreme poverty. For in Scripture poverty is called an armed man (Prov. 6:11; 24:34). Here he afflicts us. Sin torments us, etc. But as for you, against such dangers trust in God alone and say: "It is nothing else than straw and stubble." Do you think that there was a weak faith in Isaiah, who could label a huge army of the king as nothing more than blades and straw? So then, if we see the pope, the emperor, and the duke arrayed against us, let us say: "They are stubble and straw."

"Fire will consume you with your fear." It will consume us altogether, both belly and stubble, both counsel and army. This is a fine example of giving comfort to the afflicted.

12. *And the peoples will be as if burned to lime,* that is, the peoples of the Assyrians will be burned up in such a way that nothing will remain but ashes and lime. *Like thorns cut down, that are burned in*

[4] Horace, *De arte poetica,* 139.

the fire. With these two comparisons he points to their destruction. In Scripture a "fire of thorns" specifically denotes destruction, because thorns are cut off for the fire, as the psalm says, "They blazed like a fire of thorns" (Ps. 118:12). For such a fire is not extinguished like other fire, since they are of no use except for fire and ashes. So also those people have been condemned to fire. He goes on with the refutation to the very end.

13. *Hear, you who are far off.* These are all words of God. It is as if the prophet were saying: "If you will not hear this, I will shout that it will resound under heaven, so that the peoples far away may hear what you close by do not want to hear." *You who are near, acknowledge My might,* My power and victory over the king of the Assyrians. The emphasis lies on the word *My.* "No one boasts of My might instead of the king's might. Let us see who is the stronger."

14. *The sinners in Zion are afraid, etc.* The prophet confesses that he is clearly living in the midst of sinners and hypocrites, people who formerly were extremely hostile, but not in time of adversity there is nothing more afraid than they; people who used to yield to no one in their strength and uprightness now are despairing.

Who can dwell? The prophet reproduces the words of the ungodly and of their preachers: "Do you want to stay here in Jerusalem? Don't you see that the city has already been set on fire? Let the devil stay here!" With such blasphemy they attack Isaiah. And these are precisely the words of the ungodly, such as our opponents: "Let the devil remain at Wittenberg in the heresy." So also we hear in Moses: "Why did we not remain in Egypt, where we had fleshpots? (cf. Ex. 16:3). What devil told you to lead us here?" Such things the godly have to bear.

Who among us can dwell with everlasting burnings? "Who will order us to stay here with the fire?" Such is the nature of the confused, ungodly, who soon take refuge and make the fire everlasting. "Look out for your wives and children and flee!" This is what you have to hear from the ungodly.

15. *He who walks righteously and speaks uprightly, who despises the gain of oppressions.* The prophet begins to speak by making a concession full of bitterness. "On account of your ungodliness Jerusalem will truly be burned, but for the sake of you godly people it will not happen." Here he describes the godly, who walk by faith

and mercy. This is their righteousness, which is properly the mercy whereby mercy has been shown to us and we show compassion to others. This is faith and love. He speaks uprightly because upright words follow faith, as the ungodly unbelieving speak and do wicked things.

He who despises the gain of oppressions, those who do not look out for their own interests but despise and even proceed with the strongest hatred against greed and slander, by which the neighbor is harmed. *Who shakes his hands, lest they hold bribes,* bribes that blind the judge and ruin the good people. *Who stops his ears,* that is, who will not willingly hear of shedding blood and will not agree to a plot to shed blood. *And shuts his eyes from looking upon evil.* He will not participate in but will rather argue against doing evil. In short: Rely only on God and trust God, do good, and you will see that He will protect you.

16. *He will dwell on the heights.* This God will be well disposed to you, he will well protect you, and Jerusalem in the process of transition will appear to lie on the heights so as to seem impregnable. Thus at this place you hear the promise of victory among the godly. The ungodly, however, follow their own mind; they do not believe the Word and are not worthy of victory. Here, then, you have a description of the godly, who are extremely rare in the world, since even now we see nothing but ungodliness, corruption, bloodshed, etc. But the godly will be safe, because

His place of defense will be the fortresses of rocks, that is, *his bread will be given him,* that is, he will have food and clothing, there will be no poverty there, but rather he will be abundantly nourished. *His water will be sure,* certain, and will not fail but be available, that is, they will have the most certain nourishment. This is what the Hebrew word for "sure" means. These are the promises to the godly: Safety and peace and sufficiency.

17. *Your eyes will see the king in his beauty; they will behold a land that stretches afar.* These righteous people will not only have an earthly peace, but they will see a kingdom well and excellently ordered, a prosperous king with his family, with good law and an excellent administration. This is the king's glory: A flourishing realm, a well-ordered government, a just law, things that do not flourish thus in time of peace. But in peace you will see *a land that stretches afar,*

land outside the city, also cultivated, adorned, and relinquished by the enemies. You will see far into the field, where there will be nothing but peace, now that the enemy is gone. Note how the prophet exerts himself to keep his little ones in the faith so that they do not despair because of a variety of matters. The ungodly, however, always proclaimed the opposite against the prophet, and they are justly reduced to despair.

18. *Your mind will muse on the greatness of the affair.* Great and unexpected affairs create astonishment, as here the worst kind of unrest in one night becomes most peaceful, something that seemed impossible. Who would have thought that it would be achieved so soon?

You muse: Where is the scribe, where is he who weighed the tribute? Where is the scribe of the towers? Here there are two "scribes." St. Jerome is joking.[5] "Scribe," "weigher," and "scribe of towers." We understand "scribe" to refer to the teachers of the legal code and of the laws, men who are at the courts, very learned scribes, as the psalm says (Ps. 45:1), "My tongue is like the pen of a ready scribe," that is, of an expert in the law and in jurisprudence. That is what the people ought to be saying: "Where are his scribes, stewards, treasurers, directors? Where are the smart alecks now and big money men of the king of Assyria?" "Scribe of the towers, or citadels." The first are in the councils, the next are chamberlains, the next, the scribes of the citadels. They are the chancellor and his scribes, who keep a record and look after court affairs. Eating, drinking, and writing are the business of the court. These three functions of the royal court you will not see around the king of Assyria, who has been driven out, though formerly he was illustrious in them.[6]

19. *You will see no more the insolent people.* "You will fear the powerful people of Assyria, but you will not see them, for you will be delivered of them." *The people of an obscure speech,* that is, the people of Assyria, who have thick lips and complicated forms of speaking, the people who speak barbarously so that they cannot be understood. *Stammering in a tongue which you cannot understand.* This is what the Hebrews do with all barbarian people who do not speak the Hebrew language. They call their lips thick and their tongue stammering. The prophet goes on with the promises.

[5] The abbreviation *D.* probably stands for *Divus,* but it may refer to *Doctor.*

[6] Cf. *Luther's Works,* 13, pp. 215—216.

20. *Look upon our city,* מוֹעֵד, that is, established and firm. A specific city, which is found in a specific place, because no city but Jerusalem was established to be the capital of the kingdom and the priesthood. *A rich habitation.* Not only will the city be certain, but it will truly be safe, substantial. *An immovable tent,* which will not be shifted but will eternally be protected by God. As a tent that has been secured by pegs will remain, so this city will not be moved elsewhere forever.

But there the Lord in majesty will be for us. This is the reason why the city will not be moved, because the majestic Lord is there for us. *A place of broad rivers and streams,* that is, ample for grappling hooks. The Lord is for us a very wide trench around the city. As the Lord earlier called Himself the city's wall,[7] so here He calls Himself *a place of broad rivers,* a moat three cubits wide that makes the city unapproachable.

Where no galley with oars can go. By means of that pit and that trench they will be safe from the enemy so that the enemy can approach neither by ships nor by triremes. In this way, by means of allegorical language, the prophet describes Jerusalem as being strongly fortified, and this because God is the city's protector.

22. *For the Lord is our judge, the Lord is our ruler, etc.* The king of the Assyrians will not be our judge, nor priest nor king, but our God will rule over us and teach us. By way of contrast he compares the Assyrians with our king.

23. *Your tackle hangs loose.* You, Assyria, will attempt much; but you will accomplish nothing, neither on land where your ropes will not prevail, nor at sea, because they will not stretch out the banner where they ought to be fighting.

Then prey and spoil in abundance will be divided, that is, with the king put to flight, very handsome and abundant spoils are left behind, so that the able-bodied cannot carry off everything but even the lame will take it away.

24. *And no inhabitant will say: I am sick,* that is, all the people will hurry with exceeding joy and come running.

The people who dwell there will be forgiven their iniquity, that is, they will have a gracious God who forgives their sins, and therefore all will be well off.

[7] See p. 200 above.

CHAPTER THIRTY-FOUR

1. *Draw near, O nations, to hear, and hearken, O peoples! Let the earth listen.*

THE next two chapters bring us up to the remarkable story of Sennacherib. I simply take these two chapters to deal with the transfer of the Jewish kingdom to the church. The first chapter deals with the last destruction. For the Jews, trusting in past promises, were simply unwilling to listen to the new teaching concerning Christ, because in their excessive and secure presumption they dashed against the Cornerstone, and because of this they deserved the supreme and final destruction by the Romans.

Draw near, O nations, to hear, and hearken, O peoples! This is a general admonition addressed to the Jews, whereby the prophet calls on them to hear the coming wrath and rage of God, as if to say: "You are about to hear great and terrifying things about the sword of the Lord."

Let the earth listen, and all that fills it, that is, whatever is in it. This great threat has caused many to think that this refers to the destruction at the Last Judgment.[1] I do not accept this, because of what follows.

2. *For the Lord is enraged against all the nations.* This is a general sword against Jews and Gentiles, because they held a general hatred against Christ and His Word. *Against all their host,* that is, their army and people. For every affair has its own host, as the heaven has its stars. Observe: In the Scriptures "host" denotes every kind of endeavor. Ovid says: "The love of study is a kind of host," [2] and Job 7:1 says: "The life of man is warfare," that is, hard service. In short, every kind of endeavor or task, whatever endeavor and task you will. Those who in Hebrew are called its soldiers because they engage in it. So here "host," pursuing various endeavors – priesthoods, religions, etc. – denotes everything that was in opposition to the Word

[1] Jerome, *Commentaria,* X, 382.

[2] Ovid, *Fasti,* II, 9.

of God. *He has doomed them.* The Jews were put out and given over to physical slaughter as sheep of the slaughter. To put out is to destroy down to the foundation and beyond restoration. The Hebrew word is חָרִים. This is what happened to the Jews.

3. *Their slain shall be cast out.* This happened to the people of Jerusalem, that neither time nor place for burial was given them. "They will not be buried with appropriate rites." According to Josephus, pestilence and stench arose from the unburied corpses.[3]

The mountains shall flow with blood, that is, there will be so great a supply of corpses that the mountains will become soaked with blood.

4. *All the host of heaven shall rot away.* Here you have a new Hebrew theme, which is difficult for Latins to understand. He calls the religion of the Jews the host of heaven. The religion of other nations is of the earth, just as the religion of our monks is of the earth. In Daniel the priests and chief priests, the teachers and prophets themselves are called stars of heaven. As in Dan. 12:3, the prophet compares the prophets and teachers to the stars of heaven. He is speaking, however, concerning the destruction by the Romans, when the religion, worship, and priesthood were of no benefit to them without the hearing of the Word, but became rotten, had to fall into decay, and were transferred to the Gentiles.

And the skies roll up like a book. A book, that is, a scroll. For books and larger sheets were rolled up on a rod. So the sky that is stretched over the Jews in their smugness will be rolled up and hidden, and will clearly not be in use, as a rolled up scroll is no longer read. So also all their religious pomp will perish and be consigned to oblivion. The Jews do not now have a priesthood and a religion, but we Gentiles have them.

All their host shall fall. These are very plain words that are spoken concerning the most holy nation of the Jews. They show that just as the most beautiful leaves fall in winter, so the most excellent Levites, priests, and aristocrats have fallen and died. He calls them shoots of the vine and the fig tree, however, indicating that theirs is not a divinely made ingrafting into some splendid tree, and they were finally cut off because of unbelief, as we read in Rom. 11:20.

5. *For My sword has drunk its fill in the heavens.* This is a Hebrew

[3] Josephus, *The Jewish War,* V, 12.

idiom. In Deuteronomy we read (Deut. 32:42): "My sword shall devour flesh," and it is drunk with blood. The sword being drunk is an indication of a great slaughter, where the sword not only gets wet, but where it is drunk and drenched through and through.

Behold, it descends for judgment upon Edom. It is this sword in heaven that will descend and devour all ungodly peoples. The Edomites attached themselves to the Jews, and so they were all likewise slain as by the wrath of God. *Upon the people I have doomed.* Some construe this as metonymy and understand it as referring Edom to a remnant people who were not of the Jewish people.[4] My opinion: Idumea was allied with the Jews and suffered the same fate.

6. *It is gorged with fat, with the blood of lambs and goats, with the fat of the kidneys of rams,* that is, in that calamity a great carnage was made of aristocrats, princes, priests, and Levites. It was not the scum and defenseless people that perished, but the choicest segment of the nation fell. Some very important people are included in the destruction. This will be a new kind of destruction, not like the Babylonian one and like any other that has struck lowborn people, but here all the princes and chiefs have utterly perished. These are the ones called lambs and goats. That is to say, God will simply invade their kingdom.

For the Lord has a sacrifice in Bozrah. With a salty taunt he ridicules them in calling them a sacrifice, as if he were saying: "As the priests grew big and fat through the sacrifices and offerings and for these sacrifices skinned the people (as we read in Matt. 15:2 ff.), so I will kill you skinners of My people as though you were a sacrifice." So it will happen to our skinners. *Bozrah* by metonymy is a name for Jerusalem, namely, a fortified city. *Edom,* that is, bloody. By metonymy either word fits the Jews, who were *Bozrah,* that is, in a superbly fortified city that withstood all enemies. Likewise *Edom,* that is, bloody, reddish, inclined toward bloodshed, headstrong, ruddy with wrath for slaughter and bloodshed. Thus by metonymy they are Bozrahites and Edomites. God will repay the priests for their butchery. *A great slaughter in the land of Edom.* There will be a heavy carnage.

7. *There shall fall with them.* They will be brought low, they will

[4] That interpretation appears to be reflected in Luther's scholia on this passage (W, XXV, 217).

be pulled down to the very dust – they who formerly were extremely puffed up, who were *unicorns*, namely, chief priests and princes and פָּרִים, *young steers*, that is, the lusty young men. The men of power in the city they call *unicorns* and *young steers*. אַבִּירִים. This stands for men who are powerful, marvelous, and angelic. By comparison אַבִּירִים denotes a beast of burden that is fat, well fed, and strong. So here the אַבִּירִים, all the others, and the nobles will be cast down, since the entire kingdom will be laid waste. *Their land shall be soaked with blood*, that is, the slaughter will be on so large a scale that the common people will not be considered out of respect for the aristocrats and princes who have been slain and whose blood fills the land.

8. *For the Lord has a day of vengeance, a year of recompense.* This will happen because God wants to avenge the true Zion itself, that is, the church, which has not turned away from God to Edom, that is to say, they have not persecuted the Gospel.

9. *And her streams shall be turned.* This shows what will happen in Jerusalem after Jerusalem has been destroyed. The inhabitants await nothing but loneliness. The prophet has described the devastation of the kingdom and the priesthood. Now in figurative terms he depicts the city's remaining appearance after the destruction. This, too, some desire to interpret as referring to the eternal fire,[5] and that is possible; but we stay with the simple meaning. Formerly, in time of prosperity, it was called the river of God. Streams denote people. This river will be blood, and these streams will not be a large number of people but pitch, and its soil will be and turn into brimstone, as we read in Deuteronomy (Deut. 29:23): "The whole land brimstone and salt, and a burnt-out waste, unsown, and growing nothing." This is a description of utter destruction, because the most offensive stench rises from this ungodly people like smoke from brimstone and pitch. *Forever and ever*, that is, they will be forsaken, they will be turned over to their own lusts, and there they will be consumed as if in pitch. They will no longer come to the truth of the Word and have a priesthood, as we see among the Jews today, who are in pitch and brimstone. That is to say, under a curse and about to be cursed, they do not want to hear the Word of the Gospel.

10. *None shall pass through it.* The same is said in chapter 5:6 above: My vineyard "shall not be pruned or hoed." So here, in this

[5] Jerome, *Commentaria*, X, 385.

land there will be no vinedresser, there will be neither teacher nor preacher.

11. *But the hawk and the porcupine shall possess it.* These words compel us to refer this passage not to the fire of hell but to an earthly destruction, where such creatures generally live. *The hawk* is the bittern. *Porcupine,* or hedgehog. The *ibis* is an unclean bird, a native of Egypt and unknown to us. Such animals are untamed, wild, and living by themselves. By way of allegory the ungodly rabbis, who are generally accustomed to living in the wilderness, represent a wasteland forsaken by all prophets and teachers. This is what we see in the papacy today, where all its teachers are wild beasts, shouting wild and hostile words. Where Christ is not present, there is destitution, there is nothing but savage beasts. They screech and howl like hoot owls. They impart no sure and true teaching.

He shall stretch the line of בֹּהוּ *over it, and the plummet of* בֹּהוּ.[6] In Gen. 1:2 we read: "The earth was תֹהוּ וָבֹהוּ, without form and void." This is what he says here, but in inverse order. They will indeed build, but for destruction, while the inhabitants meanwhile are working to build it up. This is what we see today among the Jews, who are anxiously plying their trade as carpenters with plummet and line to preserve their teaching. But that plummet is without form and that line will be void, that is, all the endeavors of that people will be completely void and useless. They will sweat and toil in vain.

12. *The nobles there shall be named "Those who have no kingdom."* They will be princes without territory, as the king of Lorraine calls himself King of Jerusalem;[7] that is, the nobles will be called "No Kingdom There." They will be known as "Lords of No Place." The prophet ridicules their hope, by means of which they cling to the divine promises and await their fulfillment in vain. They say, "I shall have a kingdom there," but there the prophet ridicules their hope, saying: "Yes, indeed, Lords of No Place!"

13. *Thorns shall grow over its strongholds,* that is, they will have no kingdom, as we see today in the case of the forsaken Jews, who are altogether homeless. These are indirect statements about utter and ultimate desolation.

[6] This repetition occurs in the Weimar text, but not in the original Hebrew.

[7] Luther is apparently referring to the Latin Kingdom of Jerusalem created by the Crusaders in 1099—1100.

14. *Demons.* We would call them martens. *Hyena,* or jackal. צִיִּים are winged wild animals, אִיִּים are ground animals. We could not arrive at the true meaning of these animals, for even in the German language they have various names. Nor can we learn the names of all things from a grammar. In any case, by means of these animals we are to understand the utter desolation of the land.

The satyr shall cry to his fellow. שָׂעִיר is a goblin, or field demon. The word denotes a hairy creature, like fauns or satyrs, or what we Germans call "goblins," like our house spirits, likenesses of men and of devils. *There shall the night hag alight.* I have translated it "porcupine." They are witches and night hags who at night give suck to children and inflict injury on babies, as the prophet says, "Even the night hags give the breast" (Lam. 4:3). By allegory: All ungodly teachers are witches and night hags, goblins, who perplex us with false milk and teaching. They are male and female demons who cause nightmares; goblins, devils of all kinds that lie in wait for us during the night.

15. *There shall the owl nest and lay and hatch.* In a Greek proverb eggs denote "disciples." The bad egg of a bad raven. So here the owl's eggs are wild, destructive, and hermitic disciples, not tamed like chickens. Ungodly teachers will produce ungodly disciples.

There shall the kites be gathered. Their teachers are ravenous wolves, who tear their souls to pieces in the desert. This passage must be applied to our time. Once we have forsaken Christ, all monsters, beasts, and demons lead us astray, error follows upon error. This we see today, first concerning Baptism, then concerning the Eucharist, then concerning free will, so that one error follows hard upon the other.[8] As one wild beast falls in with another, so it was hitherto under the papacy. Aristotle, Scotus, etc., fell in with each other. In short: When the Word has been abandoned, there is nothing but desert, where animal meets animal, wild beast meets wild beast. That is, such people are exposed to every kind of seduction, as we see in the papacy and by the example [9] of our sectaries.

16. *Seek and read from the book of the Lord,* that is, in the book of Deuteronomy. In this book, chapter 28:15 ff., He pronounces many

[8] The controversy over infant Baptism had erupted late in 1521, that over the Eucharist in 1522, that over free will in 1524.

[9] The Weimar text has *exemplum,* but we have read *exemplo.*

curses upon the transgressing people. *Not one of these shall be missing,* for they shall be consumed. *One has not sought for the other,* that is, all things are fulfilled, and neither these nor those are desired.

For the mouth of the Lord has commanded. "It is He who orders me to speak; it is not my idea." *And His Spirit has gathered them.* "I am speaking under direction of the Spirit of God. He has imparted these things, I have not produced them out of my own brain."

17. *He has cast the lot for them,* that is, He Himself has thus set the limits for the unbelievers and those who oppose His Word, and their lot has already been predetermined. Their reward will follow in line with their work. Thou art righteous, O Lord, who dost retaliate for all things. Let those who refuse to listen to God, the truth, etc. listen to Satan and to lies. Those who will not hear their parents belong to the hangman.

They shall possess it forever, from generation to generation. Those curses will be in effect forever, He will dwell before them always. While they wait for a blessing, a curse will come to them and stay with them, because God has cast such a lot for them, so that they may be despoiled and made desolate by ungodly teachers and monsters. Now the following chapter deals with the new kingdom of Christ.

CHAPTER THIRTY-FIVE

1. *The wilderness and the dry land shall be glad, the desert shall rejoice and blossom; like the crocus.*

We have heard that in the previous chapter the destruction of the synagog was dealt with. This chapter speaks of the establishment of the church out of the remnants of the synagog. By the Spirit the prophet promises many grand things concerning the church, things which under the form of the cross are hidden from the world; and therefore the promises must be understood under the guidance of the Spirit.

The wilderness shall be glad. Thus the field, the meadow, is properly called happy when the year looks its most beautiful. By this picture he also describes the flourishing church, though there is a desert there. The church flourishes inwardly, not in power, in the wisdom of the flesh, in the gleam of splendid works; but it walks along in a simple form, not in ostentatious holiness, and therefore appears to be quite forsaken and without any glitter. Yet there are internal flowers and delights there, but these are not visible, namely, confidence, peace, life, a cheerful conscience, things that are not seen. But it does shine outwardly with obedience, love, humility, etc., which do not seem great in the eyes of the world. The world considers this to be a common run of people, meanwhile looking up to exalted things, to feasts, fasts, to a unique prayer, to ceremonial rites, to cowls, tonsures, and similar things of this kind, while it disdains the church which looks so very insignificant. Therefore the shape of the church must be discerned by the Spirit, not in the wisdom of the flesh. For here the church is in the wilderness, though it is compared with tilled and happy fields, tilled, that is, not by our merits, but by the grace of God.

2. *Like the crocus it shall blossom abundantly, and rejoice with joy and singing,* namely, enriched with spiritual wealth and with the riches of God's gifts, it will rejoice, as we read in 1 Cor. 12:4 ff.

The glory of Lebanon shall be given to it. This is so because the kingdom will be taken from them and given to the Gentiles, as we read in Matt. 8:11, 12. For all *the glory of Lebanon,* that is, of Israel, *shall be given to it. To it* means "to the desert," that is, to the church. By synechdoche Jerusalem is called Lebanon because it has been built of materials from Lebanon. In other words, all the glory, the priesthood, the ritual, and the Word of the Jews have been transferred to our church.

The majesty of Carmel and Sharon, that is, all the gifts of the Spirit that were present in this people have been given to us. Carmel was a very fertile mountain in Judea beside the sea, and nearby is Sharon. These two mountains had the boast of being very fruitful. They are now called the synagog, which was fruitful and fertile in teachers, prophets, and teaching, as the apostle points out in Rom. 9:5.

They shall see the glory, that is, the church consists in this that it sees the majesty and glory of God. The disciples are joyful in the Lord alone. For the church boasts only of the knowledge of the Lord, as we read in 1 Cor. 2:16. So Peter says, "Grow in the grace and knowledge of our Lord Jesus Christ" (2 Peter 3:18), that is, the church has the knowledge of Christ, which is hidden from the Jews. So today we observe among the blinded papists that they cannot see the glory of our church, because they have a beam in their eyes (cf. Matt. 7:4) and see nothing but a black cloud.

3. *Strengthen the weak hands.* This is wonderful comfort that is to be understood not in a physical but in an internal sense, because it shines under the appearance of the cross. For this church of Christ is extremely poor and wretched in appearance, since its poor, distressed, naked, imprisoned, and dishonored are the refuse of all and loathsome to all men for the sake of Christ's name. And the members of the church are exposed to all, to Satan and to the craftiness and power of the world and the flesh. They are like "the offscouring of the world" (1 Cor. 4:13). It is as if people were saying: "They are to be regarded as a misfortune and a monster. If we could only be rid of these scoundrels." With all their might they exert themselves to expel and exterminate this utterly loathsome Christian people. So we see today that all the most criminal people are less disturbed than the members of this church. Therefore the inward joy of the spirit fights with the grief of the body exposed to the cross. Therefore the prophet comforts them with exceedingly great consolations. *Strengthen.* This is a command. As long as Satan is awake he will

not stop attacking us. It is for us to stand in the battle line against his stratagems.

Weak hands, hands that are so weary. Give medicine to those hands so that you become strong again. For Satan has two ways of fighting. He would gladly cast the faithful down suddenly from their joy and faith and into fear and despair. Secondly, he cunningly strives by long lasting torments and by the unremitting pressure of the torments to tire them out. It is as Cyprian confesses: "Satan did not want the captive brothers to be killed in this life, but he preserved them in a long life and distressed them with unremitting aggravation to the point of exhaustion." [1] These are extremely powerful attacks. Against Satan's continuous attack we must set our continuous divine help. The devil is a spirit at leisure and thinks of nothing but to take us by storm. We ought not have slack and idle hands over against his deceptions. Have we not experienced in these ten years [2] how he tried by various forces to frighten us away from faith in the Gospel? First through the terrors of the papists, then through the world's disgrace, then through murdering tyrants, through the fanatics, the schismatics, and fatherly flatteries. The church must diligently oppose his stratagems.

4. *Say to those who are of a fearful heart.* In Hebrew: "To those who are hasty and speedy in heart," who are not steady and firm but want to run away and give Satan the victory.

Be strong. We ought to strengthen ourselves with these words and say, "Though all devils were rolled into one, my God is still greater." The afflicted must be comforted with such spiritual consolations of the Word, not with any fleshly comfort which does nothing for troubled consciences but with spiritual comfort and with the living Word of God they must be ruled and strengthened. Why? Because

Behold, our God, etc. By those words he indicates that our God is absent but will come very quickly to avenge and save us. These are words of promise for the future, for God first permits people to condemn and persecute His church, as though He were absent, and then He will come very quickly, visit vengeance upon the adversaries and

[1] See p. 201, n. 2.

[2] Since the lectures on this chapter falls somewhere between October 1528 and May 1529 (see Introduction), Luther seems to be referring to the ten years since the debates of 1518 and 1519.

tumult upon the world, and save His church. This is truly hard for the flesh.

With the recompense of God. He will come and save you. Do not avenge yourselves. He is the God of vengeance, He will fittingly requite them and save you. Thus we see that vengeance always comes before they carry out their plan. So Jerusalem, opposing the Word, was stormed by the Romans; then Rome perished, and so will our papists. Thus the Spirit comforts us, as if to say, "Remain godly and constant and be lifted up. The Lord will come in time of trial, and He will avenge and save you." So he comforts the church that is exceedingly hateful to the world and Satan and besides does not shine with outward splendor. On the contrary, it is pressed down by a very heavy cross; it is also beset and harassed by a variety of internal evils, such as weakness of faith and falling into sin. Beyond all these, Satan, the tempter, fights against it.

5. *Then the eyes of the blind shall be opened.* In that time when the church will flourish in the midst of drought and will be cultivated in the desert, the blind will see plainly, etc. This is taken literally with reference to the miracles of Christ and the church, as we read in the last chapter of Mark (Mark 16:17, 18), signs that were necessary to confirm the new Word, signs that were added to the glory of the church, signs that are not done physically in the last time of the church, now that Christ is no longer weak. They were necessary then as a witness to the Jews, who ought to have recognized the church of God. Allegorically, in the time of the Gospel there were opened (1) *the eyes of the blind,* or ignorant, as we see happening today; (2) *the ears of the deaf,* who now accept the Gospel; (3) *the lame* walking in their own superstitions, as Isaiah calls all idolators lame, people who walk around in some sect of their own. They limp on one leg. They do not walk in an upright faith. Then, however, when they accept the Word by faith, they walk upright and leap for spiritual joy in Christ.

(4) *And the tongue of the dumb sing for joy,* namely, it will glory in a strong confession, and the mercy of the Lord shown to us is proclaimed and boasted; and they will say: "See how God has rescued us from the darkness!"

For waters shall break forth, that is, they are parted and distributed. As a spring flows forth in moistening streams, so this church, which was desert, should gush out in streams of the teachings of the Gospel, always one stream leaping from another into one city and then another, although in the eyes of the world it might seem forever desert.

7. *The burning sand shall become a pool,* that is, where formerly there was total dryness, there will now be not only streams but also pools and springs. Thus the church will grow in such a way that elsewhere and in other places our streams will become springs. The Word of God will come in abundance.

In the haunt, that is, where formerly the serpent was and the dragon reclined.

The grass shall become reeds and rushes. Dragons and serpents like above all to be in dry places, as we see from experience today. As this was formerly a desert, most dreadful in dryness, but now because of the exceeding abundance of moisture has become a place where reeds and rushes grow, so there was nothing but heat, dryness, and ungodliness as long as the Word was absent, but now with the preaching of the Word it is moist and joyful. The serpents and dragons are those who teach ungodly things and with their most pestilential teachings take possession of men's souls and consciences, like Erasmus, Zwingli, and Oecolampadius,[3] whom also Christ calls a brood of vipers (Matt. 23:33). Our lazy bishops and clerics are not worthy of this name, yes, they are scarcely dung and vomit. *In the haunts* there will be the highest fruitfulness of the Gospel and of fertile hearts, which, having come to faith, are made fruitful by the Word, teach others with their gifts and help others participate. This is the fruitfulness and abundance of the Spirit.

8. *And a highway shall be there, and it shall be called the Holy Way.* Where formerly there were serpents in the haunts of dragons, that is, pestilential teachers. The Gospel condemns them all. When these have been put to flight, the place will be safe. Indeed, there will be a highway and a royal road, yea, even a holy way. By way of contrast, look at the ungodly, who promise their disciples many things, including a royal highway; but if you look with spiritual eyes, you will see nothing but impassible places and precipices from which they have been hurling down their followers, as we saw hitherto under the papacy. The Gospel has a wide road, a smoothed way by

[3] See p. 297, n. 8 above.

means of the completely firm Word in the footsteps of the holy patriarchs who have gone before. This is the royal and holy way. Meanwhile many ways will be constructed: the way of Francis, of Dominic, and of the sects. But this way alone is royal and holy before God, although there are other haughty and holy ways in the eyes of the world.

The unclean shall not pass over it.[4] This way is so guarded that it is impossible for an unclean person to walk on it. All other ways put up with the ungodly. No sect can deny this. As the proverb says, "the cowl covers many a rascal." However, no ungodly person will walk on this way of faith and the Gospel. It will not have the corrupted and unclean walk on it.

And it shall be for them, that is, this way is such for them in such a manner that no corrupted and ungodly and foreign person walks on it, but *it shall be for them,* that is, it will not be without traffic, but many godly people will be walking on it. It is not to be doubted that these are the hearers and doers of the Word.

And fools shall not err therein. The Hebrew is unclear. It appears to say, "That even the fools may not go astray there." They who are regarded as simpletons and fools in the eyes of the world are properly called fools, just as the Word, too, is a word of foolishness. Therefore he says that those who are fools before the world but wise in faith walk on the way.

9. *No lion shall be there, nor any ravenous beast.* The Hebrew word פְּרִיץ means highway robbers and thieves, who do not travel on the royal road but on byways. That is to say, this way will be safe, since the lions, that is, the disturbers and teachers of traditions, will not be there, but sincere pastors of the Gospel, who do not permit robbers and butchers that tear us apart with a variety of opinions, but rather guide us on the same unique way. The butchers are the ones who tear us apart with works, persons, places, and numberless works of righteousness. Then we indeed have lions and ravenous beasts on the way. This unique way of faith, however, gathers me up so that I may not be torn to pieces nor go off on impassible places nor fall into this or that righteousness, but that it may keep me, even me, on the one way, Christ.

They shall not be found there, that is, they will not be permitted

[4] The Latin text reads: *Ita ut transeat per eam immundus.*

to be found on this way, and to that end the pastors will be alert. What does Paul mean when he says that there are many wicked in the church?[5] I answer: They are among us, but they are not of us. They are the excrement and spittle of the body, not members of the body, the church. Therefore this way will be pure.

But the redeemed shall walk there. We have translated "Those who have been set free again will walk there," that is, in Christian liberty, when the beasts and wolves are warded off by watchful shepherds. Then they will walk safely and securely in freedom, because, redeemed by the Word, they cannot be led astray by laws and traditions, but walk in freedom of conscience. You know that Christian liberty is outwardly subject to all men but inwardly it is lord over all things.[6] It can be condemned by no sin, Satan, Law, etc. Thus it has its being in Christ alone. Meanwhile let the outer man be subject to all, but let not the conscience give in on one tittle. You will say: "However much I am an unclean sinner, sin, Satan, and Law have nothing against me. All these neither condemn nor confound me. Thus no righteousness, uprightness, etc. will deliver us. Christ alone is our deliverer. This is Christian liberty.

10. *The redeemed of the Lord.* Who are they who walk on this way? None other than *the redeemed of the Lord.* To redeem means to pay the price. For we have been redeemed and purchased at a great price, namely, with the blood of Christ. This is the thunderbolt against all our works. It has a passive significance. It means that we were all sold under sin and death. But we have been purchased by the Lord, and at great cost we are the redeemed of the Lord, not with gold and silver, but with His precious blood.[7] Not with our zeal, not by our works, but we are *the redeemed of the Lord.*

And come to Zion with singing. They will spend their time in perpetual and eternal praises, because the Redeemer will also abide forever. Therefore Paul says (Gal. 5:22): "The fruit of the Spirit is love, joy, peace" and (Phil. 4:4): "Rejoice in the Lord always."

Everlasting joy shall be upon their heads. They will display it publicly as if they were wearing a crown on their heads.

[5] Luther seems to be referring to such a passage as 1 Cor. 16:9; Phil. 3:18; or Titus 1:10.

[6] Luther is echoing his own discussion of "Christian Liberty" (W, VII, 21).

[7] Cf. Luther's Small Catechism, which falls into the time of these lectures, though probably later than the lecture on chapter 35 (W, XXX-1, 296).

Joy and gladness. There will be complete and perfect joy that drives out all sadness. This is an excellent description of the church in this very short chapter, from which many New Testament writers have drawn, namely, that this church is happy and joyful, safe from all stratagems of Satan, that consciences are not burdened with various and divergent traditions, but that it is redeemed of the Lord, redeemed by the blood of Christ, and that it goes on happy and rejoicing in gladness.

CHAPTER THIRTY-SIX

1. *In the fourteenth year of King Hezekiah.*

THESE next four chapters are easy and clear, therefore we need not expend much labor on them. One point we need there, and that is faith, which we must have to recover from such dangers, as we see both the king and a few others lifted up by the promises of the prophet. This faith is set before us as an example, as we read in Heb. 11:4 ff. We can augment this passage of the apostle by this example, so that we may consider faith and its outcome, as well as its works and dangers, as we see in these four chapters again how the attack on faith and its near destruction take shape. Let this be our example, so that the more we are assailed and endangered, so much the more we may prosper by faith. "When I am weak, then I am strong" (2 Cor. 12:10). Strength is perfected in weakness. Paul is strong in weakness. When all our strength fails, let us stand by faith alone. "As dying, and behold we live" (2 Cor. 6:9). I am a reproach to all; I am not. I am poor; I am not. This faith is clearly contrary to reason and human understanding. It is for you to enlarge this example rhetorically. First, look at the warring king, who comes with a whole army and fights after he has conquered almost the whole world. Secondly, look at his victory. He has subjected everybody and has also carried the ten tribes of Israel away to Media. And here this King Hezekiah, who is in this one city like a cornered mouse, wants to offer resistance. How absurd this seems to a reason that is trying to make things clear. "What are you going to do, you king of one city, with one to whom so many kings and peoples and even the ten tribes could offer no resistance?" Then Satan joins in with: "Do you think that you alone are upright and holy? Don't you think there were many saints and upright people among the ten tribes? [1] And yet they were conquered. Do you put faith in the fact that you are a descendant of Abraham? Those ten tribes were also the descendants of Abraham." So the faith of King Hezekiah will have wavered; that is certain. So Satan mocks our faith. He sets the victory of the adversary before

[1] See *Luther the Expositor,* pp. 98—99.

us. Then he reminds us of the destruction of our brothers. We do not think we are beyond this danger. Consider, if some tyrant had conquered all of Silesia and Meissen and were encamped before our walls. Then we would know the strength of the faith that is in us. Besides this there are the countless complaints and blasphemies of the ungodly hypocrites.

1. *Against all the fortified cities of Judah and took them.* This is a thunderbolt and battering ram against faith. If the Lord wished to deliver us, why did He not save those cities? From their destruction and capture we have our danger.

Sennacherib, that is, the spoiler coming out of the woods, a lurking thief, a savage name that frightens by its own sound.

2. *With a great army.* He is close by in the area but not yet at the wall. Read about it in the books of Kings and Chronicles (2 Kings 18:17). It speaks more clearly about the king of Ethiopia, who was deprived of victory elsewhere. Hither is sent

4. *The Rabshakeh,* that is, the master of provisions. *And the Rabshakeh said to them.* There follow the blasphemies and attacks of Satan by means of which he assails faith. Let those who were captives consider this blasphemy, how Satan assails a struggling faith by means of boastful examples in order to snatch the Word of the Lord out of the heart. They are deceitful and extremely dreadful schemes, more dreadful than all wars, and appalling blasphemies.

The great king. First he introduces the royal majesty. *Thus says the great king,* as if he were God. Here he sets the great king against the little king. The devil is good at this. I am a very small candle; the whole world is nothing but a wind. This is the conclusion Satan and reason come to on the basis of such comparisons.

On what do you rest this confidence of yours? This is an inductive argument by which he meets all arguments that could be brought up in reply: "(1) In you there is neither counsel nor power. (2) The trust you put in the king of Egypt amounts to nothing; it is vain. (3) You trust in your God. But He cannot help you and has no desire to do so." Thus these words of the Rabshakeh are the devil's own words, whereby he attacks not the walls but the faith and heart of the king himself. The devil attacks you where you are most vulnerable. So they saw the king's faith wavering, and the devil assaults this also. "Hold on, I will help you!"

On what do you rest this confidence of yours? What strength have you? Answer: None. This the king concedes. And the opponent has scored a point. Again:

On whom do you now rely? He describes the object of his trust in a remarkable manner.

6. *Behold, you trust that broken reed.* Reason might easily do this and rely on physical resources, but faith will not. Thus by a clever device, Satan, that scoundrel, here turns a most beautiful statement of the Holy Spirit against the struggling Hezekiah. It is true. We must not rely on men, as this statement shows. Every human idea is a reedy staff. This is an outstanding maxim to be written over all human reliance, because it will apply to all in line with this comparison. It has been most useful to me to this very day. The comparison is very apt. Outwardly a reed looks whole and solid, but inside it is hollow and weak. It pierces like a spear, but it is nothing, nothing at all. Thus human power is nothing but an empty show. Let us therefore not be deceived by its outward appearance. For if we should lean on it, our hand would be pierced, that is, we would be put to shame in our faith. We are disappointed in the end. The end of this is confusion and destruction. This is what it means to pierce the hand. This is the godless comparison Satan employs against faith. Now follows the third attack.

7. *But if you say to me.* Here Satan himself attacks the supreme and unique fortification, namely, to trust in the Lord, something that Isaiah the prophet has long been building up with the utmost effort. The king of Assyria is saying, "You rely on your Lord, but He cannot help you." He grants that He is their God, but he maintains that He is wrathful and does not want to help. "Imagine that your God can help (as He cannot), yet He does not want to, because you, O king, have an angry God, whose statues you have demolished. He would be on our side, not on yours." These are indeed poisonous and loathsome arrows.

Is it not He whose high places and altars Hezekiah has removed? These are the techniques of slander. He turns this most godly work of the king into the most criminal rage against King Hezekiah, as if to say: "You have destroyed these altars, where God was worshiped by the fathers. Oho, what you have done?" Satan can advance a similar argument against us, so that all the best things we have done, such as the demolition of the Mass, the liberation of monks and nuns, etc., are slandered. By such means Satan assails a struggling faith.

8. *I will give you two thousand horses.* "Experience teaches. Come on out and try it. I will give you two thousand, against which you will not stand with twenty." This is a depreciation [2] when we ironically belittle something that is already feeble. "I am sure they have scarcely ten horsemen in the city. What are they going to do?"

9. *When you rely.* "I go on the assumption that the king of Egypt is stronger than you." This ridicule is full of ungodliness.

10. *Is it without the Lord that I have come up?* That is to say: "I have a propitious God, you have an angry one." So Christ was assailed on the cross. "Let God deliver Him now, if He desires Him" (Matt. 27:43). This is what Satan wants. He moves against our faith, as if to say: "God can help you (something the flesh easily believes), but He does not want to." In this way Satan undermines the spirit of one who suffers wrong, as he did also to Christ on the cross. Above all, Satan bears down on the third confidence, namely trusting in the Lord's mercy. For he says: "Hezekiah is mortal, he is a sinner, he has destroyed the worship of God." Then he says: "I do not come on my own, but I have been ordered by God." He has made of Hezekiah not a petty sinner, murderer, or adulterer but an ungodly idolater who has transgressed the first three commandments and whom God does not favor. This was the feeling in Hezekiah's conscience as a result of the slanders of Satan, who makes us believe that all our best works are the worst. The devil makes us feel very guilty. Secondly, he frightens the king by analogy. "Yours is the guilt because you are ungodly. I am holy, and I come by God's order. Yours are the scourges because you have deserved them by your sins." By these fiery darts (Eph. 6:16), of which Peter speaks (1 Peter 4:12), Satan attacks the conscience and confidence, and he must be resisted by a very strong faith. Here the work and toil must not waver. We must say: "Whether I have committed sin or not, I shall not be condemned." Satan must not be listened to, otherwise he will put us to shame. We must not give in to him by agreeing with him, but let us say: "I do not concede this point. Even if I were in the wrong, I would not give in to you." This is what we must do when we are attacked because of the Gospel.

[2] On *tapinosis*, cf. *Luther's Works,* 26, p. 362, n. 5.

Let us not listen to his slanders but say simply, "I believe most certainly that this is true." We must flee for refuge to the Lord's Prayer, lest Satan tempt us beyond our strength. Here, then, you see with what destructive weapons Satan attacks faith. Therefore we must cling to the Word alone.

11. *Then Eliakim said: Speak to your servants in Aramaic.* Here is an example of the trial of one who is near despair. He seeks some little support and counsel (as human reason is wont to do) so that the matter might be held in check. So it is in our time. When people say that a peaceful Word should be preached, the result is that the devil becomes all the more insulting, as we see here. These people have asked for quiet, and Satan shouts all the more. Learn this: One must not debate with Satan. Keep this well in mind. The more we wrestle with him in this debate, the more we despair. Do not argue with Satan. Note this, for example: The more someone thinks about the evil lust that should be laid aside, the more he falls into those thoughts, so that one follows closely upon the other and finally he will be in a frenzy. The same happens in the case of the anger that is directed against someone and that should be laid aside. And so it goes in all dangers. When we strive for the remedies, we play into Satan's hands, so that he argues with us all the more and you finally fall into despair, hang yourself, and fall down headlong. So it is always in great trials. Other thoughts keep occurring to a person, as happens in the case of the sick and the troubled. Let go of those thoughts. Consider an example from *The Lives of the Fathers.*[3] One of them had many thoughts and complained to a brother about the evil thoughts. The brother said, "You have sometimes seen the birds in the air flying over your head. If you do not let them fly about overhead, they have not built nests on your head. So let those thoughts fly away and do not keep them in your head. Here is another picture.[4] When you pass an entrance [5] where a dog is sleeping, quickly pass by the sleeping dog, or if he is barking, do not irritate him, for the more you oppose him, the more frenzied he becomes. You must do likewise with the ambushes and deceptions of the devil. Let them pass by.

[3] The source of this story is *Vitae Patrum, Patrologia, Series Latina,* LXXIII, 940; it appears elsewhere in Luther, as, for example, in *Luther's Works,* 21, p. 88.

[4] As the scholia on this passage (W, XXV, 232) indicate, the source of this picture is John Gerson, *Opera* (Antwerp, 1706), III, 242.

[5] The Weimar text has *hostium,* but we have read *ostium.*

In short, I give you this advice (for I speak as one who knows): You must completely despise such thoughts and arguments of Satan. For Satan is in the habit of disturbing the tenderest consciences in this way, as happened to a very virtuous girl when I was young.[6] While the host was being elevated in the Mass, she thought, "What a great rascal is elevated here," and with this thought she fell to the ground and almost died. When she finally got up, she told what had happened. If such thoughts arise, let them go quickly. We must become like one of the least of the children (Matt. 18:3). Do not let the devil come near you. For when his words are listened to here, the hearers soon despair and already ask for support. But by this request the speaker gave Satan an opening to vent his rage, so that he spoke all the more and by his extremely boastful words led the people to despair.

12. *Has my master sent me to speak these words to your master . . . to eat their own dung?* With mocking and most poisonous words he confounds the weak. His endeavor is altogether contrary to the Holy Spirit. The Holy Spirit reforms, terrifies, and crushes the exalted and the proud and lifts up and nurtures the lowly. The devil, on the contrary, puffs up the proud and causes them to be haughty, but he confounds and destroys the weak and the lowly. Learn to distinguish one spirit from another. Be sure to learn this. In all dangers stop arguing with Satan altogether. Do not listen to him and think about him. If you do want to think, think about the opposite. If he argues about death, then think about life.

13. *Then the Rabshakeh stood . . . Hear the words of the great king.* This is the guile and cunning of Satan. In order to lead the people away from the ungodly King Hezekiah to the powerful king of Assyria, he says that Hezekiah is a sinner and a deceiver.

16. *Thus says the king of Assyria: Make your peace with me.* After endless terrors he offers promises by way of contrast. That is what I call real temptations. These are immeasurable promises. Not only does he promise them land, but beyond that he promises to give them a far more fertile land. Who can stand firm under these conditions? Note that Satan is the supreme orator, who can turn the worst cause into the best one, and the purest faith into treachery and disobedience. So he came to a nun who was touching branches of a tree

[6] The manuscript contains the following gloss: "This also happens to me, Anthony [Lauterbach], in confession; that is how Satan makes his attack on us."

and a leaf and drove her to despair, accusing her of being disobedient.[7] He can set all of heaven and earth afire from one little spark and make an enormous sin out of a little one. He never stops attacking us. Do not listen to him.

18. *The Lord will deliver us.* Satan cannot forget these words. He said earlier, "The Lord does not want to help you, because you are sinners." Now he draws a different conclusion. "Granted: He may be merciful to you; He wants to save you. But He cannot." That is indeed an attack! He proves it by citing an example.

19. *Where are the gods of Hamath and Arpad?* That is to say: "So many and such great gods were not able to protect their own people from me. How do you expect to be saved by one small god?" Thus you see Satan's oratory pictured in all its unlimited colors and shapes. The king's great army did not have as much force as that internal conflict of the consciences struck by Satan's words. That is: Fighting without, and fears and terrors within (cf. 2 Cor. 7:5).

21. *The king's command was: Do not answer him.* You may earnestly observe this advice of the king, for it is thoroughly dependable. This is true, because the more we hear him arguing, the more he reviles us. The more we answer him, the more he wins. Keep still. This is what Ps. 4:4 teaches: "Be angry, but sin not. Be silent." So here we see the king's counsel: "Do not answer him."

[7] Luther relates this anecdote also in his *Table Talk,* W, *Tischreden,* III, 78 (No. 2917).

CHAPTER THIRTY-SEVEN

1. *When King Hezekiah heard it, he rent his clothes.*

WE HAVE heard this passage, that one must not argue with a blasphemous spirit, because he only becomes more infuriated by argument, as the king's advice excellently convinces us. So today we see in the case of our papists that the more we write and argue against them, the more they rave. Though one mouth of Satan be stopped, ten others are opened.[1] Here, I say, the prophet depicts the heart of the holy and godly king. He saw the wavering populace and the blasphemies, and even his heart trembled, as his words show.

3. *This is a day of distress, of rebuke, and of disgrace; children have come, etc.* This is where he confesses plainly that he has altogether given up and is wavering in his faith, as if he were saying: "Already the day of distress and rebuke and of blasphemy is here." He does not say "a day of deliverance and counsel." The oxen are standing before the mountain.[2] These are clearly the words of a despairing king.

Children have come to the birth, that is, mother and child are doomed. The king is in utter despair. But note where the despairing king turns. He joins the prophet and asks him to pray for him. This is the power of despair that it does not permit a man to pray. For a despairing man cannot pray. Therefore he pleads for the intercession of others: "Pray for me." Such is Satan's attack by outside forces. Inside, in the city Satan was a sifter, who drove the people to despair, as Peter experienced at the hand of Satan, the sifter (Luke 22:31). In short: No one, not even the holiest one, can be saved from that cunning of Satan's except by God's grace alone. And God alone sees him, as He showed Peter. No one can escape his siftings. May God protect us from him!

5. *When the servants of King Hezekiah came.* Now there was no

[1] Apparently an adaptation of the myth of the Hydra.

[2] Luther seems to be referring to a proverbial term for helplessness.

longer any counsel, hope, or encouragement. Then came the prophet bringing counsel, hope, life, and encouragement.

6. *Do not be afraid because of the words.* It is as if he were saying by way of disparagement:[3] "So far these are just empty words. Do not be afraid of Satan. But the words of Rabshakeh are poisonous and they soften up the spirit. Listen to My words. They are not empty but very powerful."

They have reviled Me. This is wonderful comfort. The Lord wants to relieve you of those revilings. He will take charge Himself and repay them.

7. *Behold, I will put a spirit in him.* This is magnificent irony against Assyria, as if to say: "That king is so haughty that he is lifted up to heaven itself. Just wait, I will give him a spirit, namely a cowardly one." By way of contrast he says: "He has a headstrong and exceedingly proud spirit; it shall be turned into an exceedingly humble and downcast spirit."

He shall hear something. He shall hear something, thunder or some such thing, by which I will cast him down. I will do it by a sound alone and will draw no sword." This is the most potent kind of irony. It is as if God were saying: "I will put him to flight by a sound alone, and I want to ruin his extremely haughty victory and triumph by one rumor." The vehemence of these words is remarkable. He does not say "with outstretched hand and strong arm," but he says: "I will overthrow this most powerful king entirely by means of a rumor, simply by means of a little thing he hears. As you heard above:[4] By thunder, lightning, and hail He has overthrown his army in such a way that he will soon flee to his own country. Therefore note the tremendous power of consoling in the Holy Spirit, who comforts and helps us in the greatest dangers, when human reason has no means of help, as happened to Israel at the Red Sea. They had the sea before them, the enemy behind them, and they were hemmed in by mountains on both sides. Yet God saved them; and if He had not parted the sea, He could have moved the mountains or transported the people high up in the air. So here it pleased God to overthrow such a king with one sound and thunder, though He could have

[3] The technical name of this rhetorical figure was *tapinosis;* cf. *Luther's Works,* 26, p. 362, n. 5.

[4] Cf. p. 220 above.

overthrown him in countless other ways. Therefore the one task of the godly is to trust in God and His Word, in all trials and hopeless situations to rely on God, who can very easily save us. Let us put away our reason, hope, counsel, and power. Since these cannot save us, let us take refuge with God; He will deliver us. Such examples must be exploited for our faith. The king, who had been living in extreme despair, is now like one reborn because of the prophet's comfort.

He shall return to his own land. This is even more disgraceful, as if to say: "I do not want to consider him worthy of being killed by foreigners in a strange land. Rather, he will have to be slain and destroyed in his own country, where he should have been safest."

8. *The Rabshakeh returned, etc. . . . from Lachish,* which he had captured meanwhile. He was forced by the king of Ethiopia to leave Jerusalem; and when that king had been put to flight, the Rabshakeh came back to Jerusalem. Then he sent the city a letter full of blasphemies for the purpose of putting it to shame.

12. *Gozen and Haran,* perhaps cities of the Medes.

The people of Eden. Read about them in the books of the Kings (2 Kings 19:12). In this letter that he had written he endeavors to frighten them. But Hezekiah,[5] somewhat refreshed by words of comfort, now dares to pray to the Lord, when earlier in his despair he did not dare to pray. Now, as one reborn, he dares not only to pray but also to refute the written blasphemies. He is strong again, though not completely restored; yet his faith is constantly growing, as his very beautiful prayer shows. You must now ponder it with spiritual discernment. He argues confidently: The gods of the Gentiles were not gods. But our God is the only one, and He is exceedingly powerful. We, too, can say this. To destroy Luther is not the same task as destroying Münzer.[6] Theirs is a different kind of church altogether.[7]

14. *Hezekiah received the books,* that is, the letter. It is a Hebrew idiom. Then follows the prayer which should be an example to us.

[5] The Weimar text has *Esaias,* but the reference should be *Ezechias.*

[6] Thomas Münzer, the radical Reformer, had been beheaded for insurrection in 1525.

[7] The paragraph that follows here in the Weimar text has been moved to its proper place at v. 20.

For the words of the letter bear the same plasphemy as the words of the messengers earlier.

16. *O Lord of hosts, God of Israel, who art enthroned above the cherubim, Thou art the God, Thou alone, of all the kingdoms of the earth.* Satan readily lets God be the Lord of hosts, the God of Israel, some little deity, and [8] he permits Him to be enthroned above the cherubim, but that he should be God alone, this Satan opposes. Therefore with a strong faith Hezekiah raises up his spirit and sets his superbly confident prayer against Satan's blasphemies. This is part of the art, that we can overcome Satan, the adversary, from the opposite, as Hezekiah does here. He concedes that Satan has despoiled many lands and conquered many gods, but he does not let him conquer this God. It is as if he were saying: "In this little God he will more than meet his match." But note the king's faith: *Lord of hosts.* Some think He is so called because He leads the army of angels.[9] We, however, call Him God of hosts because He alone fights in His church on earth against Satan. All others are soldiers of the devil. *God of Israel.* This is a great thing to know a specific God. For all idolatries have some god and say that God should be worshiped. But they err in the minor premise and make many gods. The Augustinian and the Franciscan each makes a god out of his type of devotion. This form of worship is recommended in the name of the true God, and thus reason is deceived in the worship of God, just as all heathen, even the wisest among them, were deceived. That would be the true God, whose worship was divinely ordained above the cherubim and in Israel. Therefore the king here stands by faith, although his God might appear weak, hemmed in, sitting upon the cherubim in one city, while the god of the Assyrians appears strong and capable. Nevertheless, he is not made to stumble because of the weakness of his God, nor is he offended by his foolishness, nor put to shame by the power of the Assyrian. Therefore he says: "I call Thee alone the true God, enthroned above the cherubim." This is the sure method of faith, that for a sure reason we lay hold of our God not on the basis of our ideas, as the forms of righteousness which the sects hold are unsure and unreliable. We, however, cling to our God (though He may seem weak). We know God in the Scriptures, where He is re-

[8] The Weimar text has *sed,* but we have followed the suggestion of the Weimar editors and read *et* instead.

[9] See the comments in *Luther's Works,* 1, p. 74.

vealed to us, and we ought to know about this God alone and withstand all adversaries. The Jews were wrong in this matter. They all worshiped the God of Israel as the One who led them out of the land of Egypt; but one worshiped Him in the woods, another in a garden, each one in a different place and in a different way, as in the case of the golden calf they deviated from the set and definite place for divine worship. Just so all our sects have confessed the same God, but each one worships Him by means of a variety of divergent and uncertain forms of worship. There is no greater heresy on earth than if we waver in this way, with anyone at all striving to set up his own worship. The true worship is to remain with the small and weak God according to His Word and His religion and the place ordained by God. As this is foolish in the eyes of the flesh that seeks a glorious God – and we have found Him in just that foolish form of the flesh – so it is necessary for us not to be offended either by His majesty (which cannot be fathomed) or by His weakness. I have often told you to beware of investigating the Divine Majesty, because this knowledge is not for our head, but it terrifies and oppresses us.[10] As for you, place your foot and your heart in Christ the Propitiator and do not explore loftier matters. As the king says here, "Thou art the God above the cherubim." *Thou art the God, Thou alone, of all the kingdoms of the earth.* First he begins in weakness and lays hold of his God in foolishness, then he rises to higher ground in the faith that He is the only God of all the kingdoms. This is an excellent example of prayer, in which we see true faith.

17. *Incline Thy ear, O Lord.* There again he sets his faith against the blasphemy, as if to say: "The ungodly say that My God is dead, but I know that He is living." All the afflicted have these feelings. They believe that God is dead or asleep. We know by faith, however, that He is living and watchful, that He inclines His ear and opens His eyes. To Him we cry, although any delay disturbs us. This delay is a very heavy cross for the flesh, yes, for outward appearance itself, because in this delay God appears to our spirit to be altogether dead and asleep. In waiting for Him we sense the power of faith, even ours, and we may put ourselves to the test. See the passage in the Wisdom of Solomon 10:12.[11] Through His wisdom and power we learn to know Him.

[10] Cf. p. 55 above.

[11] The original has "Wisdom 6."

Hear all the words of Sennacherib. This is a most excellent prayer. First there is faith in God itself. Faith calls upon God alone. Now the king sets forth a specific concern, namely the enemy Sennacherib.

18. *Of a truth, O Lord, the kings of Assyria have laid waste.* Here he indeed grants the major premise. It is true, he has conquered many nations. But it does not follow that he can deliver me. You must say thus: "It is true, Satan is the prince of this world and is more powerful than the weak Christ Himself. But I deny the conclusion, because this foolish and weak God is wiser and stronger than all. He can deliver me and all the rest, because He is enthroned above the cherubim."

19. *The work of men's hands.* It is as if he were saying: "If you call our God the work of men's hands, as are the cherubim and the worship of God, you, Assyria, also have a god, and he is much more the work of men's hands, because your god also has temples and wood and stone. Our God, however, has a temple and places of worship in accordance with His own prophet. He says in Exodus (Ex. 20:24): 'In every place where I cause My name to be remembered,' wherever I shall have commanded, there you will find Me." This is the difference between our temple and that of the heathen, between our sure worship and that of the papists. For they have many works and temples, temples that have works and worship just as we do. But these forms of worship are of a different kind: Their works are not commanded by the Word, but our works, including the political, are commanded by the Word. For that reason they are different. So the king argues here: "We also have a God by the work of men's hands, but according to His own commandment." They are now not the works of our hands, but of God, since they are done by God's counsel and are commanded by God's institution through the Holy Spirit. They are not the works of godly men's hands but are done by God's ordinance and are therefore God's own works. The works of the ungodly are true works of their hands. They appear in their own strength, as all our schismatics do.

20. *So now, O Lord our God, save us from his hand,*[12] that is, "Hallowed be Thy name." Note, then, that God's victory consists in this, that first we conquer the enemies in our own hearts so that we may drive out the enemy, Satan, the sifter of faith. When by the power

[12] See p. 316, n. 7, above.

of faith in the heart we shall have conquered our enemies and are sure about God's mercy, then despair will leave us, then the comforts and counsels will very easily follow. This is the gist of this passage. For it is characteristic of faith that in our desperation it kills all our own resources and then through the external Word comforts and strengthens and renews us. Ponder this power of the external Word so that you do not despise it, as our Catabaptists dream.

So now, O Lord our God. The prayer is short but pregnant with spirit, strongly fortified by faith. Ardent and ready for the battle through the Word, it seeks only the glory of God, not its own advantage. It is as if he were saying: "I do not pray for my own sake, but that Thy name alone be hallowed, so that Thou mayest not seem weak, etc., as Thou art slandered by the ungodly." We have heard the prayer of this most godly king, in which it shines forth how much faith, sincerity, and ardor there was in that king.

21. *Then Isaiah the son of Amoz sent, etc.* The answer to the prayer follows soon for the purpose of strengthening faith. Such passages must be noted for the strengthening of our faith. Let us be absolutely sure that we shall soon be heard when we pray properly. For without being asked, Isaiah comes on God's part and answers: "God is more quick to hear than we are to pray." Therefore let a man learn to trust God, and let us regard our prayers as completely firm. So Ecclesiasticus says (Ecclus. 18:23): "Before you pray, prepare your soul so that you may not tempt God." But to prepare the spirit is to act in true faith. This preparation is not hypocritical. True preparation is a difficult matter, but it is not artificially generated by uncertain thoughts. I know that the prayer of a godly man is true and difficult. When such a man is in any trial, he does not play at prayer, but he prays with serious and sincere feelings. For such a man false pretenses certainly pass away. In fact he prays with very great fervor, not like the idle monks. You should, therefore, learn this word "Amen," which means that you should know for certain that you have been heard, as James says (James 1:6): "Let him ask in faith, with no doubting," as if to say: "I have asked this of my Lord in my trials; this I know, and I have the conviction that I have been heard." This is what it means to say Amen. This answer comes for the reason that (1) we have been commanded by God to pray; (2) we have God's promise that He will hear us; (3) we have a formula for praying from Christ Himself and in the Psalter. For these three reasons it is

necessary for us to pray.[13] We rely, however, on God, who has commanded, promised, and dictated the prayer to us. No wonder that our sacrificing priests pray so coldly. They do not rely on these three reasons, but rest their prayer on their own intentions, speculations, and merits.

Because you have prayed, that is, your prayer has been heard. So be it. Now the promise follows.

22\. *She despises you, she scorns you – the virgin daughter of Zion.* These are hard words. He is speaking of the future as of the present; he is speaking about a defeated Sennacherib, who is still the victor. He utters and cites the words of those who despise King Sennacherib. Does he perhaps believe them? There are three things: to despise in the mind, to scorn with words, and to wag the head. How can one show greater contempt? This makes use of Ps. 2:1 f. Therefore they might believe themselves to be victors, although they see nothing but the opposite, namely, themselves as defeated and him as the victor. Therefore we must cling by faith to these words alone, while the state of affairs, however contrary it may be, is disregarded. This is faith that is confident in the dark and that in the midst of contrary things and affairs rests on the Word alone. Just so, the conscience tormented by the Law, by hell, by sin, and by Satan ought to cling to the bare Word. "Take heart, My son, your sins are forgiven" (Matt. 9:2). So here, at the height of the assault the king believes the Word. *The virgin despises you,* although she was sitting in the midst of events that were contrary to that very Word. This is the supreme exertion of the heart and the mind that is placed in the midst of death. This is the nature of faith. Therefore take note of this efficacy of faith, so that in all tribulations we may embrace the bare Word, however much everything appears to be opposed to it. This is what *she despises you* means. The faith of the godly is such, however, that it grows and increases day by day. It is not some fixed aptitude in the mind,[14] but it is a spirit that wavers and falls and rises, as happened in the case of the king. First his faith went to ruin, but now it shines again and is revived by a new promise. This is what "The righteousness of God is revealed through faith for faith" (Rom. 1:17) means. We must

[13] A parallel to Luther's statement in his Large Catechism of 1529 (W, XXX-1, 195).

[14] An allusion to the standard scholastic definition of faith as a *habitus;* cf. *Luther's Works,* 26, p. 127, n. 43, for a definition.

through little bits of faith arrive at a general and complete faith and grow daily.

23. *Whom have you mocked?* This is mockery. They are the words of a spirit and a faith speaking of a very certain future event. They are, however, words of irony against a defeated king, as if to say: "Milord king, now you know against whom you have fought. Now you have seen Him whom you formerly blasphemed, against whom you lifted up your eyes, namely, against the Holy One of Israel. Now look at the One whom you regarded as nothing before."

The Holy One of Israel. This is a Hebrew idiom, because God dwelled in the midst of the people of Israel by Word, worship, and religion. So Christ is the Holy One of the church, dwelling in the church, sanctifying and protecting it.

24. *By your servants.* He repeats his former blasphemies and boastings. "Where are now your lofty words?"

To the far recesses of Lebanon; I felled its tallest cedars, its choicest cypresses; I came to its remotest height, its densest forest. These are threatening words. "I have climbed Lebanon and passed through its border up to its cultivated field, and beyond this I have cut down the choicest trees. I did all this with no one offering me any resistance and everything lay open to me." This is a voice full of boasting. We can easily understand what Mount Lebanon means. I apply it allegorically to Jerusalem itself, whose temple had been built out of materials from Lebanon. It is as if he were saying: "King Hezekiah, you see that you are something in this city, but I will easily take it by storm and destroy it."

25. *I dug wells and drank waters.* I have so taken control of the land that I have drunk water everywhere." But because of the drought water is very dear in that area. "Because of my exceeding power I drank even before they drank." This must be understood entirely in an allegorical manner, as though he were saying: "With my great army I have completely worn out everything, yes, I even dried it up with the sole of my feet." That is, "I am so powerful that I do not need a sword. I have completely crushed them under my feet."

26. *Have you not heard that I determined it long ago?* God reminds the king of His miracles, as though He were saying: "You, O king, have not heard what wonderful things I did to destroy the

nations, wonders that are well known to all." Therefore, by means of examples from the past the prophet mocks the boastful king, as if to say: "It is nothing unusual or new for Me to kill a king, because I have killed many before." He reproves him for not having heard these things. "Just wait, now you are going to hear it."

Long ago, that is, in the past. "This is an easy trick for Me."

I planned from days of old what now I bring to pass. The import of these words is spiritual, as if God were saying: "What you are now assuming for yourself, I have already planned it and fulfilled it a long time ago, and therefore what you are doing now you are doing because I manage it and will it. O king, do not be proud of your strength, because I have done this in you before. For this reason I have hardened you, to demonstrate My glory in you. I have ordained it like this a long time ago. That is to say, before you thought about it and wanted to do it, I did it. You are My threshing chariot and My weapons with which I shall accomplish this." *Have you not heard* me and other prophets as we foretold this? "I planned this concerning you before you existed, and thus I have determined concerning you." Note this, therefore, with regard to our rulers. When they want to plan something according to their own counsel, they ruin it. But to those who are not presumptuous but leave it in God's care their undertaking succeeds. Thus Antwerp, Ratisbon, Rome, and all large cities were led unexpectedly by God's gift to the highest glory.[15] But when they added their own plans and interfered with God's office, then they soon came to ruin. You see this example in the papacy. Thus it must happen by prior determination, because when God foretells something, it is the same as what has been done. Although it was invisible, it was visible to faith.

What I now bring to pass, that is, "this is what you are doing now." It is like a heap of stones, of cities destroyed.

27. *That you should make fortified cities crash into heaps of ruins, while their inhabitants are short of hand.* This is a Hebrew idiom. *Short of hand* means weak. Thus God very easily shortens those who are to be destroyed. Those who strive to accomplish something with their power and industry soon perish.

Are dismayed, that is, the confidence of their heart is also snatched

[15] During Luther's day Antwerp was probably the most flourishing city in the Lowlands, as was Ratisbon in southern Germany.

away from them; they are deprived of their strength and courage. Being confounded easily follows from this. "This is My work, not yours, O king of Assyria."

And have become like plants of the field, namely, these cities. These are excellent comparisons. It is as if God were saying: "I have dealt with these cities as with grass. These cities are to Me like grass and plants that wither very quickly, even though they have the best farmers." For the glory and power of the whole world are compared to plant and grass. So Christ in Matt. 6:29-30 compares all glory of the flesh to a flower, as Isaiah does below in ch. 40:6: "All flesh is grass." In short: All glory, power, and splendor are before God like flowers and hay on the roof. Let this comfort the godly so that they are not disheartened by the mask of the ungodly tyrants. For their power is doomed, like hay.

Before it is grown. You see that all the lofty plans, schemes, and endeavors of the world wither away very quickly. For all their powers are nothing but dried straw in the sight of God. "But you, O king, who have overpowered so many cities, have not done it, but you are My scythe with which I have cut this hay."

28. *Your dwelling place and your going out.* He turns the speech toward the proud and presumptuous king, as if to say: "You, O king, think that you have done it alone. But you shall find out what I have done because I know your dwelling place." The ungodly say, however: "There is no God, He does not know, He does not see," and in their excessive smugness they always think they have God on their side. This is what our papists do in their schemings, this is what the Enthusiasts do in their blasphemies. They think they have God on their side; but a foolish God, who does not appear they do not want to have. So He says here: "You regard Me as a foolish God, but rest assured, O king, I will show you who I am."

"I know where you live, namely, in Babylon. I have seen your going out and your coming in, I have watched the equipment of your army from the beginning."

And your raging against Me. Because you have raged against Me. "You have offended not the people but Me, indeed you are touching the apple of My eye (Zech. 2:8)." *Your arrogance,* a smugness that has arisen from too much abundance, an arrogance that is securely proud and lifted up because of excessive power and presumption.

This is what we see in the papists and Duke George,[16] who rail against one who speaks about God.

29. *I will put My hook in your nose.* This is figurative language taken from the handling of wild animals. "Assyria is a bear to Me, and to control him I need chain and hook." Thus you see here that as we are in God's supreme care, so that the hairs of our head are numbered (Matt. 10:30), so also it very easily comes to pass that the enemies of the godly are destroyed, because they always rise up and dare great things. Yet they do not advance, because men of blood shall not live half their days, since their end is hay and a blossom. We experience this with regard to our tyrants. Therefore we must take note of this comfort, so that we rely on God against those who attack us. Thus God here strengthens, by means of mimicking words against Assyria, a king who is wavering in his faith. Therefore apply yourselves to faith, which is the chief matter of Scripture, and strengthen your spirits by faith.

30. *This shall be the sign for you: this year eat what grows of itself.* We shall simply remain with the historical sense. Many have referred this text to demons.[17] Note: Signs are always added for the confirmation of the Word. So also here. Among the signs are some of the past, some of the future. Those that happen after faith seem foolish. But then both kinds confirm the Word. *This year eat.* "In the first year you must eat that grain that was trodden down in the straw by the Assyrian army. These grain fields ought to give you an ample supply. I will feed you by a miracle, so that you will be amply satisfied with the crushed grain. This is the first sign. The second sign is in the second year. You must eat those seeds that were trodden down in the former year and come up spontaneously this year." This is the mercy and kindness of God, who makes a double gain out of one loss, so that the second year may provide enough without the work of threshing of the previous year. The third sign follows in the third year. All the broken grapevines have by a miracle produced so much wine that it is enough. The grapes have grown spontaneously without trimming the vines. It is as if he were saying: "The Assyrians have trampled the grain. This is good. Now you do not have to thresh it. The grain has remained in the field. Now you do not have to sow it."

[16] George "the Bearded" was duke of Albertine Saxony from 1500 to 1539.

[17] Luther seems to be attacking an exegesis that interpreted the wheat here allegorically, perhaps by relating it to such passages as Matt. 12:43-45.

Thus by this miracle and sign God strengthens them, because the sign is of the future, indicating what should happen after the king has been defeated, and after they had faith. This is so because when God's miracles are performed, they are understood by none but the godly. The ungodly indeed disparage all of God's miracles and say that they happened by chance. They attribute them to some essential and formal causes, as the mathematicians do.[18] Thus our papists think that all the grand miracles of the Gospel come about not by God's act but by chance and accident. For the ungodly are disparagers of God's miracles. They say, "Well, what of it? This has happened before too."

Last time[19] we heard of the extraordinary sign which was to strengthen the king's faith. He adds a sign of the future government, which is destined to be safe; not only from that king will it be safe, but also from other kings. Therefore he says the following:

31. *And that which shall be saved shall again take root downward, etc. That which shall be saved* is the Hebrew way of saying what we term "the surviving remnant." That is, the kingdom of Judah had been uprooted completely; there was only a remnant in that city. He draws an analogy from a tree, where many trees are cut down and hardly any strong shoots remain. So he says here: "Do not look at the great destruction but look at the little root." There is a similar passage in the eighth chapter of Zechariah, where he says concerning the destroyed city of Jerusalem: "If there is one stone, I will cause it to be rebuilt, so that boys and girls and women may play and dance there" (cf. Zech. 8:5). "Do not despair." The monks have applied this passage figuratively to their own contrived humility.[20] Those coarse asses know nothing of this humiliation. Humiliation is here used metaphorically. It is the very terror of the Law, by which we are humbled and killed. Do not play this way with allegories. But where you do want to employ them, at least apply them to the Word and do it carefully; otherwise you will use them in a destructive way, as our searching monks have interpreted everything allegorically according to their own speculation. For example: Jesus went into a certain vil-

[18] In the scholia on this passage (W, XXV, 240) it is astrologers rather than mathematicians who are attacked for "looking for circumstances and causes on the basis of which they claim that it is a natural happening, so that the glory of the miracle might be obscured."

[19] See Introduction, p. x.

[20] The specific point of allegorical comparison was the devastated kingdom of Judah, which was taken to symbolize monastic self-humiliation.

lage, and Mary received Him (Luke 10:38).[21] In this way the benefit of the lesson and the building up of faith are lost. Faith must be built up on the basis of history, and we ought to stay with it alone and not so easily slip into allegories, unless by way of metaphor we apply them to other things in accordance with the method of faith. So here Jerusalem can allegorically be called our conscience, which has been taken and laid waste by the terror of the Law and then set free out of the remnant and the sprouts, and the restored conscience is saved by the Word of the Gospel, through which we grow up into mature manhood by the knowledge of God (cf. Eph. 4:13). Such allegory must be used in accordance with the Word of the Law and the Gospel, and this is the explanation of different matters by the same Spirit. These things must not be twisted to apply to works and station in life, as our papists have done, and both Origen and Jerome in their allegories are members of the same allegorical clan.[22] Therefore note that allegories properly pertain to the Word, as Paul used it in Galatians (Gal. 4:22 ff.). I have called these things to your attention so that you may beware of a vulgar use of allegories.[23] So here, where I refer it to the Word and to faith when I compare Jerusalem allegorically to our conscience that is terrified by the Law. *Root downward* I understand to mean the energy of faith that is hidden and not visible before the world. Therefore beware of clumsy and commonplace allegories. This is the summary of Scripture: It is the work of the Law to humble according to history, externally and internally, physically and spiritually. It is the work of the Gospel to console, externally and internally, physically and spiritually. What our predecessors have experienced according to history externally and physically, this we experience according to our history internally and spiritually. That is, Jerusalem, which is now cut down and made desolate, is not altogether destroyed and hopeless, because it still has roots untouched whence the roots sprout forth. However, he calls the king and the few little upright people the *root downward,* because they had no outward appearance; yet from this root the most beautiful trees, girls, boys, and many inhabitants are to come forth. Therefore do not

21 Luke 10:38-42 was the Gospel for the feast of the Assumption of the Virgin Mary; cf. Luther's sermon of August 15, 1522 (W, X-3, 268—273).

22 Despite the great differences between them, Luther often linked the names of Origen and Jerome as allegorists, e. g., *Luther's Works,* 1, p. 91.

23 The manuscript has *ceremoniarum,* but we have followed the suggestion of the Weimar editors and read *allegoriarum.*

lose heart in view of the city's remnant. For the most damaged of all physical things can be mended and restored again. Stay with the grammatical and historical sense. The downward growth of the root means that the city has no form and appearance. The sprouting again means that this almost completely destroyed city is repaired again. Allegorically we can refer it to the conscience, killed and revived, but not to the monastic humility. Beware of allegories. However, this is the comfort, that we do not despair in matters that to the flesh appear impossible to restore.

32. *For out of Jerusalem shall go forth a remnant, and Salvation,* that is, the remnant of the house of David. They will not only have a restoration but also the freest safety in carrying on their affairs, in going out and coming in, that is, in ruling and performing all human works and transactions.

The zeal of the Lord of hosts will accomplish this. Here he gives the reason in opposition to the objection of some who say, "You, O prophet, are deranged for saying that a great kingdom will come into being out of a little remnant. Are you having hallucinations? Who is going to do this?" This is the way the flesh speaks. He answers: "Not your strength and your planning, but *the zeal of the Lord,*" that is, a friendly jealousy, a wrathful love, as I interpret this word. It is the exceedingly earnest passion of zeal.

Therefore thus says the Lord. He shall not come into this city . . . or cast up a siege mound against it. These are promises of future safety. Because the king of Assyria was now besieging the city, they were looking for nothing else than a cloud of spears and a very swift entrance. Against this hopelessness of the people the prophet offers them consolation.

34. *By the way that he came.* It is absurd to the flesh that they should believe themselves to be safe in the midst of the moment of need, as they saw the army outside before the city. This is the nature of faith and of the Word of God, that we cling to the Word without anything else and rely on faith in the midst of death and life. We must not look at the shattered and weak walls, all of which are nothing against this faith in the Word. Where there is no defense, where they are forsaken without cover, walls and weapons are nothing, and they stand abandoned. Now comes their wall and weapon. *He shall not come into this city.* That is the wall that protects the city. This is an

example also of the triumph of faith, which is not apparent to the eyes by any kind of argument. By this faith in words they were able to withstand the tyrant and king in the midst of their needs. These four small and wretched words are the power of God, protecting the city and people from two hundred thousand men. Let these not be powerless and insignificant words, as Zwingli says.[24] Thus by the Word alone we are protected against the tyranny of Satan and of death.

35. *For I will defend this city.* Hear how He is building this wall. The flesh cannot receive such words.

For My own sake, "not for yours, because you are wicked, but *for My own sake,* because I dwell there, and the king of Assyria wants to lay waste My house. For that reason I shall block him *for My own sake and for the sake of My servant David,* who believed in Me." God granted that salvation and victory not for the sake of their merits but for His own sake and for the sake of David, His servant. God opposes merits. He comforts us that we shall receive all things gratis for the sake of His promise. Because He promised that He would dwell here in the temple, for the sake of this promise He protected that city. Even if we are righteous and upright in the eyes of the world, yet before God we are sinners who cry, "Forgive us our trespasses." *For the sake of David.* Although David was righteous before the world and before God by faith, yet this protection was provided not for the sake of his merits but for the sake of the compact and covenant which God made with His servant David. There is therefore no mediator and intercessor between God and us. Nor is David a mediator here (as some dream [25]), but God defended them for the sake of His covenant and grace and for the sake of His promise to David.

36. *And the angel of the Lord went forth.* This story is so well known and was described by the prophet before in magnificent words. Here, however, he depicts the slaughter in very brief words.

And slew a hundred and eighty-five thousand in the camp of the Assyrians, though until now the king had boasted in grand and sublime words. This is the reason. When the prophets are busy encouraging,

24 On this controversy, cf. *Luther's Works,* 37, p. 180, n. 32.

25 The scholia on this passage (W, XXV, 240) clarify this point: "He refers to David not as an intercessor, but as one who had the promises. For David, too, was pleasing to God by trust in divine mercy, not by trust in his own merits."

comforting, and strengthening, they use a great number of words, but in a matter of fact they use very few. The Holy Spirit's activity is more concerned with perfecting and strengthening our feelings and faith than with the matter itself and with the story. Historians and poets might have described this slaughter with very ponderous and great words in the tragic manner: How from various directions a tempest had rushed in, hail from here, lightning from there, thunder from another direction, etc., as the prophet had often called to mind above in his admonitions. So also the destruction of Sodom is very tersely described (Gen. 19:24): "Then the Lord rained on Sodom and Gomorrah brimstone and fire," where you may be sure there was a very severe storm. The task of the prophets is more deeply involved in comforting the mind and faith and strengthening them with an abundance of words, but the event itself they report in a few words. Whoever has been touched by the inclination of faith will not need detailed descriptions of the story. In his own spirit he will spout forth the mighty works of God in that slaughter, and from a single word he will derive a large commentary. *He slew in the camp,* where there were many nobles, *one hundred and eighty-five thousand.* How dreadful it would be to see five or six corpses. What do you think this vast slaughter was like? Even if the Assyrian had been made of iron he could not but despair. If I had a hundred mouths and a hundred tongues, I could not say it. I leave it to your thoughts, so that henceforth you may believe that your God cares for you.

37. *And he departed and went home.* He is a fugitive, he has no thought of restoring his army by military plans. There is nothing but fear and flight. Even if he had had a thousand Hectors,[26] his affairs would have collapsed. Take note, therefore, how quickly God suppresses the pride of the flesh by means of the supreme disgrace.

38. *And as he was worshiping.* This is the consequence of the whole tragedy. It is a pitiful tale. It is reported that as Sennacherib fled and prayed to his own gods and asked his priests how he could avenge himself, he received the answer that by offering his son Abraham had won the grace of the people of the Jews in the sight of God, so that they prospered as they did.[27] The priests are then said to have exhorted the king to sacrifice his own son, too, and to

[26] Hector, the mighty warrior in the *Iliad,* was proverbial for military valor.

[27] Cf. Lyra *ad* 2 Kings 19:37 and Is. 37:38.

surpass Abraham with his piety. Then the king wished to surpass Abraham by his piety, and he desired to sacrifice two sons, *Adrammelech and Sharezer.* When the sons found out about this, they massacred the father himself. This is what the Hebrew writers report, and it may well be true, but it must not be taught as an article of faith. The sacrifice of children according to the rite of Abraham crept far and wide into all nations, both Gentiles and Jews. Reason, that most stupid ape under the control of Satan, has followed this example according to the outward act without faith and without God's command. This is in fact idolatry before God, although it glittered in their eyes as the supreme work of piety. Against this idolatry all prophets have cried out, and David laments that the land was polluted with the blood of the children sacrified to God (Ps. 106:37-38). This aping nature and reason everywhere imitates God. So here it is believable that this king in despair of weapons adopted this religion. Beware of the examples of the saints and do not become like apes. The prophet, however, in historical manner simply records the most shameful death of the king, the one who had lost his army, his glory, and his courage and was finally massacred by his own sons, the one who wanted to kill the children of God. This is a just judgment of God. A similar most wretched slaughter will befall our tyrants. This is the most wretched and shameful death of Sennacherib, who was not killed in the field by plundering foreigners, but was most wretchedly done to death in his own court by his own sons while he was practicing his religion. This is an example for all blasphemers, who will perish by this and like examples, who in their madness blaspheme that God is foolish and weak. So it almost happened to the pope who was driven from his realm by Caesar, "his beloved son." [28] He was chanting the canonical hours and Vespers. He will surely chant Compline too. Thus you have an outstanding story that is everywhere tossed out with few words, and I recommend it to your meditations and pray that you may build up your faith against all blasphemers. As this slaughter was brought about by Isaiah, who achieved this through his faith and through the encouragement given to the people through the Word, therefore this example deserves to be added to the others in Heb. 11:14 ff. Isaiah was a great man; yet you should never read anything about his works but much about his most fervent word and faith, as you see here.

[28] A reference to the "sack of Rome" by the troops of Charles V in May 1527.

CHAPTER THIRTY-EIGHT

1. *In those days Hezekiah became sick and was at the point of death.*

WE HAVE heard about that glorious and miraculous victory which was provided not by weapons but by faith alone. It is an example for our faith, so that we may learn to be diligent in the Word, not in our powers and endeavors. However, when one trial, namely, despair, had been overcome on the left, the king soon slipped to the right in good days, because wealth, riches, and strength puff us up, yes, righteousness and victory themselves puff us up. This extremely bad downfall is ours by birth, so that we very easily become proud and are lifted up when we have received gifts. This is a most dreadful downfall of the heretics and clearly devilish, when they are proud in spirit and lifted up. It is an uncontrollable evil that they even seem spiritual to themselves and are most haughtily proud even in their humility. It is safer for any young man to boast of his appearance or his riches and possessions (because he can easily be helped) than it is for him to conquer such spiritual trials. For our nature is so corrupted and depraved that nothing is worse. Consider David and how he slipped to the right. Consider that to Peter was given the disgrace of denial, so that he might remain humble. To Paul was given a thorn in the flesh (2 Cor. 12:7), to the blessed and most spiritual Mary was given the sword of Simeon (Luke 2:35). Such a most dreadful example we see here in the king, who was puffed up with his victory and began to be proud of his uprightness and righteousness. We are most wretched men; may Christ help us when we sin! Let us pray God earnestly to guard us against such pride! This sickness is taking possession of all our adversaries, of Carlstadt, of Zwingli, of Oecolampadius, and of Erasmus. The sickness of presumption is very showy in humility, zeal, and piety, and it cannot be recognized like the sickness of despair or like gross sins. For this sickness there is need of the sword of Simeon, the adultery of David, of gross sins and thorns in the flesh, so that this sickness may be brought under control by them. Pray to the Lord and beware, be diligent students of Scripture, lest you proceed by your own powers and become haughty even in

Scripture. All pride resting on all kinds of endowments and political knowledge is not so destructive as pride based on the Sacred Scriptures. Therefore Paul admonishes all bishops not to be φιλαυτοί (2 Tim. 3:2), that is, not to be proud.

We read in *The Lives of the Fathers* [1] that a distinguished man, who was exceedingly troubled by κενοδοξία,[2] that is, ambition, and could not resist it, prayed with might and main to God to be freed from this vice. Then the Lord showed him his enemy over his head in the form of a black Ethiopian. Him he crushed with his feet and thus vanquished him. The same thing happened to me, Martin Luther.[3] When I was troubled with a similar vice, I ground my enemy under my feet and won the victory.

This chapter is an example of this sickness, so that we may see the weakness of our nature. When it has fought a battle on the left, it falls down on the right. Is this not the devil in us? All the apostles had to be humbled with a burden and a weight and a thorn in the flesh. This was necessary for the saints, the nobles and pillars of the church. What must be done to us? For our nature is such that the more it thrives in glory, the more it staggers and is presumptuous and proud. Our ecclesiastics do not recognize this sin; indeed, all schismatics are possessed by the pride of presumption. Therefore we must simply despair, because we should be set free from this sin. I, too, have despaired of myself, because our whole nature is plunged in pride. Therefore we must pray constantly.

In those days. Good Lord, how he attacks this haughty saint! That trial was not the fault of a past sin, but pride was to blame for the present swelling. Therefore God fights that spiritual inflation with a physical swelling, namely, with a pestilence. For just as the plague swells up externally and travels very swiftly, so a spiritual tumor is both swollen and proud. This needs a thorn in the flesh. It needs a spear through the whole body.

Set your house in order; for you shall die, you shall not recover. These are words that apply to the puffed up and the proud. He adds

[1] *Vitae Patrum, Patrologia, Series Latina,* LXXIII, 1155.

[2] We have corrected the Greek in accordance with the suggestion of the Weimar editors.

[3] From his statements elsewhere it is evident that this — together with prayer, manual labor, and other activities of diversion — was one of Luther's techniques for conquering the temptation of the devil.

a word to the sick man. It is as though the desperate man were shown the hangman and the sword.

2. *Then Hezekiah turned his face.* Question: Was the king heard? I answer that his prayer was heard, but not the works of the prayer. Second, the question is asked, whether the king could with a good conscience boast about his works in the way it is reported in the text. The answer is twofold: First, as far as the Word is concerned; second, as far as his attitude is concerned. First we must turn to the Word, because the king knew most certainly that what he had done he had done on the basis of the Word. Such works as are done on the basis of the Word are certain and holy. Thus Peter [4] says (1 Peter 4:11): "whoever speaks, as one who utters oracles of God." This is clearly a holy office, of which we must boast in opposition to human traditions that come into being apart from the Word. Thus I can boast: "Lord, what I have done I have done and preached according to Thy Word." And this is the very opposite of human traditions, which are observed apart from the Word. Thus the king should have boasted of his victory as having come because of the Word of God, not because of his own strength. But as far as our attitudes are concerned, this boasting is nothing, and therefore we must cry, "Forgive us our trespasses," and we must say, "Preaching the Word is right and holy, but we never do justice to this office, because we are wretched sinners." Therefore we must remain on the king's highway, lest we depart from the Word. However wretched sinners we may be, let us glory in this divine Word. Thus also King Hezekiah boasted with reference to the Word, not with reference to his own attitudes. Let us remain on the true way, and even though we limp and are like clods, we are still on the royal road, we are still moving ahead. It does not help you at all to be swift on some byway. Take note also of the lie in the trial of those who are in agony, who say and cry out: "Would that I had been a swineherd! Would that I might be destined to live long, so that by my uprightness I might acquire merit and atone for my sins! Would that I had a bagful of good works!" The proudest people, whoever they may be, toil with this sin, and nature at its most natural in our life leads people to trust in their own works. Such a person says, "God be praised, I am not so bad at all. It was not like that." He is forever looking for comfort in himself, instead of simply appealing to God's mercy, as we experience in the case of people who are in agony. It

[4] The original has "Paul."

is doubtful whether such an attitude existed in the king. When someone asks us whether the king was without sin and walked in faithfulness, as he boasted, we must answer that this king was righteous and faithful according to the Word in which he lived, but that as for his own nature, he was a wavering sinner, because together with us he prayed, "Forgive us." His kind of life was correct because it was in harmony with the Word, although his life did not achieve it. Secondly, here is the desire for merits. In this pride we were born and reared. I myself was also involved in this over my ears. There is not one of us who is without this vice. I cannot get rid of it myself. Here I neither accuse nor excuse this king, but this is the way it appears.

3. *O Lord, I beseech Thee.* The prayer itself is a godly one, flowing from faith, although there were impure thoughts.

5. *I have heard your prayer, I have seen your tears.* Here God approves of his prayer, his grief, and his weeping to the extent that he looked to the mercy of the Lord. However, God omitted praising the prayer entirely. He makes no mention of it but says, *I have seen your tears,* not, "I have seen your faithfulness and righteousness."

Behold, I will add. A severe trial was as necessary as food and drink for this proud king, and it is necessary especially for us who are in the office of the Word, because our nature itself is thoroughly corrupt. This pestilence is implanted in the innermost parts, in your intellect and your will. No fornicator or harlot is so inflamed with lust as a learned theologian is inflamed with his knowledge. The passion of the fornicator is a joke beside the theologian's presumption, yet very few recognize this sickness. The serpent's head is not yet crushed. And the more chaste and righteous we become, the more that head lives. Therefore the severest trials and divinely wrought terrors are necessary, so that we may feel these words: "You are of the devil," and "Get a hangman for your neck."

Yesterday [5] we heard the example of a faith that comes from what is heard (cf. Rom. 10:17) and that receives more than it asked for. Because of our weakness we cannot pray as much as we ought. For God gives far more than we ask, as we read in Eph. 3:20, and "the Spirit Himself intercedes for us with sighs too deep for words," as we read in Rom. 8:26. Thus this king prayed only for his health, but he got life for fifteen more years, as well as protection and peace during

[5] The beginning of a new lecture; cf. Introduction, p. x.

that time. Let this be an example for our faith that we may pray unceasingly and faithfully. God will give more bountifully than we shall ask. What is not granted, however, is not the fault of Him who hears but of him who prays. Therefore when we pray for the progress of the Gospel, not only will the Gospel move forward, but everything contrary to it will be put down. Know, then, that the Sacred Scriptures exalt the fact that always more is granted than was requested.

However, we must leave the time, the place, and the circumstance to God. Let us place only the matter itself before God. So here reason would perhaps have prayed for scarcely an hour or three days, and yet he receives fifteen years. Do not look down on the prayers of the godly, for they are great and lofty. Writers raise the question how it is that God promised the king deliverance when he was already delivered.[6] It is possible that another attack on the part of Sennacherib, who was not yet completely subdued, is indicated, and concerning this God promises Hezekiah that He will protect him forever. The meaning is: "The king of Assyria has been struck down, but perhaps you are afraid that he will take vengeance. I will protect you." Never again was Jerusalem besieged by the king of Assyria, but it was besieged by the kingdom of the Chaldeans, and all subsequent prophecies of Isaiah are to be directed toward that monarchy. Jerusalem was forever delivered from Assyria. Here is the end of this kingdom because of King Hezekiah's prayer. If we prayed thus against our tyrants, we would be delivered.

7. *This is the sign to you from the Lord. . . . Behold, I, etc.* This is a great and splendid miracle: God even goes beyond His own promise, just as if, on top of it all, great signs were to be done together with the promises. It is an amazing miracle, such as has never been heard of before. The sun has moved back ten hours. In these tremendous miracles the prophet very quickly passes by those who leave the event to our thoughts. The writers deliberate on the dial of Ahaz.[7] This King Ahaz carried the brazen altar out of the temple and in its place set up an altar from Damascus. He did not wish to desecrate this altar, so he made a dial out of it. I do not know if this is true. Here, however, it is added that this one most wonderful day becomes three. The writers report that this miracle induced the kings of the Chaldeans to send gifts to Hezekiah. None of the astrologers would

[6] The *Glossa ordinaria* says that this is said *prepostero ordine*.

[7] Cf. Jerome, *Commentaria*, XI, 405—406.

ever have observed anything in this sign. Here the king is so cheered by his good health that he did not recall much of his earlier deliverance from the defeated king, and he intones a very lovely song, although it is poorly transmitted. This song, too, has such great emotions and complaints about death that it can be understood by none but those who have had experience in dangers. This song is worthy to be incorporated by Isaiah in his prophecy for the comfort of all the dying.

9. *A writing of King Hezekiah.* This is the written form of the poem which he composed after he had recovered from his illness. This song has two parts: First, it relates the feelings of fear during his weakness; secondly, the joy at his recovery. Both death and resurrection are in the song.

10. *I said in the noontide of my days: I must depart; I am consigned to the gates of Sheol.* This is a Hebrew idiom. The Hebrew word שְׁאוֹל means what has been buried. It is indiscriminately used for hell and the grave, that is, "I go through the midst of the dead to the nether realm." "I said in the silence of my days," that is, "when I was well off, I thought of nothing less than of dying." So we read in the Book of Sirach,[8] "O death, how bitter is your memory to a man who has many possessions" (Sir. 41:1). Death is indeed bitter to those who are in their best estate, in quiet, and in peace. They are as secure as though they were in Paradise, and they do not fear death. This is what *in silence* means. In the midst of this king's feeling of safety because of a defeated enemy Isaiah comes and says: "Set your house in order." There, at the prospect of falling into an unexpected death, all laughter ceases. Here many have argued about getting ready for death.[9] Many have gone into the desert to prepare themselves for dying well. I do not disparage spurning the world, but whether we shall accomplish this by withdrawing from this spurned world, I do not know. However, victory and preparation for death must be sought in Christ, not in the wilderness and in monasteries, where bellies are fattened. You must look to Christ, in whom you see death conquered. There the serpent's head is bruised (Gen. 3:15), and there you will see the whole image and the trophies of victory against our foes. We must not look at our sins and disgraceful acts, but we

[8] The original has "Wisdom."

[9] Luther is referring to the *Ars moriendi*, a widely read medieval manual of "holy dying."

ought to get out of ourselves, away from our sins and our presumption, and go to Christ Himself, to the Lamb of God that bears the sins of the world (John 1:29); to Him we should rise, on Him we should look. None have correctly dealt with this manner of preparing for death, although countless treatises on the preparation for death have been written. As for you, do not consider your death as it is in you, but see it in Christ, the Victor.

We had begun [10] the song of Hezekiah, where two things must be considered: the obscurity of the words according to the grammar, and then the thoughts of his song. *I said in the noontide, in silence.* This is what we call it when we think everything is going well for us; and yet to die unexpectedly, to die like the ungodly, this is the central thought.

I have sought the rest of my years. This is an extension of the foregoing. "I am compelled to crave, I am compelled to be without." To crave means properly to be without, to lack, when we seek something we do not have. *I have sought,* that is, "I have not found it, and with all my seeking and planning, I do not have it, that is, in an unexpected and unhoped-for manner my years are being cut off." Plop! Death strikes. This is therefore a word of distress and of one toiling in sickness. Such emotions are not recognized in talking about them, but by experience, as when some one has come down with the plague.

11. *I said, I shall not see the Lord.* This is an argument born of distress. Not only does he say that his life is cut off, but also that he must then leave everything behind. As the ungodly say, "Where will my children and wife and riches stay now? Who will get my savings?" The dying have such feelings. Here the good king complains that he will be deprived of the worship and Word of God. In this alone he delights and for this he hopes to live, and from this purpose he is being snatched away. Because of his love of the worship of God he thinks of living on. So we read concerning Saint Martin, who prayed: "Lord, if I can be of service to Thy church, cause me to live." [11] "I have said despairingly in the groaning of my heart: *I shall not see the Lord in the land of the living.*" First he bemoans that he must forsake the divine worship. To see the Lord is to see the things that

[10] The beginning of a new lecture; cf. Introduction, p. x.

[11] This story is told in the *Legenda aurea* of Jacobus de Voragine, ed. T. Graesse (Dresden, 1846), p. 748.

are the Lord's, for we should not attempt to see anything else than what belongs to the worship of God, which is received through the Word. *I shall not see the Lord,* that is, I shall no longer hear the Word and worship of God, where all the things of God are recognized and seen. *In the land of the living.* The land of the living means the land of those who rejoice, of those living excellently, in whom there is no terror and distress, no death, nothing but life. Here he says: "I am compelled to leave all this behind and enter death." By comparing these two with each other, he creates wretched feelings.

I shall look upon man no more among the inhabitants of the age, that is, among the inhabitants and citizens who live out their life while I alone am plucked off. They remain, I become a corpse.

Nor the citizens of the age, that is, "those who live and die with me." He first complains that he must forsake the Word and worship of God, and then, that he must leave his excellent and, so to say, spiritual reign behind. You may see, then, that the excellent king complains of his distresses in an excellent order: First he laments leaving both orders, the spiritual and the political realm. In both of them he works hard, and in the midst of this work he is snatched away. He is not like us; carnal people that we are, we deplore leaving carnal things behind. Now, after these most appropriate words, there follow some comparisons.

12. *My generation is removed from me.* "Generation" means duration of time. This is the first comparison. "My generation is not fixed like a palace, but it is like a shepherd's tent which is moved away." This is an outstanding analogy. For the Arabs used to carry their homes with them, as with us the shepherds' huts are homes and yet not homes. It is as if he were saying: "I seemed like a palace to myself, but I am a tent." This is an outstanding analogy. Our life is like a tent and a shepherds' hut which is rolled along in various dangers every day. Therefore Paul calls our life and body a tent (2 Cor. 5:1). Our body and our life indeed appears very noble and seems like a house, but is hardly a tent, that is, unsure and doubtful, roving and unsteady. And removed, the way a barrel is rolled away from the well. This is the second analogy.

He cuts me off. "He cuts off my life because of its thinness." So God cuts off my life and tears it off as the weaver tears a thread. This is another excellent comparison. The former comparison refers to duration, while this one reflects unexpectedness, namely, that our life is like a web, since in the midst of weaving and working we suddenly fall down because of the plague, or hunger, or fire, etc. "He snaps me off like a slender thread."

From day to night Thou wilt bring me to an end. That is, "Thou wilt not wait until the evening, but Thou wilt kill me this very day." You have the same message in Deut. 28:66: "In the evening he shall not hope for the morning, and in the morning he shall not hope for the evening." "If I live in the morning I wonder what I shall do in the evening; if in the evening, I wonder how I shall live in the morning."

13. *I cry for help until morning.* "I would like to live tomorrow." You see the feelings of distress. "I held out, I resisted, because I wanted to be alive tomorrow," as we experience in the case of the ungodly when they die. These things cannot be expressed.

Like a lion He breaks all my bones. The distress is so great that a man simply becomes numb, so that he can neither stand nor walk nor look ahead. Thus a certain condemned man about to be executed and then set free said that he felt as if he had been walking in mud over his knees.[12] So heavy are bones and limbs of the distressed. For the prophet's answer, *Set your house in order,* was a lion to his feelings.

14. *Like a crane I clamor.*[13] That distress forced me to clamor like the cranes, birds that whoop wretchedly. So the afflicted do not express themselves in words but produce sounds like doves, coo, coo, coo. Behold, then, the wretched groans of distress. To despair, this is what it means that the bones are broken.

My eyes are weary. Those who are near death have eyes that are broken, as it were. They have much whiteness and turn the pupil in an upward direction. *My eyes are weary,* that is, they have failed, they are closed. It is not only death that produces this weakness of the eyes and of the body, but every sorrow of the heart does so. Every sorrow is a bit of death. This is a description of his distress: that his bones are broken and that his tongue has failed. He no longer had a heart for singing. Then the eyes have become weary, and all members have become weak, and all this has arisen from the inner distresses of the

[12] This is apparently based on a personal reminiscence.

[13] For some reason, the Biblical text here is printed in German rather than in Latin.

heart. Now that the distressful feelings have been described, the prayer follows.

O Lord, I am oppressed. In Hebrew: "O Lord, I am slandered; sweeten me." This is the highest art, that in the worst grief and distress we do not despair but call upon God. "Call upon Me in the day of trouble; I will deliver you" (Ps. 50:15). The Hebrew word עָרַב means to answer, or to sweeten. He does not cry out much but says quite briefly: "I am oppressed." These are sounds like those of a crane, sparks indicating that he is coming back to life again. "Relieve my lot, make it sweet for me, be gentle with me."

15. *What can I say?* These are the words of one who is rejoicing and returning to life. This part refers to the part of the prophecy that says: "Behold, I will add fifteen years to your life." Therefore we must read: "Oh, how I will speak, how I will talk and preach with rejoicing because I have been delivered."

He has spoken to me, and He Himself has done it. "This is what He promised me, and He will keep His promise." The convalescent is relying on God's promises. Because of his joy great things are embraced in very few words. He thinks that his joy has been made known in all the world.

I will confess all my years. "I will give thanks all the years of my life. I will never forget as long as I live that He has delivered me from my distress." "Bitterness" means distress. Some have applied this text to confession and have said that in bitterness one must recall the entire past up to the present day.[14] But this is not true, for here he is speaking about the joyful feelings of the king coming out of his distress.

16. *O Lord, if by these things men live.* Our translator was not far from the correct sense, if only he had left out "if" and had said, *Lord, by these things men live.* Now he recounts the things wherein his life and pleasure consist. He wants to compare the strength of the Word with the strength of all other things. For the abundance of all things is nothing apart from the Word, as we see in the case of the rich man who was enlarging his granary (Luke 12:16-20). So here the king knows by experience that there is no power to heal in the medicine, but there is power in the Word, just as nourishment is not a matter of bread and food, but of the Word. The Word accomplishes marvelous

[14] See, for example, Ambrosius Catharinus Politus, *Apologia pro veritate* (1520), Book IV, Disputation 7, ed. Josef Schweizer (Münster, 1956), p. 275.

things in the human body. Not medicines and food, but only the Word changes the body. All the natural philosophers are unable to conceive of so great and so sudden a change in one hour, that food and drink should be transformed into blood and urine. The Word does all these things. We do not live by bread and wine, but we live and are nourished under the Word. Though we should swallow all kinds of medicine, it accomplishes nothing without the Word.

In all these is the life of my spirit, that is, in the Word.

Restore me. "Without care and toil on my part Thou dost give me safety, and while I dream and sleep, Thou dost make me well." There are many such passages in David. "In peace I will both lie down and sleep" (Ps. 4:8). "He gives to His beloved in sleep" (Ps. 127:2). He will give to His beloved in sleep, while He gives to others with supreme exertion and wakefulness, but also that they cannot enjoy it. What is sown grows, and the sprouts flourish while we sleep. Thus we are safe, having cast our care upon God. All things are given and preserved through the Word. This is a remarkable statement, "He gives to His beloved in sleep." Why is it that you languish day and night? Wife, children, and cattle are given by God. As for you, just do your work, take care of your wife, your family, and your cattle, and leave the care to God. He will keep everything in His own order. Learn, then, that it is not our care and concern that does it, but that, having cast our care upon God, we leave the matter to Him. This is what it means to sleep. Take heed of this most beautiful rule in this verse if you want to be safe; go to sleep, that is, leave the care to God.

17. *Behold, in peace.* The church's double peace is the severest kind of persecution. There is no plague worse for the church than a peace in which the Word of the Spirit and its diligent use are lacking. For the purpose of obtaining the true peace, however, we need nothing but the Word. *Lo, it was for my peace that I had great bitterness,* that is, "Instead of peace I had the most bitter anxiety, because I wanted to look for peace for myself elsewhere after I had forsaken the Word." *Welfare,* that is, being well off, prospering. In all things this is a most certain rule: When we want to avoid Scylla, we fall into Charybdis. We labor and worry and exert ouselves in one kind of toil, care, and vexation, so that we may fall into something worse, because we rely on our care instead of relying on God. This worry and striving makes us insane. Yet you must use means and

commit everything to God. Use medicines, but do not rely on them; rely on God. This drive of nature, this striving to do something strictly according to one's own will, this a most pestilential thing. It is as if I were saying: "I want to eat at such and such a time, or I will die. My wife must do this or that for me, or else I will smash everything." Hence this verse is like a maxim. The fact that this most godly king in seeking peace apart from God found bitterness is something that will come to us all.

But Thou hast held back my life. "Thou hast clasped me to Thy heart. This is what happened to me. I looked for peace while forsaking Thee and found nothing but bitterness until Thou didst embrace me with Thy Word." Elsewhere (Is. 66:13) he compares the embrace of the Word to a husband's or mother's love that embraces him. Thus God enfolds us with His Word as with His arm; God embraces us also in all dangers and griefs. Even though things appear to be going in reverse for you, commit them to God, and He will embrace you.

Thou hast cast all my sins behind Thy back. Every trial has this misery that it scares man into thinking that this is sin. When sickness and misfortunes come, Satan, too, soon comes and troubles the conscience, and for that reason a Christian must fight with his conscience and with his body. Here Satan shakes us with various conscience scruples and attacks us as if he were fighting against Cerberus, the Lernaean Hydra, and other monsters. Soon Satan draws the conclusion in our consciences: "God is not at all well disposed toward you because He did not help you." Thus any affliction has a tail, namely, that we think God is unmerciful. Such a conscience thoroughly frightens man, so that we imagine death has a thousand teeth, while it has none; and the greater our weakness, the more Satan harasses us with despair, when our conscience ought to be surrounded with the more joy. Let all trials have their heartache. Therefore [15] these are the greatest blessings of God: To believe that God takes hold of us and makes us alive.

18. *For Sheol cannot, etc.* This is taken from Ps. 6:5. "Thou didst do the right thing in saving me, because the dead and the nether regions do not praise Thee. If it is Thy desire to advance Thy praise, then have mercy."

19. *The living, the living, he thanks Thee, as I do this day.* "The

[15] The Weimar text has *erga*, but we have read *ergo*.

living are those who are without care, who commit their affairs to Thee and then go to sleep. Such a person praises Thee." And the king demonstrates this by his own example.

The father to the children. This is taken from Ps. 78:5: "Which He commanded our fathers to teach to their children." We publish this praise in such a way that not we but all our children publish it. This, therefore, we must strive to do against the zeal of Satan. Note that there is no greater sacrifice for a godly man than gratitude, praise, and thanksgiving for the blessings received.

20. *The Lord will save me.* This is from Ps. 12:1.[16] Here he comes to a close, as if to say: "Let us sing this song which I have composed. Only save us. Thou hast given us health; help us to remain in it." So today we ought to sing: "Lord, preserve us in the truth that we have come to know."

And we will sing our songs in the house of the Lord. This song was concerned only with performing these praises in the house of the Lord.

21. *Now Isaiah had said, etc.* It was necessary to add this. Here Isaiah was made a physician. Here the physicians have their patron saint. For you heard in the song above that all things are kept and cared for by the Word. Then the ungodly cry: "If the Word does everything and provides nourishment for everything, we do not want to eat or take medicine." For them he takes up this example. As for you, make use of means. Do not rely on them but use them, since God has created them. If they do not help, commit the matter to God. Do not say: "Doctor, if this will not help this time, I refuse to take it anymore." Yes, you want to have your own way! So we all go beyond the proper use of means by clinging to them, as our papists altogether cling to works. Others despise works altogether, so does this song ascribe the power to the Word and not to the medicine. Yet it does not forbid that we use them, but the prophet's example supports their use, since he poultices the wound with a cake of figs. Therefore we must make use of means. We must work and produce and commit ourselves to God.

22. *Hezekiah also had said: What is the sign?* These are words spoken in irony, as if the king were saying out of his excessive and unexpected joy: "What a sign, that I shall go up to the house of the Lord!

[16] The original has "Ps. 9."

I who thought I was about to go down to Sheol must now go up to the temple." Therefore instead of "what" we must now read "how," as elsewhere. "How lovely is Thy dwelling place, O Lord!" (Ps. 84:1). "How beautiful upon the mountains are the feet of him who brings good tidings" (Is. 52:7). And in Ps. 8:4: "What is man that Thou art mindful of him?" So here we must read: "How great will be the sign, that I shall go up to the house of the Lord," as if in his sudden joy he were saying ironically: "Oho, what a sign is this, that I shall go up to the house of the Lord!"

CHAPTER THIRTY-NINE

1. *At that time Merodach-baladan the son, etc.*

THE prophet has sufficiently reported this remarkable story, namely, that the king was struck with his illness in order that his presumption might be cast out. What is there to say? If our life had no reason for desiring death, for the sake of this monster of pride and presumption our life would have to be detested. For we are all proud and lifted up by a remembrance of a well-lived life. This makes us happy, and we rejoice in prosperous and favorable circumstances. This is the worst idolatry. So here the king is extremely lifted up in his boasting about having established a good government. The memory of the defeated king of Assyria came to him, and there again came this monster of pride which was suppressed by his sickness. Third, this monster is not yet dead but is again puffed up by the envoys and gifts from the king of Babylon. What else is there to say? Ambition, presumption, boasting, and φιλαυτία (2 Tim. 3:2) are a great monster in life, and this plague vexes the life of every man and especially old people. Beyond this comes the perpetual passion of ambition, by which our whole life is besieged. What shall I say? All periods of our life are beset by the most ungodly sins. Therefore it is not evil for us to be oppressed by countless dangers and afflictions. I have asked God day by day to free me from this ambition.[1] I shall not avoid it as long as I live. So in this king this sin could not be overcome, no matter how much it was suppressed by cares. Read about it in the Books of Kings, how he was charged with the sin of unthankfulness after his illness. If this most godly king could not be freed from pride, how can Erasmus, Bucer, Zwingli,[2] and others, who are nothing but people infected with pride in their own excellencies and with hatred? I do not know how to stand up against this sin. For praise puffs us up, hatred exasperates us. Where do we want to go? Shall we run into the desert? There we will become devils. Alas, Fame,

[1] From other statements of Luther it is evident that ambition, together with pride, was a prime source of his temptation.

[2] Luther frequently accused both Zwingli and Erasmus of pride, but Bucer vexed him more because of his apparent inconstancy in doctrine.

may grief befall you! What trouble you create! This king could not be cleansed of the disease by these two extreme trials, and no man has ever been able to surpass him. Therefore we must despair of ourselves and run to Christ and beg Him to be gracious. This is a dreadful and accursed sin for the sake of which death would have to be desired, so that we might return to ashes as quickly as possible, because here a most godly king could not be cleansed of it in three cleansings. Therefore I impress upon you to have faith, because faith very urgently impresses upon you God's glory, not ours, although this pride of yours will never leave you. Beware of this pride and arrogance, you shepherds of souls. For the arrogance of humility is more potent and more pestilential than pride. The people who under the guise of humility imagine themselves to be good seemingly spurn praise and yet love nothing more than this. This is the most pestilential kind of human life, which is attacked everywhere by various sins and most of all by arrogance. Faith must fight against this above all. So here the king became puffed up and ungrateful through the flattery and honor of the envoys, so that he forgot God more than enough and exalted himself. Is this not a shameful thing? Let it be an example to our faith, so that when we have been felled by such and similar sins, we may be awakened to the mercy of God. For here the most honorable king is leprous from head to foot with this disease of arrogance. Therefore our life is full of dangers. When we have conquered all sins, if this is possible, along comes the queen of sins, pride, which seeks glory in its own goodness. Therefore our most hostile enemies and afflictions are our best agents to conquer this sin. Friends and flatterers are our worst enemies. Hence Augustine says: "If you scold me, it is bad; but if you praise me, this is worse." [3]

At that time. Books in Hebrew means letters. Here friends and gifts are the king's enemies, because Hezekiah was puffed up by their honor. I have read nothing about this king, I do not know who he might be; many have made many comments.[4] I take it simply that with the collapse of the Assyrian kingdom the kingdom and monarchy of the Babylonians came into power, as one kingdom follows another. The kingdom of the Greeks was superseded by the sultans, the sultans

[3] Luther quotes this maxim elsewhere, for example, in his sermon of September 29, 1536 (W, XLI, 685) and attributes it to Augustine; but it does not seem to appear precisely this way in Augustine.

[4] Luther seems to be thinking of the material on Merodach-Baladan assembled in the comments of the *Glossa ordinaria* on Is. 39:1.

by the Turks, and the Turks will be superseded by someone else. So here Babylon looks after its own affairs and seeks the favor of King Hezekiah to get his help against the kingdom of the Assyrians, and so Babylon strives to make covenants by means of its gifts, as is commonly done in conspiracies.

And Hezekiah was happy because of them. See how this sin, namely arrogance, now struts around! The king does not rejoice in the Lord, but, as Cicero says, "the memory of a good life is most delightful."[5] In this he rejoices and arrogantly relies on his own strength. Oh, this is a serious sin. Here this sin, which is described in more detail in the Books of Kings, is simply called joy. But this is the joy found in creatures when God has been forgotten. May God protect us!

And he showed, etc. He leads these foreigners through his entire castle and city and boastingly says: "See, this is what I have accomplished." In this way he is proud and holds his cockscomb high. What about me, Martin Luther? This is a horrible example for me. What kind of people are we? How long are we going to stand when such people fall down? Since God has forgiven them, let us not despair.

3. *Then Isaiah the prophet came to King Hezekiah.* Here is the third medicine. The prophet's rebuke is extremely impassioned, as though he were saying: "My Lord King, you have heard words of praise from strangers. You ought not to have permitted these words to enter your heart; you should have given God the credit, but you attribute it to yourself." What is there to say? The prophet's words against the king, "Why did you let them in?" are extremely sharp.

Whence did they come to you? "They came from your enemies, in whom you now trust as you forget God."

What have they seen in your house? "Did you have to let them see it?"

They have come to me from a far country. He does not say, "to the Lord." In other words, "I am so splendid that they came not for the Lord's sake but for my sake."

4. *What have they seen in your house?* "Did you have to grant them this favor?" The prophet's words are most impassioned. Read about it in the Books of Kings.

They have seen all that is in my house. This is the king's confession. The prophet extends his anger even to the king's children. The

[5] Cicero, *De senectute,* III, 9.

anger is threatened, however, because of this sin and the sin of all the vaunting citizens.

5. *Hear the word of the Lord of hosts,* namely, of the angered Lord. He says: "Because you put your trust in men, you will clash. Whence you expected help you will experience loss." This happens to all who trust in men. All alliances of the princes, of the emperor and the pope, have been broken, because they seek agreement without God. For Maximilian made an alliance with the king of France and with the pope, but this alliance did not last.[6] The emperor Charles made an alliance with the pope, whom he is now devastating.[7] In short: All covenants without God are sources of irritation. This is true because they seek help in the flesh.

6. *Nothing shall be left,* that is, of those things of which you boasted. You will be deprived of them. Thus because of this sin of pride, the prophet foretells God's supreme wrath for the king, so that the whole city of Jerusalem will be destroyed by the Babylonians.

8. *The Word of the Lord is good, etc.* This confession and this humbling brought it about that this wrath did not descend on the king in his own time, as may be read in 2 Chron. 32:8 ff.

[6] Apparently a reference to the League of Cambrai, the alliance formed in 1508 by Pope Julius II, Emperor Maximilian I, and Kings Louis XII and Ferdinand.

[7] See p. 331, n. 28.

Index

By HILTON C. OSWALD

INDEX TO SCRIPTURE PASSAGES